THE
LOST KINGS

THE
LOST KINGS

LANCASTER, YORK & TUDOR

AMY LICENCE

For Tom, Rufus and Robin

First published 2017
This paperback edition published 2019

The History Press
97 St George's Place
Cheltenham, GL50 3QB
www.thehistorypress.co.uk

British Library Cataloguing in Publication Data.
A catalogue record for this book is available from the British Library.

ISBN 978 0 7509 9211 4

Typesetting and origination by The History Press
Printed and bound by TJ International Ltd

Introduction:
The Fear of Death

Timor mortis conturbat me

The pretty little church of St Andrew's at Wickhampton has overlooked the Norfolk marshland for at least 800 years, probably more. It is situated 4 miles from the coast, on the edge of the Yare Valley, but its dedication to a patron saint of fishermen suggests it may have originally served a community who enjoyed easier access to the North Sea. Wooden vessels could have found their way along the Yare in the south, or the Bude in the north, to the port of Great Yarmouth, to take advantage of a national diet that was rich in seafood thanks to an adherence to the regular fish days of the Catholic calendar: Fridays in particular, and often Wednesdays and Saturdays too. Across the length and breadth of the country, those days saw cooks using almonds or onions, cinnamon or pine nuts to dress their herring and cod, supplied from places like Wickhampton.

Today St Andrew's lies quietly among the fields, rebuilt extensively in the fourteenth and nineteenth centuries. Yet for all its long-dead maritime connections, it is remarkable for symbolising another of the key elements of medieval life, an inescapable, all-pervasive, unceasing element as universal as the need for the people to provide and consume food. Adorning the western corner of the north wall are images of a subject that the congregation would have thought about almost as much as their meals, a subject to which the questions of eating and survival were closely allied. Along with many other English churches of the period, St Andrew's contains a series of famous *memento mori*, or paintings depicting the dead. And death, when, where and how it arrived, was nothing short of a medieval obsession.

It is unclear exactly who painted the three eerie-looking skeletons at Wickhampton and the fleshy reflections of their living descendants. The job might have gone to a skilled local painter, who also depicted the images of saints upon other walls of the church, or perhaps an artist drafted in from the royal court, recommended by a wealthy patron. Similar themes appear in churches nearby that were frequented by the well-connected Paston family. However, the artist's execution of the six figures here and the details that accompany them leave no doubt as to where he gained his inspiration. The three living and three dead figures are engaged in a hunting scene: a rabbit runs for cover, a dog handler holds leashes and one nobleman holds a falcon upon his outstretched arm. This allows the painting to be identified as an illustration of a widespread legend: that of the Three Living and the Three Dead, originating from the 1280s, and found in places as widespread as France and Germany, Switzerland and Denmark. Although the narratives vary, the most succinct English version is an anonymous alliterative poem of the fifteenth century, possibly by the Shropshire priest John Audelay.

The Three Living and the Three Dead, also called *The Three Dead Kings*, relates how three kings follow a boar hunt and end up getting lost in the mist. There, in a strange twilight world between earth and the afterlife, they encounter the figures of their ancestors, in varying states of decay, and react with a mixture of fear and bravery. The corpses berate the kings for neglecting their memories and failing to say masses for their souls, reminding the living that their hold on life was brief, and they should 'makis your mirrour be me', since 'such as I was you are, and such as I am you will be.' The dead also rue their materialistic, lascivious lives, wishing they had lived more simply and spiritually, and warning how rapidly time passes unnoticed. The three living kings heed this macabre message and combine forces to build a church, on whose walls the legend is depicted to the edification of its flock.

But such legends and images were not confined to the walls of churches, to watch over Catholic heads bent in prayer below. The dead were seemingly everywhere, adorning psalters and Books of Hours in lurid colour, creeping into the most quiet, intimate moments of people's lives. Sixty versions of *The Three Living and the Three Dead* survive, alongside eighty versions of a later manifestation of the same theme, called *The Dance of Death*,[1] but corpses also spoke up in other contemporary poems and stories, such as the graphic *Disputacione betwyx the Body and Wormes*. This unusual dialogue also raises the medieval obsession with the connection between mortality and appetite, as a decaying woman tries to dissuade the worms in her tomb from consuming her, only to be informed that all desires will be overcome by the hunger of others. Although they were ultimately silenced by worms and time, the medieval dead were difficult to ignore, being visceral and three-dimensional, carvings of their rotting corpses glimpsed underneath cadaver or transi tombs, such as those erected for Archbishop Henry Chichele in Canterbury Cathedral and Bishop Richard Fleming at Lincoln. In fact, Chichele's tomb prompted the passer-by to remember 'you will be like me after you die' and was completed before his death, so that he might sit and contemplate it in his final years. It also bore a reminder of his humble origins, 'a pauper born then to Primate raised', and echoed the imagery of the *Disputacione*, asserting that he was now 'cut down and ready to be food for worms'.

First, one had to survive birth. With complications arising from delivery, puerperal fever and infection, it has been estimated that mothers faced around a 1 per cent chance of mortality as a result of giving birth, a statistic that marks the process as around 150 times more dangerous than it is today. Spread through the average woman's childbearing career, that led to a risk of 6 or 7 per cent. Around one in five children died before they reached the age of 1, and more before their fifth birthday. After this, their life expectancy improved again before another dangerous peak between the ages of 10 and 14. The middle to late teens introduced a new swathe of potential killers, as the medieval child straddled the adult world and engaged in warfare, sexual activity and greater independence.

Sometimes death came knocking at the door. Plague was a regular occurrence, sweeping away huge portions of the population and going into abeyance only to resurface again later. After the first catastrophic outbreak of 1348–49, major outbreaks hit Europe in 1360–63, 1374, 1400, 1438–89, 1456–57, 1464–66, 1481–83, 1500–03, 1518–31 and 1544–48. England was particularly battered by a specific resurgence in 1361, another in 1471, which might have claimed as much as 10–15 per cent of the population, followed by the onslaught of 1479–80, which is considered to be responsible for the deaths of around a fifth of England's inhabitants.[2] Then there was the dreaded and highly contagious Sweating Sickness, which arrived in 1485, and rampaged through the country for the next sixty-five years before vanishing as mysteriously as it had arrived.

If medieval people successfully navigated these epidemics, their fellow men might prove just as lethal. The English upper classes represented a very small gene pool from aristocratic families with a tendency to intermarry going back generations. Many of their young men were directly affected by the civil wars of the second half of the fifteenth century, commonly known as the Wars of the Roses, a struggle for dynastic supremacy which was fought out among this elite group, with the inevitable results. When each side took up arms, they were not unaware of the possibility of capture, injury and death, although the prevailing chivalric code meant that it still took some by surprise. Brutal attacks upon the battlefield and merciless executions in its aftermath meant that these courtesies of warfare were eroded, marking a new savagery and finality between enemies. Blue blood or not, those who got in the way needed to be removed.

Despite its constant presence, death was only one of many facets of medieval life. It does not appear to have created a mood of excessive fatalism, morbidity, pessimism or even thanatophobia. On the contrary, the proximity of death seems to have bred a sense of opportunity, not exactly a 'seize the day' mentality, but a fighting spirit in the face of a force that might be eluded for a while. Death, personified, was an adversary to outwit. In contemporary literature, there is almost a sense of glee in the notion that death could be cheated of its prize, held at bay, even though it would always gain the final victory. A sardonic, dark humour pervades accounts and images of the Devil being outsmarted in his search for corruptible souls. This is not to suggest that people pursued hedonistic lives, since the dance with death was balanced by the influence of Christian teaching; it was more a game of chance, a cultural motif that recurred very often throughout the period. By snatching back a few more weeks, months or years, and living to fight another day, medieval people embraced the moment while keeping their eye on the eternal. Death was not considered to be the end, of course, within the context of the Catholic faith. Medieval people hoped to make a 'good death', which could determine their ultimate fate just as much as their deeds during life. This meant having time to prepare oneself for the end, in terms of deathbed provisions, confession and setting one's affairs in order.

Yet more than anything, death could be unexpected. While modern mortality rates remain fairly constant, the fifteenth and sixteenth centuries experienced wild fluctuations which created more of a fear of being unprepared for death, especially of being unshriven, than of death itself. The century 1450–1550 certainly saw sudden episodes of mass annihilation, through battle and epidemic, as well as changes in population and life expectancy. According to monastic records, especially those collated at Westminster Abbey, the latter half of the fifteenth century was marked by a greater tendency towards premature death, which may have correlated with the most devastating conflicts of the Wars of the Roses. The birth rate took a slight turn upwards in 1470 and again in 1520. By this point, the national population is estimated to have reached around 2.5 million, nowhere near the pre-plague figure of between 4 and 6 million in 1300.[3]

Death may have been commonplace, but there is no denying the grief of the bereaved. Loss had a huge impact upon the personal lives of loved ones and relations, changing the prospects of their children, spouses and siblings, often catapulting them into unexpected positions of power, or the lack of it. This book explores the lives of ten young men in the century 1450–1550 who were products of this visceral environment and died prematurely. Each loss represented the absence of a life, of a future path forsaken, the laws of inheritance resulting in serious changes for dynasties. Each death broke a branch of the tree, created a man who would not father children, a king who would not rule, an established household to be disbanded, dependents to seek another master, subjects to find another lord and a group of allegiances lost. The social standing of these lost youths meant that the political and national consequences of their deaths vastly outweighed the personal impact of their loss. And each loss left a very brief vacuum, or window of opportunity, into which others might step. Of the ten young men analysed here, four died of illness, three in battle, two by execution and one disappeared under mysterious circumstances, probably smothered in his bed. Their youth and the suddenness of their ends, made it less likely that they had taken the necessary legal steps to ensure a smooth transition of their legacies or created the spiritual conditions conducive to the salvation of their souls. In some cases, they were deliberately denied the opportunity for closure by those who wished to exploit their demise. The only one to write a lengthy surviving will was Edward VI, but even then his wishes about the succession and religion were quickly overridden.

Those who were facing death at the start of this period were concerned about their salvation, the distribution of their property and the future of their families. The will of Thomas atte Bregge in Kent, written on 31 October 1443, left certain rents, lands and tenements to his son Thomas, the remainder going to his other son John; 40 marks went to each of his three daughters and a priest received a sum to say masses for his soul at Lydd church for the next three years.[4] Similar wills of the era provide for meat and drink to be served to those attending mass on the anniversary of the subject's death, bequests to monasteries and for the comfortable living of widows, providing, in the will of Sir Ralph Rochefort, they 'behave properly or marry well'. Ralph's son and heir was still underage at the time of his father's decease, but he was to inherit all his manors and pass them on to the legitimate heirs of his body.[5] Failing that, the next preferred family line was identified, with clarification for the transfer of property in the event of their deaths. Blood and inheritance mattered. Medieval nobles had a strong sense of themselves as temporary custodians of dynastic possession, which it was their job to tend, increase and hand on to the next in line. From this came their sense of identity and duty, their position in society, their career and choice of marriage partner, their lifestyle and the manner and significance of their death.

Wills were also the last opportunity to exercise influence that was available to the dying. The medieval belief in purgatory, still so strong at the start of this period, meant that the fates of those in spiritual limbo could be influenced by their acts of charity and the prayers of the living. To obtain their good will, and their active influence, the dying might leave bequests to individuals or churches, for the benefit of the entire congregation, or establish chantry chapels where priests could pray for their souls in perpetuity. Their gifts of money, clothing and objects, their devout effigies, hands clasped together, might encourage those left behind to appeal to the saints on their behalf. The fires of hell were very real. They did not just exist inside class-exclusive manuscripts such as Dante's *Inferno*, or on the illuminated pages of rich women's prayer books; they were painted in lurid colour on the walls of churches and preached in sermons. They crept right up behind people and insinuated themselves into their lives, in popular stories, legends and customs. And just as material wealth could exalt the conditions, comfort and diet of the upper classes, so it was thought to ease the path to heaven. The wealthy could not take their riches with them, but they might put them to good use in the service of their souls, or purchase papal indulgences to pardon their sins. To an extent, access to heaven in the late medieval period could still be bought. Writing his will in 1454, the priest Nicholas Sturgeon bequeathed his soul to 'the great mercy of almighty God', his 'wretched body to the earth sanctified and hallowed' and 'all my worldly goods to be demened for the merits of my soul'. He paid for a new steeple for the parish church of St Augustine's in London, a costly chalice for St Nicholas in Henstridge, vestments for priests in St Andrew's of Asperton to observe the anniversary of his death for the next seven years, and asked the abbeys at Canterbury and St Albans to pray for his soul.[6] A century later, when Guildford Dudley met his death in 1554, the concepts of prayers for the death had been rejected. The dead were dead, and those ties with the living had been severed. England's religion, its beliefs about the afterlife and its methods of memorial had undergone a revolution.

This book is about death and its impact but, even more so, it is about life. Life as an opportunity to be seized with both hands, to be fought for amid difficult and overwhelming circumstances, to be celebrated and exploited, valued and revered, in all its brutal brevity. Death is always of significance, in any era, but the concentration of these ten young losses fed into a complex process by which the dynasties of York, Lancaster and Tudor were redefined. These deaths shaped the Wars of the Roses and the families' descendants, as much as its key adult players, by virtue of the young men's birth, the offices they held and their actions or inactions. The cultural, social and dynastic impacts of death cast particularly long shadows over the living during this century and helped to shape the posthumous reputations of these ten young men, often casting them as martyrs and victims. Their lives and the manner of their ends require fresh evaluation to place them in the context of their family trees, assess their contribution and counter the knowledge of hindsight that hung a sword of Damocles above their youthful heads. It is the fate of death to always be written about by the living, but the trails these young men left, like temporary lines on a beach, are worth recording before the waves wash them away.

This book is also about history and the way it is written. It is impossible for the historian of any era to shake off the specific combination of factors that formed their particular consciousness and dictated their education. It is almost as difficult to divorce interpretation from hindsight, so its influence must be recognised and viewed from an alternative platform, from as detached and timeless a perspective as is humanly possible. The nature of premature death means that some questions must be left open-ended and all likely conclusions considered, mapped out around the actual course that events took, and the measurable facts. It may seem a fruitless exercise in fiction to speculate what might have been had they lived, but it is possible to examine what did happen as a result of their deaths; the people who took their land and position, seized the opportunity and stepped into their shoes, either by design or accident of birth. These results, these lives and events, are the opportunity cost of the lives lost.

Amy Licence
Canterbury, August 2017

I that in heill wes and gladnes,
Am trublit now with gret seiknes,
And feblit with infermite;
Timor mortis conturbat me.

Our plesance heir is all vane glory,
This fals warld is bot transitory,
The flesche is brukle, the Fend is sle;
Timor mortis conturbat me.

The stait of man dois change and vary,
Now sound, now seik, now blith, now sary,
Now dansand mery, now like to dee;
Timor mortis conturbat me.

No stait in erd heir standis sickir;
As with the wynd wavis the wickir,
Wavis this warldis vanite.
Timor mortis conturbat me.

On to the ded gois all estatis,
Princis, prelotis, and potestatis,
Baith riche and pur of al degre;
Timor mortis conturbat me.

William Dunbar, 'Lament for the Makers'

1

Edmund, Duke of Rutland (1443–60)

I

Edmund, Duke of Rutland was born into the world depicted by John Lydgate, court poet to the Lancastrian kings. It was a world in which Lydgate could produce his heroic verse *Troy Book*, a Middle English translation in decasyllabic couplets of Guido Delle Colonne's Latin *Historia Destructionis Troiae*, and simultaneously confess that he 'stole apples … gambled at cherry stones … [was] late to rise and dirty at meals, [a] chief shammer of illness'. It was a world where the early painters of the Italian Renaissance used jewel-bright colours equally to depict the birth of Venus or the Marriage of the Virgin, where saints' shrines were buried under gifts of golden coins and the dead were piled up in plague pits, sprinkled with lime and covered over to await the next layer of bodies. In Edmund's world, explorers might reach the coast of Africa and Lollards call for religious purity, but comets blazing through the sky heralded disaster and crops might be blighted by an old woman muttering charms. It was a world of paradox, of extreme sensitivity and vision, juxtaposed with an essential pragmatism, often a brutality, of approach. Sickness and health, poverty and riches, squalor and art, piety and war, life and death sat alongside each other.

In 1443, England was in the twenty-first year of the reign of Henry VI and the hundred and sixth year of the Hundred Years' War. It was still a green and pleasant land, largely covered with fields of wheat, barley and oats or where sheep, pigs and cows dotted the landscape, around a fifth of which was owned by the Catholic Church. A small number of very wealthy families held the reins of government but the country's administration was riddled with corruption and abuses, and the Crown itself was in a desperate financial state. The previous decade had seen a number of harvests fail and livestock fall prey to disease, driving up prices and rents, resulting in higher taxation. Henry had succeeded to the throne before his first birthday and spent the next two decades under the influence of several unpopular ministers. The country was just seven years away from the eruption of violence that was Jack Cade's rebellion, when peasants ran riot across the south-east, executing bishops and claiming that Henry had lost control of his kingdom.

The costly war with France had been started by Henry's great-great-great-grandfather, Edward III, and had run its course of highs and lows through several generations. England had experienced some terrible losses but also some resounding victories. No doubt the young king had heard tales of armies crossing the Channel in a huge fleet, marching through the Norman countryside and laying siege to walled cities: the names of Crécy, Poitiers and Agincourt were the foundation of the young king's international heritage. Agincourt itself had been won by his own father, who led his troops against a much stronger opponent on St Crispin's Day, and later took as his wife the King of France's daughter. The beautiful Catherine of Valois had borne their only child in December 1421: thus Henry VI was half-English and half-French, the blood of two long-standing enemies mingling in his veins. By the Treaty of Troyes, negotiated by his father in 1420, he was to be king of both countries, so he had been crowned in both Westminster Abbey and Notre-Dame, Paris. The body of Henry VI, his physical person, his very duality, was to be the solution incarnate to the century-old conflict. It was a heavy mantle for his young shoulders.

In 1443, Henry's man in Normandy was Richard Plantagenet, Duke of York. A decade older than the king, York had attended both of Henry's coronations and succeeded Henry's uncle as Lieutenant of France. In practical terms, though, this meant ruling a patchy empire including Normandy, Picardy, Touraine, Poitou and the southern Languedoc region while Catherine's half-brother, Charles VII, held the remainder of France in the Valois name. If nothing else, Charles had Paris, the traditional heart of the country, which the English had abandoned in a disastrous state in 1436 following a prolonged siege. The new capital of the English region was Rouen, and it was there that Richard, Duke of York arrived with his family in the summer of 1441 to take up residence in the city's castle. Today, nothing more than the keep remains of Rouen Castle, the Grosse Tour, standing out as a turreted *donjon* to the north of the city, on Bouvreuil Hill, which had once been the site of a Roman amphitheatre. The Yorks would have known a substantial complex of several towers enclosing an inner courtyard with buildings, all ringed about by walls and ditches. The surviving tower, 30m tall with walls 4m thick, gives some impression of the vast scale of the castle and its defences, but is also a reminder of the Anglo-French conflict that was very recent history for the Yorks. Referred to today as Joan of Arc's Tower, the Grosse Tower actually never held her captive; her prison was demolished in 1809. In 1441, though, the castle, both towers and the city, would still have been ringing with memories of the young girl who believed herself called upon by God to free the French and was burnt by the English in Rouen's marketplace. Only a decade had elapsed since her pyre had cooled.

Richard, Duke of York had been born in 1411. He was Anne Mortimer's third child, but this labour proved too much and she died the following day, at around the age of 20. Descended from both the second and fourth surviving sons of Edward III, the boy had a strong claim to the throne; in fact, his mother's Mortimer ancestors had been the preferred heirs of Richard II before he was deposed by the Lancastrian line, by Henry VI's grandfather. This had diverted the line of succession away from York, whose family's reputation had been further besmirched by the failed attempt his father made to reclaim their right in 1415. Death touched the family twice in this significant year. Richard, Duke of Conisburgh was executed for his role in the Southampton Plot, but this had not prevented his 4-year-old son from inheriting his ducal title upon the death of his uncle at Agincourt – reported alternately to have sacrificed himself to save the king, or been trodden into the mud because of his heavy armour, Edward of Norwich, Second Duke of York passed the family inheritance on to the orphaned boy.

Richard had been raised as a loyal subject to the Lancastrian crown and, in 1429, had made a good marriage into a family who shared the king's bloodline. His 14-year-old bride was Cecily Neville, a granddaughter of John of Gaunt, fifth son of Edward III, founder of the Lancastrian line and father of the man who had usurped York' position. Cecily may have been of the 'usurping' line but the marriage proved a strong one, based on personal esteem and affection, and she appears to have transferred her loyalties completely to her husband. Reputedly a great beauty, Cecily has gone down in history for her strength of character, her determination and loyalty, and her belief in York's cause. By the time of their arrival in Rouen, she had already borne a daughter, Anne, in 1439 but had also lost a son, Henry, in February 1441. This lost infant would have been the head of the York family, significantly changing subsequent history, had he survived; the death of an heir in such a dynasty was a great loss but his parents were still young, and able to have more children. Richard and Cecily's departure for France may even have been delayed while she lay in and recovered from her ordeal. Both the duke and duchess were aware that their children had a triple claim to the throne, stronger than that of the reigning king.

While York was busy governing the region and repelling attacks from the Valois royal family, Cecily was running the household and entertaining guests and dignitaries. Soon after their arrival, she was called upon to act as hostess for the visiting dukes of Brittany and Alençon. The castle would have been run sumptuously, with the best food and wine, linen and table ware, and comfortable furnishings such as the cushioned privy seat Cecily ordered especially for their new home. York's financier, John Wigmore, also had to settle bills for a gold cup the duchess purchased from a London goldsmith and clothing to the tune of £680.[1] It was a proper sense of their social position, a requirement of rank, that prompted the Yorks to live like kings in Rouen. The status-conscious medieval world was accustomed to translate visual symbols of power into actual respect; thus the more opulent a lord and his household the better. Properties, servants and retinue, clothing and jewels, food and hospitality, poise and behaviour were essential tools of the aristocracy. Sometimes those with new money sought to ape such a position, giving rise to sumptuary laws and conflicts between established families and newcomers. It was especially important for the Yorks to be seen to be powerful in France, as seeing was believing. The convincing demonstration of power was power itself. Against the backdrop of the recent bitter conflict, the duke and duchess were effectively king and queen in France.

The Yorks were a very prolific couple. A profusion of heirs was an obvious dynastic advantage, especially as, across the Channel, Henry VI was still in his early twenties and had yet to marry and father a son. Until such time, the Duke of York, as a descendent from a senior bloodline, was effectively his heir. Soon after their arrival in Rouen, Cecily fell pregnant for the third time. She gave birth to Edward on 28 April 1441, who was given a quiet christening, either in one of the castle's two large chapels, or the smaller one adjoining their private quarters.[2] This expediency was probably the result of simple proximity. Perhaps Edward was premature, or else overdue; perhaps the labour was difficult or lengthy. Only fourteen months had elapsed since Cecily had lost her first son during birth or very soon afterwards. It is unlikely that she was prepared to take any risks with Edward's immortal soul. Swift action in such a case was considered crucial.

In later years, rumours would circulate about the paternity of this new son of York, initiated by his enemies once he had displaced Henry VI and taken the English throne. His low-key christening has also been cited as evidence that he was the product of an adulterous liaison. Yet York never doubted the child's paternity, which Cecily repeated on her deathbed, when circumstances would have allowed her to maintain a diplomatic silence or piety prompted her to confession. The timing of York's campaign at Pontoise has been offered as proof that he was not in the city at the time of conception, but this alone is inconclusive, as it does not record Cecily's whereabouts or take account of the variation in duration of 'normal' pregnancies. Just four months after Edward was born, Cecily fell pregnant again. Edmund arrived on 17 May 1443 and was christened in Rouen Cathedral. The fact that Edmund had a grander ceremony than his brother may be due to any number of reasons that are unrecoverable now. Perhaps there was fear of plague in Rouen, or uprisings, or the weather was unseasonable, all of which would have affected the removal of a newborn through the narrow city streets. There is also the possibility that York had already decided that Edward would inherit his titles in England while Edmund continued his work in France, hence his more public reception. Yet the Anglo-French dynamic was to change completely in the coming years.

By the time Edward and Edmund were joined in the Rouen nursery by Elizabeth, a year later, the question of government had already become more complicated for their father. Maintaining law and order in a divided country was costly and difficult. Even before they engaged in any conflict, armies needed to be paid, fed, clothed, sheltered, moved and equipped. On top of this, York had to constantly repel efforts by the Valois and their supporters to encroach upon the ever-shifting borders, with little support from home. The English crown was already in financial difficulties but when Henry decided to allocate more funds to France, they were given instead to John Beaufort, Duke of Somerset to lead an army in Gascony, leaving York to fund his armies and expeditions out of his own pocket. Worse, the Gascon venture failed and the army was forced to return empty-handed to Normandy. When York's tenure came to an end in 1445, he and his young family returned to England in the expectation of it being renewed. However, it soon became clear that the Yorks were out of favour, losing out to the Lancastrian Beaufort line, with the job being given to Somerset's younger brother. Settling back into the family properties at Fotheringhay and Ludlow, York felt sidelined and frustrated that someone with his proximity to the throne was not allowed greater influence. By this time the crown owed him over £28 million in today's currency.

By the end of that year, when he was 2 years old, Edmund was already being formally referred to as the Earl of Rutland. It was a fairly new title, having been created for York's uncle Edward of Norwich, who no longer needed it once he inherited the family dukedom. York chose to resurrect the title for his second son, possibly as an honour to his uncle, as his elder son Edward had been given the earldom of March. It would also bring rents, revenues and other resources on which Edmund might draw. Rutland itself was a small county in the East Midlands, but Edmund had little actual connection to the place during his lifetime. His investiture was more important for the association it gave him to a hero of Agincourt and demarcated his status within the English aristocracy.

Very little else is known of Edmund's early life and education beyond that which was dictated by his father's career. When Edmund was 6, York was appointed Lieutenant of Ireland and sailed from Beaumaris, on the tip of Anglesey, over to Dublin, landing on 6 July 1449. Cecily was definitely with him, but the whereabouts of the two York sons are unclear. Edward and Edmund might have accompanied their parents and stayed in Dublin Castle, taking their lessons behind the solid stone walls overlooking the River Poddle, welcoming their new brother George, who was born in October and visiting Trim at Christmas. The family seem to have been genuinely popular in Ireland, York commanding loyalty from the Irish, and their stay there was a success, but the same question of money plagued them, as King Henry would not grant them enough for their expenses. Equally, this might have been the occasion that prompted the boys' parents to set them up in their own establishment. At the ages of 6 and 7, Edmund and Edward formed something of a unit, as brothers and friends, who could more easily be left behind than a single child, alone. It was customary among aristocratic families to send children away from home to be raised, or trained, for their future positions and the age of 7 was considered a significant point of transition in childhood development. If this was the case with the Yorks, Edmund would have accompanied his elder brother to Ludlow.

II

The little Shropshire town on the Welsh Borders would have already been familiar to the two boys. It was the base from which York administered his Welsh estates, where he had a considerable following, holding the title of Earl of March from his Mortimer ancestors. But Ludlow was not just an important administrative centre, its defensive position harked back to earlier conflicts, when the castle dominated the rise of land overlooking the Welsh hills. The town nudged up close to the castle walls, ensuring adequate supplies for the boys' household as they went about their education and recreation. The castle itself contained an inner bailey with a round chapel, great hall and apartments, and a large outer bailey with service buildings and a gatehouse. Later, Edward would leave strict instructions for the regime of his own son, who was sent to Ludlow at an even younger age. The boy was to follow the usual format of religious devotion and academic study, courtly manners and combat, but must be allowed time for leisure and playing with his dogs. Those who served him were carefully vetted and no bad behaviour was to be tolerated. No doubt York appointed trusted guardians to oversee his sons in his absence. They were being raised to become the great English magnates of the future.

While Edward and Edmund were reading French chronicles and practising their archery, news arrived at the castle of the changing political scene. It seems likely that, given their intended futures, at least some of this information would have been shared with the boys. English territories in France were falling rapidly to the Valois. In April 1450, following a huge victory at the Battle of Formigny, where around 3,500 English were killed or wounded, the French pushed into Normandy, claiming other victories all the way north to Calais. This was a particularly bitter blow, given that York had been passed over for the position of Lieutenant in favour of the Duke of Somerset, whom he now blamed for these losses. It may well have been a defining moment for Edmund too, if his career had been envisioned as part of the long tradition of the English governance of France. The job had long been reserved for the king's uncles and cousins but, with the empire crumbling, there would soon be nothing for Edmund to govern. With this identity snatched from under his nose, compared with the vast inheritance of his elder brother, his path seemed uncertain. He had been a future ruler of France; he was now merely a younger son. Nothing survives to record his reaction. At 7 years old it was probably less meaningful to him in a real sense, than his close relationship with his brother.

In the spring of 1450, a figure known to history as Jack Cade emerged as the focal point for people's dissent. Born in the south-east, from the lower class, he voiced their concerns in a manifesto called The Complaint of the Poor Commons of Kent and rallied huge numbers to his side. In late May, the rebels began to march to London and reached Blackheath at the start of June. There they were joined by disgruntled soldiers and sailors returning from the wars, as well as a few members of the middle and upper classes. This would not have directly affected the Duke of York and his family, had Cade not then adopted the name John Mortimer, with its obvious allusions to the rival royal line. This gave rise to rumours that York was in alliance with the rebels, prompting him to write to Henry in earnest from Ireland, assuring him of his loyalty.

The situation in London rapidly escalated. Leaders of the royal army were ambushed and killed, Baron Saye and the Bishop of Salisbury were murdered, then Cade declared himself Lord Mayor. King Henry fled the capital. York hastened back to England, gathering troops in the name of the crown, but also in his own defence, as the king made attempts to intercept him. York and Henry met in London and the duke called for reform and the removal of unpopular royal favourites, such as the Duke of Somerset, whom he considered to have failed the English cause in France. In some quarters this seemed to confirm York's sympathy with the rebels' demands. For a brief while, Somerset was imprisoned but, after his release and Cade's death, York retired to Ludlow and was reunited with his sons. Two years later, when he made another attempt to remove his enemy, Edward and Edmund certainly were informed of his movements. At 10 and 9, they now had a better understanding of the precarious situation their father was in, and Edward at least had been keen to assist

York, offering to march to London with 10,000 men and liberate him after he was captured by the king.[3]

The question of Edmund's future was settled in 1451, when he was appointed Lord Chancellor of Ireland by his father, then still holding the Lieutenancy. It was essentially an honorary title for a child, but made clear the direction his father intended for him. Rouen was lost, so Edmund's future career would be in Dublin. Due to Edmund's youth, his duties were carried out by Sir Edmund Oldhall, brother of Sir William, who was York's chamberlain. The Oldhalls were originally a Norfolk-based family, and Sir Edmund was a Carmelite priest and judge, well-placed to fulfil this role until 1454. After that, the role of deputy chancellor was taken over by the Lancastrian John Talbot, Earl of Shrewsbury, further distancing Edmund from his intended path.

The next time Edmund appears in the records is in two letters composed by himself and Edward in the spring and early summer of 1454. Edmund was then approaching, or had just passed, his eleventh birthday and was resident with his brother at Ludlow Castle, whence they wrote to their father. The political situation had changed considerably at court, following King Henry's lapse into a catatonic state the previous August. During his incapacity, Parliament had continued to rule in his name, employing the great seal which was in the keeping of John Kemp, Archbishop of Canterbury. Kemp's death in March 1454 meant that this was no longer possible, so Parliament appointed York as Protector of the Realm until Henry's recovery, despite the protests of his Beaufort opponents. At the time they wrote their letters from Ludlow, there was no guarantee that the king would recover his wits, so York's appointment took the duke and his sons a step closer to the throne.

The first letter is dated 'on Saturday in Easter week', which would have been 20 April, just over two weeks after York's protectorship began. The boys had been informed by loyal servants of the challenges and successes their father had experienced at court and wrote to wish him 'honourable conduite and good spede in all your matiers and besynesse, and of your gracious prevaile ayenst thentent and malice of your evilwillers'.[4] They also asked for York's blessing 'thrugh whiche we trust muche the rather to encrees an growe to vertu, and to spede the better in all matiers and things that we shall use, occupy and exercise'.[5] Then, in a little domestic touch that reminds us of their age, they thanked him for sending them some green gowns and requested some new bonnets. It is a letter of two boys aware of their position on the threshold of young adulthood, keen to prepare themselves for the time when they might be of service to their family.

The second letter is dated 3 June, and was written in response to one their father had sent six days before from York. The boys thanked God for York's 'worschipful and victorious spede ageniest your enemyse to ther grete shame' and found these 'the most comfortable tydinges that we desired to here'.[6] They informed their father that they were in good health and were obeying his instructions to 'attende specially to our lernyng' in their 'yong age' which would cause them to grow in 'honor and worship' in their old age. In particular, this second letter gives the sense that both boys were at the beginning of a journey which would propel them into public affairs, the best preparation for which was to study their lessons and observe their father's example. The emphasis is not on power for its own sake, but on being honourable, on being a good lord, of fulfilment of their birthright as a responsibility rather than a privilege. In 1454, as the two boys signed their names at the bottom of the paper, there was no way of knowing that one of them would complete that journey while the other's path would be cut short.

Three mentions of the earl in the close rolls from 1456,[7] in formal legal documents relating to property, refer to York, Edward and Edmund as a unit, which seems to confirm that the duke was planning to divide his Anglo-Irish responsibilities between them. There was never any suggestion of sidelining Edmund into the Church and no mention in the rolls of the two younger York brothers, who had both been born by this point. Thus the males in the family fell into pairs according to age: Edward and Edmund, who were educated and raised with the intention of fulfilling the duke's duties in the future, and George and Richard, both still in the nursery in 1454, whose futures may have lain in clerical and administrative fields. Previous royal generations had found roles for clusters of brothers, such as the sons of Edward III and Henry IV, among whom seniority was significant but did not always dictate prosperity and fortune. In this light, the establishment of the two elder York boys at Ludlow would seem a conscious choice to foster ties of friendship and devotion between the brothers and to prevent rivalry. In fact, it would be the absence of Edmund, rather than his presence, that would later confirm just how divisive the English system of primogeniture could prove.

III

By the late 1450s, relations between the Crown and York were strained to the limit. The Battle of St Albans had given the Yorkists the upper hand, leading to a second Protectorate but, despite various shows of peace, hostilities were brewing between the duke's faction and the queen's party. When York and his allies were summoned to attend a Parliament at Coventry in 1459, they correctly suspected their attendance would lead to their arrests, and so stayed away. The extent to which Edward and Edmund were involved is unclear, but both were identified along with their father as rebels, guilty of 'high treason' and intent upon 'raising insurrection'. Now described as the '*late* Earl of Roteland', Edmund was attainted by an Act of Parliament, meaning that he was deprived of his title and that any manors, estates and lands formerly in his possession were now in the hands of the royal receivers.[8] His capture would mean certain death. The brothers chose to fight and that October they were considered old enough, at 17 and 16, to engage in combat alongside their father. Prompted by a surprise attack upon their allies, they rendezvoused just outside the city walls at Ludlow, as the king marched down from the north. No doubt Edmund experienced a mixture of emotions on the eve of his first battle, praying and recalling his martial training, listening to the advice of seasoned campaigners such as York, his Neville cousin the Earl of Warwick, and York's brother-in-law the Earl of Salisbury. Yet the planned encounter at Ludford Bridge did not take place. Overnight, King Henry was spotted in the opposite camp, causing numbers of York's followers to desert, fearful of dying a traitor's death. It was impossible to win on such terms. Under cover of darkness, York and his sons took the difficult decision to flee the country. For the first time, the brothers were divided: Edward went to Calais with Warwick and Edmund accompanied York to Ireland.

It was a wise move to go to Ireland, where Henry had no real jurisdiction. Ten years after his first visit, York was still the country's Lieutenant and had retained the support of its Parliament, including the influential FitzGerald family and their adherents. The Sixth Earl of Desmond, James FitzGerald, had even been chosen by York as godfather to his son George back in 1449. Edmund only just missed meeting his deputy, Edmund Oldhall, who had died that August and now the youth was able to take over the position for himself. A few records survive from transactions made by the duke during this time, including the reward of loyal Yorkist Sir James Pickering, who was appointed Clerk of the Common Pleas and 'searcher' of customs at the ports of Dublin and Drogheda that November.[9]

On 7 February 1460, York summoned Parliament to meet at Drogheda, in a session which ran until 21 July. Two weeks after the summons, the duke formally confirmed the full-time appointment of Edmund as Chancellor of Ireland, 'to exercise the office in person or by his sufficient deputy for whom he is willing to answer, taking yearly the accustomed fees, wages and rewards, profits and commodities, due and accustomed to that office of old'. During York's rule, the Irish Parliament took the significant step of declaring itself legally independent from England, its subjects bound only to follow the laws and statutes of 'the Lords Spiritual and Temporal and Common of Ireland, freely admitted and accepted in their Parliaments and Great Councils'. This effectively made York King of Ireland. Any officials attempting to enforce decrees from Henry VI would lose their land and face a fine. One of the assembly's final actions was taken in response to news that Edward, Warwick and Salisbury had returned from Calais and won a decisive victory at Northampton. The death of York's enemy John Talbot, Second Earl of Shrewsbury, allowed the duke to reassign his lands in County Wexford, granting them to Patrick Ketyng and James Prendergast.[10]

York and Edmund might have remained indefinitely in Ireland, where they were as good as kings. In time, Edmund might have become the country's sole leader and built on York's foundation with the long-standing support of its aristocracy. His year in Ireland would have established and cemented his position as his father's heir in the country, in preparation for his future government. Yet the Yorks' bloodline placed them so close to the English throne that at times it must have felt as if it was at their fingertips. With Edward's conquest changing the political climate in London, the way was clear for York to formulate a new plan. His position of authority, almost regality, in Ireland gave him a new determination and it is likely that he took Edmund into his confidence. On 9 September, York and Edmund landed in Wales. As they rode east, York commanded that a drawn sword be carried before him, in the tradition of kings. When they arrived at Westminster, on 10 October, the duke laid claim to the English throne by right of conquest.

York's actions took Edward, Warwick and the English lords by surprise. Henry VI had been captured after the Battle of Northampton and returned to Westminster where he was, once again, the puppet of the Yorkist faction. As far as the duke was concerned, the attainder of 1459 made his former position untenable, so seizing the throne was justifiable as a defensive act. How Edmund reacted to this decision is unclear. It may have been something his father discussed with him, and which Edmund approved. The English lords, however, disapproved. Their compromise was the Act of Accord, passed on 25 October, by which Henry retained the throne for the duration of his life but York was named as his heir, after which the crown would pass to Edward and Edmund. They were given incomes in accordance with their new status and it became a treasonable offence to conspire against, attack or kill them. Henry VI's son, the 7-year-old Edward of Westminster, was excluded from the succession, which York must have known would not be accepted by the queen. York might now have the protection of the law but it would not be enough to save his life.

Edmund's position had now changed considerably. After the initial switch in direction from France to Ireland, it seemed that his life would be spent in the governance of English territories abroad, in service to a Lancastrian king. The Act of Accord changed everything. Edmund was now third in line to the throne, after his father and brother. If the terms of the Act were adhered to, there was a reasonable chance that Edward would inherit, but if he were to die in battle, of illness or without issue, Edmund would become England's king. For a few weeks that autumn, stability and hope returned for the York family, who finally believed they had been restored to their rightful position. That November, Edmund received a bequest in the will of Sir William Oldhall, brother of his deputy in Ireland, Sir Edmund. William had been attainted for aiding and abetting the Yorkist uprising of 1459 and died the following November. While Edward was left a grey walking horse, Edmund got the value of the horse in money.[11]

Soon, it became apparent that there were still battles to be won. The Act of Accord had settled certain questions but it had raised others and Queen Margaret was raising an army in the north on behalf of her disinherited son. That December the York party divided again: Edward went west to intercept the arrival of the king's half-brother, Jasper Tudor; Warwick stayed in London to guard Henry; while York, Edmund and Salisbury headed north with a commission of array, a group of men needed for recruiting purposes, which may have only numbered a few hundred.[12] Again, Edmund was partnered with his father while Edward acted independently. Separating the two brothers is likely to have been a precautionary measure, to prevent the capture of both heirs, but it also indicates that Edward was considered to have come to maturity and, perhaps shows an ease or connection between Edmund and his father. They encountered appalling weather on the way north, which caused flooding and unpassable roads, and their troops were ambushed on at least one occasion. With Edmund were two other young men, Salisbury's son Thomas and his son-in-law Thomas Harrington, who was 18. There was also Sir Thomas Parre, who had been in exile with Edward, and Sir James Pickering, who had been in Ireland with York and Edmund. On 21 December, twelve days after leaving London, they arrived at Sandal Castle, on the edge of Wakefield in Yorkshire.

Edmund, York and their party spent the Christmas period at Sandal, aware that some of the queen's forces were in the vicinity. They may have believed that the Act would protect them, or that a truce negotiated to cover the festive season would be honoured. On 30 December, perhaps in need of more supplies, they ventured out of the castle and encountered a large army waiting for them in the surrounding forest, led by the son of York's great enemy, Edmund Beaufort, Duke of Somerset. The details of the battle are not known, as no contemporary account survives, but York was killed in the fighting, Salisbury captured and beheaded, and Edmund was killed about a mile away from Sandal Castle. He was 17. The chronicles offer differing accounts of his final moments, but none of the writers had been present to witness his death and some were writing centuries after the event.

There is no doubt that Edmund would have fought bravely and well. He had been trained to do so. The one contemporary writer who would have seen him in person was William Gregory, Lord Mayor of London 1451–52, who was aged around 60 at the time of the battle. He described Edmund as 'one of the best disposed Lords in the land' when it came to the use of arms.[13] Most other accounts agree that the earl was dispatched by John, Lord Clifford, later known as 'the butcher' for his actions, in revenge for York's killing of his father at St Albans in 1455. Two other contemporaries, William Worcester and the author of *The English Chronicle*, simply state the fact of Edmund's death, without detail. Writing around eighty years after the battle, chronicler Edward Hall makes one major error in getting Edmund's age wrong. Believing him to be 12 rather than 17, Hall wove a scene of great pathos and sentiment, which has coloured interpretations of the event ever since: the child Edmund kneels, 'a fair gentleman and maiden-like in person … imploring mercy and benefitting grace, both with holding up his hands and making dolorous countenance'. His chaplain pleads for him but Clifford 'struck the earl to the heart with his dagger' and made the priest take the news to his mother. It is more likely that Edmund had fought his way out of Sandal and met the 25-year-old Clifford in an evenly matched encounter.

Most accounts agree that Edmund died on or near the bridge over the River Calder about a mile to the north of the battle site. He may have been trying to reach the safety of Wakefield and the sanctuary of St Mary the Virgin's Chantry Chapel, which sat midway along the bridge. The Elizabethan antiquarian John Leland visited the site in 1544 and wrote that Edmund had actually died a little above the barres or gate, beyond the bridge, 'going up a clymyng ground' into the town. He drew on what appears to have been an oral tradition, recording that 'the commune saying is that the Erle wold have taken ther a poore woman's house for sucore and she for fere shet the dore and strait the erle was killid.'[14]

Later writers have located the site of Edmund's death further on, near a medieval building called the Six Chimneys at the bottom of Kirkgate, although some reached that conclusion centuries after the event. The difference is a distance of around a third of a mile, along the route of the present A61, which is quite compatible with a drawn-out chase from the chapel, perhaps with the mortal wound inflicted at one location and the finality of death lagging a little behind. Wherever his killing took place, the end result was the same. Shortly afterwards, Edmund's corpse was decapitated, just as those of York, Salisbury and others had been, as a warning to their allies, and their heads were displayed upon Micklegate Bar in York. They remained in place until Edward was in a position to order their removal, when they were interred at nearby Pontefract Abbey. Clifford was killed on 28 March 1461, shortly before Edward's decisive victory at the Battle of Towton.

IV

In February 1462, Edward, now King Edward IV, honoured his father and brother in a way that illustrates an aspect of late medieval piety. The living could undertake or instigate a range of acts which were designed to commemorate the memory of loved ones, offset the nature of their deaths and speed their journey through purgatory. This had the added advantage of casting spiritual merit upon the benefactor, not just in the eyes of the community, or justification for the new regime, but as a mark in their favour against the moment of spiritual reckoning. Acts of honour might be carried out by the individual themselves, such as a pilgrimage or even an act of penance, but it was more often through the bequest of money for the creation of a tomb or the establishment of regular masses or an obit, which were prayers to be said on the anniversary of the departure of the deceased. Edward chose to continue his father's work at Fotheringhay by completing the college begun by their ancestor, Edward, Duke of York, the new king's great uncle, hero of Agincourt, from whom they had inherited the title:

> Considering the zeal of Edward, late Duke of York, in the foundation of a college at Foderinghay [sic] on a site of six acres in his demesne there, for a master, twelve chaplains, eight clerks and thirteen choristers or a smaller number, there to celebrate for his soul and those of his progenitors and heirs, the King desiring from pious motives to complete this foundation ... to celebrate for the souls of his progenitors, for his happy state during his life and for that of his mother, Cecily, Duchess of York, and for the health of his own soul after death ... Richard, Duke of York, the King's father, true heir of the realms of England and France and the Lordship of Ireland, and of Edmund, late Earl of Rutland the King's brother ... and all of the King's progenitors and all of the faithful departed. [15]

Edward appointed a Thomas Buxhale to be master of the college and granted him six acres for the building of dwellings necessary for those employed in the establishment, supported by revenues from lands and other existing religious foundations. [16]

On 20 July 1463, Edward established obits to be said for his father and brother by harnessing a former Lancastrian pious foundation. Having deposed Henry VI, who was then a fugitive in the north, Edward had no qualms about building on the former king's patronage for St Peter's Church, Westminster, as a Lancastrian location for devotion to the soul and memory of Henry V. Perhaps Edward meant this as a conciliatory gesture, using religion to span the divide between opposing dynasties.

Given Henry VI's notorious piety, the former king may have been pleased to hear that the devotions to his father were being respected, not neglected, in the spirit that all enemies were equal in death. He had also had a particular affiliation for St Peter. However, Edward went further and ordered that prayers be said for 'the good estate of the present king and of his mother Cecily, Duchess of York, during life and for their souls after death, and may also celebrate and observe an anniversary for the souls of the illustrious prince Richard, Duke of York, and the mighty lords Edmund, Duke of Rutland, and Richard, Earl of Salisbury', on 30 December, with a mass the following day.[17] It is difficult to know quite what Henry VI thought of the harnessing of his piety and ancestry to the memories of those who had fought against him. He was hardly in a position to do anything about it, but there does seem to have been a universal respect for the dead, even if they had been one's opponents in life, a sort of superstition about their influence and the harm that could come from speaking ill or them or damaging their memory. This was typical of late medieval piety and would not be challenged on a large scale until the iconoclasm of the Reformation seven decades later.

It was not until 1476 that Edward arranged for the removal of his father and brother from Pontefract to Fotheringhay where, initially, York was buried in the choir and Edmund in the Lady Chapel. The event was witnessed by Thomas Whiting, a herald, who left a detailed account of the magnificent proceedings:

On 24 July [1476] the bodies were exhumed, that of the Duke, 'garbed in an ermine furred mantle and cap of maintenance, covered with a cloth of gold' lay in state under a hearse blazing with candles, guarded by an angel of silver, bearing a crown of gold as a reminder that by right the Duke had been a King. On its journey, Richard, Duke of Gloucester, with other lords and officers of arms, all dressed in mourning, followed the funeral chariot, drawn by six horses, with trappings of black, charged with the arms of France and England and preceded by a knight bearing the banner of the ducal arms. Fotheringhay was reached on 29 July, where members of the college and other ecclesiastics went forth to meet the cortege. At the entrance to the churchyard, King Edward waited, together with the Duke of Clarence, the Marquis of Dorset, Earl Rivers, Lord Hastings and other noblemen. Upon its arrival the King 'made obeisance to the body right humbly and put his hand on the body and kissed it, crying all the time.' The procession moved into the church where two hearses were waiting, one in the choir for the body of the Duke and one in the Lady Chapel for that of the Earl of Rutland, and after the King had retired to his 'closet' and the princes and officers of arms had stationed themselves around the hearses, masses were sung and the King's chamberlain offered for him seven pieces of cloth of gold 'which were laid in a cross on the body.' The next day three masses were sung, the Bishop of Lincoln preached a 'very noble sermon' and offerings were made by the Duke of Gloucester and other lords, of 'The Duke of York's coat of arms, of his shield, his sword, his helmet and his coursers on which rode Lord Ferrers in full armour, holding in his hand an axe reversed.' When the funeral was over, the people were admitted into the church and it is said that before the coffins were placed in the vault which had been built under the chancel, five thousand persons came to receive the alms, while four times that number partook of the dinner, served partly in the castle and partly in the King's tents and pavilions. The menu included capons, cygnets, herons, rabbits and so many good things that the bills for it amounted to more than three hundred pounds.

A list of the burials at Pontefract, compiled in 1504 by John Wriothesley, states that the Duke of York's heart remained there when his bones were translated to Fotheringhay. This was not unusual, as the internal organs were removed during the embalming process and sometimes stored separately in urns, which might allow for burial elsewhere, especially if there had been several locations of significance during the life of the deceased. The same went for Edmund's heart, although his ties to Pontefract were not particularly strong in comparison with Fotheringhay or Ludlow. It may have been a practical question of accessing the organs in 1476, if they had been sealed in stone or in an inaccessible part of the abbey. The medieval belief in the final day of judgement encompassed the idea that all the body parts of an individual would be reunited as a prerequisite for their endowment with eternal life. No details survive about the original tombs of Richard or Edmund. The abbey at Pontefract was completely destroyed during the Reformation and the tombs at Fotheringhay were disfigured. During the reign of York's great-great-granddaughter, Elizabeth I, the remains were moved again from the choir and Lady Chapel and placed in a communal vault under a new alabaster memorial.

V

It is only hindsight that allows us to consider Edmund's death in terms of the absence of the individual. Without speculating what kind of Lieutenant of Ireland he might have made, or even what manner of king he could potentially have become, it is possible to examine what actually did happen as a result of his death. And what happened was that his mantle fell to his next York brother in line, George. After Edward became king in 1461, the 11-year-old George stepped into Edmund's position as his heir. He was also granted the Lieutenancy of Ireland, and appears in the Parliament records in that capacity as early as October 1462. Given George's age, his godfather's son, Thomas FitzGerald, Seventh Earl of Desmond, acted as his deputy, continuing those ties of loyalty that had been established by York and Edmund. George's influence is also suggested in a 1463 grant to the inhabitants of Ireland's Dungarvan giving them the same rights as the inhabitants of Clare in Suffolk, as Clare was the town whence the dukedom of Clarence originally derived.[18]

Initially, all seemed to be going well, one brother seamlessly replaced by another. On 24 February 1464, the Irish Parliament wrote to Edward in praise of George as Lieutenant, who was fulfilling his father's memory:

> Advertisyng your highnesse of the full grete and notable service that your faithful subject and true liege man or especiale good Lord your most derrest Brothir of Clarence lieutenant of this your land of Irland hath dooun as well unto your highnesse as to the Right noble and famouse Prince your fadre of blessed memorie whom god Rest of the importable charges and costes by the same depute aswel afore thoffice of depute lieutenancy of this your said

land as after unto the said Erle committed hath daily susteined he there of not
failing but daily continuyng his faithful service right ordinate and worshipfull
at al tymes.[19]

In 1464, the 15-year-old George was clearly a loyal adherent of his elder
brother, Ireland and the Yorkist dynastic cause. Yet everything would
change later that year, when Edward made an unpopular marriage and
tensions began to appear in his court that would lead, in time, to George
rebelling against his brother. Until Edward fathered a legitimate son of his
own, which did not happen until November 1470, George was next in
line to the throne. When George joined Warwick to rise against Edward
in 1469–70, it was to challenge his brother's authority; to depose and
kill him may not have been his initial intention. Angered that Edward
had vetoed an important marriage for him, George absconded to Calais,
where he married Warwick's daughter and, along with the earl, cast
aspersions upon Edward's legitimacy. At first Edward could not believe
that his brother was acting against him, but George's flight and the issue
of a rebel manifesto from Calais confirmed his treachery. This was the
moment that clarified just how much Edward had lost an important ally
and support in Edmund.

Despite this, when George and Warwick's coup foundered, they were
forgiven and the brothers were briefly reconciled. Yet George was not
content and, following a second rebellion, Edward was deposed in favour
of the Lancastrian Henry VI and forced into exile. Although Edward
returned and reclaimed his throne six months later, killing Warwick in the
process, he was not prepared to afford his errant brother any more chances.
Five years later, George's repeated challenges and erratic behaviour
prompted his brother to sign his death warrant. It is not possible to know
what position Edmund would have taken as his brothers clashed and
threatened the stability of the realm but his former closeness to Edward
might suggest where his loyalties would have lain. It is not unfeasible to
imagine that Edmund could have provided an anchor for George, keeping
him grounded, curtailing his ambition. If nothing else, his mere existence
would have removed the very impetus of George's claim, as any doubts

concerning Edward's fitness to rule would have simply turned the spotlight upon Edmund rather than George. He could not have realistically argued that both his elder brothers were illegitimate. There would have been no point in George's rebellion had Edmund still been alive. Edmund's death put the throne within George's reach. His unrealised career and actions cannot be imagined, but his absence allowed the advancement of a man whose ambition and instability ultimately proved fatal.

It is tempting, with hindsight, to preserve Edmund as the figure of Yorkist salvation, the buffer between the early years and the Edwardian disintegration and reign of the final brother, Richard III. Knowing the tragic path Edward's relationship with George would take, and that the former would die a premature death and his sons be lost in the Tower, Edmund emerges like a shining beacon of lost Yorkist opportunity, the piece in the jigsaw that would have ensured continuing dynastic dominance and serene Yorkist rule into the next century. Obviously, Edmund's life is too narrow a pin upon which to hang such fabulous visions but this possibility illustrates the very real dangers of interpreting history. He might have been all this, and equally, he might not. But this is a very human failing. The romantic trap of recovering the dead as final solutions, as retrospective answers to unfathomable problems is not just a modern phenomenon. In every chantry tomb, every lit candle, every remembrance day feast, medieval memorial had an aspect of lost potential, forever idealised as it was eternally unrealised. No wonder the fascination with, and attachment to, those who die young continues.

Shortly after the final translation of the earl's bones to Fotheringhay, Shakespeare portrayed the deaths of York and Edmund at Wakefield in *Henry VI Part III*. The impact of such a scene, frequently enacted upon the stage to a wide audience, had the effect of countering other narratives with a sympathetic popular history of the event, which would shape the subsequent artistic interpretations of the eighteenth and nineteenth centuries. Apart from the obvious inaccuracies of placing Edward and a highly precocious 8-year-old Richard at the scene, Shakespeare creates a scene of pathos between Edmund and Clifford with the metaphor of a lion bent over its prey as the youth pleads for his life:

> So looks the pent-up lion o'er the wretch
> That trembles under his devouring paws;
> And so he walks, insulting o'er his prey,
> And so he comes, to rend his limbs asunder.
> Ah, gentle Clifford, kill me with thy sword,
> And not with such a cruel threatening look.
> Sweet Clifford, hear me speak before I die.
> I am too mean a subject for thy wrath:
> Be thou revenged on men, and let me live.

At this critical moment, it is the awareness of ancestry, of recent and past deaths, that shapes the mood. Clifford's immortal justification that Edmund's 'father slew my father' makes the murder an act of honour to avenge his family, and one that will allow the soul of his father to rest more easily. Yet this murder of an 'innocent' was contrary to Church teaching, as Edmund's tutor asserts in the play, promising that the Clifford would be 'hated both of God and man'. This seems to represent a religious struggle between the concepts of honour and 'good' acts in the name of the dead; the interpretation of dynastic duty which can seem incompatible with piety to a modern audience. To avenge and honour a loss was admirable, but not when the victim was as young as Shakespeare portrayed Edmund, or when it invoked further bloodshed. Rutland himself tells Clifford that he should take his revenge to York, who was a fully-grown man, and the author of his loss.

Clifford's response inverts the notion of suffering in hell for his deed: until his revenge is enacted, he is experiencing a hell upon earth. His graphic, grisly imagery of digging up the bones of Edmund's ancestors is a reminder that remains could be subject to acts of desecration as well as veneration, but this was so socially unacceptable that, setting the imminent murder aside, it establishes Clifford in the minds of the audience as a damned villain:

> Had thy brethren here, their lives and thine
> Were not revenge sufficient for me;

No, if I digg'd up thy forefathers' graves
And hung their rotten coffins up in chains,
It could not slake mine ire, nor ease my heart.
The sight of any of the house of York
Is as a fury to torment my soul;
And till I root out their accursed line
And leave not one alive, I live in hell.

As Clifford's opposite, as his literary foil, Edmund counters the lord's damnation with his own imminent salvation, begging to be allowed to pray, thus easing the path to heaven. He appeals to Clifford for the sake of future generations, not past ones, reminding him that he has a son and, as God is just, that son will surely be taken from him. Edmund's final words are in Latin; 'Di faciant laudis summa sit ista tuae!' (May the Gods grant that this be your crowning praise!). The use of the language of the Church establishes a link between the youth and divinity, suggestive of his imminent salvation. The audience has no doubt where Lord Clifford is bound.

Centuries after his death, Edmund was claimed by art as something of a romantic hero, a *cause célèbre* which exaggerated his innocence and the pathos of his demise. Many artists took their cue from Shakespeare. In 1800, an edition of *Henry VI Part III* was illustrated by Scottish artist Robert Ker Porter, including an image of Edmund's death. Kneeling, the earl clasps his hands in supplication, appearing simultaneously childlike and robust, well rounded and sturdy beside Clifford, whose billowing cloak, fashionable boots and headdress depict him as something of a rake. It is not an image that evinces great sympathy, despite Edmund's cowering. The crudeness of translation from image to engraving and the depiction of the victim lose something of an aesthetic battle in the viewer's eye.

The same year as Waterloo, 1815, genre painter and Royal Academician Charles Robert Leslie's iconic picture foregrounded a child-like Edmund with long blonde curls, dressed in pearly white and gold, far closer to a boy of 12 than a young man of 17. In contrasting chiaroscuro shades of black and gold, Clifford stands over the boy, wearing full armour, with a rippling red sash intimating the violent spillage of blood to follow. Kneeling upon the ground, hands clasped in prayer, Edmund's head is held back by his enemy, revealing angelic features and wide eyes. Tucked beneath him, his childish legs and little soft shoes fastened by a strap are passive beside Clifford's great thigh, metallic and almost serpent-like in its scaly decoration. With his dagger poised, his visor raised to reveal brutal features, this enemy of innocence and religion is as terrifying as a Caravaggio killer or a Fuseli nightmare. The skies behind him broil in a menacing mix of pink and grey as if the very heavens disapprove. It is a scene designed to tug the heartstrings, to overplay the emotional response in contrast with the facts such as they can be established. As a piece of art, it is a success, it achieves its aim and, although exaggerated, it foregrounds Edward's loss in a way that historians had failed to do at that point.

Leslie's pathos found a receptive audience in the Victorians. Two texts of the 1870s retold Edmund's story as part of a wider narrative of Irish rule. James Roderick O'Flanagan reminds us that Edmund was also Earl of Cork and gave a positive account of York's tenure as Lieutenant, giving 'Early indications of a better policy towards the Irish than was usually observed' and 'employing the arts of peace' instead of 'attacking the native chiefs'. He was so popular that it was said that 'the wildest Irishman in Ireland would, before twelve months, be sworn English', and he endeared himself 'not only to the English in Ireland but the natives'. At the time of the Battle of Wakefield, Flanagan portrays Edmund as having 'a fair and almost effeminate appearance' and 'a brave and intrepid spirit'. Needless to say, this is something of a romanticisation and may have been prompted by Leslie's picture, as no contemporary images of Edmund survive, nor do any suggestions that he was in any way effeminate. Flanagan has Edmund taken prisoner by Clifford, who was unaware of his identity until it was revealed by 'the richness of his armour and equipment', prompting the lord to drive his dagger into his heart.[20] In his 1879 book on the lives of the Irish Chancellors, Oliver J. Burke also described Edmund's identification by his 'noble appearance', as well as the pleas of his chaplain and the moment when Clifford 'rushed on the hapless youth' and struck him in the heart, repeating the lines attributed to the Lancastrian by

Shakespeare. In *Henry VI Part III*, Burke's evocative account has him die 'in the flower of his youth'.[21]

The loss of Edmund, Earl of Rutland, Chancellor of Ireland and Earl of Cork sent ripples through history that underpinned his brother's reign. Had he still been alive in April 1483, at the age of 40, he would have been faced with the question of loyalties that defined the reign of his third brother, Richard, Duke of Gloucester. Should he support his 12-year-old nephew as Edward V or attempt to claim the throne for himself? Yet the attempts to discredit the boy had arisen through George's rebellion, so the likelihood is that the child would have been untainted, and ascended the throne. Edmund might have ruled Ireland, or attempted to regain England's foothold in France, or perhaps even taken the role of Protector towards his young king, ensuring the survival of Edward V. Today, Edmund lies with his parents behind the central limestone and chalk façades that flank the altar. His contribution to the House of York was brief but complete and his lost potential forever a cause for speculation.

2

Edward of Westminster, Prince of Wales (1453–71)

I

The story of Edward of Westminster returns this narrative to the winding streets of medieval Rouen in 1445, when the city was still in English hands and Richard, Duke of York was Lieutenant of France, and his two eldest sons, Edward and Edmund, were learning their letters in the nursery. Henry VI had not yet fallen ill and the trials of the coming decades were yet to unfold, so the families of York and Lancaster were working in unison, each focused on their individual service for the greater good of the realm. York had every reason to anticipate his imminent reappointment and was considering a match between his eldest son and a Valois daughter, as King Henry VI's future heirs, while Edmund's future lay in Rouen. York was not the only one arranging marriages and, that spring, it fell to the duke to conduct a very important visitor into the city.

The 23-year-old Henry VI was about to marry the niece of the Valois Charles VII, in the hopes of creating a lasting peace between the two countries. His bride, the 15-year-old Margaret, was the daughter of René of Anjou, whose swathe of titles included Count of Piedmont, Count of Provence and Forcalquier, Lord and Count of Guise, Duke of Anjou, Lorraine and Bar, King of Naples, titular King of Jerusalem and Aragon, which included Corsica, Majorca and Sicily. In reality, though, René's list of possessions was far more impressive than the extent of his actual power and finances. His daughter travelled to meet her bridegroom without a dowry and in the expectation that Henry would reverse tradition and pay for their wedding. One impressive item that René did own was a book of hours, known as the London Hours, which was produced and illuminated two decades before it came into his possession. Adding to the work, René commissioned an image of himself as *le-roi-mort*, an artistic *memento mori* that captures him as an animated corpse, looking back at the viewer in a state of decay. It is a disturbing image, clearly fashioned to be a portrait in allegory, with his body scarred, flesh taut and his stomach split open to reveal his intestines. A magnificent white castle on the hilltop behind, and his crown studded with pearls and topped with *fleur de lys*, serve as a reminder of his worldly status, in contrast to the scroll he holds, which bears the legend 'dust thou art and to dust thou shalt return'. The king would commission a similar image from his artist Coppin Delft in 1450, as part of a fresco to sit above his tomb in the Cathedral of St Maurice at Angers.

On 22 March, the future queen, nemesis of the House of York, arrived in Rouen. No direct record of her appearance survives, but an Italian who had never seen her reported that she was 'a most handsome woman, though somewhat dark'. Otherwise, she is portrayed conventionally as blonde in all but one of the contemporary manuscript illustrations. Around this time, she was described as 'already a woman: passionate, proud and strong-willed'. Margaret and Henry were technically already married, as the bride had undergone a proxy ceremony in the French city of Nancy in February, at which the Duke of Suffolk represented Henry. A month later, York travelled to Pontoise to meet her and conduct her north, travelling by barge along the Seine, to a reception worthy of a queen that awaited her in Rouen. Accounts of her time there are mixed. Some state that the journey made Margaret unwell, so that she missed the ceremonies and the Countess of Shrewsbury took her place, while she was conducted to her lodgings. She was probably taken to the royal suite in Rouen Castle, where she would have been greeted and attended by Cecily, Duchess of York. Other sources proclaim her presence at the head of a troop of nobles, preceded by 600 archers and knights, followed by a dizzy round of events. One of her biographers, Jock Haswell, has her pawning her silver wedding presents in order to pay for gifts to reward her boatmen and sailors.[1] Whatever the truth of her situation, Margaret remained there for two weeks over Easter, before York accompanied her on the next leg of her trip to Honfleur, which she reached on 9 April. As the duke returned to Rouen for his final months of the lieutenancy, Margaret sailed for England aboard the *Cokke John*, enduring such terrible conditions that she was carried ashore by the Duke of Suffolk and the Privy Council records state that she was 'sick of the labour and indisposition of the sea'.[2] Margaret's formal marriage to Henry VI took place on 23 April, followed by a coronation in Westminster Abbey on 30 May. By the time the York family returned to England that October, Margaret was an established wife and queen. Her next duty was to provide the country with an heir.

In many ways, Henry and Margaret were temperamental opposites. She was mature beyond her years, driven, ambitious and resolute. He was a more ascetic character, reflective, sensitive, humane, pious and serious; a founder of colleges, a pardoner of traitors and murderers, a generous patron and well-intentioned. This combination did not always sit well with his contemporaries' expectations of medieval kingship, which valued a more martial, physical sort of virility. The king was considered eccentric, choosing to wear a long drab gown and round-toed shoes, in contrast to the fashionable pointed Crakow style. Henry was also chaste in his dealings with his wife, although not so chaste as to eschew her bed, as some of his detractors claimed. He may have been abashed at the sight of naked dancers and encouraged his courtiers to reject sexual vices, but he did keep 'his marriage vow wholly and sincerely, even in the absence of the lady ... neither when they lied together did he use his wife unseemly'.[3] Yet eight long years passed before Margaret fell pregnant. The couple spent the Christmas season of 1452 together at the Palace of Pleasaunce at Greenwich, enjoying masques and feasts, and it was at the end of this happy time that Margaret finally conceived. That April she undertook a pilgrimage to the shrine of Our Lady at Walsingham to give thanks for her advancing pregnancy. Henry was delighted to learn of her condition, awarding Richard Tunstall a life annuity of £40 for bringing him the news to his 'singular consolation … grete joy and comfort'.[4] However, the nation's consolation and comfort was to be shaken that summer when Henry fell ill and was unable to comprehend, let alone witness, his son's birth.

Edward of Westminster was born on 13 October 1453. In the Catholic calendar, it was the feast of Edward the Confessor, who had built an earlier version of Westminster Abbey and whose remains had been translated into his tomb on that day. This probably lay behind the decision to name him Edward, breaking the royal use of the name Henry for three generations. He was christened in the abbey by William Waynfleet, Bishop of Winchester with the font arrayed in russet cloth of gold and a mantle embroidered with pearls and precious stones costing almost £555.[5] Henry had been unable to recognise his son, as recounted by the Duke of Norfolk: 'at the Prince's coming to Wyndesore, the Duke of Buckingham toke hym in his armes and presented hym to the Kyng in godely wyse, besechyng the Kyng to blisse him and the Kyng gave no maner answere.' The duke tried again, but then the queen arrived and 'toke the Prince in her armes, and presented hym in like fourme as the Duke had done, desiryng that he shuld blisse it, but alle their labour was in vayne'. Henry still made no answer, only once did he look at the prince and then cast his eyes downwards again, saying nothing.[6]

At Pentecost 1454 Edward was created Prince of Wales, Duke of Cornwall and Earl of Chester at Windsor Castle. He was to receive an annual allowance of £1,000 until he was 8 years old, transferring all other revenues from his lands and estates to the king, in whose household he was intended to reside until his majority at 14.[7] If it seemed that all was now settled for the royal family, their detractors still had the powerful weapon of gossip. While Edward's arrival had been long anticipated, and should have made the Lancastrian inheritance secure, the timing of his birth was unfortunate. Henry's illness and character, coupled with the factional nature of politics and the influence of certain advisors upon the queen, led to rumours about the child's paternity. The birth also brought the question of authority to the fore, with the dual problem of an incapacitated king and an heir who was an infant. Until Edward's birth, Henry's heir had been the Duke of York, an experienced adult, who was now displaced by the child. There was no guarantee that Henry would ever recover sufficiently to be able to govern, suggesting a long regency and the potential for rivalry for influence over Edward as he grew. Keen to retain her influence, Queen Margaret proposed herself as Protector, but her gender, inexperience and nationality counted against her and the role was awarded to York. For the time being, though, young Edward remained blissfully unaware of the thunder rumbling around the throne.

II

As unexpectedly as he had fallen ill, Henry VI recovered. At the end of 1454, he was finally able to recognise his son, in an encounter described by a letter written by Edmund Clere to his cousin John Paston. Writing from Greenwich on 10 January, he related how:

> On Monday afternoon the Queen came to him, and brought my Lord Prince with her, and then he [Henry] asked what the Prince's name was, and the Queen told him, Edward; and then he held up his hand, and thanked God thereof. And he said he never knew him till that time … and he asked, who were godfathers? And the Queen told him and he was well apaid [content].[8]

The fissures appeared between the houses of Lancaster and York while Edward was in his infancy. He was learning to walk when the first clash took place at St Albans, when his father was brought back to London humiliatingly as a puppet, and 2 years old during York's second Protectorate. It is likely that the boy was with his mother during this time, in Cheshire, at Kenilworth and at Coventry, as she tried to establish an alternative royal support base to London, which was loyal to the Yorkists. Legends that they were captured and robbed, and that Margaret appealed to the men's sense of loyalty to her son as their future monarch, may date from this period. They were essentially popular in the north, and the Welsh shires gifted the prince over £12,000, to be paid over six years.[9] Margaret and Edward's considerable support was also reflected in pageantry designed to welcome the family to Coventry in September 1456, featuring Edward's namesake Edward the Confessor, prophets, Roman emperors, the four cardinal virtues and nine worthies who honoured the Lancastrians as the future rulers of England, treating the prince as a future king:[10]

> Like as mankynde was gladdid by the birgth of Jhesus
> So shall this empire joy the birthe of your bodye
> The knightly curage of Prince Edward all men shall joy to see.[11]

He was presented as inheriting the qualities of his grandfather, Henry V, and adopting the mantle of Julius Caesar, all under the guidance of his mother. Edward spent almost his entire life living closely with Margaret of Anjou; the two were hardly ever parted, and her influence was recognised in Coventry as formative in shaping a desirable English king.

A group of four loyal Lancastrian knights was established to manage and administer the prince's estates during his troubled period of his infancy: the son-in-law of the Duke of Somerset, James Butler, Earl of Wiltshire and Fifth Earl of Ormond had replaced York as Lieutenant of Ireland; John, Viscount Beaumont had served in France and was Lord Great Chamberlain and Steward of the Duchy of Lancaster; John Sutton, Lord Dudley was a favourite of Henry VI and the family of Thomas, Lord Stanley had supported the Lancastrian takeover in 1399. Edward would have come to know them well, as their job was to authorise his expenditure and supervise his officials. He was also served by Robert Wittingham as his receiver-general, Thomas Throckmorton as his attorney-general and Giles St Lo as the keeper of his wardrobe.[12]

Edward's sixth birthday was approaching when the Yorkists were defeated at Ludford Bridge, and his enemies were exiled and attaindered. It was a high point for his cause. In the Parliament of late 1459, the Lords made a solemn vow in the presence of the king to honour the prince and accept him as Henry's heir, and receive him as their king when the time came. It was around this time that the visiting Italian Raffaelo de Negra reported that Edward was 'a most handsome boy, six years old'.[13] The following February, the young prince was issued with a powerful commission of *oyer* and *terminer,* allowing him to preside as a judge over local Assize court hearings. Months later, though, the Yorkists returned with a decisive victory at Northampton and regained control of the king.

Edward was just 7 years old when his future was greatly altered by the Act of Accord that named the Duke of York as heir to the English throne. Henry was forced to sign under duress, meaning that the prince was formally disinherited of his titles, future and lands. Exactly what role the Yorkists imagined Edward fulfilling in the future cannot be imagined. Margaret's response was to appeal to her Valois relations to invade England but when this came to nothing, she fled, taking Edward north to the Scottish court. In Edinburgh, they were received by the newly widowed regent, Mary of Guelders, who was ruling for her infant son. Mary's situation must have provided Margaret with a vision of exactly what she had hoped to achieve in England. A letter to the city of London composed on Edward's behalf that December objects to the actions of the Duke of York in the strongest possible terms, describing him as 'a fals traitour that ceasith not his said malice but utterly entendith the distruccion of my lord and of my lady and the disherityng of us'. He was acting in self-interest, not for 'the wele of this my lords reaulme and the seurete and welfare of his subgettes to the same' and had rejected the prince's 'rightful and lineal' descent and place in the succession. Edward vowed to free his father from captivity in a way that protected the city from harm and any who threatened its stability and peace would be punished.[14] What Edward offered, even as a 7-year-old boy whose literary skills were unlikely to have been equal to such a composition, was hope. With Henry VI locked away and their enemies in control, it was the vision of a Lancastrian future, in the martial tradition of Henry V, that the boy embodied.

Margaret and Edward were staying with Mary of Guelders at Lincluden Abbey in Dumfries when the Battle of Wakefield was being fought in December 1460. She was not riding among her troops on a white palfrey, encouraging them to die for her cause, as narrated by the chronicler Waurin,[15] or in a position to order the decapitation of York or relish his head being placed upon Micklebar Gate, topped with a paper crown, as some historians have claimed. She and Edward were 170 miles to the north. News that the Duke of York and Edmund, Earl of Rutland had been killed would not have arrived in Scotland until early in the New Year, but the young prince must have been old enough to realise its significance. The previous March, his mother had made the decision to dismiss his governess, Lady Lovell, in the belief that it was time for him to commit 'to the rules and teaching of men, rather than stay further under the keeping and governance of women'.[16]

Yet whatever triumph the queen and prince felt at York's death was to be short-lived; the Italian priest Francesco Coppini wrote to warn them that Wakefield was only a 'trifling victory' and advised Margaret to make peace while she was in a strong position. In response, Margaret headed south, wearing the crimson and black badge of the Prince of Wales, featuring a plume of white feathers, the unruliness of her Scottish army instilled fear into her subjects. Margaret's troops won a victory at St Albans, after which she was reunited with her husband, and Prince Edward with his father, after nine months apart. Waurin relates that Margaret encouraged her son to order and witness the executions of their enemies, and Henry VI's formidable biographer, Professor R.A. Griffiths, accepts and repeats this incident. Waurin had been wrong before and his account must be treated with caution, but the possibility cannot be ruled out. If Edward was encouraged to witness Lancastrian acts of justice, it was to put his legal commission into perspective and, modern sensibilities aside, must be seen within the context of threats to his realm and future kingship. The prevalence of death in the fifteenth century would have made it far more of a reality for a child than a single traumatic event. Any scruples might also have been lost in the euphoria of success. Prince Edward was knighted by his father on the evening after the battle. He wore a regal costume of purple velvet covered in goldsmiths' work and then took up the sword himself to knight his allies.

Just as it seemed as if the Lancastrians were again in the ascendant, their momentum was dramatically lost. York's eldest son, Edward, Earl of March had been absent from St Albans in order to intercept the troops of Jasper Tudor, coming from the west. March won a convincing victory at Mortimer's Cross, forcing Jasper to flee, and then another in a final encounter at Towton, where the Lancastrians suffered catastrophic losses. For some reason, Margaret failed to capitalise on her success and return to London, allowing March to enter the city and proclaim himself Edward IV. For the young prince, this was a worse blow than the Act of Accord. Now his dynasty had been displaced, his father usurped and himself relegated to the status of outsider. In the coming years, this other Edward, the first Yorkist king and the prince's namesake, would become his nemesis.

With the Yorkists in the ascendant, the only option for the Lancastrian royal family was flight once more. Margaret and Edward rode at speed to Berwick, with their enemies in pursuit, then on to Linlithgow Palace, where Mary of Guelders provided them with lodgings in the convent of Blackfriars in Edinburgh. Henry made his way separately to join them, landing at Kircudbright. He was soon followed by a delegation sent by Edward IV, requesting that Mary surrender 'Harry, late usurpant King of our said Realm, Margaret his wife and her son', a request that was backed by Edward's allies Philip of Burgundy and the Valois Dauphin Louis. Under this strain, Mary was able to offer the exiles a safe place to stay but no help in terms of an invasion force or finances. Margaret retaliated by sending ambassadors to France, to appeal to her father's family and to Burgundy, but the general mood of the moment was tending towards peace, not the renewal of war. A letter from her ambassadors in France lists the twenty-one men who had fled with Margaret and were to form her court in exile over the coming years. The following April, Margaret set sail for France, determined to return at the head of an invading force. Yet the death of her uncle Charles VII meant the accession of his estranged son Louis XI, who quickly came to terms with the new Yorkist regime. Recognising that his supportive words would not be backed by action, Margaret returned to Scotland and bid farewell to her husband at Bamburgh. With Prince Edward, she sailed for the

Burgundian port of Sluys in July 1463, to seek assistance from Duke Philip. Edward was three months off his tenth birthday. He would never see his father again.

Having failed to inspire Philip the Good to back Henry as the rightful King of England, Margaret was forced to admit that she was temporarily defeated. Mary of Guelders was unable to offer more support; she was likely to have been incapacitated by the illness that would kill her on 1 December that year, at the age of 30. In the autumn of 1463, therefore, Margaret accepted an offer from her father of a pension of 6,000 French crowns and the residency of Château Koeur-la-Petite, lying 4 miles to the south-west of Saint Mihiel-en-Bar, near a bend in the River Meuse, in the Duchy of Bar, Lorraine. It was to be their home for the next seven years, the most permanent and significant home that the young prince would know.

III

The two villages of Koeur-la-Grande and Koeur-la-Petite sit about a mile apart and look, to all appearances, to be typical small settlements of the area. The Voie des Koeurs, which connects them, reveals flat lands on both sides, its route lined by a handful of square, beige houses, and most landmarks, including the church, small square and pond, dating to a later period. Much of the village was destroyed in fighting during the First World War but two surviving postcards show images of an 'ancien Château' and 'vieux Château', clearly the same building, in existence shortly before this time. The two images are taken from a similar perspective, showing a building of substantial size, with a long wing of two storeys, flanked by seven large decorative archways containing smaller windows. At the far end it abuts a taller section with three storeys and, on the near end, closest to the photographer, another part contains a small doorway up three steps and a shuttered window. One photograph shows that the building is constructed of old, substantial stones at the foundation level. Children sit on the step, a broom leans against the wall and local people stand on the path before it, alongside a small expanse of grass and a tree. It may well be that this was the place where the Lancastrians stayed, repaired and improved by later generations, or else this building was erected on the foundations of the original. The existence of a Ruelle de Château midway between the main road and a tributary of the river suggests its original location, although the building there is listed as dating to the first part of the eighteenth century. Here, or near here, the exiled queen and prince established their own Lancastrian court.

A veteran of English law, and loyal servant of Henry VI, Sir John Fortescue, was appointed as tutor to the 10-year-old Edward. Born in 1394, Fortescue was an MP and chief justice, trusted by Henry to the extent that he appointed him Lord Chancellor in exile, although this was technically invalid as he was not in possession of the great seal, the essential ingredient to make the matter legal. In France, he composed a number of works on subjects like the nature of law and the law of nature, on the differences between an absolute and a limited monarchy, on England's constitutional framework and the conceptual and political basis of English law. As Edward's tutor, he wrote *De Laudibus Legum Angliae* around 1468–71, a manual to assist a future monarch. It takes the form of a dialogue between tutor and pupil, with Fortescue proposing certain areas of study and the prince replying. Although some artistic translation has occurred between the reality and the record, the details appear to derive from essential truths in Edward's character, or at least record a literary version of him. Fortescue compliments his pupil on his inclination to employ himself 'in such manly and martial exercises', as it was his duty to fight battles for his people and judge them 'in righteousness'. While Edward engaged in 'feats of arms', Sir John, referring to himself as 'Chancellor', wished him to turn to 'the study of the laws'. On hearing this, 'the Prince looked very intently at the old knight' and replied that law was merely human, when he should be studying the divine.[17] Through their debate of the law, Edward is 'overcome' by the Chancellor's 'reasonable discourse' but discouraged 'lest I employ all my younger years' to reach the required proficiency. The debate continues. The literary Edward asks a number of questions pertinent to the era and English dynastic conflict, such as how it may come to pass that one king can rule over his people absolutely while such power is unlawful for another and how a man might protect himself while living under a corrupt government.[18] It seems unlikely that, cast out by usurping Yorkists, the pair did not discuss such matters during their exile.

De Laudibus Legum Angliae also rings true in its attempts to teach Prince Edward about his native land, which are worth quoting at some length for the depiction they give of England in the 1460s:

> At the time your highness was obliged to quit England, you were very young, consequently the natural disposition and qualities of your country could not be known to you … England is a country so fertile that, comparing it acre for acre, it gives place to no one other country; it almost produces things spontaneous [*sic*] without man's labour or toil. The fields, the plains, groves, woodlands, all sorts of lands spring and prosper there so quick [*sic*], they are so luxuriant … the feeding lands are likewise enclosed with hedgerows and ditches, planted with trees which fence the herds and flocks … there are neither wolves, bears nor lions in England, the sheep lie out a nights without their shepherds … the inhabitants are seldom fatigued with hard labour, they lead a life more spiritual and refined … from hence it is that the common people of England are better qualified and inclined to discern into such causes which require a nice examination than those who dwell upon their farms.[19]

England, explained Fortescue, was 'so thick-spread and filled with rich and landed men' that each village contained at least one, and they comprised the local juries. 'Other countries, my Prince', he continued, 'are not in such a happy situation, are not so well stored with inhabitants'. Fortescue praised the English geographical concentration of 'persons of rank and distinction' and the way in which society was arranged and justice delivered, concluding that Edward should cease to be surprised that 'that law, by means of which in England the truth is enquired into, is not in common to other countries, because other parts of the world cannot furnish juries of such great sufficiency or equally qualified'.[20] The Chancellor continued to compare life in England with that in France, calling certain examples to mind in a way that indicates they had been witnessed by the prince while living at Koeur-la-Petite. He prompted Edward to recall:

> a condition you observed [in] the villages and towns in France ... during the time you sojourned there. Though they were well supplied with all the fruits of the earth, they were oppressed by the King's troops and their horses, that you could scarcely be accommodated in your travels ... [and] the soldiers treated them at such a barbarous rate.

He also criticised the taxes which obliged the villagers to offer up a quarter of their earnings annually, the hardship and misery of the peasants and the secretive, illegal way in which justice was administered. In comparison, he stated, the English drank wine not water, were well clothed 'in good woollens' and fed 'in great abundance'.

These contrasts between countries, and Edward's response, are illuminating. Firstly, the prince disputed the differences between civic law and that of the Scriptures, keeping his mind on the standard set by religion, in a move that sounds very much like an utterance made by his father. Edward has often been characterised by historians in the bloodthirsty mode offered by a couple of hostile chroniclers, in complete contrast to the pious, reflective King Henry. Yet, if there is truth in Fortescue's reported dialogue, the prince's constant concern with spiritual matters closes this divide considerably. The Edward of *De Laudibus Legum Angliae* is a young man who not only understands the medieval concept that temporal life is brief in comparison with the divine, but seeks to apply this to his life. He chooses to 'give the preference to that law which does most effectually cast out sin and establish virtue'.[21] He was also merciful, like his father, in contrast to the accounts of him being 'blooded' at executions, giving his opinion that the law was most 'eligible which shews more favour than severity to those parties involved in it'. In addition, Edward was generous, stating that 'all matters of hardship are odious and were as much as possible to be restrained' while 'favours are to be amplified'.[22] The text also exposes a small personal detail about the prince's character, which is valuable amid so little surviving information. Twice, the reader is informed that his favourite saying is 'comparison is odious'.

These extracts raise an interesting new identity for Edward. He may have been English-born, and created Prince of Wales, but through exile to Scotland and France at such a young age, he lost something of his identity as an Englishman. Lacking in experience of the customs of his land, his absence recast him as a foreigner, already half-French by birth, he became even more 'other' and 'different' by virtue of his circumstances. The years he had spent as a child travelling in the north with his mother, often in flight from danger, would not have equipped the prince with a comprehensive understanding of the country, which was essentially London-centric. He had not been in England since around his seventh birthday and, by the time he reached 17, those experiences would have receded enough to seem distant. When he considered the conquest of England, as he and his mother did frequently, it was almost as foreigners. This distance was in stark contrast to the new king, Edward IV, who might have been born in Rouen, but whose childhood and adolescence were spent in England, and who enjoyed great popularity in London. Although the prince drew allegiance as a figurehead of the Lancastrian cause, the implications of his difference from the ruling Yorkists should not be dismissed.

There were other figures in Koeur-la-Petite who influenced the growing youth. Along with the ever-present Margaret was a group of her chaplains, headed by a Thomas Bird, Bishop of Asaph, who had formed part of the queen's entourage upon her entry to England in 1445.[23] There was also the poet George Ashby, who arrived at the castle in 1464. He was a former keeper of the signet to Henry VI who had either just been released, or had escaped, from the Fleet Prison in London, perhaps having been incarcerated there by the Yorkists. His poem *The Active Policy of a Prince* is dedicated to Edward, in the anticipation that he would follow its maxims once he had taken the throne. Divided into three sections representing the past, present and future, it exhorted him to live within his means and not make the same mistakes as his father. He praised Edward for his circumspection, for living without funding from Parliament, for choosing his advisors carefully and listening to them, for paying debts, being quick and decisive, and staying in charge. The prince was encouraged to remember the recent conflicts as well as those of the past, and to think carefully before beginning fresh conflict:

> I would fain you keep in remembrance
> The be right well advised by good sadness
> By discreet prudence and faithful constancy
> Before you begin a war for any riches,
> Or out of fantasy or simplicity.
> For war may be lightly commenced
> The doubt is how it shall be recompensed.[24]

With Margaret were about fifty members of the exiled Lancastrian court, including the dukes of Exeter and Somerset, the earls of Ormond and Devon, Edward's receiver-general Sir Richard Wittingham, his chamberlain Sir Edmund Hampden and his chancellor John Morton, later to be the Archbishop of Canterbury who would build his own *memento mori* tomb. Jasper Tudor, the king's half-brother, was in France during the first winter of the prince's exile and may have travelled the 170 miles east to report on his efforts to raise funds from Louis XI. Their resources were stretched but, through her prudence, Margaret used her income to sustain them. As Sir John Fortescue wrote to the Earl of Ormonde, who was then in Portugal, 'we are all in great poverty, but yet the Queen sustaineth us in meat and drink, so we be not in extreme necessity. Her highness may do no more than she doth.'[25]

A surviving letter written by Prince Edward to the Earl of Ormond shows his focus on his enemies and his desire to prove how good a writer he was, a touching combination of adult military concerns and childishness:

> Cousin Ormond, I grete you heartly well, acerteyning yow that I have hearde
> the gode and honorable report of your sad, wise, and manly guiding ageynst
> my lordis rebellis and your adversaries, in the witche ye have purchased unto

yow perpetuall lawd and worship. And I thank God, and so do ye also, that ye
at all times under his proteccione have escaped the cruel malaise of your said
adversaries; and for as much as I understand that ye are nowe in portingale, I
pray yow to put you in the uttermost of your devoir to labore unto the kyng
of the sayd realme, for the furtherance and setting forthe of my lord, in the
recovering of his ryght, and subduing of his rebells. Wherin, if ye so do, as I
have for undowted that ye wyll, I trust sume frute shall follow, w' god's mercy,
witche spede yow well in all your workes. Writen at seynt mychacl, in Bar, w'
myn awn hand, that ye may see how gode a wrytare I ame.[26]

In 1465, two lots of distressing news arrived from England. At the end
of May, Edward IV's wife, Elizabeth Woodville, was crowned Queen of
England in Westminster Abbey. This was an insult to Margaret on a number
of levels, given Elizabeth's social status and her previous widowhood, as
well as the fact that there were now two rival queens, a blow which must
have specifically hurt Margaret. Then, in July, King Henry was captured
again by the Yorkists. Having spent the last year in flight, trying to avoid his
enemies, Henry VI had made himself a base of sorts at Bamburgh Castle
in Northumberland. Eventually, he was tricked into accepting hospitality
from his enemies and taken hostage in Lancashire, whence he was led
south, tied to his saddle, and incarcerated in the Tower of London. With his
father no longer at liberty, a greater burden fell upon the shoulders of the
young Prince Edward, representing as he did the hopes for the Lancastrian
dynasty: from this point, if not before, his thoughts and preparations must
have been dominated by the idea of regaining his kingdom.

In February 1467, Prince Edward's character was reported to the Duke
of Milan by Giovanni Pietro Panicharolla, the Milanese Ambassador to
France, who was then at Berri with King Louis, who had embarked upon
a pilgrimage. On the way, he encountered Margaret's brother, the Duke
of Calabria, with whom he dined and talked. The ambassador reported
that it had recently been suggested that the Earl of Warwick, dissatisfied
with Edward IV's foreign and marital policies, might join with Margaret
and oust the Yorkists. At dinner, Louis XI considered the possibility that
Prince Edward might be offered as a hostage to guarantee loyalty to the

earl, but this would have been a totally unacceptable option to Margaret, even an outrage. Panicharolla wrote that 'this boy, though only thirteen years of age, talks of nothing but cutting off heads or making war, as if he had everything in his hands or was the god of battle or the peaceful occupant of that throne.' The meal ended in argument, Calabria accusing the king of having 'never loved their house' and Louis retorting sharply that they had given him reason not to.

Panicharolla's report of Edward's character requires further examination. Neither Margaret nor Edward was present, so it is difficult to know whether this description came from life, or from hearsay, or whether the ambassador had ever met the prince, or was passing on rumour, or what he believed his Milanese employers wished to hear, just as the Duchess of Milan was flattered that Margaret was not as fair as herself. Given his situation in exile, following the death of loyal friends and the incarceration of his father, the suggestion that Edward thought of 'making war' upon his enemies might be an understatement. At 13, he was on the threshold of manhood, of legal majority, the age when young kings were traditionally allowed to rule alone. If it is true, the notion of 'cutting off heads' likely sprang from adolescent enthusiasm, frustration and the suppression of his ambitions in exile. Dynasty and birthright were everything to a young man of the nobility: as far as Edward was concerned, he had been robbed of both, and his parents dishonoured. Yet there is also another dimension. His enemy, Edward IV, was often cited by contemporaries, and later historians, for his military prowess, his focus on the chivalric arts and martial rituals. In order to defeat him, the prince would have to compete on an equal playing field. There was something chivalric and romantic about the court of an exiled prince, about the dreams and ambitions he cherished for the future, the certainty of the belief that he would one day return as the avenger and rule England. It was what kept him going; he was the answer to his parent's woes, his nation's avenging knight. The legacies of Henry IV and Henry V hung about his neck. Sir John Fortescue presents the other side of this 'bloodthirsty' prince, describing first-hand how Edward 'applied himself wholly to feats of arms, much delighting to ride upon wild and unbroken horses, not sparing with spurs to break their fierceness ... he practised also sometimes with the pike, sometimes with the sword', dealing his partners 'savage blows'. He was a young man of focus and determination who was preparing himself for the time when he would face experienced grown men in battle.

In May 1467, Louis made the suggestion that Margaret and Edward might come to live at the French court. Panicharolla related to the Duke of Milan that Margaret's nephew, son of the Duke of Calabria, had gone to visit her at Koeur-la-Petite, but also that Louis had dispatched the Count of Vaudemont to accompany her back to the king. It appears that Margaret never went, though. The reason may appear in the ambassador's letter of four days later, which reports that Louis was on his way to Rouen to meet the Earl of Warwick.[27] Sensing that she was being summoned to comply with the French king's plan to join her to the earl, the exiled queen may have refused. Margaret was not yet ready to sign a deal with her mortal enemy; three more years would pass before she would consider it. It may also have been that Edward was ill during this time, preventing their departure. Apparently, that year he recovered from a serious malady, after which his mother undertook a pilgrimage to the shrine of St Nicholas de Port, the patron saint of Lorraine, to give thanks for his recovery.

IV

In 1469, the Yorkist dynasty fractured. Edward IV's younger brother, George, Duke of Clarence fled to Calais with the Earl of Warwick and was married to Warwick's elder daughter, Isabel. From there, they launched a first challenge to the king. This failed but by May 1470 Warwick was determined to topple his former friends. That April, a false report arrived in France that the earl had defeated Edward IV in battle, and that the Yorkist king was dead. The new Milanese Ambassador, Sforza di Bettini, reported that Louis XI was announcing the news 'very joyfully'.[28] No doubt a similar report reached Koeur-la-Petite, giving cause for celebration, even prompting plans for a Lancastrian return.

But the messenger was partially mistaken: Edward was not dead, although he was indeed defeated, and forced into exile in Burgundy while his pregnant queen sought sanctuary in Westminster Abbey. Perhaps it was due to the advocacy of Sir John Fortescue that Margaret finally agreed to travel to meet Louis and discuss a possible marriage alliance between Prince Edward and Warwick's younger daughter, Anne. Bettini also reported the rumour that Warwick was intending to return to England with the prince, who would rule for his father: 'accordingly it is believed that he will return soon, taking with him, so they argue, the Prince of Wales, son of King Henry, and will take the part of that King to see if, in that way, he will enjoy better success'.[29]

By 25 June, Edward and Margaret had arrived at the Château of Amboise, on the Loire, 300 miles to the west of Koeur-la-Petite. They were received 'in a very friendly and honourable manner' by Louis, who spent 'every day in long discussions with that queen to induce her to make the alliance ... and to let the prince, her son, go with the Earl to the enterprise of England'. Initially, Margaret showed 'herself very hard and difficult' and would 'on no account whatever' allow Edward to go with Warwick 'as she mistrusts him'.[30] Instead, it was suggested that the prince remain behind and Jasper Tudor take his place at Warwick's side. On 22 July, Margaret finally met the outlawed earl in person at Angers. Bettini reported that Warwick knelt before her 'with great reverence' and 'asked her pardon for the injuries and wrongs done to her in the past'. Margaret 'graciously forgave him' and he 'did homage and fealty' to her, swearing his loyalty to Henry, Margaret and Edward 'as his liege lords unto death'.[31] The formal betrothal between the 16-year-old Edward and the 14-year-old Anne took place on 25 July, at Angers Cathedral, with oaths sworn on fragments on the 'true cross'. Warwick set sail for England. The others were to join him after he had restored Henry VI.

Anne was not the bride that Edward and Margaret had once anticipated. As he was a future King of England, they would have sought a princess of royal blood, and previous suggestions had included daughters from the Valois and Burgundian houses. There was also the advantage that a foreign alliance could have brought a new player into the York–Lancaster dynamic, a potentially powerful backer for Margaret's cause, had she looked beyond the triumvirate of England, France and Burgundy. It is a mark of how low the Lancastrian cause had been brought that Margaret was prepared to marry her only son to the daughter of her enemy. What Edward thought of the match is not recorded. They must have seen Warwick as their best, perhaps their only, hope of restoring the dynasty. Bettini was under the impression that the wedding and consummation would take place straight away[32] but in the end, the actual ceremony was delayed until 13 December. Historians have doubted whether this was followed by a full wedding night, with the young couple sharing a bed, but it was imperative for the Lancastrian cause that Edward father an heir, and crucial that the marriage was considered legitimate once they all arrived in England. Warwick had restored Henry VI to the throne, and the King had been led through the streets to a ceremony at St Paul's. All that remained was for the Lancastrians in exile to return and claim their rightful places. Yet Margaret delayed. It was to prove fatal, literally and metaphorically.

Perhaps Margaret was being cautious, waiting to ascertain that Warwick's success would prove lasting and that he would remain loyal. Perhaps she was doubtful of her reception, having not set foot in England for seven years. Prince Edward might have urged her to leave sooner; equally he may have counselled her to delay until they were ready. The weather certainly held them back, returning their battered ships to port when they finally attempted to sail on 24 March 1471. For whatever reason, Edward, his wife and mother did not land at Weymouth until 14 April. By then it was too late. Edward IV had already returned, coming ashore in Yorkshire the previous month and gathering supporters as he marched south. On that very day, he had met and killed Warwick at the Battle of Barnet. Hearing the news, the Lancastrians would have been devastated, but they chose not to give up. They hurried to the shelter of Cerne Abbey to plan their next move and loyal Lancastrians flocked to join them.

On 4 May, the 17-year-old prince prepared for battle. This was the culmination of his years of preparations, of dreaming about avenging his parents and destroying his enemies. Beside him in the field were the Beaufort brothers Edmund and John, sons of the Duke of Somerset, who took the right of the field. On the left was John Courtenay, Earl of Devon, who had been with Edward in exile, while in the centre was the veteran soldier Lord Wenlock, who had defected from the Yorkist side, accompanied by Prince Edward himself. The Lancastrians had a slight advantage in numbers, with around 6,000 men against the Yorkists' 5,000. They also had the advantage of arriving first, enabling them to take position, meaning that their enemy found it difficult to advance upon them and resorted to their archers first. Edmund Beaufort then led an attack but was beaten back and driven into the way of 200 Yorkist spearmen who had been concealed in the trees. His flank scattered and headed for the river, where they were cut down in a 'bloody meadow'. Beaufort then turned on Wenlock, accusing him of not coming to his aid and, reputedly, attacked and killed him. The rest of the Lancastrians tried to flee for sanctuary in the nearby abbey, but Prince Edward did not reach it. The questions of when and how he died, as in the case of Edmund, Earl of Rutland remain controversial.

Weeks after the battle in 1471, Bettini reported that the Yorkists had 'not only routed the prince but taken up and slain him, together with all the leading men with him'.[33] Another contemporary source, the pro-Yorkist *Historie of the Arrival of Edward IV*, stated that Edward, 'called Prince', was put 'to discomfiture and flyght' and 'was taken, fleinge to the town wards and slayne in the fielde'.[34] It also contained a miniature depicting the execution of Edmund Beaufort by axe shortly after the fighting, with Edward IV looking on. The prince may have met a similar end. Two years later, a French chronicle, the *Histoire de Charles, dernier duc de Bourgogne*, claimed that Edward had been surrounded by his enemies and killed in cold blood. Polydore Vergil, the Italian historian of Henry VII, who first visited England in 1502, based his account of the battle on primary sources which have now been lost. He described a scene in which Edward IV questioned the prince about his opposition, whereupon the 'excellent yowth' replied his purpose was to free his father from oppression and regain the usurped crown. The king then reputedly struck him in the face with a gauntlet and waved him away for execution. A similar story was reported by Robert Fabyan, a London chronicler and sheriff writing before 1512, in which the king 'strake him with his gauntlet upon the face, after which stroke, so by him received, he was by the King's servant incontinently slain'.[35]

This account became the general version of Edward's death, being repeated by sixteenth-century writers Hall and Holinshed. Shakespeare's depiction of the event in *Henry VI part III* is a dramatisation of their narrative, with a defiant prince speaking for his father and challenging Edward IV's right to rule:

> Speak like a subject, proud ambitious York!
> Suppose that I am now my father's mouth;
> Resign thy chair, and where I stand kneel thou,
> Whilst I propose the selfsame words to thee,
> Which traitor, thou wouldst have me answer to …
>
> I know my duty; you are all undutiful:
> Lascivious Edward, and thou perjured George,
> And thou mis-shapen Dick, I tell ye all
> I am your better, traitors as ye are:
> And thou usurp'st my father's right and mine.

Although Edward speaks heroically, his moment in the limelight is brief. The prince is sidelined in the drama, a supporting figure in the anti-Ricardian narrative, a view informed by the hindsight that overrides the possibility of the youth's opposition and potential kingship in 1471. Shakespeare even has Edward insulting Richard as a 'scolding crookback', which seals his fate. He is defiant, angry and brave, and perhaps foolhardy as he meets his end. There is none of the pleading, praying and pathos with which Edmund, Earl of Rutland dies, earlier in the same play. It was to Edward's mother, Margaret of Anjou, that Shakespeare gives any comparable sentiment:

O Ned, sweet Ned! speak to thy mother, boy!
Canst thou not speak? O traitors! murderers!
They that stabb'd Caesar shed no blood at all,
Did not offend, nor were not worthy blame,
If this foul deed were by to equal it:
He was a man; this, in respect, a child:
And men ne'er spend their fury on a child.
What's worse than murderer, that I may name it?
No, no, my heart will burst, and if I speak:
And I will speak, that so my heart may burst.
Butchers and villains! bloody cannibals!
How sweet a plant have you untimely cropp'd!
You have no children, butchers! if you had,
The thought of them would have stirr'd up remorse:
But if you ever chance to have a child,
Look in his youth to have him so cut off
As, deathmen, you have rid this sweet young prince!

It is to be expected that the Lancastrians would present Edward as a martyr, their lost hope, and that the Yorkists would attempt to belittle his abilities, making him into a caricature of contrasts, bloodthirsty but essentially cowardly, unlike the martial virility epitomised by Edward IV. The pro-Lancastrian Warkworth chronicle depicts Prince Edward 'crying for succour' to his brother-in-law Clarence, before he was 'slain in the field',[36] creating more of a sense of pathos and pity for the young man, but this is a rare voice. Over the course of time, many historians have been swayed by the narrative of the victors, which is why a re-evaluation of the prince is so long overdue.

Edward's remains were buried in the choir of Tewkesbury Abbey but the exact location is uncertain today. A brass memorial plaque in the floor of the choir records the event in Latin, which broadly translates as: 'Here lies Edward, Prince of Wales, cruelly slain whilst but a youth. Anno Domini 1471, 4 May. Alas, the savagery of men. Thou art the sole light of thy Mother, and the last hope of thy race.' It seems unlikely that

Edward was ever given anything more in terms of a tomb or memorial. His mother was not in a position to insist upon it, or to finance it, and the Yorkists might have been reluctant to erect such a monument to the last Lancastrian prince, as a potentially dangerous reminder for his supporters. It would have been appropriate for Edward IV to order masses said for the youth's soul, as a violent death was considered significant in the individual's experience of the afterlife. Death in battle, however honorable, would have necessitated a period of time in purgatory, which could be sped up by the prayers and intercessions of the living. However, following the battle, the abbey was closed for a month and reconsecrated as a result of the bloodshed and the violation of its sanctuary; it may by that this process also included arrangements for Edward's bodily remains and spirit. The path to heaven was determined not just by the manner of one's death but also one's good deeds during life. Not to make such arrangements would have been a heinous act in the eyes of the Church and a black mark against King Edward's own future salvation.

Prince Edward's death put an end to Lancastrian hopes. The alternative ending, had his side somehow defeated the Yorkists at Tewkesbury, is of the complete restoration of Henry VI, with his son ruling as Protector until his natural death. Edward could have fathered children with Anne, and subsequent wives after her death in 1485, ensuring a strong continuation of the Lancastrian dynasty. The Yorkists' brief interlude would have been merely a blip in generations of kingship by inheritance. This would also have transformed the life and reputation of Margaret of Anjou, who would have retained her close influence and lived out her days in comfort but, critically, she would have been able to return to the epitome of quiet, dedicated queenship she modelled before her husband's illness. Later historians would have praised her tenacity, resourcefulness and patience in exile, rather than painting her as a 'she-wolf' with an unnaturally masculine focus on war. Margaret of Anjou's name would have become a byword for successful medieval queenship, of stepping into the breach when the need arose, then retiring with dignity. But the Battle of Tewkesbury was one of those visibly defining moments of history, when the outcome turned upon a knife edge, balanced between outcomes that were absolute in their finality. The moment of Edward's death may alternatively have been his beginning, but it turned out to be his end. He was buried in Tewkesbury Abbey.

The immediate result of Tewkesbury was the collapse of one dynasty and the empowering of another. Just over two weeks later, Henry VI was killed inside the Tower of London. Until the battle, his life had been guaranteed by that of his son, who presented a far more formidable opponent. Following the prince's death, there was no point in the Yorkists keeping Henry alive as a figurehead for subsequent rebellion. The *Arrivall* states that Henry died of grief on hearing the news but the timing of Edward IV's recrowning, the following day, suggests that it was by design. The broken Margaret of Anjou was forced to submit to Edward IV, captured by Sir William Stanley and taken through the streets as a prisoner to Wallingford Castle, then to the Tower of London. She was ransomed to the French in 1475 and spent her seven remaining years living in France, in poverty, and reliant on a pension from Louis XI. Later, Lancastrian supporters would transfer their loyalty to the prince's half-cousin, Henry Tudor, the future Henry VII.

Most subsequent descriptions or portrayals of Prince Edward tended to recast him according to the taste of the moment. An early eighteenth-century illustration by Royal Academician Thomas Stothard was made into an engraving by Augustus Fox in 1824, to appear in editions of *Henry VI Part III*. It depicts the prince as a Blakean figure, draped upon the earth, childlike and vulnerable having lost his armour, with curls and folds of fabric loose around him. A woman in white, presumably Margaret, hovers behind him in a low, flowing robe, half-bent, with arms outstretched, hair long and untied, in line with Romantic sensibilities. Her body shields her son from the armed figures behind, poised to draw their swords as they contemplate his demise.

Prince Edward's death did not give rise to much outcry, or to a devoted following, as did the deaths of some young men in battle. The majority of his supporters had been killed and those remaining recognised that they had little choice but to suppress their grievances and fall in line with the victorious Yorkists. Undoubtedly, his long absence in France meant that

Edward had grown up out of the sight of the English, so there was less sympathy for him than if he had been able to maintain a high profile in the country he hoped to rule. The death of his father, Henry VI, drew a greater reaction from the English people, many of whom had been born under his reign, or still felt the ties of four decades of loyalty. The death of a young man trained for battle was one thing, but the murder of an old man, ill and unstable, in prison and helpless, and an anointed king, was quite another. Unable to openly condemn what was probably his murder, sympathy for the Lancastrian king was channelled into a religious cult, which reported miracles at his first burial place of Chertsey Abbey, then followed him to St George's Chapel, Windsor. Towards the end of the century, when his half-nephew, Henry VII, was seeking to have the former Lancastrian canonised, miracles dating from between 1471 and 1500 were recorded in chronicles. Out of 400 instances, 174 were selected to form the text *The Miracles of King Henry VI* – curing the sick, saving the innocent and similar acts. The cult rapidly died out as the sixteenth century advanced, suggesting that it had sprung more from the loyalty of his contemporaries than from a strictly pious cause. Yet in those crucial years of the aftermath, when history was being rewritten, it took the focus off the prince. Edward remains an unsympathetic figure in modern treatments of the Wars of the Roses, his shadowy life too brief, and too Lancastrian, to evince much unbiased investigation. It should be remembered that the Battle of Tewkesbury was by no means a forgone conclusion, and the evidence of his life suggests that he would have made a formidable English king in the model of Henry V.

3

King Edward V (1470–83?)

I

When the Duke of York's eldest son, Edward, Earl of March displaced Henry VI in 1461, he was 18 years old. Tall, handsome and athletic, in contrast with the pious, conscientious and mentally fragile Lancastrian, Edward looked the part, fighting at the forefront of his troops, dressing in gorgeous colours and fabrics, dazzling with jewels and quickly establishing a reputation as a devotee of women. After forty years of Henry VI's rule, Edward IV was the perfect foil for his opponent, and his attraction lay partly in this difference. His reign began in a blaze of military and chivalric glory, as he followed his devastating victory at Towton with not just one coronation, but three. On 28 June, he was crowned in the traditional way at Westminster Abbey, but to his superstitious contemporaries, Sunday was considered an unlucky day, so he returned on the Monday for another crown-wearing ceremony. The day after that, Tuesday 30 June, Edward was at St Paul's Cathedral, which was larger and could accommodate an audience of his subjects, summoned to witness the crown being lowered into place again. He was a man who understood the importance of ceremony and had a wide appeal for the citizens of London.

It was expected that Edward would make an important international marriage. A wife with powerful European connections would cement his position in financial, commercial and military terms, to secure the house of York's new hold upon the throne. Such a match would deter Lancastrian challenges, but it was also the logical next step of his family's evolution. Even during Edward's youth, his father had intended him to marry into royal blood, believing it commensurate with his family's ancient right and their projected future. While still resident in Normandy, back in the mid-1440s, the duke had made overtures to Charles VII of France, in an attempt to win the hand of Madeline or Joan, princesses of the Valois line, for his son. The little girls had been 2 and 10 at the time, but had both since been married and were out of Edward's reach by 1464. However, their brother was now king and his second wife, Charlotte of Savoy, had an unmarried sister. Thus, a delegation led by the Earl of Warwick crossed the Channel to forge a union with the 14-year-old Bona, whose eighteen siblings would have afforded the Yorkists support in places as widespread as Geneva, Cyprus, Milan, Luxembourg, Brittany and Scotland. This was a popular choice at court, if not only to secure peace, but to curb the young king's roving eye. As William Gregory's chronicle relates, the royal advisors had implored him to send 'into some strange land to enquire for a queen of good birth, according unto his dignity', just as his Lancastrian predecessors had done.

When Edward's second Parliament met at Reading in September 1464, it was in expectation of hearing the treaty concluded and to make plans for a royal wedding. Instead, Edward took the opportunity to inform the assembled lords that he was already married. His new wife, Elizabeth Woodville, could not be faulted in terms of her beauty, but she was a widow with two young sons from a large Lancastrian family. She could bring Edward nothing in terms of international relations, but this clearly mattered little to the king, who had chosen her for her personal qualities alone. It was another sign that Edward intended to reign on his own terms, rather than conforming to expectations. Yet the question of motivation when it came to the marriage still causes controversy today. Clearly Edward fell in love with Elizabeth, or in lust,[1] but the choice to wed her in secret might betray more than a straightforward concern about his minister's disapproval. Two decades later, Richard III would argue that Edward had been precontracted to another woman, rendering his match with Elizabeth illegal and their children unlawful. It is also not entirely out of character that Edward made promises to at least one woman in order to bed her, but found himself caught on this occasion. The secret ceremony is reputed to have taken place on or around May Day, at the Woodville's Northamptonshire estate of Grafton Regis. Whatever the king's motives on that occasion, five months later he chose Elizabeth to be his queen. She was presented at court and crowned in Westminster Abbey on 26 May 1465.

The marriage rapidly produced three children. Elizabeth gave birth to a girl named after her in February 1466, followed by Mary in August 1467 and Cecily in March 1469. What Edward most needed though, was a son to secure his dynasty. Until a boy arrived, his heir was George, Duke of Clarence, who had already been inspired to rebel by this fact. When George joined forces with Warwick for the second time in the summer of 1470, when Edward of Lancaster was betrothed to Anne Neville and Margaret of Anjou was planning her return, Queen Elizabeth was pregnant with her fourth child. That September, Edward was hurrying south to repel his enemies when he was taken unawares by the defection of Warwick's brother, and forced to flee at once into Burgundy, to save his life. There was no time to say goodbye to his wife and daughters, whom he hoped would be safe in the Tower of London. At the start of October, Elizabeth had just four weeks left until her delivery, which was the traditional time that a queen would have formally entered her confinement. Her rooms in the Tower had been prepared and provisioned for her lying-in, but now her circumstances had changed dramatically and she had no idea whether Edward would return, be killed in battle or drown in the turbulent conditions of the North Sea. At this point, Henry VI was still resident in the Tower, and Elizabeth realised that the Tower would become a focal point for her enemies. On the night of 1 October, she fled with her three daughters and mother to the safety of Westminster Abbey, where they signed the register as 'sanctuary women'.

The conditions in which the women found themselves were far from what they had been used to in the palace nearby. The abbot offered

Elizabeth rooms in the Deanery, but the surrounding area was crammed full of poor tenements bordering Thieving Lane, potentially home to common criminals seeking to escape the law. The poem 'The Recovery of the Throne by Edward IV' describes her 'in langowr and angwiche … to here of hir wepyng it was grett pity', while Thomas More claimed that she was 'in great penury and forsaken of all friends'.[2] Yet she had not moved a moment too soon. Warwick arrived at the Tower just a day or two later and moved Henry VI into the very apartments Elizabeth had vacated. As ever, though, the Lancastrian king was inclined to mercy, issuing a proclamation forbidding any man to 'defoul or distrouble' those within the Tower, on pain of death. He also appointed Lady Scrope, a doctor and midwife, to attend Elizabeth, and allowed John Gould, a London butcher, to supply the family with meat. On 2 November, the queen gave birth to a son, whom she named Edward. His godparents were among those who shared his sanctuary: the abbot Thomas Milling, the prior John Eastney and Lady Scrope. As the *Croyland Chronicle* relates, 'those faithful to King Edward drew some consolation from the event,' while the more numerous Lancastrians thought it 'of no importance'.[3]

Baby Edward spent his first six months at Westminster, then his existence and status changed completely. In the spring of 1471, his father returned from exile and made his way to London on the pretext of wishing to regain his father's former title of Duke of York. Arriving in the city on 11 April, he returned to the scenes of his coronation: St Paul's and Westminster Abbey, where he gave thanks and revealed his true hand by having himself recrowned by Cardinal Bourchier.[4] There, Elizabeth presented to him 'a fair son, a Prince, to the King's greatest joy, to his heart's singular comfort and gladness, and to all them that truly loved and served him'. He was reunited with his daughters too, and did 'full tenderly' kiss his 'sweet babes' and bore his son in his arms. As the *Arrivall* relates, all his sorrow 'was turned to bliss'. The family moved to Baynard's Castle on the Thames, a large fortified Yorkist possession between Blackfriars and Queenhithe. Edward went on to regain control of his kingdom, killing the Earl of Warwick at Barnet and

Prince Edward of Lancaster at Tewkesbury and ordering the death of Henry VI.

On 11 June 1471, baby Edward was formally created Prince of Wales and Earl of Chester at Westminster Palace, 'with the assent of the lords of our blood'. He was later assigned the dukedom of Cornwall with its corresponding lands and estates, as well as his own household, with council, Chamberlain Thomas Vaughan, Chancellor Abbot Milling and Steward Lord Dacre, along with the traditional employees of the royal nursery. His nurse was Avice Welles, who is likely to have suckled the prince for two years, before being given a tun of red Gascon wine in November 1472 as severance payment.[5] On 3 July, the king summoned a meeting of the great council, whose members, following the lead of the Archbishop of Canterbury, swore an oath of allegiance to the new prince. Thomas Bourchier's promise acknowledged the 'first begotten son of our sovereign lord … to be the true and undoubted heir to our said sovereign, as to the crowns and realms of England and of France and the lordship of Ireland'. In addition, the lords swore that if it was the will of God that the prince should outlive his father, they would 'then take and accept you for true, very and righteous King of England … and in all things truly and faithfully behave me towards you and your heir'.[6] The prince's uncles, George and Richard, were among the forty-six men present at this council meeting and signed the oath with their own hands.

Edward's power and importance continued to grow, despite his young age. The following April he was made a knight of the garter at the annual Windsor ceremony, receiving the honours at the hand of his father. That September he was brought into the presence of a special visitor, his father's ally-in-exile, Louis de Gruuthuyse, who was a guest at Winsdor Castle, in order to bid him welcome. Edward's biographer Michael Hicks states that the child had probably 'not yet learned to talk'[7] but at two months off his second birthday, the prince would have been capable of offering a greeting. He would also have been interested in the gift his parents bestowed upon their friend, a jewelled gold cup containing a fragment of 'unicorn's' horn. The boy was present as the company processed in their robes to Westminster Abbey to make offerings at the shrine of St Edward, although on this occasion he was carried by his chamberlain Thomas Vaughan. One surviving clothing account for him, the only one, lists a long gown of cloth of gold on damask worth £1, doublets of velvet and satin, and two bonnets, one of which was purple velvet lined with green satin.[8] His father understood the importance of maintaining regal magnificence, in the Burgundian style, as a crucial demonstration of influence and power. There would have been many other gowns, doublets and bonnets ordered for the future king.

The year 1473 was to prove significant for the young prince. His council was enlarged, and charged to manage his affairs until he reached the age of 14. Among its members were his mother Queen Elizabeth, the archbishop, his paternal uncles, his maternal uncle Anthony Woodville, Lord Rivers, and Chancellor Robert Stillington, Bishop of Bath and Wells. That September, when Edward was just 3, plans were made for the establishment of his own household at Ludlow Castle, in the Shropshire town on the Welsh Borders. A list of ordinances was created by his father, outlining the boy's routine, education, rules of the house and job descriptions for employees. The cultured and chivalric Anthony Woodville was appointed as his master, or governor, to guide him in 'truth, honour, cunning, virtue and knightly demeaning' and to 'oversee that all [Edward's] servants now being and hereafter do duly and truly their service and office'. Dr John Alcock, Bishop of Rochester was charged to 'teach and inform our said son in all spiritual cunning and virtue' and replaced Milling as chancellor, while John Giles was given the specific job of teaching him Latin. The young prince's day began with Matins in his chamber, followed by breakfast, mass and lessons. At dinner, he was to be served meat while listening to 'noble stories' before returning to more learning. Afterwards he was allowed some playtime in the form of 'disports and exercises', or playing with his pets, games and sports, before supper and evensong in his chamber. A final session of recreation was intended to make him 'joyous and merry' before he retired to bed at eight in the evening.[9] But Edward was not always at Ludlow from this point, as he frequently travelled with his family, visiting Coventry in April 1474, where he was presented with a gilt cup decorated with allegorical figures including Edward the Confessor and St George, and appearing at Windsor that May.

Early in 1475, when the king was planning an invasion of France, this council would have stepped in to supervise the boy even more closely. The prince was knighted at Westminster on 18 April, along with his younger brother Richard of Shrewsbury, who had arrived two years before, along with a number of other peers and boys his age, establishing ties of loyalty. This was a significant moment for Edward, as his father's absence encompassed certain responsibilities that would be undertaken in his name, and the possibility that the king's death in battle, at sea or through that traditional scourge of the English in France, dysentery, would propel his son onto the throne. That July, the prince was at Westminster to be appointed Keeper of the Realm until the king's return; this made him the nominal head of government, whose authority would be exercised by his mother. As such it was essential that he was present in London and Elizabeth was allocated an additional £2,200 to cover his household expenses. A council of twenty, based on those appointed two years before, was appointed to guide him and he was issued with patents affording him small powers such as approval of the election of clergymen. The king's will was drawn up at Sandwich shortly before his departure that June, clarifying his son's succession in the event of his failure to return. Had he been killed on campaign, it is impossible to know how events in England would have played out, or whether his wishes would have been honoured. In fact, his war turned out to be as brief as it was bloodless, and Edward IV returned to his kingdom, significantly richer, just three months later.

On 9 November 1477, shortly after Edward's seventh birthday, Richard, Duke of Gloucester led the other lords of the Council to offer loyalty to the prince. Following a dinner hosted in Edward's honour, Gloucester went 'on both his knees' and put 'his hands between the prince's hands' to do 'him homage for such lands as he had of him and so kissed him'. The boy replied by thanking 'his said uncle that it liked him to do it so humbly'.[10] Two years later the boy was created Earl of March and Earl of Pembroke, making him a powerful magnate in the Welsh Marches, an inheritance from the Yorkist Mortimer ancestors. As Edward passed through his early boyhood, it seemed that long-standing patterns of allegiance and loyalty were being established for him, in anticipation of his future rule.

His future was also being considered in terms of international marital alliances. The Prince of Wales would not be allowed to choose his own wife as his father had done and matches were considered with the eldest daughter of the Spanish monarchs Ferdinand of Aragon and Isabella of Castile, the daughter of the Emperor and a princess of Milan. In 1480, negotiations were begun for an alliance between Edward and Anne, Duchess of Brittany, who was then 3 years old, followed by a treaty in 1481. The wedding was scheduled to take place when Anne reached her twelfth birthday, which gave a projected date of January 1489, when Prince Edward would be 18 years old.

In the meantime, the education of the future king continued. The few books known to have been among Edward's collection included a French copy of the *Testament of the Sultan*, Woodville's translation of *Dictes and Sayings of the Philosophers* and *The History of Jason*, which was dedicated to him by the printer William Caxton. An Italian visitor to England in 1482–83, Dominic Mancini, whose source of information was Edward's own doctor, John Argentine, described the boy's feeling for literature, which enabled him to 'discourse elegantly, to understand fully, and to declaim most excellently from any work whether verse or prose that came into his hands'. He was in possession of 'talent and remarkable learning … far beyond his age'.[11] Edward was still based at Ludlow, but he did join his family for Christmas – at Greenwich in 1479, Windsor in 1481 and Eltham in 1482 – as well as other occasions. Some of his visits were educational, such as the occasion in May 1481, when he visited Sandwich with his father to view the fleet which Lord Howard was to lead against Scotland. Two years later, Edward was scheduled to visit Canterbury with his mother but their plans were cancelled because of an outbreak of measles in the city.

At the start of 1483, Edward was a couple of months past his twelfth birthday and was clearly considered to be in transition from childhood to adolescence, growing up and requiring greater independence to prepare him for his majority. On 25 February, a new set of ordinances for his household were issued to update those which had been in place since he was 3. New appointments were made, although all the key staff remained in place, but now Edward was to be constantly accompanied by two 'discrete and convenient' people and he was not to issue any orders unless he took advice from Anthony Woodville, John Alcock or Sir Richard Grey, his half-brother from his mother's first marriage. This trio were to watch over Edward's behaviour and warn him if he broke any of the ordinances, to correct him and keep the king and queen informed of his progress. Might these stricter controls imply that Edward was asserting himself, or misbehaving? On the verge of young adulthood, he was clearly a youth who had a mind of his own and was conscious of his status.

It was just at this delicate point, as he was beginning to emerge as an individual, when he was most in need of guidance to steer him towards his future kingship, that the prince's world collapsed. On 14 April, news arrived at Ludlow in mid-April that Edward IV had died at the age of 40. On the surface, it appeared that the prince's power and influence had increased. Overnight he had become King of England and was at once to prepare for his departure for London and his coronation. In practice, it transpired that his reign was over before it even began.

II

It was never the intention of Edward V to attend his father's funeral. That took place swiftly, while he was still in Ludlow, according to the protocol of the time. Immediately after his death, the former king was lain out in Westminster Abbey for the inspection of the mayor and aldermen, lords and bishops, less a macabre spectacle than confirmation that he was truly dead. Then, he was embalmed, wrapped in strips of waxed linen and dressed in regal finery, from his red leather shoes to his cap of estate. In this condition, his body remained in St Stephen's chapel for eight days, watched over by members of his court while requiem masses were sung. On 17 April, Edward IV's body was lifted onto a bier and covered in cloth of gold. Above him was carried a canopy of imperial cloth fringed with gold and blue silk, with banners at each corner depicting St George, St Edward, the Trinity and the Virgin Mary. Archbishop Rotherham, Edward's chancellor, led the procession into the abbey, followed by the Duke of Norfolk who carried the king's own banner before the bier, after which came a number of lords and knights. A life-size effigy of Edward wearing a crown and dressed in royal robes, holding orb and sceptre stood before the bier as offerings were made.

The next day, Edward's body was taken from Westminster to Charing Cross and on to Sion Abbey for the night. Then it travelled to Eton, where the bishops of Lincoln and Ely censed him as he was brought into the chapel of St George, the architectural masterpiece of his reign. Nine knights and other loyal servants kept an overnight vigil at the king's side and in the morning the final masses were read and Edward's shield, sword and helmet were placed upon his tomb. The members of his household ceremoniously broke their white staves of office and cast the pieces into the grave. In 1475, Edward had outlined a design for a cadaver tomb, featuring the image of Death dressed in armour and a depiction of the king in life, made of 'silver and gilt or at the least copper and gilt'. In 1482–83, casks of black marble were shipped from the Netherlands for the completion of the tomb but Edward's premature death curtailed the completion of these plans. Instead, he lay under a simple slab, where his wife Elizabeth would later join him. He had been buried for almost a week before his son set out for the capital.

Edward left Ludlow on 24 April, accompanied by the trio appointed by his father to guide him: Anthony Woodville, Thomas Vaughan and Richard Grey. But the young king and his party would have needed to travel quickly, as a coronation date had been set for 4 May, allowing only two weeks for him to travel the 150 miles, conduct necessary business and be received in London. Parliament may have anticipated that he would leave Wales sooner, but ten days elapsed between the news' arrival at Ludlow and the boy's departure. This delay allowed Edward's uncle,

Richard, Duke of Gloucester, to leave his home in Yorkshire before them and ride south to meet them at Stony Stratford on 29 April, just 50 miles north of the capital. It was clearly arranged in advance, probably at Richard's instigation, as Edward's party could have taken a more direct route, south-west through Gloucester and Oxford, instead of the path through Banbury and Grafton Regis to Stony Stratford. Leaving the king behind at the Rose and Crown Inn, Woodville rode 12 miles to meet Richard in Northampton. According to the *Croyland Chronicle*, Edward urged his uncle to go and pay his respects and 'submit the conduct of everything to this will and discretion of … the Duke of Gloucester'.[12] The pair dined with Henry Stafford, Duke of Buckingham, Edward's uncle by marriage, and appeared to part on good terms. However, early the following morning, Richard arrived in Stony Stratford, confiscated the keys to the inn and arrested Woodville, Grey and Vaughan.

But the young king was not prepared to accept the arrest of men who had cared for him for as long as he could remember. According to his latest household ordinances, at 12½, Edward had already shown himself to be capable of independent thought. He challenged Richard's actions, only to be told that the three had been plotting to take control by force and had concealed a number of weapons in their luggage from Ludlow. Croyland relates how Richard and Buckingham bowed before the boy, bare-headed, with 'every mark of respect' and explained that their 'only care was for the protection of his person, as [they] knew for certain that there were men in attendance upon the King who had conspired against both his honour and his very existence'.[13] Mancini's account goes further, stating that Richard blamed the death of Edward IV upon the dead man's friends, claiming that they had 'little regard for his honour, since they were accounted his companions and servants of his vices, and had ruined his health'. It was essential, Richard added, that the boy should not fall into their hands and that, due to his youth, he would be 'incapable of governing so great a realm by means of puny men'. He justified the arrests by saying that Woodville and the others were planning to ambush him on the road and cause his death, but their accomplices had revealed the plan to him just in time. It was 'common knowledge' that they were attempting to 'deprive him of the office of regent conferred on him by his brother' and their 'previous licence' proved them capable of anything.[14]

Young as he was, Edward was intelligent enough not to be convinced by arguments that seemed to contradict his own experience. In response, he reminded Richard that he was attended by men appointed by his father and that, 'relying on his father's prudence, he believed that good and faithful ones had been given him' and he wished to retain them 'until otherwise proved to be evil'.[15] He had every confidence in his servants and had put his trust in the lords and the queen, who awaited him in London. Buckingham disabused the boy of this belief, telling him that women had no business ruling kingdoms and that 'if he cherished any confidence in her he had better relinquish it'. According to Mancini, the real intention of Richard and Buckingham was apparent despite their initial show of deference, 'for although they cajoled him by moderation, yet they clearly showed that they were demanding rather than supplicating'.[16] Edward had little choice but to agree to submit himself to the care of his uncles, conscious of their greater power at this point. He must have wondered what was happening but probably hoped that all would be resolved once they arrived in the capital.

The news of Richard's actions reached London that night. Awaiting the arrival of her son, the Queen Dowager Elizabeth realised the danger she was in and fled to seek sanctuary again at Westminster with her children. It took another five days for the boy to reach the city, making a ceremonial entrance on the very day intended for his coronation, 4 May, accompanied by Richard and Buckingham. Initially all seemed well, with Edward appearing in blue velvet to be welcomed at Hornsey Park by the mayor and aldermen in scarlet and 500 citizens in violet, who joined to swear an oath of allegiance to him. He was lodged in the Bishop's Palace at St Paul's and received visitors, although this venue was quickly judged to be too small for the scale of entertaining required. He was thus moved to the Tower, some time between 9 and 16 May. With the benefit of hindsight, it is difficult not to read this as sinister, as the 'Prince in the Tower' being manoeuvred into place for the final act of the drama, but it may not have been so. Several sites were suggested as lodgings for the boy, including Westminster Palace and the Hospital of St John, before Buckingham proposed the Tower. This plan was 'at last agreed to by all, even those who had been originally opposed thereunto', which implies pressure on the duke's part, even though the palace was more suitable, right beside the abbey, where the coronation was scheduled to take place. It should be remembered, however, that the Tower was the location the queen had originally selected to deliver Edward, back in 1470, and it was only to acquire its sinister reputation after the boy and his brother disappeared behind its forbidding walls. A new coronation date was set for 22 June. Edward's first Parliament was to meet three days later. Instructions were given for new coins to be minted in his name. His name appeared on official grants until the middle of June. It appeared that the transition between kings would now take place smoothly. But Edward was never seen again.

By the second week of June it became clear that things were changing. Awaiting his coronation in the Tower, Edward was placed at a significant distance from his council, who were meeting to discuss arrangements for the event, his father's will and the question of who would guide the boy once he was crowned. A letter written by a Simon Stallworthe, in the service of the Bishop of Lincoln, to John Stoner, stated that negotiations between the Council and the queen had broken down and the members were refusing to visit her in her sanctuary. He continued that 'there is great business against the coronation' and a surviving fragment from the book of a London merchant indicated that 'divers imagined the death of the Duke of Gloucester'.[17] A mood of unease set in when Richard summoned troops from the north and Edward IV's old friend Lord Hastings was dragged out of a meeting and executed on the spot, at Richard's request. Three days later, on 16 June, Edward's younger brother, the 9-year-old Richard, Duke of York, was removed from sanctuary with his mother by Archbishop Bourchier. Gloucester had argued in a council meeting that the boy should be with his brother for the coronation, so a ring of armed men surrounded the abbey and the prince was sent to the Tower despite Elizabeth's protests.

In the meantime, arrangements were proceeding for Edward's coronation and the opening of his first Parliament. John Russell, Bishop of Lincoln and newly appointed Lord Chancellor, prepared a speech for the first sessions, to honour the estate of the nobles, the commons and 'owre glorious prince and King, Edward V'. Russell intended to say on Edward's behalf that 'Godd hath called me in my tendire age to be yowre kynge and soverayne' and to remind those assembled of the 'fluctuation and changing among the nobles' which had lately occurred in the realm. He appealed to the people represented by those assembled lords to obey them in the name of the law they shared, as members of the same metaphorical body of England. God had called Edward, as 'a yonge creature coming out of the wombe', to heal that body as a whole and recognise its rotten members. He recognised that Edward would require guidance through the early years of his reign, 'which yn the tyme of the kynges tender age must nedely be borne and supported by the ryght noble and famous prince the Duke of gloucestir hys uncle, protector of this' realm. Russell continued to praise Gloucester as wise in the defence of the realm and opposed to 'the open ennemies as ageynste the subtylle and faynte fryndes of the same', and anticipated he would have the tutelage and oversight of 'the kynges most roialle persone durynge hys ... yeres of tendirnesse'. Although his father had passed away, Edward was perfectly placed between the former king and his uncle, with Gloucester 'ordeigned as next in perfyt age of the blod Ryall, to be hys tutor and protector'. The duke's power and authority were established, Russell observed, as was his martial experience, so that 'the kynge oure soverayne lord may have cause largely to rejoyse hym selfe and congruently say'[18] to his uncle how glad he was to be in his protection. Russell had already been instrumental in the education of one young man anticipating future kingship, Edward of Lancaster, and would no doubt have proved a valuable guide during the youth of Edward V. But this fulsome praise of Richard was never delivered.

On 16 or 17 June, the meeting of Edward's first Parliament was cancelled. Edward may not have been informed of this latest development. Increasingly, he and his brother were out of touch with developments in the Council. Mancini relates that the two boys were observed playing and shooting in the Tower gardens or at the windows on a couple of occasions over the coming weeks. His source was his fellow Italian, Dr John Argentine, who was still employed as Edward's doctor and visited him regularly in his apartments. In the week of 17–22 June, though, the boys were moved to the innermost apartments of the Tower and were seen less and less; his last signature as king was made on 17 June. All their household servants were dismissed. Eighteen of them were paid off early in July. On Sunday 22 June, the day that should have been Edward's coronation, the first decisive move was made to depose the uncrowned king. Dr Ralph Shaa preached a sermon entitled 'bastard slips shall not take deep root' at St Paul's Cross, claiming that Edward IV had been precontracted to marry Eleanor Butler, meaning that his marriage to Elizabeth Woodville was invalid and their offspring illegitimate. The same message went out from a number of pulpits across the capital in a concerted attempt to prove that Edward was not entitled to rule, and that the crown should pass instead to his uncle Richard. The young king's reign formally ended on 25 June, after which he was referred to as 'Edward, bastard, late called King Edward V'. At the same time, his former guardians, Anthony Woodville, Richard Grey and Thomas Rivers, were executed at Pontefract.

Within the Tower's walls, it is impossible to know what the young Edward's experience of all this was, or to what degree he was informed of the changes taking place outside. He must have been aware that the day of his coronation had passed and is likely to have asked questions. He had the intelligence to understand that his deposition and the accession of his uncle put his life in danger. A report by Dr Argentine gives a glimpse of the boy's state of mind and his last miserable days: 'like a victim prepared for his sacrifice [Edward] made daily confession because he thought that death was facing him.'[19] On 4 July, Richard, Duke of Gloucester, now proclaimed Richard III, and his wife Anne, arrived at the Tower in advance of their coronation, which was scheduled for two days' time. A 10 p.m. curfew was imposed in the city and Richard's northern soldiers were positioned in the streets. After this point, there was no recorded sighting of Edward or his brother. Not a single source has them alive from this day forward. If, as one argument goes, Richard was seeking an opportunity to kill the two boys, the night of 4 July certainly afforded one. Nine days later, when Mancini left England, he was able to state that the princes had 'ceased to appear altogether' and that he had 'seen many men burst forth in tears and lamentations when mention was made of [Edward V] after his removal from men's sight, and already there was a suspicion that he had been done away with'.[20] The next question arising is exactly when this took place. The contemporary evidence suggests that Edward was killed between July and November that year.

Writing in the next reign, Thomas More drew on information from Bishop Morton, who had been arrested at the same time as Hastings, to state that Richard had ordered the deaths of his nephews on 29 July. This was the day Richard left the capital to head north on royal progress. Morton might have heard this from Buckingham, who was with Richard on this occasion and remained in his company until 2 August. After overhearing this command, the duke rode home to Brecon, where Morton was currently his prisoner. More believed that Buckingham was upset by the revelation that Richard intended to put the boys to death, which is why he rebelled against him a few weeks later. It was indeed a strange moment to quit the new king's side, as Buckingham had been with Richard throughout the summer, urging him forward, facilitating his succession, officiating at his coronation. He could, rightly, have taken his place in the splendid ceremonies planned in York, but he chose to retreat into the countryside. More's account states that the new king dispatched his servant Sir James Tyrrell to London to commit the murders, and a reputed confession by Tyrrell in exile, in 1502, would seem to support this. However, the confession was recorded while he was under arrest for treason and the relevant document appears never to have been produced. But this does not mean it never existed. Buckingham was executed for rebellion that November, at the same time as the rebels rose in the belief that Edward V had been murdered. While a couple of contemporary sources cite Buckingham as the instrument used by Richard to bring about the boys' demise, this may well have been propaganda circulated following his treason.

Historian Alison Weir speculates that the deed was done on 3 September, when Richard sent Tyrrell to collect hangings and robes from the Tower and bring them to York, for the investiture of Richard's son as Prince of Wales. It was two weeks later, in the middle of September, that the Recorder of Bristol, Robert Ricart, wrote that the boys had been 'put to silence' in the Tower. Then there is the allegiance of the rebels who raised their standard in November to support Henry Tudor, who planned to marry the boys' eldest sister. Initially it was hoped that Henry would restore Edward but support for Tudor as a candidate for the throne grew rapidly as the rumours arrived from London. The *Croyland Chronicle*, which historians believe to have been written by a member of Richard's council, confirms that the princes died late that summer. Initially the writer asserts that at the end of July, the princes were 'under special guard' and that an attempt was being planned to release them by people in the south-west, who 'began to murmur greatly and to form assemblies and confederacies, many of which worked in secret'. Soon afterwards, though, he was reporting that 'a rumour arose that King Edward's sons, by some unknown manner of violent destruction, had met their fates.'[21] Tudor himself was convinced of Richard's guilt, referring to him as a 'homicide' guilty of 'the shedding of infant's blood'. By the following January, their deaths were being assumed on the continent, the French Chancellor, Guillaume de Rochefort, describing how the boys, 'already big and courageous, have been put to death with impunity and the royal crown transferred to their murderer'. The French chronicler Jean Molinet stated that they had been held prisoner for around seven weeks before being smothered. In March 1486, the Spanish historian Diego de Valera claimed that Richard had 'poisoned his nephews', while Alvaro Lopes de Chaves, the secretary to the King of Portugal, asserted in 1488 that they were starved to death.

Other sources express uncertainty about the fates and locations of the two boys but, with one exception, these are datable to after the event. Visiting England in 1484, Nicolas von Popplau wrote glowingly of Richard, adding that 'many people' believed that the princes were 'still alive' and 'kept in a very dark cellar', although he could offer no evidence to this effect, merely a report of rumour. Thomas More also records such rumours but, given the mysterious nature of their demise, caution and doubt are more the sign of a reflective chronicler than a real indication that they may have survived. The suggestion that the boys were allowed to leave the Tower and live out their days in the countryside with their mother betrays a naivety regarding the realpolitik of the fifteenth century and has no basis in fact. Such theories are the result of circular rumours, coming into being through the efforts of the pretenders Lambert Simnel and Perkin Warbeck, which fired the imaginations of those reluctant to believe the worst.

Writing in the 1580s, antiquarian John Stowe related that there had been a plot to liberate the princes in July 1483, which involved lighting a fire within the Tower's walls to distract the attention of their gaolers. It may have been the same plan, or a different one, which intended to send the boys' sisters to safety overseas, prompting Richard to set a guard around their sanctuary. This conformed to the usual standpoint, in the century following Bosworth, for historians to assume the boys' death and the guilt of Richard III. John Rous described how the 'usurper King Richard III then ascended the throne of the slaughtered children', and contemporary poems, such as the *Ballad of Lady Bessie*, *The Rose of England* and *Ode on the Battle of Bosworth*, depicted the evil murdering Richard that found full development in the work of writers such as Polydore Vergil, More, Hall, Holinshed and Shakespeare.

The deaths of the boys are not depicted directly on stage in Shakespeare's *Richard III*. Instead the audience learns that the deed has taken place through the soliloquy of James Tyrell, who paints a romantic picture that tugged the heartstrings of even the two murderers, whom Shakespeare names as Miles Forrest and John Dighton, identified as early as More's history eighty years before:

> The tyrannous and bloody deed is done.
> The most arch of piteous massacre
> That ever yet this land was guilty of.
> Dighton and Forrest, whom I did suborn
> To do this ruthless piece of butchery,
> Although they were flesh'd villains, bloody dogs,

Melting with tenderness and kind compassion
Wept like two children in their deaths' sad stories.
'Lo, thus' quoth Dighton, 'lay those tender babes:'
'Thus, thus,' quoth Forrest, 'girdling one another
Within their innocent alabaster arms:
Their lips were four red roses on a stalk,
Which in their summer beauty kiss'd each other.
A book of prayers on their pillow lay;
Which once,' quoth Forrest, 'almost changed my mind;
But O! the devil'--there the villain stopp'd
Whilst Dighton thus told on: 'We smothered
The most replenished sweet work of nature,
That from the prime creation e'er she framed.'
Thus both are gone with conscience and remorse;
They could not speak; and so I left them both,
To bring this tidings to the bloody King.

Upon hearing this news, Shakespeare's Richard comments that 'the sons of Edward sleep in Abraham's bosom', which alludes to the contemporary view that a small number of exceptionally good individuals bypass purgatory altogether and proceed straight to heaven. The connotations of 'bosom', taken from the story of Lazarus in the New Testament, are that of comfort and contentment, suggesting a place reserved for a special guest. Not only was this intended to offer a contrast with Richard himself, but something of a comfort to the audience, to salvage something of a retrospective 'happy ending' for the boys.

The most likely end to the mystery of Edward V's deposition is that he died in the Tower in the summer of 1483. One certainly arrives at this conclusion based upon incomplete information, but motive and opportunity can be established, in terms of the dangers of keeping the boy alive, the days on which the murders could have occurred and who could have committed them. With Edward already emerging as independent around the time of his twelfth birthday, he could have represented a formidable future opponent to Richard. At the time of the last known sighting of the boys, in early July 1483, Edward was four months off his thirteenth birthday. One more year and he would have been considered of age, able to rule as king in his own right. Even when he was deposed he was rapidly growing into a man and would have continued to provide a figurehead for rebels, and a thorn in Richard's side, while he remained alive. Although Richard's first Parliament passed the act *Titulus Regius*, establishing the boys' illegitimacy, this would have proved no barrier for Edward's supporters, had they been able to restore him to power. Such acts were easily overturned, as Henry VII was to prove in 1485. Act or no act, Edward V was too dangerous to be allowed to live and no reports suggest that he survived his incarceration in the Tower. Had he and his brother survived, and been successfully smuggled out of London, or even out of England, their claims to the throne make it unlikely that they would have been content to live out their days in obscurity. Yet nothing was ever heard of Edward V again.

III

It is the sad fate of Edward V that the circumstances of 1483 have generated more interest in his death than in his life. This is partly explained by the young age at which he met his end, but also the immense constitutional significance of his removal from a throne to which he had already succeeded. This act, apparently followed swiftly by his death, represents either a deposition or a usurpation, depending upon one's interpretation, but cannot deny the boy's sovereignty. Whatever the truth of Richard III's claims about Edward's legitimacy, the fact remains that they were not made public until 22 June, a full ten weeks after the death of Edward IV. This means that Edward V had already reigned for two and a half months, so the decision made by Richard to replace him was a decision to remove a reigning king, rather than a Prince of Wales or a hopeful rival. Edward had not yet been crowned and anointed, but he was still legally recognised as ruler, and had been from the day after his father's demise. In this respect, the events of that summer take on a magnitude beyond the facts of the boy's existence and his loss. For the historian, it is not simply a question of what type of kingship he and his potential offspring might have adopted, it is a matter of the reversal of a process believed to be a question of divine law.

And yet, Edward's case is even more complex. Late medieval kings had been removed before, but when Henry Bolingbroke replaced Richard II and Edward IV deposed Henry VI, each was acting against a different branch of the family, a distant cousin, a fully grown adult, an individual who was perceived to have failed in his duty. Neither of them, nor their predecessor Edward II, survived the process, all dying violently in mysterious circumstances soon afterwards. These cases established precedents for the killing of a deposed ruler but none of them encompassed the death of a minor. The removal of Edward V was unprecedented and shocking, even to his contemporaries, for three reasons: because the instigator was his uncle and Protector, the king was a child who had shown potential and he was removed before he had had the chance to prove himself. It is easy and natural to be sentimental about two children who likely met a violent end but the facts in the case of Edward V are such that sentimentalisation is hardly required to reveal the horror and significance of the case. And this is even before the question of culpability arises.

The immediate consequence of the death of Edward V was the reign of Richard III. This set in motion a chain of events that led to the Battle of Bosworth in August 1485 and the advent of the Tudor dynasty. It was in the name of Edward V, or perhaps in his memory, that Henry Tudor launched a first invasion of England in the winter of 1483, just months after the boys' disappearance. The initial plan was to remove Richard and restore Edward, Tudor's reward being marriage to the young king's elder sister, Elizabeth of York. But during Richard's reign something changed. It was the certainty of Edward's death that underpinned Tudor's second invasion and his proclamation as king. He claimed the throne by right of conquest, but would not have done so had Edward V remained a prisoner in the Tower or in exile, given his stronger claim. In a section of the *Croyland Chronicle* composed in April 1486, the author includes a short poem which states that the third Richard had 'destroy[ed] his brother's progeny' but their cause was 'avenged' at Bosworth. When the first Tudor Parliament reversed *Titulus Regius*, ordering the destruction of all existing copies, Henry legitimised all Edward IV's children, re-establishing Edward V's superior claim to the throne. That document's inclusion of the accusation that Richard had been guilty of shedding infants' blood is a further indication of the Tudor-York royal family's belief in Edward's murder.

Further evidence for Edward's death can be found in the actions of his cousin, John de la Pole, Earl of Lincoln. The eldest son of Edward IV's sister, de la Pole rose against the Tudor regime in 1487, offering a 10-year-old boy, Lambert Simnel, in the role of Richard, Duke of York. Had the rebels believed that the younger prince was still genuinely alive at that point, by which he would have been 15, they would have rallied behind the real duke, rather than an imposter. Later, Simnel dropped the claim to be Richard of York, instead adopting the identity of Richard's cousin Edward, Earl of Warwick, son of George, Duke of Clarence. This acknowledged the death of the little duke, but was far easier for Tudor to refute, as the real Earl of Warwick was then incarcerated in the Tower. Thus, Henry was able to expose the fraud and eradicate de la Pole's cause at the Battle of Stoke. A few years later, another claimant also attempted to adopt the identity of Richard, Duke of York, but Perkin Warbeck later confessed to have been a native Fleming and was never identified by Queen Elizabeth as her long-lost brother. No pretender ever assumed the identity of Edward V. Even Warbeck's cover story, that his brother's murderer took pity on him and helped him escape, allowed that the former king must be dead. Although sympathy, even a romantic hope, might linger into the twenty-first century, the overwhelming silence regarding the survival of Edward V after July 1483 must be considered conclusive.

The trail may have gone cold there, but for a controversial discovery. In 1647 workmen excavating a stairwell in the White Tower found a box of bones, including scraps of velvet, an upper-class material, which convinced the current king, Charles II, that they belonged to the princes.

The remains were reinterred in Westminster Abbey as such in a white marble urn designed by Sir Christopher Wren, and there they remained for almost 300 years. In 1933, the urn was opened and the contents examined by Lawrence Tanner, archivist of Westminster Abbey, and William Wright, President of Great Britain's Anatomical Society.

The skeletons were incomplete, mixed with other matter and animal bones, but portions of two skulls were present, allowing the use of dental evidence. This suggested that the elder child was aged 12 or 13 and the younger 9 to 11, which was consistent with the ages of the princes at the time of their disappearance. As neither boy had yet undergone puberty, there was no way of establishing the gender of the bones, but estimates of their height put one at around 4ft 9in or 4ft 10in and the other just under 4ft 7in. Examination of the two jaw bones later revealed dental similarities with the skull of Anne Mowbray, child-bride of Richard, Duke of York, who was also related to the princes by blood. Mowbray's skull was discovered and examined in 1965, whereupon it was noticed that she suffered from hypodontia, or the failure of some teeth to develop, exactly as had been noticed in the jaws bones discovered in the Tower. It was also suggested in 1934 that the skull reputed to belong to Edward V bore a red bloodstain but this has since been discredited and there was no other visible sign of the cause of death on the bones, leaving poisoning, smothering, drowning and neglect as the most likely.

One other interesting discovery arose from the examination of the bones. Tanner and Wright concluded that the elder skull bore signs of disease, suggesting that Edward V suffered from osteomyletis, an inflammation of the bone caused by a bacterial infection. This could be very painful, stemming from an infected tooth socket and, before the age of antibiotics, it could prove fatal. No records survive of Edward experiencing anything of this kind during his lifetime, although it is conceivable that the royal family might have wished to keep it quiet, as a sign of weakness. It may be that the illness was recent, post-dating the boy's accession, as the condition is judged chronic if the infection has lasted more than one month. Symptoms include facial pain and swelling, chronic fatigue, fever, difficulty opening the mouth and swallowing, but may not have been so severe in Edward V, for lack of time. Conditions in the Tower, or the neglect of his health during this time, may have contributed to it. The possibility cannot be decisively ruled out that Edward actually died of this infection while in the Tower, facilitating Richard's eradication of the line. Even in the event of the king's death by illness, Richard is unlikely to have made a public announcement, as the crown would have automatically passed to the 9-year-old Duke of York. It is not impossible that the uncle killed the younger brother but not the elder.

Even if the urn in Westminster Abbey were to be reopened today and examined using modern forensic techniques, many questions would remain unanswered. If the identity of the bones could be established using DNA, the fate of Edward V and his brother could potentially be settled, yet the identity of their killer would not be settled. It would remain assumption, albeit the most logical, that they died in 1483, and it would still be assumption. though he is the likeliest candidate, that Richard had ordered it. However, even if Richard himself had not carried out the act, or appointed someone to do it for him, the responsibility still lies with him as the boys' uncle and their monarch. There is no doubt whatsoever that he removed Edward V from the throne and both boys' welfare was his responsibility: the fact cannot be ignored that their disappearance happened on his watch.

Edward V and his brother Richard feature in several iconic paintings from the late Georgian and Victorian period, all of which take the expected approach of sentimentalising the boys' last moments. In 1786, James Northcote portrayed the two princes asleep in bed, the moment before they were smothered. Pink and white, with flowing curls, they appear the very image of innocence as they sleep in each other's arms, with an abandoned book to one side and a crucifix above them. Their murderers loom over them, swarthy and crude, one in armour with his helmet pulled low over his eyes, the other with sleeves rolled up, exposing the boys with a lamp, seeming like a servant. In 1831, French artist Paul Delaroche created a more historically accurate image of the boys which allows for the uncertainty of their demise. Rejecting more sentimental potential titles, he called his version *The Children of Edward IV*, although the image depicts only two of them. Delaroche places the boys on the end of an ornately carved bed, with Edward seated and Richard either leaning against him or seated on a stool which is concealed by his long gown. They have been reading, but appear to have heard a noise and while Edward looks straight out from the canvas, the attention of his brother and their small dog is drawn by the imminent arrival of an unknown person, presumably their killer. Possibly the most famous of all the later images of the princes was created by John Everett Millais in 1878. Millais places two delicate, scared children at the foot of a flight of steps, in a reference to the location where the bones were discovered two centuries before. The boys appear holding hands, dressed all in black against a dark surround, their bright faces and golden hair standing out as angelic. Their wide eyes appear alarmed as they stare out of the canvas, unaware that the glimmer of light at the top of the stairs behind them heralds the arrival of their murderer. It is a simple, powerful image by a pre-Raphaelite artist famous for sympathetic depictions of the innocent who went on to produce the sentimental image *Bubbles*, used for advertising by Pears' Soap. Millais' *The Two Princes Edward and Richard in the Tower* is the most frequently reproduced image of the boys, instantly recognised even by those who know little more than their identities. It immediately evokes sympathy and demonstrates the reverse side of the Ricardian coin, of which their historical reputations will always be a function.

The most significant effect of Edward V's death was the damning of Richard III. Of course, if the decision to depose and kill the boy was entirely Richard's, he was indeed the author of his own damnation, as judged by many of his contemporaries and the majority of later historians. But the death of Edward and his brother was to prove inescapable for Richard, leading directly to challenges that created a sense of unease throughout his brief reign and which culminated with his death in battle. Despite the best efforts of Ricardians to exonerate him from the crime, they remain in the minority, against the evidence of the remaining facts. Other enthusiasts explain his actions within the context of late medieval realpolitik, without denying the significance of Edward V's deposition and death, or the impact upon Richard's reign. In personal terms, Edward was an unexpected, possibly avoidable, casualty. He was not cut down on the battlefield, executed for treason or removed for incompetence. He was an untried king who was destroyed for reasons beyond his control. Whether the victim of his father's youthful licentiousness or his uncle's ambition, more than any other individual of the era, he was a victim of his times, of the intrigues of the adult world.

IV

The deaths of Edmund, Earl of Rutland, Edward, Prince of Wales and Edward V belong to the first phase of the conflicts that have come to be known as the Wars of the Roses, or the Cousins' War. Each died as a result of dynastic conflict but at different levels of engagement. Edmund was fighting in defence of the rights given to his family by the 1460 Act of Accord. With his father nominated by Parliament as Henry VI's heir, a right which then devolved upon his sons in order of birth, Edmund was protecting his dynasty and his own claim to the throne, righting a wrong he believed went back to the displacement of the Yorkist line by the Lancastrians back in 1399. He had not expected to be attacked at Wakefield. This attack constituted an act of treason, by the terms of the new act. When the battle came to him, he fought valiantly but lost his life in the aftermath. The Act of Accord also underpinned the actions of Edward of Westminster, Prince of Wales. Its change to dynastic focus left him disinherited for no reason other than York's ambition. Edward had been born in legal matrimony, the son of a reigning king raised in anticipation of rule. When he returned to England in the spring of 1471, he did so in the belief that his father had been usurped and his bloodline displaced. At 17, he made the active decision to engage the enemy in battle, although he could not have anticipated the loss of the Earl of Warwick, who had been a vital component of the campaign. The case of Edward V differs vastly from these two in its details. At only 12, he would not have been expected to fight on the battlefield, although he might soon have brought his persuasion to bear in the Council chamber. Assuming that his death took place in the Tower in 1483, Edward was killed as a result of dynastic conflict, but to say that he was a victim of war is too simplistic and denies the personal involvement of those in whose care he had been placed. He was the victim of whoever ordered and carried out his death, and the dynastic struggle at this point had turned inwards. With the leading Lancastrians dead or in exile, York was fighting York. Edward was murdered because he was the eldest son of Edward IV and an obstacle to Richard.

These three deaths encompass an important phase in late medieval history. They delineate the span of the first Yorkist reign, Edward IV's rule, the means by which it came about and the results of its premature end, when the king passed away unexpectedly at the age of 40. During this period, illness, plague and accident also threatened the lives of young men, but the most frequent cause of adolescent deaths among the aristocracy was their engagement in battle. This was by no means consistent though, since certain families took a cautious path and avoided committing to conflict, but for those who did, such repeated warfare had devastating effects. It would be going too far to say that the late medieval aristocracy was decimated by the Wars of the Roses, but several branches certainly took a body blow.

One such family was the Staffords. Richard of York's wife Cecily, mother to Edward IV, Edmund, Duke of Rutland and Richard III, was one of twenty-four siblings and half-siblings born to her parents in the decades either side of the turn of the fifteenth century. Her closest sister, Anne, was married to the loyal Lancastrian Humphrey Stafford, First Duke of Buckingham, back in the days before the question of York and Lancaster had reached a crisis. In the 1420s, '30s and '40s, Anne bore Humphrey ten children – four girls and six boys. The eldest son and heir to the family title died before his father (who was killed in battle in 1460), perhaps of the plague, or of the wounds he had received while fighting for the Lancastrians at the first Battle of St Albans in 1455. He was dead by 1458, but had reached his thirties at this point, old enough to have married and fathered a son, named Henry. This son, the Second Duke of Buckingham, would become the closest companion of Richard III, helping him to the throne and then rebelling against him in the autumn of 1483. Henry had fathered four children, including two sons, and it was to his eldest, Edward, that his title passed. Edward became the Third Duke of Buckingham but was executed by Henry VIII in 1521, for pretensions to the throne. Thus, through this direct line, four generations of the Stafford male heirs died in violent circumstances: Humphrey and his eldest son in battle, Henry and Edward on the executioner's block. Going further back, more violent and premature deaths are revealed. Humphrey's father had died in battle at Shrewsbury in 1403, yet he had been the youngest of four brothers, the rest of whom had predeceased him violently. It is necessary to go back to Humphrey's grandfather, Hugh de Stafford, to find a male in the family who died peacefully, on pilgrimage in 1386, at the Hospital of the Knights of St John, on Rhodes.

Humphrey and Anne Stafford produced another five sons. The second, Henry, was in his forties when he died as a result of wounds he sustained at the Battle of Tewkesbury. He had been married for over a decade to Margaret Beaufort, mother of the future Henry VII, but the couple had no children. Lingering for about six months after the battle, Henry had time to put his affairs in order and prepare himself to make a 'good' death by accepting and embracing his fate. He drew up his will on 2 October 1471, requesting that his body be buried at the Collegiate Church at Pleshey, in Essex, with which he was associated through the line of his paternal grandmother, Anne of Gloucester, granddaughter of Edward III, and from the Essex de Bohun line. The church had been founded in 1394 by Anne's first husband, Thomas, while the couple lived at nearby Pleshey Castle and Henry's father Humphrey had already been laid to rest there, after requesting that money be paid to the local poor to pray for his soul.[22] Henry left the sizeable sum of £160 'for the finding of an honest and fitting priest to sing for my soul in the said college for evermore'; a horse cloth and four new velvet harnesses for his stepson Henry Tudor; a good horse, a 'bay courser', for his only surviving brother, John Stafford; a 'grizzled horse' for his friend Reginald Bray; and the rest of his goods for his wife, Margaret.[23] Henry died two days later, on 4 October 1471. He was buried at Holy Trinity Church, Pleshey.

How long was Henry Stafford's 'for evermore'? Some wills specify terms of prayer of one, five or seven years, perhaps in the hope that their soul would have left purgatory by this point. Henry Stafford can hardly have imagined that his request would be honoured *ad infinitum*? When it came to the observance of prayers for the dead, the following century would witness the almost complete rejection of this practice. Henry could not have foreseen this religious sea change, but did he really hope that £160 would cover it? It is plausible that he was hoping, after the duration of this time, that his surviving relatives, his brother, wife and friends, would have made similar bequests in their wills, or continue to pray for him, extending his period of grace piecemeal until he had passed out of living memory? Wills certainly did make reference to already deceased family members, often spanning many decades. When Jasper Tudor recorded his last wishes in 1495, he requested prayers for his mother, Catherine of Valois, who had died almost sixty years earlier; for his father Owen Tudor, then dead for thirty-four years; and for his brother Edmund, dead for almost four decades, as well as 'the souls of my other predecessors'.[24] It seems that in many cases, after an individual passed from living memory, unless they were a notable figure, or the founder or benefactor of a dynastic line, they were absorbed into the catch-all prayers for 'predecessors' or 'ancestors'. It gives us pause for thought regarding the late medieval belief in the duration of purgatory and also the meaning of 'evermore', in the same way that the contemporary marriage vows of 'until death do us part' might only mean a couple of years, with swift remarriage on the horizon.

Henry had four other brothers, born to Humphrey and Anne Stafford. Edward appears to have died young, as did the twins George and William who arrived in 1439. That left John, who was born in November 1427 and outlived Henry to receive the good horse in his will. John survived the conflicts of the 1460s and '70s, although he fought for the Yorkists at Hexham in 1464 and was imprisoned by the Earl of Warwick in 1470, which may have prevented him from fighting at Tewkesbury. He died of unknown causes on 8 May 1473, in his mid-forties, leaving behind a single son, Edward, who was then just 3 years old. Edward succeeded to his father's title of the earldom of Wiltshire, but his junior status in the family meant that the dukedom of Buckingham passed through his uncle's line, out of his reach. He became a ward of the king, carrying the queen's crown at the coronation of Richard III and Anne Neville in 1483, and was present when their son Edward was created Prince of Wales, around six weeks later. He survived the change of regime to the Tudors and was present at the coronation of Elizabeth of York, helped defend Henry VII against a rebel army and entertained the king at his Northamptonshire home. He must have suffered from some unspecified illness, as he drew up his will on 21 March 1499, at the age of 28.

In death, Edward, Earl of Wiltshire remembered his ancestors, but it was the maternal side of the family that he chose to honour, requesting to be buried in St Peter's church, Lowick, Northamptonshire, 'in Oure Lady's aisle by my grandfather Greene'.[25] This is significant, as his loyalties clearly lay not with the main Stafford branch, that of the lost dukedom, but with his mother's father, Henry Greene, who lay in a chest tomb in the south transept, his effigy dressed in full armour above a shield of the family arms. With no surviving male heir, Henry had passed his inheritance to his daughter's husband and on to his grandson, so Edward received the impressive Drayton House, which had been in the Greene family for six generations. Edward was clearly grateful, and mindful of the need to actively give thanks, as he refounded the chantry chapel and left money for the chapel to be remodelled. Lacking children in 1499, Edward left gifts to his wife, cousin, uncle and aunt, requesting that his executors make him 'a convenient tomb'. He died three days later, of unknown causes. His 'convenient' tomb has survived, though, on the south side of the south chapel. It is not quite typical of its time, perhaps even harking back to earlier medieval practices in contrast with the funerary advances made in the construction of Westminster's Lady Chapel and the work of the Italian Renaissance artist Pietro Torrigiano on the tomb of Henry VII. The Renaissance had not reached Lowick, and Edward lies under a chest tomb of white alabaster, decorated with arms inside lozenge panels, inside cusped squared panels. Above this, the young man reclines in alabaster, in partial armour, his clasped hands gloved but his head bare. His Stafford ancestry is represented in the iconography of knots that referenced the dynastic emblem – the Stafford knot that featured eleven times upon their family flag.

The Stafford family are a strong example of how the premature death of young aristocratic men impacted upon a dynastic line. Confining the data to two subsequent generations, the marriage of Humphrey and Anne resulted in seventeen live births, of which eleven were male. Out of these, only three men went on to produce sons of their own. Of the four daughters born to Anne Stafford, three had no known offspring, or daughters, and only one, Catherine, had two sons. The only little flourish of fecundity is to be found in the next generation, when Catherine's eldest boy, George, fathered eleven children of his own, although they bore their mother's surname by marriage, which was Talbot. The continuation of the Stafford name had depended upon a single birth line, that of the eldest sons: Humphrey, Henry and Edward. And although their genes appeared to dwindle for a while, curtailed by battle, early death and execution, Edward's son would father fourteen children, his seven sons ensuring the continuity of the Stafford name through the sixteenth century.

Similar losses were experienced by other leading medieval families as a result of dynastic and political conflict. Of the ten children born to Edmund Beaufort, Second Duke of Somerset and Eleanor Beauchamp, four were boys. After the death of their father at the Battle of St Albans in 1455, the eldest, Henry, was killed at Hexham in 1464, aged 28, leaving a single, illegitimate son. His youngest brother, Thomas, died at the age of 8, while the middle two, Edmund and John, both perished at Tewkesbury, aged 32 and 16 respectively. Neither left issue. The only Beaufort grandson born through the male line was the illegitimate Charles Somerset, but neither of his grandparents were alive to see him legitimised in 1514 and created Earl of Worcester. Where the Stafford name had narrowly survived, depending upon just one individual, this branch of the Beaufort name was lost because the one male child had been born out of wedlock. The fortunes of aristocratic lines were easily lost or broken during this period, as much in the bedroom as on the battlefield. Yet, as some were to discover, the birth of legitimate, healthy, peaceful male heirs was no guarantee of continuity in the face of an enemy determined to eradicate the threat they posed. In the coming years, fewer young men would die in battle; the greatest danger they faced was untreatable illness.

4

Edward of Middleham, Prince of Wales (1473?–84)

Very little is known about Edward of Middleham, the only legitimate son of Richard III. His arrival, his childhood, character, appearance, death and the location of his bones all remain a mystery, although the boy was once in line to become King of England. Even his birthdate is uncertain, with estimates ranging from 1473 to 1477, meaning that he could have lived as many as eleven years, as few as seven, or even just short of that, depending upon when his birthday fell in the year. Edward was one of a group of male cousins born to the three surviving York brothers, the next generation of a dynasty whose fortunes had climbed to their height with the martial victories of Edward IV, and would plummet again as a result of the chaos of 1483. That next branch of Yorkist blood included the Princes in the Tower, Edward V and Richard, Duke of York, Edward, Earl of Warwick and Edward of Middleham, all of whom were born in the early to mid-1470s and should have been in their prime as rulers, warriors, patrons and parents by the end of the century. Not a single one of them made it.

Of all his peers, Edward of Middleham was closest in age to the younger Prince in the Tower, Richard, Duke of York. Both were second in line to rule and both died young but their fates could hardly have been more different. While Duke Richard is likely to have perished at his uncle's command, by violence or neglect, Edward of Middleham was cherished and promoted by his father to take the very throne that had been denied his cousin. The *Croyland Chronicle* described Edward as 'this only son, on whom, through so many solemn oaths, the hopes of the royal succession rested'. Yet all the care Richard III lavished upon the boy could not prevent his premature death. No doubt some of his contemporaries saw the irony in this and, possibly, due to the beliefs of the time, the hand of divine justice at work.

Edward's existence was the result of an extraordinary marriage that could not have happened but for the outcome of the Battle of Tewkesbury. That game-changing day not only ended the direct Lancastrian line, it also redefined the lives of the victors. On the death of the 18-year-old Prince of Wales, Edward of Westminster, his wife Anne Neville became a widow at the age of 14. Their marriage had been an unusual one, forged out of necessity, of opportunity, perhaps of desperation, as the Earl of Warwick sought out allies to strengthen his invasion attempt of 1470. Yet for years his family had been the closest friends of the Yorkist dynasty and his support of Edward IV earned him the epithet of 'Kingmaker' from later historians. Likewise, his two daughters, Isabel and Anne, had grown up viewing Edward's younger brothers as potential husbands, rather than enemies. Isabel had even married George, Duke of Clarence, so it was no real surprise when Anne married Richard, Duke of Gloucester in the spring or early summer of 1472.

The newly-weds retired to the Neville family home of Middleham Castle in North Yorkshire, to take over administration of the north during the second half of Edward IV's reign. Within a year or two of the marriage, Anne gave birth to a son, whom they named Edward, after Richard's reigning brother. The location of his delivery is unknown, but the two most likely places are London and Middleham Castle. Tradition favours the latter, placing the event in the nursery tower, or Prince's Tower, in the south-west corner of the complex. However, there is no guarantee that this location was not named later, perhaps in response to local legend about the boy's birth. Edward had certainly arrived by 10 April 1477, when his name was included in the list of benefactors to be prayed for by clerics at the church of Fulmere, Cambridge, along with his parents.[1] The following year, the boy was given the title of Earl of Salisbury, which had once belonged to Anne's grandfather. Referred to as 'Edward Plantagenet', he received £20 annually from estates in Wiltshire, as approved by the leading clerics and lords of the day.[2]

Wherever he was born, Edward did spend a portion of his childhood at Middleham Castle, if not most of it. Situated in the rolling green countryside of Wensleydale, the castle had come into the Neville family in the late thirteenth century, added to over the years to create a substantial defensive base. Shortly before Richard and Anne's occupancy it had been developed further, to become a more comfortable family home, with residential wings built up around the large, central keep. Situated on the first floor in the castle's west wing, the nursery would have been warm for the new arrival, as it was above the fires of the bakehouse. The other adjoining wing to the Prince's Tower, in the south, housed the privy chamber or lady chamber, allowing access for Anne to her son. A bridge connected these rooms to the central keep, which housed the great hall and gave access to the chapel. Life for a child in a medieval castle was fairly insular, much of the family's needs being provided on-site, or brought in from the surrounding countryside. Edward would have had his own establishment from birth, which functioned within the wider context of castle life, with nurses, rockers, domestic servants and those required to authorise and administer his accounts. It would have been a far more secluded life than that experienced by his cousin Prince Edward, even after the future king had been sent away to Ludlow. In comparison, Richard was raising his son to play a supporting role to his cousin, as a great magnate in the north; it appears Richard never considered sending the boy to be educated at the Ludlow establishment as a young henchman to the future king, as often happened with the sons of the nobility. It seems very unlikely that the two young Edwards ever met.

Edward's life at Middleham contrasted with that of his cousin in other ways too. The prince's advantage of age and destiny defined his household as a predominantly masculine one, shaped by chivalric models, while Richard's son remained under the care of women. Yet Edward of Middleham does not appear to have made the transition to a more adult, male establishment that might have come through advancing age or better health. The court rolls list an Isabel Burgh as his wet nurse and Anne Idley (née Creting) as the 'mistress of the nursery'. Isabel was the wife of one Henry Burgh, probably also a recent mother, and later received an annuity of twenty marks for 'good service to the family'. Isabel's initial role would have ended when Edward was weaned but it was Anne who would have defined the boy's daily routine and education, approved by his parents and implemented by the mistress, especially during their absence on business. Anne came from Market Drayton in Oxfordshire, where she had been the second wife of one Peter Idley and although she appears to have borne no surviving children of her own, she had been stepmother to at least one of Peter's sons. It was for this son, John, that Peter had composed a book of manners, or instructions for the education of a boy, called *Instructions to his Son*, of which Anne must have been aware.[3]

Idley was contributing to an established tradition. The late fifteenth century saw a glut of instruction books aimed at improving the manners of the aspirational middle classes in every respect, from dining etiquette, to appearance and protocol. The *Boke of Nurture*, the *Babees Book*, the *Young Children's Book* and the *Book of Courtesy* were among many texts advising medieval youths to wash their hands and face, tell the truth and 'let no foul filth' appear on their clothing. Idley's *Instructions* were composed in the late 1440s, during his first marriage, but three decades later his widow Anne had become the guardian of both his book and his legacy. After she arrived at Middleham, her stepson John refused to pay her the annuity they had agreed, leading her employer, Richard of Gloucester, to intervene to ensure the debt was settled. His father's advice apparently had little impact on John but the future king's son would have benefited from it.

As mistress or 'lady governess' of Edward's nursery, Peter's widow would have overseen the arrangements for his education. It is not impossible that Anne taught him directly from the book herself. At the time that she was employed by the Duke of Gloucester, Edward was never expected to be anything more than the nephew of the king, although it was crucial that he received a suitable training for this prestigious role. Idley's advice filled two volumes, the first dealing with the theme of 'wise business' and fickleness of fortune, while the second includes religious teachings and the handling of sin. Family connections and loyalty were important. A young man should leave idleness until his old age and 'set his mind' to business, for the advancement of his friends and relatives. He should also honour his parents and see their blessing as a reward. His father's advancing age should serve as a reminder to a 'negligent' child that 'after warme youth coometh age coolde'. In all dealings, he should be humble and honest to rich and poor, in both word and deed, and respectful of his masters and superiors. It is no coincidence that the maxim 'manners maketh man' dates from this period.

Discretion was considered important too. Idley advised keeping 'within thi breste that may be stille' and not letting the tongue 'clakke as a mille'. The avoidance of unnecessary conflict and offence are considered essential to personal control, as the 'tonge' could give 'moche pain' and 'a grete worde may cause affray'. In fact, caution was a constant theme in the book. A boy should keep his ideas close 'as thombe in fiste' and not be too keen to express an opinion, as it may lose him friends. He should aim for 'meekness' as many had been 'cast adoun' for 'grete pride'. Loyalty should be tempered by wisdom when it came to personal feelings.[4]

Even as a child, boys like Edward were advised to exercise self-control. Not for him the games, japes and 'evil company' that could lead him into mischief, even if he had had the opportunity or the good health to enjoy them. Friendship was the greatest treasure the author could recommend, more precious than silver or gold. According to Idley, a man without friends was a man without a soul. Nor should a boy be too hasty in making promises to friend or foe, or too quick to take vengeance. Equally, he should not ask for advice when he was angry as 'it is harde than the trouthe to feele' nor accept it from those who were 'greene' or inexperienced. He should beware of 'covetous' men who could show 'two faces in one hood'. Interestingly, as Edward's father would find, Idley warns that 'a man may somtyme wade so depe, it passeth his power to turn ageyn.'[5]

Although many similar manuals existed, Edward's almost certain access to this text encourages speculation as to the lessons he was taught and, by projection, the man and king he might have become. Idley advocated loyalty, hard work, caution and discretion, characteristics that Richard himself had amply displayed as Duke of Gloucester, until he took the throne. This raises the question of how Anne came to work at Middleham. Having spent her married life in Oxfordshire, there is little to connect her with the Yorkists. Peter acted as the comptroller of the king's household from 1456 to 1461 under the Lancastrian Henry VI, leaving the position on the succession of Richard's brother Edward IV. He may also have been the Peter Idley who was listed in the court of common pleas as having been in debt to a London tailor in 1466. Did he fall on hard times after losing his job at court? Given how closely the advice in the *Instructions* tallies with Richard's character, it is not implausible that Gloucester had read the book and on hearing of Idley's death, offered his widow a home. Anne was clearly a valued employee, remaining with the family throughout Edward's short life.

In April 1483, Edward of Middleham may have been as young as 6 or as old as 10. Either way, he would have been old enough to understand the news that Edward IV had died and that his cousin, only a few years older than himself, had become Edward V. He would have bid farewell to his father, who first rode north to offer masses for his brother's soul, then south, to intercept his nephew's party at Stony Stratford. News of the rapid developments taking place in the capital may not have all reached Middleham, or else his mother, Anne, may not have passed it all on, but the next certain step for Edward was the dramatic news in June that his cousin was illegitimate. His mother prepared to leave Yorkshire and travel to London, leaving Edward behind in the nursery as the news sunk in that his father was to be crowned king. What was Edward told about the implications of this change, about the fate of his cousins? Did he understand that his elevation came at the cost of their lives? Perhaps the boys were simply not mentioned again, passed over as casualties of a legal detail, not permitted to impede the true succession.

Suddenly, the young boy was catapulted from relative obscurity at Middleham to heir to the throne. His parents clearly had their reasons for not taking him to London at this point. The final weeks of late June and early July were tumultuous and they may have judged the situation too volatile for the small boy; perhaps the journey was too long, or his health not sufficiently strong. In fact, Edward never visited London at all. His parents were crowned on 6 July as he waited at home, trusting that his time would come. But he was not forgotten. The mayor and aldermen of York made the trip to the castle to present the boy with gifts, food and wine on the day of the coronation. It must have been an exciting occasion for Edward and a taste of what was to come.

II

Today, Edward of Middleham is barely remembered, but between July 1483 and the following April, his future kingship was a very real possibility. For that brief window of time he was his father's sole heir to the throne and the slender shoulders on which the dynasty rested. Two weeks after his parents' coronation, Edward was appointed Lieutenant of Ireland,[6] a role that had once been held by his grandfather, Richard of York, a decisive move that indicated what the new king had in mind for his son. And yet he was their only son. Anne Neville never bore another surviving child, although she may have had other unsuccessful pregnancies. His parents' future and, technically, England's future, was bound up in the health of a small boy few had seen outside Middleham. His father was determined that the public should see Edward as a viable king.

In late July, Richard III began his progress north. Queen Anne stayed at Windsor while the king visited Oxford, Tewkesbury, Gloucester, Worcester and then went on to Warwick on 8 August, where the pair were reunited and stayed for a week in the castle. At Warwick, Anne was presented with a chronicle by the Warwick family historian, John Rous. It depicts the royal couple and their son, in probably the only contemporary image of Edward, although Rous is unlikely to have seen the boy in the flesh. The image of him is just a smaller version of the one of his father, with no identifiable individual features. They were also joined by Edward's young cousin, Edward, Earl of Warwick, son of George, Duke of Clarence, who was then aged 8. It is impossible to know which of the two boys was the elder but it can be stated that they were close in age, probably a year or two apart at the most. Warwick was also a reminder of the dynasty's rebellious past and potentially dangerous. George's seniority of birth would have seen the crown pass to his children following the allegations about Edward V's legitimacy. However, Clarence's attainder and execution in 1478 deprived his surviving children, Edward and Margaret, of their inheritance and their chance to rule. The pair had become wards of Richard and Anne, and were based at nearby Sheriff Hutton by 1484. With their nephew in tow, and perhaps their niece, the royal couple left Warwick on 15 August, travelling through Coventry, Leicester and Nottingham.

Edward left Middleham on 19 August, although his exact movements are unclear. Some sources have him staying in York, then joining his parents at Pontefract, while others place him at Nottingham, 120 miles south of his home. What can be stated for certain is that he was created Prince of Wales on 24 August, either at Nottingham or Pontefract, in advance of the family entering York. It was a precursor to the highlight of his life. At York, he was to briefly enjoy a lavish spotlight that was intended to be the first step of an increasingly illustrious career. His father went to considerable lengths to ensure the magnificence of the occasion, to put a seal upon his own reign and the right of his son. Richard's secretary, John Kendale, wrote ahead to the citizens of York to request they put on the most elaborate pageants and finest speeches, to make an impression of local loyalty upon the lords accompanying the king. Thousands of badges depicting the white boar of King Richard's device were commissioned to mark the occasion.

According to the city's council proceedings of 4 August, it had been decided that the local dignitaries would be the first to welcome the king:

At the which day it was agreed that my lord the Mayor, and all my masters his brethren, the aldermen in scarlet, and all my masters of the twenty four, and the Chamberlains, and also all those that have bought out their charges of all offices in this City, shall, in red gowns, on horseback, meet our most dread liege lord the King at Breckles Mills, and over this, the Bridgemasters and all other that hath been Bridgemasters, and all other honest men of the City, shall be in red … and that all other persons, of every occupation, in blue velvet and muster devers, shall meet on foot our said sovereign lord at St James's Church.

When they arrived on 29 August, Richard and his family passed through Micklegate Bar, where the heads of his father and brother had been displayed twenty-three years before. It was a symbolic choice to vindicate the dead duke's claim. As part of their welcome, they watched a series of pageants before retiring to the archbishop's palace. It has been suggested that Edward was ill at this point, too sickly to walk and carried upon a litter,[7] but it is difficult to find contemporary evidence to corroborate this. Sixteenth-century historian Edward Hall has the boy playing a more active role, but his sources cannot be verified:

At the day appointed the whole clergy assembled in copes richly revested, and so with a reverent ceremony went about the City in procession after whom followed the King with his crown and sceptre, appareilled in his surcoat robe royal, accompanied with no small number of the nobility of his realm; after whom marched in order Queen Anne his wife, likewise crowned, leading on her left hand Prince Edward her son, having on his head a demi crown appointed for the degree of a Prince. The King was had in that triumph in such honour, and the common people of the North so rejoiced that they extolled and praised him far above the stars.[8]

Edward had time to rest before his formal investiture as Prince of Wales. On 7 September, the Corpus Christi Guild in York performed the Creed Play for Edward and his parents, an entertainment that was part-pageant, part-miracle play, and took a processional route past various stations in the city, featuring prophets, apostles and scrolls. Although the original text has been lost, the York Creed Play would have conformed to type, with each of the apostles offering an article that contributed to the final Apostle's Creed, or statement of beliefs. As the centre of this attention, fêted by the city, Edward's future would have been brought sharply into focus. He would already have been instructed in his family's history, and that of the recent rulers of England. Perhaps he had also been read the classical stories, French romances and Arthurian myths that had shaped the education of his doomed cousins. Did young Edward allow himself to dream of such a future, following one of these models?

The following evening, Edward attended the archbishop's palace with his parents, where he was invested by the touch of a sword and the placing of a cap of office on his head. An account in the York Minster Record book relates how 'the Bishop of Durham was the officiating prelate, and the High Altar was decorated with silver and gilt figures of the twelve apostles and many other relics given by the Lord King'. A translation of the king's words upon the occasion indicates the level of ceremony and the affection that Richard III had for his son:

> We therefore, following the footsteps of our ancestors and with the assent and advice of the said prelates, Dukes and barons of our realm of England, we have determined to honour our dearest first born son Edward, whose outstanding qualities, with which he is singularly endowed for his age, give great and, by the favour of God, undoubted hope of future uprightness, as prince and Earl, with grants prerogatives and insignia and we have made and created, and do create, him Prince of Wales and Earl of Chester ... And we invest him as the custom is by the girding on of the sword, the handing over and setting of the garland on his head, and of the gold ring on his finger, and of the gold staff in his hand, to have and hold to him and his heirs, Kings of England, for ever.[9]

It was during the ceremony at York that Edward met his older illegitimate half-brother, John of Pontefract, who was knighted along with Edward, Earl of Warwick. John of Pontefract emerges in the historical records after Richard's succession and is likely to have been born in the early 1470s, perhaps to an Alice Burgh identified as Richard's 'beloved gentlewoman', a relation of Edward's wet nurse Isabel who was awarded an income in 1474. Alternatively, he may have been conceived during Richard's residency at Pontefract Castle in 1471–72, in an encounter with a local woman. This would have made John around 12 years old at the time of his knighthood in York. In fact, Edward of Middleham had two half-siblings, both illegitimate children of his father. It is difficult to know exactly when he became aware of their existence, but such children were not usually looked upon with shame, rather accepted as part of life, unless they were in line for the throne. The second was a sister, Katherine Plantagenet, who was married between March and May 1484 to William Herbert, Earl of Huntingdon. She is likely to have reached the age of consent of 14 by this time, placing her birth in the first half of 1470 at the latest, making her at least three years older than her half-brother Edward. She died before 1487, possibly in childbirth, as her husband was described by that time as a widower. It is not clear whether the brother she outlived ever met her or was even aware of her existence.

Edward remained in York with his parents for a few days after the ceremony. Then, around mid-September, his mother accompanied him back to Middleham. This may be telling: there must have been a good reason why the Prince of Wales did not travel to Westminster, which he might be expected to have done, in order to observe and participate in the governance of the country. It had been common practice for the heir, especially once he was invested, to undertake an educational regime or to a least be involved in administration or ceremonial occasions. Edward could not do this tucked away at Middleham, nor could he be seen by the people among whom Richard would hope to establish ties of loyalty for the future. Either the boy's health did not allow it or it was not safe for Edward to travel to London. It is true that rebellion was brewing, headed by the Duke of Buckingham, who wrote to Henry Tudor in his exile on 24 September, encouraging him to invade England the following month. Yet Richard was unaware of this when Edward returned to Middleham.

Tudor was not ready to sail until 3 October and the first signs of revolt erupted in Kent a week later. Perhaps the king had received other intelligence, since lost, or was expecting a continuation of the volatile situation of the summer. Middleham was certainly a safer place for his son during these months. Yet after September 1483, Prince Edward drops out of sight. He was not even brought to Westminster that Christmas, to celebrate with his parents. This was unusual for a Prince of Wales. Bearing in mind that he had only just over six months to live, his immobility might be indicative of illness or weakness.

As the year progressed and Richard was involved in fighting the rebels and preparing for the threat of Tudor's invasion, Edward's investiture looked increasingly like a formality. He was included in prayers for the royal family that formed part of grants to a church in Yorkshire on 4 December 1483, All Hallows, London on 2 March 1484 and again at Nottingham three weeks later, but never engaged with the world he had hoped to rule. He may have been as young as 8 or as old as 11, both ages considered sufficient for him to have been active with his father in tasks such as overseeing the fleet, or representing authority in court or council. Yet there are no surviving accounts of him having visited nearby locations or written letters to encourage support, as would have been manageable from his base in the north, nor records of his movements. The complete silence regarding his activities would seem to support the notion of worsening illness or a perceived weakness. The suggestion that he was unwell at the time of his investiture may have arisen from reliable contemporary sources, or subsequent ones, and may have a basis in truth.

One interesting aspect of Richard III's rule helps shed light on contemporary beliefs about death, mourning and memory. Richard had been a mere boy of 7 when his brother Edward won his decisive victory amid the snow at Towton and claimed the throne for the Yorkists. Described by historians as one of the bloodiest encounters ever, during which Edward ordered that no mercy be shown, Towton possibly claimed the lives of as many as 28,000 men. Afterwards, the bodies had been hastily buried in mass graves near the villages of Towton and Saxton. When the area was excavated in 1996, the extent of the battle's legendary brutality was underlined by the discovery of forty-three bodies packed into a tiny space measuring 6m by 2m and 50cm in depth. The battle was an iconic part of the Yorkist legend. By 1484, looking back at it, Richard could afford to be charitable to the souls of his family's enemies, in contrast to his brother's brutality. He ordered the grave pits to be exhumed and the bodies to be given a decent Christian burial:

> Their bodies were notoriously left on the field ... and in other places nearby, thoroughly outside the ecclesiastical burial-place in these hollows. Whereupon we, on account of affection, contriving the burial of these deceased men of this sort, caused the bones of these same men to be exhumed and left for an ecclesiastical burial in these coming months, partly in the parish church of Saxton in the said county of York and in the cemetery of the said place and partly in the chapel of Towton ... and the surroundings of this very place.[10]

In 1461, Edward had either planned, or actually built, a chapel at the battle site in atonement for the massacre. Twenty-three years later, Richard granted £40 for the chapel, or its foundations, to be 're-edified', and fragments of masonry and glass found in 2013 suggest that the work went ahead. He also appointed a permanent chaplain, funded from revenues from the Honour of Pontefract, to continue the work of helping the slaughtered men to salvation.

Chantry chapels were a common feature of late medieval piety, usually founded by a wealthy patron for the sole purpose of one or two priests to say daily masses and annual obits in their name and those of their family. On the anniversary of their death, or certain saints' days, the priests might also light candles as a reminder of that soul's ultimate destination. It was believed that after death, the soul lingered in purgatory while certain sins were expunged, allowing it to progress to heaven. The wicked went straight to hell, but the balance of good and evil meant that the majority of people were in limbo for a certain period of time. Exactly how long they had to wait was determined by their conduct during life, the manner of their death, their good works and the prayers of the living. Therefore, death became a process rather than an event, a journey begun when a soul relinquished its physical body and only completed when it reached its final resting place. Technically, there was a final stage too, the resurrection upon Judgement Day, but that was at a remove. Those souls who had experienced particularly violent deaths, especially those in battle, were considered by some contemporary European sources to remain trapped on earth, as *anima*, or ghosts. Having been wrenched too soon from their bodies, they mourned their loss and were reluctant to move on. Jerome de Raggiolo's fifteenth-century *Miracles of John Gualbert* even depicts them returning to repossess the living, in a vain attempt to experience life again. It was as much in the interests of the living to assist the dead, as it was the dead to seek assistance.

A chantry chapel might be an altar or discrete section of existing churches, or it might be a free-standing building dedicated entirely to the purpose, such as the one on Wakefield Bridge, which Edmund of York had attempted to reach in 1460. Usually established in wills, chantries might cater for a handful of individuals, so the creation of one for the benefit of such a large number of souls, by a non-relative, was not unique, but quite unusual. It worked like a trust fund, allowing the benefactor some degree of control over the perpetuation of their memory as long as their wishes were respected. If the bequest did lapse, the fabric of the chantry itself, the very solid stone presence and the carvings and paintings upon it, was an everyday reprimand. Typical of the times was the chantry chapel founded in 1460 by Sir John Wenlock, later Lord Wenlock, in Luton Church, Bedfordshire. The east window served as a constant reminder to the congregation to remember the knight in their prayers, assisting his path through purgatory, featuring his portrait and a verse:

> Jesu Christ, most of might
> Have mercy on John le Wenlock, knight
> And on his wife Elizabeth
> Who out of this world is passed by death
> Which founded this chapel here.

Help them with your hearty prayer
That they may come to that place
Which ever is joy and solace.[11]

Winchester Cathedral also provides an excellent history of the chantry chapel, housing seven that were established from the fourteenth century through to the sixteenth. One of the most spectacular, and the closest contemporary to Richard's reign, is that of Bishop William Waynflete. Dying in 1486, Waynflete's career spanned the entire spread of the Wars of the Roses, including the baptism of Edward of Westminster over thirty years before. His chantry chapel is a self-contained unit within the cathedral, a fantasia in stone dedicated to Mary Magdalene, the construction of which he had overseen during his lifetime. Situated at the east end of the nave, almost as a partner to that of Cardinal Beaufort, it is likely to date from 1470, when the cathedral's great screen was completed. On a floor of Purbeck marble, two pillars enclose the chapel, flanked by two screens decorated by a series of open arches which culminate in canopied niches. Inside, the tomb's plinth is also made of marble, topped with a life-size coloured effigy of Waynflete, presumably taken from life, dressed in blue, red and gold robes, a blue mitre and white jewelled gloves. The bishop wears black shoes with red-edged soles and carries a crozier.[12] The intended duration and impact of chantries is illustrated by the fact that the Waynflete obit continues to be read on the anniversary of his death.

Richard's chantry at Towton was incomplete at the time of his death. It is a sad irony that his effort on behalf of those souls who died violently in battle was so swiftly followed by his own bloody end. A year later, in July 1486, Thomas Rotherham, Archbishop of York offered to issue indulgences for anyone willing to contribute towards the completion of

a certain splendid chapel expensively and imposingly erected from new foundations in the hamlet of Toughton, upon the battleground where the bodies of the first and greatest in the land as well as great multitudes of other men were first slain and then buried and interred in the fields around, which chapel in so far as the roofing, the glazing of the windows, and other necessary furnishings is concerned, has not yet been fully completed.[13]

Richard's intention to honour the dead of Towton in such a way was perfectly consistent with late medieval piety and his own personal religious mission. This was a mixture of social convention, faith and individual redemption, which makes it not quite as altruistic as may appear. It cannot be overlooked that such an act, on such a scale, would have earned Richard himself great credit in the eyes of the Church and effectively bought him more direct access to heaven. Yet all members of Richard's social class were concerned to purchase memorials and prayers for themselves, to save their souls by the exercise of their worldly goods and status, as even a cursory glance at contemporary wills indicates. Late medieval piety actively encouraged the relationship between wealthy benefactors, the fabric of the Church, the congregation and the dead, for the mutual benefit of all. Richard's actions serve as a reminder that the dead, and recent history, were not forgotten but still very relevant, and the living were active in the facilitation of their afterlife.

III

Edward died in the spring of 1484. Richard and Anne were at Nottingham Castle on 20 April, when the news reached them. Even if his health had been poor, his state may not have been considered life-threatening, or might have been complicated by an additional infection or setback. The *Croyland Chronicle* suggests that his end was not anticipated at that time:

> this only son of his ... was seized with an illness of but short duration, and died at Middleham Castle, in the year of our Lord, 1484, being the first of the reign of the said King Richard. On hearing the news of this, at Nottingham, where they were then residing, you might have seen his father and mother in a state almost bordering on madness, by reason of their sudden grief.[14]

The Neville historian, Rous, called it an 'unhappy death', although this is more likely to have been a description of the political consequences than the circumstances of the boy's end. Perhaps Rous had in mind the irony of the situation, which Croyland refers to as a judgement on Richard's ambition, stating that 'it was fully seen how vain are the thoughts of a man who desires to establish his interests without the aid of God.' Rous's term was also a deeply emotive one for the times, when the emphasis on making a good or happy death, of embracing the end with not just resignation, but acceptance, was critical to the afterlife. A 'good' death, met without impatience or complaint, was just as important as good deeds throughout life, but in cases of illness, it might be a drawn-out process, lasting days, weeks or months. With the lack of surviving evidence, we do not know the circumstances of the boy's death, but then Rous was at a remove from the family, and may not have known more than us. Rous's comment seems to relate more to the timing and the impact upon Edward's parents. The chronicler's reminder that it was a year since the demise of Edward IV indicates a possible approximate date for the boy's death, around the anniversary on 9 April. The effect of his loss upon Richard and Anne, though, is not in doubt; 'In a state bordering almost on madness, by reason of their sudden grief', they left Nottingham at once and arrived back at Middleham on 5 May. In an era that saw the hand of God in every action and reaction, the loss of the king's only son – on the anniversary of the death of his brother, whose sons he had usurped – would have been seen as significant.

The location Edward's parents chose as his final resting place remains a mystery. It had traditionally been thought that the tomb of a young fifteenth-century male in the church of St Helen and the Holy Cross at Sheriff Hutton contained his bones, but the carved white alabaster memorial has proved to be a cenotaph, and completely empty. The figure on top appears to be that of a boy of 10 or 11, his features rubbed away over time, dressed in a belted robe and coronet. According to a local story, Edward's body was brought to Sheriff Hutton while his parents travelled north in order to witness his burial, and the alabaster memorial was created for him but his bones were laid to rest opposite, on the church's south side, in a vault of the Neville family. This is geographically plausible. The journey from Nottingham to Sheriff Hutton is 100 miles, which Richard and Anne could have covered in a week, perhaps less. If they had left Nottingham the day after hearing the news on 20 April, they could have reached the church and buried their son by the end of the month. They would then have had ample time to cover the forty-five remaining miles to Middleham Castle, to arrive on 5 May.

Yet there are problems with this story. Recent research suggests that the alabaster tomb dates from the first half of the fifteenth century and, therefore, cannot be Edward. Even if his bones lay in the Neville vault, the church of St Helen and the Holy Cross is a small and insignificant choice for the final resting place of an invested Prince of Wales. After the recent ceremony in York, it might seem a natural choice for the boy to have been buried in the cathedral there, in a city which would have mourned and revered him, where Richard could be certain that masses would continue to be said for his soul. Yet there may have been good reasons why the king deliberately chose a quiet location for Edward, to echo the quiet life he had lived. Edward's death immediately made his father more vulnerable. Anyone seeking to remove Richard's crown would previously have had to contend with the existence of a son, to whom the title would legally have passed. Perhaps, amid such unrest, Richard did not want to publicise his son's demise, in case it emboldened his enemies. Perhaps he deliberately kept it quiet, hoping that nothing would be suspected the capital. This might be why Edward was still being named in Commissions of Array that were issued in Westminster on 1 May.

Contemporary protocol also offers an argument against the theory that Richard and Anne witnessed Edward's burial at Sheriff Hutton. It was against custom for royal parents to attend the funerals of their children, as well as those of their spouse, as their status would place the focus on them rather than the deceased. Elizabeth Woodville did not attend the funeral of Edward IV and neither of them were present when their children Mary, Margaret or George were laid to rest, at Windsor or Westminster, in the 1470s. Richard III would not attend Anne Neville's funeral, nor Henry VII those of his wife and eldest son, also a Prince of Wales. Royal parents provided for their children's interments by appointing suitable officers to plan and oversee the details and service, then retreated into private grief. A monarch could not be seen to grieve publicly. However, it would have been fitting for Richard and Anne to visit the church at Sheriff Hutton on their return journey to Middleham, a few days after their son had been laid to rest there. The possibility also arises that Edward's burial was intended as a temporary measure. Just as Edward IV had reinterred his father and brother Edmund, Richard may have planned to relocate his son's remains once he had established the collegiate church he was planning at Middleham. However, he ran out of time, so Edward remained in place. It is also possible that Edward's remains already lie unmarked in the parish church of St Mary and St Alkelda at Middleham, just a five-minute walk from the castle where he lived.

There seems to be no question that Edward of Middleham was deeply mourned by his parents. Very little evidence survives to suggest the boy's character or suitability for rule, although educated guesses might be made about his education. Yet the dynastic significance of his death for Richard's reign was even more far-reaching. Without an established successor of his blood, the king was a vulnerable target for his enemies, as his removal could now more easily pave the way for a new dynasty. Richard could hardly turn to the young Edward, Earl of Warwick for to embrace his claim would necessitate recognition that that claim was superior to his own. There was his illegitimate son, John of Pontefract, but Richard could not overlook the very same problem that he had used as grounds to disinherit the sons of Edward IV.

It appears that he now sought out his sister's son John de la Pole, Earl of Lincoln, possibly as a temporary solution to the succession question. Although this was never formalised, Lincoln was given Prince Edward's old position of Lieutenant of Ireland, significant for being a title often bestowed upon the heir, and he was already President of the Council in the North. John also had the advantage of being a fully grown adult, able to offer immediate support to his uncle, even immediate succession to the throne, should Richard be defeated by his enemies.

With hindsight, it is easy to identify Edward of Middleham's death as a turning point for his parents. In a superstitious age, the irony of Edward's death would not have escape the attention of his enemies, less than a year after Richard had been considered responsible for the death of Edward V and the usurpation of his throne. The threat of invasion persisted through the autumn and winter of 1484, and Richard prepared his army and naval fleet to repel Henry Tudor. He and Anne spent that Christmas at Westminster, which the Croyland Chronicler described as full of scandalous and self-indulgent behaviour, the origin of the rumour that Anne was ill and Richard was intending to marry his own niece, Edward IV's eldest daughter, Elizabeth. After Anne's death on 16 March 1485, Richard had to make a public statement that he had no such marital intentions. It seems like this was the beginning of the slippery slope for the Plantagenets. But the Battle of Bosworth had not yet been fought. In fact, hindsight could easily cloud this occasion, as Richard may have viewed the spring and early summer of that year in quite different terms. He had lost his wife and son, but these tragedies presented a new opportunity for remarriage and the fathering of sons. Richard was only 33 and might have anticipated ruling for another decade or two. Henry Tudor was a rank outsider, an exile with a tenuous claim and no military experience; his threat should have been relatively easily dealt with, leaving Richard to remarry and reign in peace. To this end, he began negotiations for a joint match, for himself and Princess Elizabeth, to members of the Portuguese royal house.

Edward has made little mark on history, with few representations in art and literature. While his death was no less a tragic loss than that of his cousins in the Tower, the element of secrecy and lack of surviving information makes him one of history's notable absences. Having died quietly at home in his bed, even as a Prince of Wales, his fate did not capture the popular imagination or have as immediate, obvious an impact as the possible death of Edward V in the Tower. Edward of Middleham almost passed away unnoticed and unmourned, save for his immediate family and the loyal servants who had raised him in seclusion. After 1485, the king's name was vilified and aspects of his humanity downplayed or forgotten, including his fatherhood. The identity and historical reputation of Edward of Middleham was a casualty of this. Yet one small shift occurred as a result of his loss, which could have repercussions within a few years. With the passing of the Yorkist mantle to John, Earl of Lincoln, the stage was set for violent conflict that would surface to haunt the new Tudor regime.

5

John de la Pole, Earl of Lincoln (1462/4?–87)

I

On 22 August 1485, the armies of Richard III and Henry Tudor met at Ambion Hill, south of the Leicestershire town of Market Bosworth. The outcome should have been a foregone conclusion. Tudor's army may have been as small as half that of the more experienced king, composed of a mix of paid mercenaries and Welsh, Scots and English exiles. Also to his disadvantage was the fact that he had not set foot in England since he had fled after the Lancastrian defeat at Tewkesbury, at the age of 14. He was fighting a reigning king, an experienced military leader who had ranged his troops along the high ground and had trained his cannons down the hill, right into the Lancastrian line of advance. While he waited for Tudor's forces to assemble, Richard had ordered his armies to be blessed, and a cross carried before them, in the conviction that God was on his side. But battles can be unpredictable. The fortunes of war, and life, turn upon single decisions.

Mid-fight, Richard III made one such decision. Spotting Henry Tudor relatively unguarded on the battlefield, he led a direct charge in an attempt to cut his opponent down. It is likely that he took a small group of mounted men with him, anticipating that the fight would soon be won, breaking his way through to the place where Henry had taken shelter behind his archers. This took the Lancastrians by surprise, allowing Richard to get close enough to kill Henry's standard bearer, but a combination of marshy terrain and Tudor's Welsh guard brought the king to the ground. It was a bold, decisive move and, in other circumstances, might have won the day and reaffirmed Richard's reign for years to come. Yet it was at this point that Lord Stanley, Henry's stepfather, committed his troops on Tudor's side.

In fact, the tide may have turned earlier. Sources writing soon after the event suggest a reluctance on the part of Richard's men to come to his assistance; his officers deflected his order to execute Lord Strange and his instructions were not followed by key figures like Lord Brackenbury and Lord Stanley, on whom he was relying. The chronicler Molinet described how Richard's death took place as the result his horse being stuck in a bog, whereupon he was killed with a halberd. The discovery and forensic analysis of Richard's body in 2013 confirmed that this was likely, and that other blows to his head and body followed. Richard's circlet, especially designed to sit upon his helmet, was found nearby and used to crown the invader as Henry VII. Control of England had passed out of Yorkist hands and a new dynasty was established. The Tudors had arrived.

Bosworth is often considered an historical watershed, a line in the sand between dynasties, a demarcation between the medieval and modern world. In reality, while the fortunes of England's nobility did experience some change, the story was largely one of continuity. After the battle, the majority of Yorkist survivors recognised that their personal and dynastic futures depended upon them submitting to the new regime. Some did so enthusiastically, while it was more a question of tolerance than acceptance for others, an exercise in pragmatism. The example of frequent regime changes in recent years allowed for the possibility of Tudor's overthrow, if the right challenge was mounted at the right time. With Henry cleverly backdating his reign to before Bosworth, England's aristocracy swore an oath of allegiance that allowed them to retain their liberty and property. As a result, almost all of Richard's supporters were pardoned; of the thousands who had fought at Bosworth, only twenty-eight men were attainted. People moved into the spaces that had been vacated, mopping up the lands, titles and jobs, even the widows, of the dead. Yet there was one individual who found this particularly difficult. Richard's nephew John de la Pole had fought at Bosworth, and witnessed the aftermath of his uncle's death. After being informally adopted as Richard's heir the previous year, John's claim to the throne meant that he was not prepared to countenance the Tudor regime for long. He swore the oath and escaped attainder merely to abscond and plan his assault upon the new king.

Like many of his contemporaries, John came from a family which united the Lancastrian and Yorkist bloodlines. His grandfather William de la Pole, First Duke of Suffolk had been married as a child to Henry Tudor's mother, Margaret Beaufort, although the union was dissolved before they reached the age of consent. William had gone on to marry Alice Chaucer, granddaughter of the poet, friend and ally of Margaret of Anjou, but later endured an horrific death at the hands of his enemies, beheaded with a rusty sword on board ship on his way to exile. On the day before Suffolk died, he wrote a touching letter to his young son John, telling him to look after his mother and 'always obey her commandments, believe her counsels and advices in all your works.'[1] It may seem strange, therefore, that William's son John, Second Duke of Suffolk sought a bride from a prominent Yorkist family, but the match had taken place by 1458, in a period of ceasefire and was, perhaps, a tacit admission of the importance of the Duke of York and his family.

The wife of the Second Duke of Suffolk came from the same Rouen nursery that had nurtured Edward IV and Edmund, Duke of Rutland in the mid-1440s. Elizabeth was the third child born to Richard, Duke of York and Cecily Neville during York's tenure as Lieutenant of France, arriving less than a year after Edmund, on 22 April 1444. Like her mother, she was married as soon as she came of age, around the time of her fourteenth birthday, although given that the earliest birthdate suggested for their eldest son is 1462, a delayed consummation of the marriage is suggested. The match was probably made to reconcile the de la Poles with the York Plantagenets in the brief interval of peace in the spring of 1458.[2] The young couple lived together at Wingfield Castle, in the village of the same name in Suffolk. Today only the south curtain wall and gatehouse survive of the medieval building but the local church, St Andrews, has an octagonal font dating from 1405. It is quite plausible that John, Earl of Lincoln was baptised there at some point between 1462 and 1464.

Between the de la Pole marriage and the birth of baby John, the Yorkist fortunes had undergone a significant change. Upon her marriage, Elizabeth Plantagenet had been the daughter of the most able and ambitious aristocrat of the era, second in line to the throne after Edward of Westminster, the king's own son. Even though York had amply proven his ability to rule as Protector, Henry VI was still King of England and had produced a male heir. Four years later, father and son had been displaced and Elizabeth was now sister of the king. Her husband, John, had fought for Edward at the second battle of St Albans in February 1461 and then alongside him at Towton and was soon to benefit from the victory. The first sign of his changing fortunes was Suffolk's appointment as a Steward of England for Edward's coronation, which took place that June.[3] Two months later, the duke was granted the office of the Constable of Wallingford Castle and other lands, yielding them an income of £40 annually;[4] four years later it was increased to 100 marks.[5] The following February, he received a commission of oyer and terminer, to hear local cases[6] and in March 1463 his income was confirmed and he received a licence to 'enter into all the castles, towns, lordships ... and other possessions in England and Wales and in the marches of Wales' over which his father had enjoyed jurisdiction.[7] Of course there were also benefits for their children: an annual provision of £40 drawn from the fee farm of Gippewich was made for their male heirs in June 1466.[8] John was created Earl of Lincoln by his uncle in October 1467, and the sheriff of Lincoln was ordered to pay 'the King's nephew, son and heir of John, Duke of Suffolk' an annual income of £20 for life.[9]

In July 1471, John's parents were granted the wardship of Francis Lovell, who had been a ward of Richard Neville, Earl of Warwick, recently killed at Barnet. Lovell was in his teens at this point, already married and living with his wife's family, the FitzHughs; the control of his estates was a further privilege of proximity to the throne.[10] In 1472, the family were trusted even further when John's grandmother, Alice, Duchess of Suffolk, was appointed the keeping of the defeated Margaret of Anjou. The former Lancastrian queen stayed in Alice's care at Wallingford and Windsor for the remainder of the duchess's life, after which she was ransomed and sent back to her native France.

John's family were typical in following contemporary patterns of aristocratic piety and patronage. In December 1473, when John was between 9 and 11 years old, Alice and her son received a licence to found a fraternity or guild of parishioners in Leighton Buzzard, Bedfordshire. They were to appoint two guardians annually, have their own seal and appoint a chaplain to say masses for the souls of the royal family, the de la Poles and the members of the congregation. Although 100 miles from Wingfield, the family had an existing connection with the town's church of All Saints, which perhaps came through the Chaucer family, as it was Alice who also paid for the church roof to be embellished with angels in the East Anglian style. It was a common act of piety undertaken as benefactors neared the end of their life, and Alice was to die in May 1475. Wills of the 1470s illustrate the extent of bequests made by wealthy widows for the creation of roods (crosses), statues, banners and wall paintings. Another widowed Alice, an Alice Chestre of All Saints in Bristol, left extensive gifts to her church when she died in 1485, including a new front for the altar carved with the images of five saints, gilding for Our Lady's altar, a tabernacle for the image of Jesus and a black velvet hearse cloth embroidered in gold with her initials and those of her late husband.[11] When she died, the church book recorded that because of these 'good deeds' the parish was 'bound to pray for her'. These tokens were a way of embedding Alice Chestre's memory into the fabric of the church, just as Alice Chaucer's angels were. They were a reminder to the living to behave themselves and to pray for the women's souls. Just as money and influence could offer comparative luxury and protection for the nobility in life, it was also considered able to assist the passage to heaven.

Alice Chaucer's final resting place, St Mary the Virgin in Ewelme, Oxfordshire, is one of the best surviving examples of the late medieval cadaver tomb. This should come as no surprise, as she accumulated considerable wealth during her three marriages and died at the time such forms of memorial reached a peak of popularity. It goes without saying that Alice's servants and tenants do not repose in such graves: the material demonstration of piety and the purchase of a swift path through purgatory were the preserves of the rich. For secular worshippers, the cream of religious benefits was available only to an elite minority.

The alabaster effigy of Alice lies on top of an ornate box tomb decorated with angels under canopies, her head resting on pillows borne by feathered angels, her features finely drawn and ageing. She is dressed in her ducal coronet, wearing the garter insignia upon her arm, full wimple and kirtle in folds, her hands clasped in prayer. Yet below the effigy, through apertures in the tracery panel, another glimpse of the duchess is visible. While the top figure presents the pious public face of the medieval aristocracy, death has ravaged the corpse below, wrapped in its shroud with hair spilling out. The duchess allows us to peep, voyeuristically, into the privacy of her death, through small holes that serve to heighten the terror, making more of an impression than if the tomb simply exposed the entire figure beneath. However, just inches above the cadaver, painted on the underside of the tomb is an image of the Annunciation, offering hope of redemption.

Hope and redemption were exactly what the Yorkist dynasty needed in 1470–71. John's father offered solid support for the crown during the hiatus of Henry VI's readeption, fighting alongside his brother-in-law at Losecote Field, Barnet and Tewkesbury. Among the Paston collection is a letter written at Wingfield, dated 22 October 1471, in which the Duke addresses the baileys, constables and chamberlains of the Suffolk town of Eye. Two of the Duke of Suffolk's men had served in a skirmish at Stamford, putting down a rebellion that was led by Sir Robert Welles against the king. Welles was defeated and executed, and the duke was writing to insist that the men be paid in full, at once, for their service. In fact, as John was writing this letter, Edward had been forced to flee as a result of the actions of the Earl of Warwick and Duke of Clarence. In all probability, his brother-in-law was not yet aware of this new downturn in the family's fortunes.[12]

Otherwise, the Paston letters do not show John, Duke of Suffolk in a particularly positive light, detailing his property dispute with the Paston family and his men's attack upon the Paston property of Hellesdon, ransacking the church, standing upon the altar, stealing images and forcing out the parson. This desecration appears to provide quite a contrast to his mother's piety, but the medieval world was more complex than that. It was not incompatible with Alice's faith to lavish gifts upon one parish while supporting her son's brutal attack upon another. Margaret Paston made an extensive list of what had been stolen and destroyed by the duke's 500 men, including many personal and household items and buildings but, in addition, gowns, money, a silver collar in the king's livery, a purse and three gold rings from the church.[13]

Most of John, Earl of Lincoln's childhood at Wingfield left little mark upon the surviving records. During Edward IV's reign, he witnessed the arrival of ten more siblings, eight of whom survived to adulthood. Perhaps he shared a tutor with his brothers Edward and Edmund, but he was in his late teens by the arrival of the youngest de la Pole, Richard. In April 1475, he was created a Knight of the Bath alongside his cousin the future Edward V, in a move intended to create a bond of loyalty between them. Three years later he attended the marriage between the young Duke of York and the Norfolk heiress Anne de Mowbray and, in 1480, he carried the salt at the baptism of Edward IV's youngest daughter, Princess Bridget of York.[14] In the late 1470s or early '80s, John made a Yorkist match of his own, marrying Margaret FitzAlan, another cousin, who was the daughter of Queen Elizabeth's younger sister, Margaret Woodville. The couple may have had a son but, if so, the child appears to have died young.

With his father and grandmother involved in such political and religious activities, John, Earl of Lincoln grew up within a narrative of unquestioning service to the Yorkist crown, and the paradoxes of piety and violence so characteristic of this era. This absolute loyalty might have been shaken in the spring of 1483, when John attended the funeral of Edward IV and watched the bastardisation of his royal cousins in the Tower. Yet neither Suffolk nor Lincoln challenged this; it was simply a matter of transferring loyalties to the next uncle, Richard III, and accepting the new king's justification for his reign. John was around 20 when Richard succeeded the throne and, although his devotion to his dynasty would reap short-term rewards, it would ultimately cost him his life.

II

When Richard III was crowned at Westminster Abbey on 6 July 1483, both the Duke of Suffolk and John, Earl of Lincoln played prominent ceremonial roles. Behind the king and queen, Suffolk's role was to hold the sceptre while Lincoln carried the cross and ball. John's mother Elizabeth walked alone in the procession, as a mark of honour, with twenty ladies behind her. After the anointing and crowning, they would have taken their place on one of the top tables at the coronation feast in the palace nearby, among the 3,000 guests. The same month, John was appointed President of the Council of the North, which Richard established as a court of justice to oversee the north of England. It was based at Sandal Castle and Sheriff Hutton, the latter property John knew well, and he joined Edward, Earl of Warwick there the following year. Little more than ruins now remain of the quadrangular castle of sandstone and limestone.

When Buckingham and other rebels rose against Richard in the autumn of 1483, John supported his uncle and received rewards of lands worth £157, followed by the reversion of Beaufort estates worth £187 in the event of the death of Lord Stanley. In 1483, Stanley was still alive and well, though, so until such time as John could benefit from this arrangement, he was granted an annual income of a similar amount, to be drawn from the Duchy of Cornwall.[15] After the death of Edward of Middleham in 1484, Richard III tacitly accepted John as his heir by granting him lands worth over £300, although his position was never formally clarified. It is likely that Richard had a more long-term plan to remarry and father more sons, so he kept John in reserve but never officially invested him with the title of heir. In the summer of 1485, John was aware of the new threat posed to his uncle by Henry Tudor's planned invasion. He was with Richard at Nottingham Castle at the start of August, waiting to hear where the enemy would land; he was probably still with him when the king had marched to Leicester and on to Market Bosworth. Although John's presence is not mentioned by contemporary chroniclers, he would have fought at Richard's side, as he was mistakenly listed among the Yorkist dead afterwards.

After Bosworth, the trail goes cold for a few weeks. No doubt John was coming to terms with the change in his fortunes, perhaps even recovering from battle wounds. With the Yorkist cause at its nadir, he made the pragmatic decision to play along with the new king, attending Henry VII's coronation that October and, probably, the king's wedding to John's cousin Elizabeth of York, eldest daughter of Edward IV, which took place the following January. Not to attend would have been a political statement that he could ill afford, considering his bloodline. Yet it is difficult to know whether this appearance of amity was instigated by John himself, or whether he responded to overtures made by the king. It was Henry's policy to keep his enemies close, so he may have invited John to be with him at York that spring, and put him in charge of the investigation into a rebellion mounted by Francis Lovell and Humphrey Stafford. It would have been typical of Henry's methods to send John a veiled warning through the medium of this legal process, to remind him of the fate awaiting those who challenged him. It was doubly poignant given the de la Pole family connection with Lovell, who had also been a close friend of Richard III. For the time being, Francis escaped justice and fled to Burgundy, where John's aunt Margaret of York was duchess.

Still, John followed the Tudor line. He attended the baptism of Queen Elizabeth's first child, Prince Arthur, at Winchester that September and was with the court at Greenwich early in November. The following February, of 1487, John was at Richmond Palace when the court was abuzz with news of a pretender to the throne. A 10-year-old boy, known to history as Lambert Simnel, had been claiming to be the young Edward, Earl of Warwick, reputed to have escaped from the Tower. However, Henry was confident in the knowledge that the real earl was securely locked away in London and decided to put him on display to demonstrate the falsity of this claim. This was a turning point for John. Perhaps he was already involved in the Simnel story or perhaps this development triggered a desire to join the rebels. As the eldest surviving Yorkist son, any challenge to the Tudor regime should have given him a central place in its plans, if not offered to champion his own claim to the throne. Either he intended to harness his cause to that of the rebels and use their dissent to overthrow Henry, or he planned to mount a counter-claim, to prevent them from stealing his thunder. John absconded from Richmond soon afterwards and crossed the North Sea to join Francis Lovell at Margaret's sympathetic court in Burgundy. Tudor issued an act of attainder against him on 19 March.

Margaret of York was the sister of Edward IV, Edmund of Rutland, Elizabeth and Richard III. She had been born in 1446, after the family left Rouen and returned to the York estate of Fotheringhay in Northamptonshire. Just two years younger than John's mother, Margaret's marriage prospects had changed completely upon Edward's succession in 1461. Whereas Elizabeth made a good but safe marriage to John, Duke of Suffolk, Margaret's new status gave her a wealth of international candidates for her hand. In June 1468, she had married Charles the Bold in a magnificent ceremony described as the wedding of the century. John may have attended the London festivities as a child, before her departure, but he is more likely to have been present at Greenwich when she returned for a visit in 1480.

Margaret had been backing the restoration of the York dynasty ever since its defeat at Bosworth. She had no reason to feign obedience to Henry VII and openly backed both Lovell and Simnel in 1486, in the belief that Simnel might be Warwick, as he had claimed, or that he might open the door for another member of the family. In June that year, she made a gift of eight flagons of wine to 'the son of the Duke of Clarence from England'[16] but it is not clear whether this was intended for Simnel or the actual Earl of Warwick. As a wealthy widow, Margaret had time and resources to devote to the cause and a deep hatred of Henry VII, who had killed her brother. Between 1486 and 1487, her home town of Malines (Mechelen) raised a sum of 750 livres for her English cause, either for her to visit in person or to support an army.[17] By this point, John, Earl of Lincoln was between 23 and 25, a suitable man, according to the Jacobean statesman Francis Bacon, 'of great wit and courage'.[18] The historian's judgement of Margaret was stereotypical of his age, that she had 'the spirit of a man and the malice of a woman', but he recognised her complete commitment to the cause. By the time John was welcomed at her Mechlen court, and reunited with his friend Francis Lovell, Margaret was already assembling her troops. She offered John 2,000 men under the leadership of Colonel Martin Schwartz, a German mercenary who had been a veteran of her husband's campaigns. Other exiles arrived in Mechelen, including Thomas David, captain of the Calais garrison, and Sir Richard Harleston, former governor of Jersey. Back in England, Henry moved north in anticipation that they would land somewhere on the east coast, only to learn that they intended to bypass him and sail round to the traditional Yorkist stronghold of Ireland to unite with the Earl of Kildare and his brother Thomas FitzGerald, Ireland's Chancellor.

Exactly when John and Simnel met is unclear, although it was probably soon after the earl's arrival in Ireland on 5 May. He was faced with a boy who must have looked familiar, reputedly bearing strong facial similarities to the children of Edward IV and, perhaps, to John himself. He had been tutored by an Oxford priest by the name of Richard or William Symon or Symonds, and proved himself adept in courtly accomplishments and graces, to the extent that 'had he ruled, he would have as a learned man.' Simnel was paraded through the streets of Dublin, carried on the shoulders of the tallest man in the city. On 24 May, he was crowned as Edward VI in Christchurch Cathedral, Dublin, sanctified by two archbishops and twelve bishops.[19] When John was confronted with the boy, he presumably maintained the pretence of allegiance, paying homage at the coronation, while keeping his own intentions secret. For centuries historians have pondered his motivation and whether the child was simply an opportunity he chose to seize. As his uncle, Richard III, had proved, medieval kingship sometimes involved acts that were ruthless and cynical, even towards children. John would have believed himself justified in manipulating Lambert Simnel, a commoner and pretender, just as Richard had been in displacing his nephews.

It seems most plausible now that John's ultimate aim was to rule in his own right. Strangely, though, the lone voice believing that he had been deceived by Simnel comes from Henry VII's historian, Bernard André, a French Augustinian friar who was working from official papers and blamed the cleverness of the boy's advisors:

> thanks to the false instructions of his sponsors, he was believed to be Edward's son by a number of Henry's emissaries, who were prudent men, and he was so strongly supported that a large number had no hesitation to die for his sake … In those days such was the ignorance of even prominent men, such was their blindness, (not to mention pride and malice), that the Earl of Lincoln had no hesitation in believing.[20]

It cannot be completely ruled out that John was taken in by Simnel's pretence but it seems more likely that the earl kept his true intentions concealed and his thoughts on the matter were assumed by Henry and others after his death.

A century later, Francis Bacon took the opposing view and was convinced that Lincoln had not been deceived by Simnel's claims, but had used him in the hope that he 'might open and pave a fair and prepared way to his own title'. It was intended, Bacon believed, 'that if all things succeeded well, he [Simnel] should be out done, and the true Plantagenet received, wherein nevertheless the Earl of Lincoln had his particular hopes'.[21] He also thought that the rebels grew too confident of their own success while in Ireland, believing that 'they went in upon far better cards to overthrow King Henry, than King Henry had to overthrow King Richard.' There is no doubt that they posed a serious threat to the Tudor regime, with the backing of the Burgundians under Margaret, the

Irish under Kildare and the two Yorkist figures of Lincoln and Lovell. With the 2,000 missionaries, a crowned 'king' and 4,500 Irish troops, their confidence was not misplaced and Henry knew it. On 5 June, the army of 'Edward VI' landed at Piel Island near Furness on the Lancastrian coast and marched through the Pennines towards York. Henry was at Coventry and marched to meet them at the village of East Stoke. But things were looking very encouraging for the rebels. On 10 June, Francis Lovell led 2,000 men in an attack upon Lord Clifford's Lancastrians, who were waiting at Bramham Moor to join the king, winning a decisive victory. Two days later, John ordered Lord Scrope to create a diversion by attacking Bootham Bar in York. This had the effect of drawing the Earl of Northumberland away from the impending conflict, taking out more of Henry's support. This was very encouraging for John and his supporters.

And yet there may have been dissent among the rebels. Days later, a rift arose between John and Margaret's military commander, and the *Great Chronicle of London* includes a letter written to the earl by Martin Schwartz on the eve of the battle, suggesting that he and Margaret had been deceived as to John's intentions:

> Sir now I see well that ye have dyssayvyd yoursylf and alsoo me, but that not wythstandynd, all such promyse as I made unto my lady the duchess I shall perfform, Exortyng th'Erl to doo the same. And upon thys spedd theym towards the feel dwt as good a corage as he had 20m [20,000] men more than he had.[22]

By this point, it was too late. Schwartz was committed to fight, but misunderstanding or disillusionment on the rebels' side can hardly have helped their cause. As John prepared for battle, praying for the same success that Henry Tudor had enjoyed, he faced the tantalising possibility that he might be wearing the crown himself within a few hours or days.

The armies met at Stoke Field on 16 June. Tudor's men were led by the Earl of Oxford and Henry's uncle, Jasper, Earl of Pembroke, and outnumbered the rebels. Many of the Irish soldiers were poorly clothed and equipped, suffering heavy losses from the Lancastrian longbows, while the German mercenaries made some headway against Oxford's flank, using new handguns. Molinet's chronicle describes how the rebels were unable to retreat due to the position of the river and they soon plunged into the ravine while the Irish were 'filled with arrows like hedgehogs'. According to Bacon, they did not lack courage but their nakedness made the confrontation 'rather an execution than a fight upon them'.[23] The battle lasted for three 'fierce and obstinate' hours. Henry's historian Polydore Vergil tells us that the king had hoped to capture John alive, in order to question him about the extent of Yorkist support, but the earl was killed along with Schwartz and Fitzgerald, while Kildare and Lovell escaped. Lambert Simnel was arrested and exposed as a fraud but, due to his youth, he was pardoned and given a role in the palace kitchens. He later became a royal falconer, married and died peacefully.

Henry VII did not treat John's body in the same way he had that of Richard III. The excavations following the discovery of Richard's body in 2012 confirmed the treatment the king received after his defeat: his hands tied, carried naked across the back of a horse through the streets of Leicester, publicly displayed and buried with minimal rites in a cramped grave in the choir of the Greyfriars church. There were good reasons for laying out the corpse of a rival in full view, to create witnesses to the fact of his death and quash any future rumours of escape, but other elements might speak of humiliation and speed. At the time of Stoke, Richard still lay under a simple slab, but in 1495 Henry commissioned him a proper tomb of alabaster and coloured marble, paying out £60 to two different craftsmen for the work. The sixteenth-century writer Holinshed states that the memorial had borne an inscription and a picture of Richard, which was perhaps a two-dimensional carving or painting, rather than the usual three-dimensional effigy. Henry may have decided that it was fitting for an anointed king to have a proper tomb or, in line with medieval notions of violent death, that this went some way to making amends to Richard's unquiet soul. John, Earl of Lincoln received no such rites or tomb. His body was buried in an unmarked grave on the battlefield and never retrieved. It would have been left to his parents to arrange masses for his soul. No records survive to confirm whether they did.

III

When Henry's Parliament met in November 1487, it passed a lengthy and unequivocal act of attainder against Lincoln and his followers:

The 19th day of the month of March last past, John, late Earl of Lincoln, nothing considering the great and sovereign kindness that our Sovereign Liege Lord that now is, at divers sundry times, continually showed to the said late Earl, but the contrary to kind and natural remembrance, his faith, truth and allegiance, conspired and imagined the most dolorous and lamentable murder, death and destruction of the royal person ... and also destruction of all this realm, and to perform his said malicious purpose, traitorously departed to the said persons beyond the sea and there accompanied himself with many other false traitors and enemies ... by long time contriving his malice, prepared a great navy ... and arrived in the ports of Ireland ... where he conspired and imagined the destruction and deposition of our said Sovereign ... and for the execution of the same thereon 24 day of May last past ... contrary to his homage and faith, truth and allegiance, traitorously renounced, revoked and disclaimed his own said most natural sovereign ... and caused one Lambert Simnel, a child of ten years of age, son to Thomas Simnel, late of Oxford, joiner, to be proclaimed, erected and reputed as King of this Realm, and to him did faith and homage, to the great dishonour and despite of all this realm, and from thence, continuing in his malicious and traitorous purpose arrived with a great navy ... accompanied with a great multitude of strangers, with force and arms, that is to say, swords, spears, marespikes, bows, guns ... and many other weapons ... with many other ill disposed persons and traitors, defensible and in warlike manner arrayed, to the number of 8,000 persons, imagining, compassing and conspiring the death and deposition and utter destruction of our said Sovereign Lord ... [and] passed from thence from place to place to they come to Stoke in the county of Nottinghamshire, where, the 16 day of June last past, with banners displayed, levied war against [the King] and gave him mighty and strange battle, traitorously and contrary to all truth, knighthood, honour, allegiance, faith … intending to utterly have slain, murdered and cruelly destroyed (the King). For the which most malicious, compassed, great and heinous offence … against the universal and commonweal of this realm [Lincoln and others] were to be taken, judged and reputed as traitors and convicted and attainted of high treason and that all [honours, lands and titles] the late Earl … had or was possessed of … be forfeit to our sovereign lord the King.[24]

John, Duke of Suffolk appears to have played no part in his son's rebellion. In fact, he rode out the storm convincingly and remained loyal to the Tudors. The parliamentary attainder against John, Earl of Lincoln specifically protected rights of his father: 'this act of attainder, made in this present parliament against John, late Earl of Lincoln, extend not, nor be prejudicial unto John, Duke of Suffolk during his life time.'[25] Suffolk served as a trier during the same session and was entrusted with the muster of troops against Brittany the following year. The duke did not live much longer, dying in May 1492, upon which his next son and heir, John's younger brother Edmund, forfeited the title in exchange for lands. John's mother Elizabeth survived into the next century, although she lived quietly and left little trace in the records. It is highly likely that she adopted a similar stance to other royal widows of the era, including Cecily Neville and Elizabeth Woodville, in living a quasi-religious life, perhaps even taking vows. The role of a vowess was a safe, reflective end for women whose lives and families had been shattered by the dynastic conflicts of their menfolk. Elizabeth was described as deceased in 1503, although she may have died long before. She was buried beside her husband at St Andrew's church, Wingfield. The alabaster tomb shows Sir John dressed in armour, his head resting upon the bleeding head of a Saracen while Elizabeth lies on his left, her clothing virtually identical to that on the effigy of Alice Chaucer. Both have their feet upon curly maned lions.

John's rebellion was the last realised effort of the Yorkists to regain the throne. As one of the eldest 'young men' included in this collection, he had the advantage over the others of having reached adulthood. But this didn't mean he was not subject to restrictions, even a sort of imprisonment at the Tudor court: he may not have been imprisoned in the Tower, but the expectation of his compliance made a cage for Lincoln which he was unable to endure. The existence of Lambert Simnel may have been the trigger for the earl's revolt, or else he harnessed the child to his intentions, which he had hitherto kept secret. Given the role he played during the reign of Richard III and his Yorkist ties of affinity, John's actions fell within Henry's expectations despite his outward signals of conformity. However, they display a very different pattern of loyalty to that of his father. Both exhibited exceptional devotion to their family, although this followed two convergent paths and yielded contrasting results. Throughout his life, Lincoln modelled dedication to the continuation of the Yorkist dynasty, as a supporter of Edward IV and Richard III and in his attempt to restore its favours. He did not question Richard's ascendancy in 1483, as this would have led to disruption and conflict, even the resumption of war, had the Princes in the Tower been rescued and the rule of a minor re-established. Lincoln preferred the transfer of power from one adult male to another, and is likely to have accepted Richard's narrative about the boy's illegitimacy, or at least accepted its necessity. After the arrival of the Tudors, he played a diplomatic game before rebelling as soon as the opportunity presented itself. He upheld the ideal of the Yorkist men as kings of England and took his place in that succession when he perceived the mantle had fallen to him. By contrast, Suffolk's devotion was to the survival of his family, whether they were rulers or not. To this effect, he was prepared to accept the sacrifice of individuals and the loss of the throne, if it permitted the continuation of his bloodline. His was a pragmatic loyalty rather than the dedication to an ideal followed by his son.

In a political sense, John of Lincoln had a valid claim to the English throne. Leaving Simnel aside, his personal challenge to Henry was a valid one and had the potential to be a success. While Henry claimed right of conquest, and had married Edward IV's eldest daughter, Lincoln had the advantage of being Richard's implied heir, although he was equal to Tudor in that their bloodlines passed through a female descendent. The Yorkist dynasty had previously suffered an interruption and regained its footing under Edward IV; surely John reasoned that Henry Tudor's rule might be a similar blip before the family fortunes were restored under his own kingship? With Burgundian and Irish support, he was confident that he stood as good a chance as his rival and he was right. In the planning stages, in theory, the battle might have gone either way, determined by an incident as unexpected as Richard III's charge upon Henry into marshy ground. In theory, the rebellion would have seen Simnel swiftly removed and England ruled by John II. In all likelihood, he would have fathered more children, or passed the throne to his brothers, and established the continuation of Yorkist rule well into the sixteenth century. In practice, though, the various elements under his command did not come together in the battle and the day went against him. It is easy to speculate about the 'what-ifs'. Had the Irish been properly clothed and equipped, had Lincoln chosen another location, had more former Yorkists offered their support, had the weather been different, had the experienced earls of Oxford and Pembroke failed to make the rendezvous, the outcome may have been the restoration of the dynasty.

John may have represented the last plausible Yorkist assault on the throne but he was not the last claimant. After his death, his brothers continued to be a thorn in Tudor's side. Next after John to survive to adulthood was Edward de la Pole, born in 1467. In 1481 he was attending lectures in Oxford, where he was praised as a precocious scholar. Richard promoted Edward to the position of Archdeacon of Richmond, Yorkshire, in January 1484,[26] but he was referred to as being dead in October 1485, so it cannot be ruled out that he was killed at Bosworth, although some sources claim that he died of natural causes.

After Edward was Edmund, born in 1471, who was created a Knight of the Bath at Richard's coronation but was too young to be involved at Bosworth. He managed to make the transition to the Tudor regime by being a close friend of his cousin, Queen Elizabeth, and frequently attended court at Christmas and other festivities, including her coronation in 1487. After John's death at Stoke, Edmund became the leading Yorkist heir and inherited his father's title upon the duke's death but agreed its reduction to the rank of an earldom in exchange for some forfeit lands, which was in keeping with Henry VII's policy to weaken the influence of the nobility. Edmund took part in the siege of Boulogne in 1492 and jousted at the investiture of Prince Henry as Duke of York in 1494, a title which must have struck particularly close to home. At Christmas 1495, he entertained the king and queen at Ewelme Manor, took part in disguisings at court and resisted invitations to join rebellions, leading troops against the pretender Perkin Warbeck in 1497.[27] By 1499, though, Edmund's loyalty to the Tudor regime was running thin as his finances were curbed by Henry, and his implication in a murder provided the king with an opportunity to impose humiliating conditions.

Edmund fled to Picardy, possibly in the hope of receiving assistance from Margaret of Burgundy as John had done. None was forthcoming and her stepson Philip the Fair negotiated Edmund's return as part of a trade agreement with England, with serious financial penalties for the earl. Henry kept his enemy close, and Edmund was present at court during the negotiations and proxy marriage of the king's eldest son Prince Arthur to the Spanish Infanta Catherine of Aragon. In August 1501, Edmund left England again, without Henry's permission, this time with his younger brother Richard. Based in Aachen, he began to plan an invasion while living on funds supplied by Emperor Maximilian. Yet this scheme only came to fruition in 1504, when Edmund left Richard behind as surety for his debts and headed for Friesland, only to be captured and imprisoned. He was attainted in Henry's Parliament of 1504 and remained in custody for two years, until Maximilian's son, Philip, was blown off course in the Channel and forced to land in England. Under duress, he agreed to hand Edmund over so long as the exile's life was spared. Henry duly placed Edmund in the Tower upon his return but his son, Henry VIII, did not feel bound to honour the agreement and executed the earl in 1513.

The next de la Pole brother, Humphrey, was born in 1474 and educated at Gonville Hall, Cambridge, where he became a Doctor of Laws.[28] Humphrey became the rector of St Andrew's church, Hingham, in Norfolk. He died the same year as his brother Edmund was executed, 1513, but of some ailment rather than the axe. Four years his junior, William de la Pole lived quietly as the keeper of Wingfield Castle but suffered as a result of Edmund's absconsion abroad. In 1502 he was considered untrustworthy despite little evidence to prove that he had supported his brothers, and imprisoned in the Tower. He would remain there for the next thirty-seven years, the place's longest prisoner, until his death 1539.

Finally, Richard, the youngest de la Pole brother, born in 1480, came to be known as 'The White Rose'. After escaping abroad with Edmund and remaining in Aachen as security for the Emperor's loans, he made his way to Hungary, despite being pursued by Henry's ambassadors. After the accession of Henry VIII, Richard attempted to gain a royal pardon but this was not forthcoming, so he allied himself with the French and was backed by Louis XII as a claimant to the English throne. He led German troops on Louis's behalf during his invasion of Navarre in 1512 and against Henry VIII when the English lay siege to Thérouanne in 1513. After receiving the news of Edmund's execution, Richard adopted the title of the Duke of Suffolk and announced his intention to seek the crown. By the following summer, of 1514, he had assembled troops in Brittany and including disaffected Yorkists abroad, funded by Louis, with the possibility of Scottish assistance. As they were poised to depart, the invasion fleet was cancelled when England and France made peace through a marriage treaty between the newly widowed Louis and Henry's younger sister. Richard moved to Metz, under the protection of the Duke of Lorraine, and remained there until 1519. His next opportunity to launch an invasion came in 1522, when the Duke of Albany arrived in France, but again this came to nothing when Richard's followers refused to rise, and his Scottish support returned home. Richard did not give up. He appealed to Louise of Savoy, the mother of the new French king, Francis I, for assistance and hoped to mount an invasion via Ireland but instead he took part in Francis's invasion of Italy. In February 1525, Francis was taken prisoner by the Holy Roman Emperor Charles V at the Battle of Pavia and Richard, fighting as one of his captains, was killed. He was the last member of the house of York to actively seek the throne. News of his death provoked Henry VIII to respond with relief that 'all the enemies of England are gone.'[29]

It was around the time of John's rebellion that his aunt, the dowager queen Elizabeth Woodville, retired from public life. As a 50-year-old widow, this may well have been Elizabeth's natural reaction to this stage of her life, or a response to the dangerous political situation and loss of her nephew. It was more usual for widows of comparable status to spend their final years in the seclusion and contemplation of a religious retreat and Bermondsey Abbey, on the bank of the Thames, had a history of housing royal women, including Catherine of Valois, Henry VII's grandmother, in the year of Elizabeth's birth. However, some have questioned the timing of the dowager's withdrawal, speculating that it was not voluntary, but was instead a punishment imposed by Henry VII for her support of her nephew, John of Lincoln. It seems unlikely that Elizabeth would have supported her nephew over her own daughter, the king's wife, and she was still receiving a reduced allowance from Henry, made over to 'oure right dere and right welbeloved quene Elizabeth moder unto our most dere wif the quene'. It would have been quite consistent with her lifelong piety to have offered to withdraw from public life and return many of her assets to the crown for the use of her daughter and grandchildren. Beyond the reasons advanced above, she could have withdrawn due to increasing ill health, as she was to die in 1492. That April she drew up her will, outlining the simplest of funerals for a former queen, and its initial lines betray the reason for her choice: 'being of hole mynde, seying the world so transitory and no creature certayne whanne they shall departe from hence'. It was humility, after years of turbulence, that dictated Elizabeth's final statement to be interred 'without pompe entreing or costlie expensis'. After her death on 8 June, she was placed in a wooden coffin and taken by barge with a small company to Windsor, where she was placed on a 'low herse suche as they use for the comyn peple' with four wooden candlesticks and a dozen old men carrying torches.[30] Her funeral represented a contrast with the opulence of her life, but that was exactly the point she intended to make. In this, she was unusual among her peers, whose wealth might buy them a magnificent tomb flanked with gilt angels, wall paintings and gifts for the church, chapels dedicated to them with priests singing masses and marking their month's mind and year's mind. Elizabeth's was a simpler piety, ahead of its time. The coming years would see a move towards a more direct, less ornate means of approaching death.

Three Dead Kings, St Andrew's church, Wickhampton. This medieval frieze captures a common motif of the living being confronted by the dead, acting as a warning about the brevity of life and a prompt to pray for one's ancestors. Large and brightly coloured, it would have proved a powerful *memento mori* for the parishioners worshipping below. (Mary Sholter)

Catholic saints at Rouen Cathedral. Late medieval Catholicism was populated by a panoply of saints, to whom mortals might pray and ask to intercede with God on their behalf. These statues survive, as there was no full-scale destruction of religious icons like the one that destroyed similar statues in England. Edmund, Duke of Rutland, was christened in the Cathedral in 1443. (Hans Splinter)

Inside Rouen Cathedral. Here Edmund, Duke of Rutland's first public appearance, days after his birth in May 1443. (Geoff Licence)

Ludlow Castle. This remote castle on the Welsh Borders was home to a number of young royals: Edward, Duke of Rutland in the 1450s, his nephew the future Edward V in the 1470s–1480s and the first Tudor heir, Prince Arthur, who brought his bride there at the end of 1501. (Luke's-photos)

Remains of Sandal Castle. In December 1460, Edmund of Rutland and his father, the Duke of York, were staying at Sandal Castle when they were taken by surprise by the forces of Queen Margaret of Anjou. The recent Act of Accord had displaced her son Edward in the line of succession, and the inevitable clash took place just outside the castle walls. (Techiedog)

Chantry Chapel, Wakefield Bridge. Fleeing from the scene of the battle outside Sandal Castle, the 17-year-old Edmund of Rutland attempted to reach the sanctuary of this chapel, located between castle and town. He was killed nearby. (Tim Green)

Interior of St Mary's Fotheringhay. In 1476, Edward IV arranged for the remains of his father, the Duke of York, and his brother, Edmund, to be exhumed from Pontefract Abbey and brought home to Northamptonshire. Amid much pomp, Edmund was interred in a side chapel and York in the main vault. The present monument dates from the Elizabethan era. (AES69)

Lincluden Abbey. After the defeat of Henry VI by Edward IV, Margaret of Anjou fled to Scotland, taking her 8-year-old son Edward, Prince of Wales. While considering their next move, they were offered shelter by Mary of Guelders at this remote twelfth-century abbey. (Library of Congress)

Approach to Windsor Castle from the park. Perhaps the most iconic of all English castles, Windsor would play a significant role in the lives of many young royals of this era. The annual ceremony of the Knight of the Garter took place here every April and Edward IV developed the chapel of St George, making a fitting residence for his great-grandsons Henry Fitzroy and Edward V. (Charles D.P. Miller)

The nave, Angers Cathedral. Exiled from home, Edward of Westminster married Anne Neville in December 1470 at Angers Cathedral. With the help of her father, the Earl of Warwick, Edward and Margaret of Anjou hoped to return to England and reclaim the throne. (Fourthandfifteen)

Cadaver tomb in Tewkesbury Abbey. A beautiful example of a cadaver tomb, showing vermin crawling over the decomposing corpse. It was built by Abbot John Wakeman in the 1530s but he subsequently surrendered the monastery and so was buried at Gloucester. (Bazzadarambler)

Tewkesbury Abbey. The 1471 Battle of Tewkesbury was fought in sight of the Abbey, during which Edward, Prince of Wales was killed. A plaque on the floor records his final resting place. George and Isabel, Duke and Duchess of Clarence, the parents of Edward, Earl of Warwick were also buried here. (David Merrett)

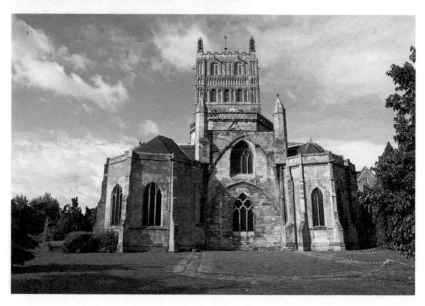

Founders' Chantry, Tewkesbury Abbey. A typical late medieval chantry chapel, established to honour the founders of the abbey, and serving as a constant reminder of their memory and journey through purgatory. (David Llewelyn)

Murder of the Princes in the Tower. Edward V and his younger brother, Richard of Shrewsbury, disappeared within the Tower of London while awaiting Edward's coronation in the summer of 1483. Tradition holds that they were smothered during their sleep. (Cassell's *History of England Volume II*)

Patron saints on the rood screen at Southwold church. The church of St Edmund's in the Suffolk town of Southwold escaped the worst of the reforming zeal, keeping its rood screen intact. This screen features the twelve apostles in bright colours and gold, but others featured patron saints and biblical figures paid for by wealthy local patrons. (Amy Licence)

Middleham Castle, with the Prince's Tower (extreme left). Edward, son of Richard III and Anne Neville, was born between 1472 and 1476, probably at their North Yorkshire home of Middleham, where he spent most of his childhood. (Erin Brierley)

Remains of Sheriff Hutton Castle. Edward of Middleham also spent time at nearby Sherriff Hutton, which was used as a base for Richard III's Council in the North. The location was home to his cousins Elizabeth of York and Edward, Earl of Warwick for a short time. (summonedbyfells)

Left: Cenotaph at Sheriff Hutton church. Reputed to mark Edward of Middleham's resting place, this alabaster figure may date from slightly earlier than Edward's demise and contains no human remains. It is not impossible that the boy was buried in the Neville chapel with a separate commemoration, but the whereabouts of his bones are unknown. (alh1)

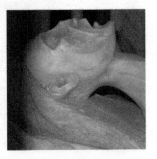

Above: Cadaver tomb of Alice de la Pole, Duchess of Suffolk, St Mary's, Ewelme. The grandmother of John, Earl of Lincoln, Alice was an influential figure in her own right, ordering that her effigy be created in likeness of herself, as she experienced her death throes. (Bill Tyne)

Left: Archbishop's Palace, York. Edward of Middleham was invested as Prince of Wales in a lavish ceremony in the palace shortly after his parents' coronation. The location suggests that Richard wanted to display his northern powerbase to any London doubters, but also might hint that the boy was too ill or too young to go to the capital, or else that it was considered too dangerous politically. (summonedbyfells)

External shot of Alice de la Pole's tomb. On the top of her tomb at Ewelme, Alice lies in peace but the corpse below is glimpsed through the apertures in the stone. (Bill Tyne)

Memorial to John, Earl of Lincoln at East Stoke church. John's attempt to reclaim the throne for the house of York ended in disaster at the Battle of Stoke in 1487. He was buried in an unmarked grave on the battlefield but this memorial was established more recently in the nearest churchyard of St Oswald's. (Fleur Hardyng)

Tomb of John de la Pole and Elizabeth, Duchess of Suffolk, Wingfield church. John, Earl of Lincoln was outlived by both his parents, who were laid to rest in this alabaster tomb near their home. His father's head rests upon the severed head of a Saracen. (Fleur Hardyng)

Warwick Castle. In 1475, Edward, Earl of Warwick was born at Warwick Castle to Isabelle Neville, elder daughter of Warwick the 'kingmaker', and George, Duke of Clarence, brother of Edward IV. (David Evans)

The Deanery, Winchester. The birthplace of Prince Arthur Tudor in September 1486. Henry VII deliberately arranged for his arrival to take place in the mythical capital of England, where Edward III's round table hung on the wall, to link his son to the Arthurian legends. (Elliot Brown)

Inside Prince Arthur's chantry chapel at Worcester Cathedral. Arthur was interred in Worcester Cathedral soon after his death in April 1502. This magnificent chantry, with its intricate carvings and saintly figures, was constructed in the following years, one of the last significant chantries to be built before the Reformation. (Hugh Llewelyn)

Tomb of Henry Chichele, Canterbury. The tomb of Henry Chichele, Archbishop of Canterbury, who died in 1443, serves as a reminder of medieval beliefs in the transience of mortality and eternity of the afterlife. His memorial survived the mid-sixteenth-century reforms and is regularly maintained in Canterbury Cathedral. (Amy Licence)

Lady Chapel, Westminster Abbey. Begun by Henry VII in 1502, this splendid chapel was still in construction when it became the resting place of Elizabeth of York. Today, Henry and his queen lie side by side under what is, arguably, the first Renaissance tomb in England. The bronze by Pietro Torrigiano stands in striking stylistic contrast to other memorials of the time. (Amy Licence)

St Lawrence's, Blackmoor, Essex. In 1519, Henry VIII's mistress, Elizabeth 'Bessie' Blount, retired to the village of Blackmoor to bear her illegitimate child. Henry Fitzroy was born near this church, in a house named Jericho, and brought to St Lawrence's to be christened. (Amy Licence)

Ruins of the chapel at Pontefract Castle. The castle and its little chapel would have been familiar to Edward of Middleham, of which little remains today. Henry Fitzroy also spent considerable time here as a child, including much of 1527 and the early part of 1528. (Tim Green)

St Giles' church, Tonge, Kent. Henry Fitzroy's estate at Tonge brought him into the parish of St Giles. The church and nearby almshouses were familiar to him, although he was not well enough to make his final visit there, planned for the summer of 1536. His household was resident at Tonge when he died and are likely to have prayed for him and ordered masses said at St Giles. (Amy Licence)

Thetford Abbey, showing the original location of the Fitzroy and Howard tombs. Once one of the most significant religious buildings on the Norfolk-Suffolk border, the abbey was traditionally the resting place of the Howard family, and it was here that Henry's father-in-law, the Third Duke of Norfolk, brought his body. The original tomb was close to the high altar, but within a few short years, the Reformation closed the abbey and Fitzroy's remains were removed. (Amy Licence)

Hampton Court. The birthplace of Edward VI, the long-anticipated surviving Tudor heir, who arrived on 12 October 1537. His mother, Jane Seymour, passed away twelve days later. (Amy Licence)

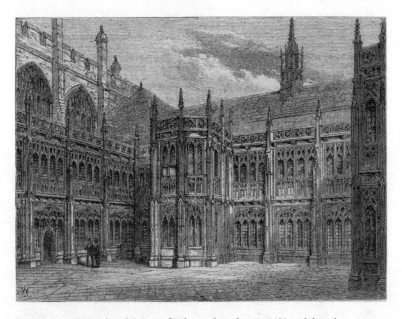

Westminster Palace. Edward, Prince of Wales was born here in 1453, and the palace was also well-known to Edward V and Arthur Tudor. For centuries, it sat at the heart of English government, close to the abbey, before being destroyed by fire in 1513. Henry VIII created Whitehall Palace, down the road, to replace it. (Library of Congress)

Left: Walsingham Abbey. Once the seat of the most significant late medieval cult, Walsingham welcomed pilgrims from all round the world to the lavish shrine of the Virgin Mary. Henry VIII visited the place at least once, removing his shoes in the famous slipper chapel to walk the last mile barefoot, but this did not prevent him from ordering its closure in the 1530s. (Amy Licence)

Right: Bell Tower, Tower of London. Guildford was kept prisoner here in 1553–54, following the failure of his father's attempt to place him and his wife upon the throne. (Abel Cheung)

Below: Dudley Castle in the West Midlands. The birthplace of Guildford, son of John and Jane Dudley, in 1535. (Tony Hisgett)

6

Edward, Earl of Warwick (1475–99)

I

Of all the sons of York associated with the Tower of London, it is Edward V and Richard of Shrewsbury, the 'Princes in the Tower', whose stories are the most well-known. Their disappearance prompted the sinister connotations of a royal palace turned into a prison, its thick stone walls no longer welcomed as defensive, but as the means of incarcerating two innocent children for nothing but the circumstances of their birth. It is a concept that has fired the imagination of historians and tourists ever since but, rightfully, their third Yorkist cousin, Edward, Earl of Warwick, is equally deserving of the association. The princes may have spent the final months of their lives in captivity there but, after their disappearance, Edward was incarcerated behind the same forbidding walls for thirteen years, more than half his life. Another potential King of England, perhaps with a greater claim to the throne than Richard III or Henry VII, lived and died within the Tower's walls. Just like his cousins, his bloodline rendered him too dangerous to live.

Edward, Earl of Warwick is a shadowy figure about whom little information survives beyond the threat he posed to the throne. Unusually, he had claims on both the Yorkist and Lancastrian side, through his parentage and by nomination respectively. His Lancastrian credentials were established five years before his birth, as the result of his father's treason against his elder brother, casting a long shadow over the existence of his future children. In 1469, George, Duke of Clarence had allied with Richard Neville, Earl of Warwick out of disaffection with Edward IV, by marrying Neville's daughter Isabel. The following year, Henry VI recognised Clarence as heir to the Lancastrian throne after his own son, Edward of Westminster. When Isabel bore a surviving son, Edward, in 1475, Henry VI had been dead for four years, as had his son, Prince Edward. Technically, according to the wishes of the last Lancastrian, George and Isabel's son could be seen to have a stronger claim to the Lancastrian throne than Henry VII.

Edward's parents were never supposed to have wed. Yet this was no romantic elopement, no love match; they were hardly the Romeo and Juliet of their age, as their flight might suggest. It was the fruition of a daring plan which saw Edward IV's two closest companions turn against him, fleeing England after the king vetoed the marriage. Warwick had been considering the 19-year-old duke as a potential son-in-law for at least two years and given that the king had not yet fathered a son of his own, any male heir born to George would be next in line to the throne. Clarence was 'seemly of person and visage', but a more volatile figure than his older brother, driven by ambition and frustrated by the restraints he felt the king imposed upon him. His household at Tutbury Castle in 1468 cost an annual £4,500, making it larger and more expensive than that of the king.[1] Isabel was two years younger, the elder of Neville's two daughters, between whom his vast inheritance would be divided. Aware of the king's opposition, Warwick had sent his own representative to the pope that March to obtain a dispensation for the match to go ahead, and then secured a special licence from Cardinal Bourchier, Archbishop of Canterbury for it to take place. They sailed from Sandwich in July for the safety of Calais, where Warwick had recently been captain. In the castle chapel dedicated to the Virgin, or in the main Calais church of Our Lady, they became man and wife on 12 July 1469.

The wedding was celebrated with conspicuous display. Warwick planned several days of festivities suitable for a royal wedding and invited various important guests, including five knights of the garter, and various Neville family members. The ceremony itself was conducted by Warwick's brother George Neville, Archbishop of York. It was crucial to the earl's plans that the proceedings were legitimate and public, above question, unlike the secret nuptials of the king and Elizabeth Woodville five years earlier. Warwick was establishing an alternative royal family, whose progeny he hoped would inherit the throne. Any lingering suspicions of romance regarding the match can be dispelled by the fact that Clarence and Warwick did not linger long to enjoy the event. Five days later they sailed for England with a manifesto of grievances, modelled on that of Jack Cade's revolt in 1450, with which to challenge Edward IV.

The challenge of 1469 failed, as did Warwick's coup and readeption of Henry VI in 1470. The earl was killed in battle, Clarence was forgiven and fought at his brother's side at Tewkesbury. However, his transgressions were not forgotten. George and Isabel settled at Warwick Castle and their London residence of Coldharbour House. Having lost a first child, Isabel was at Farleigh Hungerford Castle in Somerset when she bore her daughter Margaret in August 1473 and back home at Warwick Castle for the birth of Edward in February 1475. His uncle and namesake was one of his godfathers, ordering that the boy be called Earl of Warwick from his birth. Edward was two months short of his second birthday when his mother died, probably from complications or injuries following the birth of her fourth child, possibly from consumption. She was only 25. This event precipitated a crisis in the family, setting Clarence on the path to destruction and disgrace that would determine the future path of his son's life.

Four months after Isabel's death, George became convinced that she had been poisoned by one of her ladies-in-waiting, an elderly woman named Ankarette Twynho of Keyford in Somerset. Travelling down from Warwick on 12 April, with around eighty men, he abducted Ankarette from her house and took her to Bath. The next day, he carried her to Cirencester, Gloucester and then to prison in Warwick, where she was deprived of her money, jewels and goods. He ordered Ankarette's daughter, son-in-law and servants out of the city and convened a court at the Guildhall before the justices of the peace who were sitting in the Easter Assizes. There, he 'caused her to be indicted, of having at Warwick, on 10 October 1476, given to the said Isabel a venomous drink of ale mixed with poison, of which the latter sickened until the Sunday before Christmas, on which day she died'. The nature of the poison was not specified, although it must have been exceptionally slow-working for its effects not to have proved lethal for over seventy days.

Also standing trial with her was John Thursby, another former servant of the family, whom Clarence accused of having poisoned Isabel's newborn son with ale administered on 21 December. The child, Richard, had died on 1 January. Under considerable pressure from the duke, the justices arraigned the pair, the jury convicted them and they were hanged 'within three hours of the said Tuesday, and the jurors for fear gave the verdict contrary to their conscience, in proof thereof divers of them came to the said Ankarette in remorse and asked her forgiveness'. Many said that:

> in consideration of the imaginations of the said Duke and his great might, the unlawful taking of the said Ankarette through three several shires, the inordinate hasty process and judgement, her lamentable death and her good disposition, the King should ordain that the record, process, verdict and judgment should be void and of no effect.[2]

However, by then it was too late.

Clarence's erratic behaviour worsened. At 27, he might realistically have anticipated taking a second wife with international connections and independent wealth. Yet Edward rejected his plans to remarry, first to Mary of Burgundy, stepdaughter of his sister Margaret, then to a Scottish princess. Clarence felt this deeply, and became convinced that the king was seeking to poison him 'as a candle is consumed by burning'. When two members of his household were arrested on the charge of being necromancers and 'imagining the King's death', for which they suffered the full fate of traitors at Tyburn, Clarence burst into a meeting of Edward's council and read aloud their declaration of innocence from the scaffold. Edward had forgiven much, but this time George had gone too far. He was summoned to Westminster, where Edward denounced him for 'most serious [misconduct] … in contempt of the law of the land and a great threat to judges and jurors of the kingdom', and ordered his arrest.

The act of attainder against George, delivered by Edward to a specially convened Parliament in January 1478, reveals the king's deep sense of betrayal over his brother's continuing hostilities. Edward began by recalling 'the manifold great conspiracies, malicious and heinous treasons' that had so far arisen by 'unnatural subjects, rebels and traitors' against his realm, with the 'intent and purpose to have destroyed his most royal person and with that to have subverted the state and well-being' of the country. But Edward had repelled them, with 'great labour and diligence', with chivalry and war, and the help of God, punishing them by the sword or other means. Yet, as a 'benign and gracious prince, moved to pity', he had not only often spared them, but taken them to his mercy and pardoned them. Despite this, it had lately come to his attention that a 'much higher, much more malicious, more unnatural and loathly treason' had been hatched against himself, the queen and their children, which proceeded from the most extreme malice, 'incomparably exceeding any other that had been before'. Worst of all, it had been 'contrived, imagined and conspired by the person that of all earthly creatures, beside the duty of allegiance, nature, benefit and gratitude' was the most 'bounden and beholden, to dreaded, loved, honoured and ever thanked the King most largely'. To name the perpetrator 'greatly aggrieved the heart of our Sovereign Lord, save only that he was compelled by necessity for the surety, wealth and tranquillity of himself and all his realm'. 'We sheweth you, therefore', the speech went on, 'that all this hath been entended by his brother, George, Duke of Clarence'. The king had 'ever loved and cherished him' due to his tender age, and given him 'so large proportion of possessions' that no one could recall a king of England formerly rewarding a brother so. Edward had trusted that, not only by the bonds of nature, but by those of so great benefit, George would be 'more than others loving, helping, assisting and obedient' despite the times he had previously given great offence to the king and the realm. Now George had daily increased in malice and conspired new treasons against Edward and his family, attempting to entice away the affection of the king's subjects and speak out against his justice. Thus he must die.

George's ultimate aim was the throne and, to this end, he was responsible for spreading the rumour that 'the Kinge oure Sovereigne Lord was a bastard and not begotten' to reign. George had also cited Henry VI's statement that 'if the said Henry and Edward his first begotten son died without issue male of their body, that the said Duke and his heirs should be King of this land'. The indictment also included a strange clause about George's son, Edward, still only 2 years old. Apparently, the duke had ordered an abbot and two other men to 'cause a strange child to have been brought into his castle of Warwick, and there to have been put and kept in the likeness of his son and heir' while his true son, Edward, 'was conveyed and sent … into Ireland, or into Flanders out of this land, whereby he might have gotten him assurance and favour against our said sovereign Lord'. The two men concerned denied delivering such a child, but the implications of the claim for the appearance of pretenders during the reign of Henry VII are significant.[3]

On 18 February, Clarence was executed in the Tower of London, although his relationship with his brother may have allowed him to choose the means of his death. The chroniclers Mancini and Jean de Roye both state that he was drowned in a butt of Malmsey wine; the continuer of the Croyland text, who witnessed the trial, was also aware of this rumour, but unsure of its veracity. It seems telling that no other source cites any other method, suggesting that Edward allowed his brother this final indulgence. He also paid for an expensive funeral and a monument to be erected in Tewkesbury Abbey. Isabel's bones had lain in state in the abbey for thirty-five days so it is likely that George's also went through a similar process of observation before being interred beside her in a vault located behind the high altar, close to the Beauchamp Chapel. The monument has long since been destroyed and the tomb opened so many times to be cleaned that all traces of the original burial have been lost. The bones on display in a glass case, reputedly belonging to George and Isabel, have been tested and identified as being too advanced in age to be either. When the vault was opened in 1826, it was discovered to be 9ft by 8ft, and 6ft 4in high, carved from Painswick stone with a large central cross made of painted bricks. Upon these bricks were the arms of England, of Clarence and other heraldic families, birds, *fleur de lys* and ornamented letters. It was concluded at the time that the vault had been ransacked during the Reformation.[4]

Edward was a week short of his third birthday when his father was sentenced to death, while his sister was 5. Though they might have had different establishments within the castle, surely his sister would have noticed the substitution of her brother? Assuming that it was the real Edward who had been left behind in Warwick Castle, not an imposter, all was set to change. It is unlikely that he retained any memories of either of his parents but he would have learned, as the years passed, that the extensive lands he should have received were taken into royal custody, technically for the duration of his minority. He could look forward to a rich inheritance once he finally came of age. After his father's death, Edward was placed in the royal custody of his uncle and aunt, the king and queen, presumably attached to their court. A single surviving payment in the accounts for 1480 lists five pairs of shoes with double and single soles for his use. The following year, when he was 5 or 6, Edward's wardship was bought for £2,000 by Thomas Grey, Marquis of Dorset, the queen's son by her first marriage. Grey was then 25 and may have lived at the family's seat of Groby in Leicestershire. He had married his second wife in September 1474 and their young family included boys who were just a little younger than Edward himself.

At the change of regime in 1483, Thomas Grey was among the Woodville relations who lost royal favour. This did not affect Edward adversely, unless the removal from Grey's wardship upset him, but this can only be speculation. He was taken under the wing of Richard III and Queen Anne, attending their coronation and being knighted alongside Edward of Middleham in York on 8 September 1483. After this,

Warwick was established at Sheriff Hutton Castle with his sister Margaret, Richard's illegitimate son John of Pontefact and possibly other children with Yorkist connections. On 8 June 1484, Richard commanded lengths of cloth of gold, silk and velvet to be ordered for clothing to be made for Edward and Margaret, as well as for Richard's illegitimate daughter Katherine and her husband-to-be, William Herbert, Earl of Huntingdon. Given that Katherine's marriage took place that year, this was likely in preparation for that event, suggesting that Edward and his sister attended the ceremony.

After the death of Edward of Middleham, his cousin Warwick could potentially have become Richard's heir. He was of a similar age to the dead boy and had a strong claim to the role. Richard may have considered this briefly but by 1485 seemed inclined to prefer John of Lincoln, leading some to suspect some infirmity or defect in Warwick. Decades later, Edward was described as being unable to distinguish between a goose and a capon, but this was after long years in captivity and indicates his naivety and inexperience rather than any want of intellect. We are told this by the chronicler Edward Hall, who was born two years before Edward's death, and his words were prefaced by the explanation that Edward had been 'kept in the Tower from his tender age, that is to say from his first year of the King [Henry VII] to this fifteenth year, out of all company of men and sight of beasts'.[5] Richard's advancement of John over Edward may also have been decided by the fact that Lincoln was then a full-grown man, while Edward was only 9 at time of his cousin's death and far less likely to be of assistance in facing challenges to the throne. Technically, too, Lincoln had the senior claim, being descended from the Duke of York's fourth surviving child, although this was through the female line, while Warwick came from the sixth survivor. Yet there is a far more significant reason why the new king wished to pass over this young nephew. Richard is unlikely to have wanted to draw attention to the fact that Edward had a better claim to the throne than himself, being the son of his elder brother. He had used the illegitimacy card against Edward IV's sons, but there was no question that Warwick had not been conceived in lawful matrimony, so the earl had to remain under the cloud of his father's attainder. To recognise Edward would be to acknowledge a weakness in Richard's own right to rule.

II

Edward was living at Sheriff Hutton with his cousins Princess Elizabeth and her sisters during the summer of 1485. He was 10½, quite aware of the danger the Yorkist regime was facing but likely to have been confident in his uncle's military ambitions compared with the inexperience of his Tudor challenger. No doubt his lessons proceeded as usual, perhaps even under the care of Anne Idley, whose pedagogical skills had been redundant at Middleham since the death of Richard's son. Edward would have mourned the loss of the little cousin beside whom he had been knighted, and then the death of his aunt Anne, the queen, that March. Perhaps he was dressed in mourning still. Yet there was a very real possibility that, after Richard's victory, he would marry a Princess of Portugal and Edward would be summoned to Westminster to grow up at court, in training as a future Yorkist magnate. Soon after 22 August, though, Sheriff Hutton received news that snatched away this hope and consigned Edward to a much darker path. Richard had been killed and the invader had been crowned Henry VII on the battlefield.

After the defeat at Bosworth, Edward was fetched under heavy guard from Sheriff Hutton and placed in the care of the new king's mother. Margaret Beaufort, then in her early forties, was an astute, energetic, pious and immensely capable woman. Edward may have been with her at court, or dwelt at one of her many properties in London or in the country. Yet Margaret had a conflict of interests. She had shown interest in the Ware estate in Hertfordshire, which was part of Edward's inheritance from his mother Isabel, securing the right to appoint a steward there that September and being granted the place in 1487. The same year, she received the rich Warwick property of Canford in Dorset and, four years later, petitioned Parliament for four other estates that were part of the boy's legacy.[6] By this time, Edward had left her care and was lodged in the Tower, diminishing the likelihood that he would ever enjoy the lands left to him by his parents. Margaret was fully aware that her actions were unscrupulous but her conscience did not trouble her until later. In 1504, she obtained a pardon for all the 'purchases, alienations or intrusions … that had occurred during the minority of Edward, Earl of Warwick and Salisbury, son and heir of Isabel, Duchess of Clarence'.[7] But by this point it was safe for her to show contrition about her possessions, as Edward had been dead for five years.

While living with Margaret, Edward and his sister may well have attended the wedding of their first cousin, the 19-year-old Elizabeth of York, to England's new king, which took place at Westminster on 18 January 1486. It was a good move for the new king, as Elizabeth represented the Yorkist claim and came from a notoriously fertile family, which was critical given that Henry was an only child. Edward could have been a guest at the ceremony in Westminster Abbey and the feast that followed in the hall. Eight months later, 'my lady Margaret of Clarence', was listed as being among the guests gathered in Winchester to attend the birth of the couple's first child, Prince Arthur. Given that their other male cousin, John de la Pole, was also in attendance, it seems likely that Edward witnessed the occasion too. Henry usually practised the policy of keeping his enemies close, under his exacting supervision, which argues in favour of Edward's attendance. However, there was a difference between Edward and his sister and cousin. Just like Edward, Margaret and John were close members of the Yorkist family, cousins of the bride but, unlike them, Edward had a better claim of descent to the English throne. In terms of bloodline, Margaret and John did not pose the immediate threat that Edward did as the heir to the former ruling dynasty.

The opening years of the new Tudor regime were marred by threats of invasion and rebellion. Unless any of these came to fruition on his behalf – which they did not – Edward could only suffer, being a dangerous figurehead for the new regime. In April 1486, Humphrey Stafford and Francis Lovell attempted to seize Henry during a visit to York. Lovell escaped to Margaret of Burgundy in Flanders, where he would soon be joined by John, Earl of Lincoln, but Stafford attempted to raise troops against the king in Worcestershire. Worryingly for Edward, Stafford's followers were indicted for shouting pro-Warwick battle cries, suggesting that they were rising in his name or with the intention of using him as a figurehead. In May, an unruly mob gathered near Highbury in London bearing banners depicting the badge of the earls of Warwick – the bear and ragged staff. The uprising was defeated, and Stafford was forcibly removed from his sanctuary in Culham and executed in July. This rebellion, or similar sentiments, gave rise to rumours that Edward had escaped from England and was also in Flanders, or else in Guernsey. It was probably this episode that prompted Henry to lodge Edward in the Tower of London. Around this time, John, Earl of Lincoln stole away to join Lambert Simnel and further rumours reached the king that the imposter was claiming to be Edward. In February 1487, when he was 11, Edward was brought out of the Tower and made to walk to St Paul's to hear mass and show himself praying, and talking afterwards to people in the nave of the church. He was allowed out of the Tower again after the Battle of Stoke. That July, on Relic Sunday, Warwick walked through the streets beside the captured Simnel: two young boys symbolising the dangers faced by the Tudor regime. Perhaps he was also allowed out that November for the coronation of his cousin Elizabeth, on whom his sister was in attendance. Edward may have also been permitted to witness the wedding of the 14-year-old Margaret to Richard Pole, which appears to have taken place around this time. Or it may be that by this point, Edward was considered too dangerous to be permitted such freedoms.

It is impossible to determine just how far Edward understood his situation. He was certainly aware of his inheritance and proximity to the throne, but if he ever coveted it, no record remains of such intent. Nor is it clear that he understood what was happening outside London, and that Simnel had been crowned in Dublin after assuming his name and impersonating him. Edward was still a child, and was carefully schooled in advance of his two appearances in the city that year,[8] but he can hardly have been unaware of the disappearance of his two cousins, the sons of Edward IV, or that he was now at the mercy of an enemy regime. With hindsight, it seems that his fate was inevitable. It may have appeared so at the time.

The plots against Henry continued. By the early 1490s, three men in particular were focused on ousting the new king in favour of Edward, Earl of Warwick, whom they saw as the rightful King of England. The first, Robert Chamberlain, had been in exile with Edward IV in 1470 and had been Chancellor of Ireland. He also had links with Scotland and France. He had been placed under house arrest in 1487 and forbidden to travel more than a mile from his Chertsey home due to suspicion of treason, perhaps the result of a connection to the Simnel/Lincoln uprising. Second, a Norfolk gentleman, Richard White, entered into treasonous arrangements with the King of France to attack and kill Henry in the summer of 1490, although this was conceived as a murder or assassination rather than a conflict in battle. White was arrested in 1491 as he attempted to flee to Flanders. The third man was John Taylor, a former servant of the Duke of Clarence, later a yeoman of the king's chamber in the households of Edward IV and Richard III. Taylor held Clarence's son to be the rightful King of England and although he was still living in London in January 1489, he had escaped to France by September 1491.

Taylor seems to have been the driving force behind it all. His objections to Henry prefaced the main threat to his reign that was about to arise in the person of the imposter Perkin Warbeck, then neatly allied with them. Initially, Taylor wanted a rebellion of the English people against the Tudor regime, drawing on the old affinities of the Neville family, the Duke and Duchess of Clarence, the Beauchamps, Richard III's northern allies and those loyal to the Duke of Norfolk. Taylor was a rallying point for Yorkist loyalists as John, Earl of Lincoln had formerly been; he was of more humble social status, but his loyalties were firmly with Edward, Earl of Warwick. Taylor had fled to Rouen but returned in secret to visit friends based in the south-east, including Thomas Gale, a Neville supporter, and John Hayes, a long-standing servant of Clarence, with whom he discussed the earl's claim.[9] Taylor also managed to harness the support of the French king. After he had returned to Rouen, he wrote a letter to Hayes, which was delivered to him that November, describing how Charles VIII of France had decided to back the cause of Edward of Warwick and considered the plotters to be his allies, 'knowen for true men to the quarell'. Charles would support any rebels who chose to flee into exile 'for the wrong he did in making Henry King of England and for the gode he oweth unto the Sonne of youre maister Clarence for they be nere of kin'.[10] Hayes was asked to select a suitable location for the French invasion force to land. It may have been on his suggestion that, when the rebels left Honfleur in November, they headed for Ireland. But Hayes was being closely watched. He couldn't escape to join Taylor, and was arrested in December 1491.

It was in Cork, in late 1491, that Taylor and his companions reputedly discovered Perkin Warbeck strolling along the street and saw the opportunity he presented. The young man seems to have been the son of a Flemish couple based in Tournai; he confessed as much under duress, and research undertaken by James Gairdner in 1898 supports the claim. Having been apprenticed to a merchant, Warbeck was in the employment of a Breton trader named Pregent or Pierre Jean Meno, who had taken him to Ireland. Here, dressed up in silks as a kind of mannequin to display the wares on offer, he drew the attention of Taylor and former mayor John Atwater, with his looks and regal bearing. Either Taylor and his friends induced him to become the figurehead of their rebellion or convinced him that he was King Edward IV's illegitimate son.[11] An alternative version of events suggests that Warbeck was already pushing his claim to the English throne and had tried to gain Burgundian support in 1490, without success, so he willingly embraced the chance offered by Taylor, perhaps even instigated it. Whichever way around it happened, here emerged a young man with whom Edward's future would become bound.

Behind the solid walls of the Tower, Edward could only be aware of any developments in the outside world that his gaolers drew to his attention. In February 1489, he had turned 14, officially of age to rule, had he been king. Even though 'full' age was not considered to have been reached until 21, Edward was now of an age to question his position, his inheritance and his unjust lot. Perhaps he started asking when he might receive his lands, or if he would be able to administer them. The attainder against his father for treason and the confiscation of his lands by the crown was never reversed. However, it made no mention of his children and such acts were frequently overturned, or lands reinstated to those heirs who had been innocent of wrongdoing. It was precisely because young children were considered blameless that Edward's grandfather, Richard, Third Duke of York, had been able to inherit his uncle's titles even though his father had been executed for treason.

Edward may have heard that Henry had sent a fleet to France in retaliation against Charles VIII in June 1492. One thousand five hundred men landed on the coast of Normandy and proceeded to destroy the countryside and burn forty-five ships in the harbour over the space of a month and a half. The following year, he might have been told that the pretender Perkin Warbeck had been recognised as King Richard IV by the Emperor Maximilian. In 1495, when Edward was 20, Warbeck attempted to land off the English coast at Deal in ships supplied and equipped by Margaret of Burgundy. Due to the resistance of the people of Kent, the invasion failed before it had begun, sending Warbeck fleeing to Ireland, then Scotland. It did, however, claim one significant victim. Sir William Stanley, a long-standing Yorkist, had fought for Edward's grandfather as far back as 1459. He had served under Edward IV and Richard III, but defected to the Tudors at Bosworth, for which he was rewarded with the positions of Lord Chamberlain and Chamberlain of the Exchequer in Henry's household. Now, though, he was arrested on flimsy evidence for supporting Warbeck as a Yorkist prince. In hopes of leniency, Stanley admitted his crime, but found himself sentenced to death after having offered the necessary evidence. He was executed in February 1495. A year later, Edward, Earl of Warwick turned 21 and reached full age. He had spent the last decade locked in the Tower for good reason: there were still many dissident voices who believed that he was the true King of England.

Shortly after Stanley's execution, the matriarch of the York dynasty died. Cecily Neville was the mother of Edward IV; George, Duke of Clarence; Margaret, Duchess of Burgundy; Elizabeth, Duchess of Suffolk; and Richard III. Among her many grandchildren were Edward V and his brother in the Tower, Richard of York, Edward of Warwick and his sister Margaret, John de la Pole and his brothers, and Edward of Middleham. Her death marked the end of a dynastic era, but also illustrates an aspect of late medieval death practices which bore similarities and differences to those of the other royal grandmother, Elizabeth Woodville. In the final years of her life, Cecily had withdrawn to Berkhamsted Castle in Hertfordshire, where she lived as a vowess, in contemplation and seclusion. Her daily regime was similar to that in a nunnery, but on her own terms, in her own home: she rose at seven, prayed as she dressed, heard mass, followed by divine service and more masses; after dinner she heard religious texts read aloud, spent an hour on business, napped briefly and read prayers until evensong, dined and then related the day's sermon to her household. She began to dictate her will in the first days of April 1495, in 'hole mynd and body', surrendering her soul to God and requesting that her body be buried beside that of her husband, who had lain at Fotheringhay since his reinterment in 1476. Death had separated them over thirty-four years earlier. Cecily distributed bequests among her surviving family members, including Henry VII, to whom she left money and two gold cups; to Queen Elizabeth she left a diamond cross, a psalter and a reliquary; to their eldest son, Prince Arthur, she gave embroidered bed hangings; and to his brother, Prince Henry, the future Henry VIII, she left three arras hangings. Many of the items in other bequests were religious in nature, from books on the lives of saints and mass books, to altar cloths, copes and chasubles. All her remaining plate was to be sold to pay for her funeral, for the 'carrying of my body from the castell of Barkehampstead unto the college of Foderinghey' and, with that imminent event in mind, she signed her name and added the imprint of her seal to the document on 31 May. Cecily was buried in the church of St Mary and All Saints, in the tomb she had seen created in 1476. Ninety years later, after her resting place had been disturbed by the Reformation, Cecily's grave was opened. The bodies of the duke and duchess were observed, 'very plainly to be discerned', including the silk ribbon Cecily wore around her neck, from which was hung a papal dispensation, a remission for earthly sins 'penned in a very fine Romane hand … as faire and fresh to be read, as it had been written yesterday'.[12] It was typical of a late medieval aristocrat facing death to purchase such an item in the hope that it would ease their passage through purgatory. Soon after Cecily's soul had faced its own personal battle, a new threat was about to engulf her descendants.

In May 1497, heavy taxation in Cornwall sparked an uprising. After marching to London, the rebels were swiftly dispelled by a royal army at Blackheath but returned to the south-west to regroup and invited Warbeck to lead them. Hearing of this development, Henry pursued them to Exeter, where he won a decisive victory, forcing the pretender to seek sanctuary in Beaulieu Abbey. Warbeck made a full confession after the king offered to treat him leniently and was brought back to London, where he was kept under close guard at court. This state of affairs continued until June 1498, when Warbeck escaped from Richmond Palace during the night, reputedly by climbing out of a window. It is likely that Edward of Warwick's servants and gaolers kept him informed when the fugitive was recaptured, for now the earl was to have company of a sort. Perkin Warbeck, around the same age as him, and claiming to be his cousin, was to be brought to the Tower. Soon they were lodged one above the other, as Warbeck occupied the room directly beneath Warwick. Before long, they were in communication.

The plot against Henry VII, which would claim Edward's life, centred around the two men who were responsible for keeping the prisoners secure in the Tower. Robert Cleymond, a 'gentleman of London', was Warwick's 'keeper', sleeping beside him in confinement, while the same role was taken by a John Astwood for Perkin Warbeck. Astwood and Cleymond were already interested in the fate of Edward, Earl of Warwick. In February 1498, they had visited the house of a London haberdasher named John Finch, who told them of a prophecy stating that the bear (Warwick) would 'shortly beat his chains within the city of London'.[13] Finch wanted Edward informed of these prophetic words and also charged Cleymond to pass on a gift for the earl of two pairs of gloves and a pot of green ginger. At the time of Warbeck's arrest later that year, Cleymond and Astwood were working closely together, in proximity to the two young prisoners. Soon a hole had been knocked in the floor between the two rooms to allow for communication and letters were passed from one window to another on a long white thread.[14]

Then, early in 1499, another imposter appeared. A young man named Ralph Wilford, or Wulford, presumably bearing some physical similarities to the York family, announced that he was Edward, Earl of Warwick. He was actually the son of a London cordwainer from the Black Bull, Bishopsgate, who was then studying at Cambridge, and was slightly younger than the earl, being aged around 20. Like the boy Lambert Simnel, Wilford was encouraged by others, in this case a priest, who trained him in the necessary arts, although Wilford claimed that the idea had come to him in a dream. His appearance was preceded by a whispering campaign purporting to warn Henry VII that he was rapidly approaching the worst year of his reign. Henry sat up and took notice. Wilford surfaced in Kent, claiming to have escaped from the Tower but, before he could take any action, he was swiftly arrested and confessed his true identity. He was hung on 12 February, showing Henry again that such claims would continue so long as the earl was alive. Perhaps Wilford's effort was the final straw that prompted the king to act. Warwick would be dead nine months later.

Many historians have long been of the opinion that the case against Warwick and Warbeck was a convenient fabrication at best, a cynical trap at worst. Reputedly, it was Warbeck who instigated the plan. However, just how much prompting and suggestion he received from Cleymond and Astwood can only be guessed at. The intention was to seize the Tower, take money from the treasury, gunpowder from the ordnance and blow the place up. In the resulting chaos, they were to escape to a boat on the Thames and sail to France. There, they would issue a rallying cry to rebels to join their cause, offering them 12d a day from the stolen funds.

According to the evidence which Henry passed to his Council, Warwick had agreed to help Warbeck if he proved to be his cousin, Richard, Duke of York, as he claimed. If not, then he said he would claim the throne for himself. Warwick was given a dagger or short sword in preparation for the attempted break out, but other sources suggest he hardly knew what he was supposed to do with it.[15] The circumstances of the two young men could hardly have been more different, even though they had ultimately led them to the same place. It seems most likely that Warbeck was a pretender to the throne who had stuck to his plans over almost a decade, despite repeated opportunities to repent, or to disappear. He had put himself in the king's way, wishing him harm, and Henry thus had justification for his incarceration. Warwick, on the other hand, had never put a foot wrong, and the danger he posed to Henry was entirely due to his parentage and the schemes of Yorkist supporters. Potentially naïve, but facing the remainder of his life in the Tower, it is not surprising that Warwick was tempted to go along with an individual to whom he may have genuinely believed he was related.

The plot developed through the spring of 1499, by exchange of messages enabled by the two keepers. Exactly how much Henry knew about it is cause for speculation. It may be that the entire thing was his scheme from the start, or else he was informed by a subject, or spy, once it was underway. Early in August Cleymond told Warwick that the plot had been discovered and he was fleeing into sanctuary, No record survives of what happened to Cleymond and Astwood subsequently. They don't appear to have suffered the traitor's death that was inflicted upon Warbeck, or gone to the block like Warwick, which makes it difficult to resist the suggestion that they were, in fact, working for Henry, leading the two young men into the plot. The whole thing may have been a trap originating with the king, who used Cleymond to rid himself of two significant enemies. In addition, there appears to be no shred of evidence to support the claims or accounts of treasonous conversation, all of which relied solely upon the word of the accusers.[16] Warwick and Warbeck must have endured anxious months before being summoned for trial in November.

There is no doubt that the continued existence of Warwick and Warbeck proved a stumbling block for the negotiations that Henry was attempting to conclude for his eldest son's Spanish marriage. He finally decided to be rid of the two young men, after years of trouble from them, or on their behalf, and oblige the Spanish at the same time. This is not to deny that both did pose a significant threat to his throne as figureheads of discontent and that it was a sound policy to ally with the powerful Spaniards against the French. As far back as 1493, Margaret of Burgundy had written to Ferdinand and Isabella to endorse Warbeck as a real son of York, to which the pretender had added his own version of his 'escape' from London as a child. Two years later, the Spanish ambassador, de Puebla, wrote to Catherine of Aragon's parents about the threat posed by Perkin Warbeck, comparing it to that of Lambert Simnel, but calling him the Duke of Clarence, 'who was crowned King of Ireland and afterwards discovered to be the son of a barber'. He advised the Spanish that if the emperor supported Warbeck, it would prove 'very difficult to conclude what your highnesses wish'.[17] Just how significant was the role of Spanish pressure in this case must be balanced beside the cumulative years of threat and uncertainty that Henry VII had experienced. He had shown leniency towards Warbeck in a time when rebels and traitors were far safer dead, and Warbeck had continued to plot against him, as had others. In the autumn of 1499, Henry resolved to draw a line under these dangers and to move his dynasty forward with the validation of the most important dynasty in Europe. Harnessed to Warbeck's cause at the last minute, Edward, Earl of Warwick was an inevitable casualty of all these factors.

III

It is not clear exactly what Edward knew, or understood, about the process of his indictment and sentence of treason. He must have been told that Warbeck had been found guilty and hanged at Tyburn on 16 November. Five days later, during a brief, formal trial at Westminster, Edward confessed to the charges against him and was sentenced to death.

No matter how unjust, or contrived, he had little choice but to accept it. What can be stated for certain is that he is the first young man included in this book to have had some warning of his imminent end, some time to prepare himself for when death came as a controlled act, rather than on the battlefield, at the hand of an assassin or through illness. In the medieval mind, the ability to prepare for the final moment, to pray and be at peace, was essential in making a 'good' death. While living a good life was important, it was not the deciding factor for the afterlife, as those who had sinned could be accepted into heaven so long as they died well, having repented and asked for forgiveness. Death was considered to be a great battlefield on which the Devil made his final assault for the human soul, and needed to be resisted with every possible spiritual weapon.

A text printed by William Caxton in the 1490s, possibly by the prolific fourteenth-century writer Richard Rolle, captured the importance of approaching death in the right frame of mind by elevating it into an art form. *The Book of the Craft of Dying* captures the stages that Edward's confessors would have tried to make him accept as he lived through his final hours. All medieval people knew that death was inevitable and imminent. It had not yet become the distant abstraction that better health, medicine, sanitation, emergency care and safety have made it; the conclusion of every mystery play is the soul's departure into heaven or hell and it was a stage to be welcomed. 'Death is nothing else but a going out of prison and an ending of exile,' according to the book: 'a discharging of an heavy burden that is the body, finishing of all infirmities, a scaping of all perils, destroying of all evil things, breaking of all bonds, and entering into bliss and joy'. Edward, and anyone else who had warning of their death, should embrace what was to come, according to the teachings of St Paul: 'I deserve and covet to be dead, and be with Christ.' Caxton's volume continues with the advice that 'to die well is to die gladly and wilfully … without any grudging or contradiction … to learn to die is to have an heart and a soul ever ready up to Godward, that when that ever death comes, he may be found all ready.'[18]

Caxton also published a copy of *Speculum Artis Moriendi*, a version of a tract composed around 1415, as part of a swathe of writing about death in the wake of the plague. It follows the same pattern as the Rolle version, conforming to a six-part structure which includes sections on consolation, avoiding temptation, questions for the dying to lead them to the light, the imitation of Christ, rules for the behaviour of family and friends at the bedside and the final prayers. In his final hours, Edward would have been exhorted not to die doubting his faith, losing hope and despairing, not to die in impatience, or complacence or in pleasing himself, or in concerns about his worldly state. Edward had no wife, children, friends, riches or properties whose loss to regret, no actual life beyond his existence within the Tower's walls. Whatever the injustice of his cause, the result of his parentage, he would have resigned himself to leave life behind and embrace death. It was considered essential that a crucifix and image of Our Lady be kept in the presence of those about to die and Edward would have directed his prayers towards them, as well as to any other particular saints he favoured. His priest would have blessed him and sprinkled him with holy water as the final prayer was recited. These would have been among the last, if not the last, words of comfort that Edward heard:

> Lord Jesu Christ, son of the fatherly charity, I beseech thee by the Love that Thou, right much worthy, right innocent and most delicate, madest Thyself to be as man, to be wounded and die for the health of man, that Thy wilt pardon and forgive this Thy servant (insert name.) Jesus, right merciful, forgive him all that by thought, by word or deed, by affections or movings, by his strength and by his wit, of body and of soul, he hath trespassed. And for remission, give to him, Lord, that right sufficient emendation by the which Thou unboundest the sins of all the world; and, for the fulfilling of all negligences, join to him that right ready and valiant conversation, that Thou haddest, sith and from the hour of Thy conception unto the hour of Thy death. And moreover give to him the fruit of all the good works made and done by all the chosen saints, sith the beginning of the world unto the end. Qui vivis et regnas

Deus per omnia secula seculorum. (Who lives and reigns as God for ever and ever.)

In the honour of the right fervent love by the which the life of all living constrained Thee to be incarnate, and in anguish of spirit to die on the cross, we remember on, anew, Thy right benign heart to the end that to this, Thy servant (insert name) our brother, Thy put away all his sins, and that Thou forgive him all, by Thy right holy conversation and by the merit of Thy right holy passion; that Thou make him to experiment the superabundant of Thy miserations, and that Thou make ready us all, and in especial this person, Thy brother (insert name) whom Thou has disposed hastily to call to Thee by right pleasant manner; and that it be to him right profitable by Thy sweet patience, by very penance, by plain remission, by rightful faith, by steadfast hope, by right perfect charity; in such wise that in right perfect state he may blessedly depart and expire between Thy right sweet embracements and company, to Thy praising eternal. Amen.

Edward had a week to make his final confession and set his affairs in order. Given his sheltered life in the Tower, it cannot have taken long. He was executed on 28 November on Tower Green, at the age of 24. No accounts survive of how he met his end, which rather suggests it was a straightforward event. Edward, Earl of Warwick was buried at Bisham Abbey, where his rebellious grandfather, Richard Neville, Earl of Warwick, had been laid to rest twenty-eight years earlier. The abbey is no longer standing, having been a victim of the Reformation, but the thirteenth-century manor house remains, close to the place where Edward was finally buried. No details survive about his tomb, if he had one. Just like his young cousin Edward V, Warwick had lived a blameless life, guilty only of being born where and when he was. Thus, like the little murdered king, he can be said to be a victim of his circumstances, and more than most. The only suggestion of any wrongdoing on Edward's part was put forward in the final indictment against him, which rested entirely on the words of those who were also implicated, or had led him into his friendship with Warbeck.

The initial significance of his death, along with that of Warbeck, was for English national security, allowing Henry VII's match with Spain to proceed. On 11 January 1500, de Puebla wrote to Ferdinand and Isabella that:

England has never before been so tranquil and obedient as at present. There have always been pretenders to the crown of England but now that Perkin and the son of the Duke of Clarence have been executed, there does not remain 'a drop of doubtful Royal blood,' the only Royal blood being the true blood of the King, the Queen, and, above all, of the Prince of Wales. Must forbear from importuning them any more on this subject, as he has written so often concerning the execution of Perkin, and the son of the Duke of Clarence.[19]

Catherine of Aragon arrived in England the following year to be married to Prince Arthur, the Tudor heir.

Henry VII's conscience would later trouble him over Edward's death. According to a letter written by Edward's nephew, Reginald Pole, in the 1540s, the king had talked to his son about Edward, Earl of Warwick on his deathbed in 1509 – 'By the grace of God repenting of the acts of injustice committed by him during his reign, and amongst the rest calling to mind one of the most notable done to our uncle the Earl of Warwick' – and ordered the restoration of his lands and titles to his sister Margaret. The young man's death was also of concern to the Spanish princess, for whose sake he may have died. Catherine of Aragon was ten years younger than Edward, and just 14 at the time of his execution, which paved the way for her first marriage, to Henry VII's eldest son Arthur. After her death, Pole wrote that she had come to believe that her misfortunes were an affliction from God for her culpability in the act. Edward was 'frequently alluded to by herself ... that a great part of her troubles emanated from God, not through any fault of her own, but for the salvation of her soul', as during her marriage negotiations, 'some disturbances took place ... owing to the favour and goodwill borne by the people to ... the Earl of Warwick ... who being the son of the Duke of Clarence, brother of King Edward, became, by the death of that King's sons, next heir to the English crown'. At the time of the negotiations, Catherine's father, Ferdinand of Aragon, had:

> made a difficulty about it, saying he would not give her to one who was not secure in his own kingdom and thus, by inciting the King to do what he already desired spontaneously, he was the cause of the death of that innocent Earl, who had no more blame in those commotions, nor could anything else be laid to his charge.

Pole also believed that the premature death of Henry VII's eldest son, Arthur Tudor, was an act of 'divine justice' for the king's killing of Edward, Earl of Warwick.[20]

The story of Perkin Warbeck has continued to capture the imagination of writers since his execution, some of the most famous portrayals being Thomas Gainsford's 1618 *The True and Wonderfull History of Perkin Warbeck*, John Ford's 1634 *The Chronicle Historie of Perkin Warbeck: The Strange Truth* and, in 1827, Mary Shelley's *The Fortunes of Perkin Warbeck*. Something about the romance and colour of the pretender's dramatic life has ensured that his story, with its battles and daring escapes, continues to be told. No such works of literature have been inspired by the Earl of Warwick, whose youth spent behind bars and whose uncomplaining conformity and acceptance of his plight did not serve him well in life either. And yet, although Edward's existence lacked the high and low points of the exciting figure who brought about his downfall, he had something else far more significant in his armoury, which should not be forgotten. Edward, Earl of Warwick was the true King of England. Setting aside the technicalities of the act of attainder against his father, he was next in line to the throne by virtue of seniority after the deaths of his cousins the Princes in the Tower. While the fates of Edward V and his brother Richard are rightly lamented, upon that unfortunate king's death, probably in the autumn of 1483, the crown should have passed to Warwick as Edward VI. It suited both Richard III and Henry VII to preserve the taint the young man had acquired by association, although both were aware of the danger his continuing existence posed to them and kept him within sight. Richard dealt with him by incorporating him in his extended household, and while Henry initially attempted the same, his long-term solution was incarceration. The Clarence family were only restored to respectability in 1513, when Henry VIII permitted Edward's sister Margaret to hold the title Countess of Salisbury and returned some of her inherited lands. Blameless as he might have been, Edward, the rightful King of England, was simply too dangerous to be allowed to live. Henry VII had children of his own, and he was determined to ensure that they inherited his throne smoothly and went on to reign over England.

7

Arthur Tudor, Prince of Wales
(1486–1502)

I

Arthur was an unusual choice of name for an English prince. The one precedent was unfortunate: the twelfth-century Arthur I, Duke of Brittany, had been named heir by one of his uncles, Richard the Lionheart, only to be brutally killed by his other uncle, King John, after a period of captivity. It was not this historical figure that Henry VII wished to associate with his son, but another, legendary Arthur, the most popular romantic and action hero of medieval romance. After a tradition which had lasted centuries, from Chretien de Troyes to Thomas Malory, the story of King Arthur of Camelot reached its cultural apogee just months before his namesake was born. It was quite a legacy for the first Tudor prince's slender shoulders.

One of Henry VII's first acts as king was to lay the foundations for his marriage to Elizabeth of York. The 19-year-old princess was the eldest daughter of Edward IV, sister of the Princes in the Tower. Although Henry had claimed the crown by right of conquest, the beautiful Elizabeth had always been part of his plan, dating back to the Christmas Day oath he swore in Rennes Cathedral following the failure of his first invasion attempt. Immediately after his victory at Bosworth in August 1485, Henry summoned Elizabeth under escort from Sheriff Hutton to London. Then he set about repealing *Titulus Regis*, the act passed by Richard III to justify his disinheritance of the Yorkist royal children, ordering that all copies were to be 'cancelled, destroyed ... burnt and utterly destroyed'. Parliament approved the marriage on 10 December and Henry went ahead and ordered the wedding rings, which arrived at court at New Year. He had already obtained one papal dispensation in March 1484 on account of his affinity with Elizabeth – they were third cousins – but Henry was taking no chances and applied for a second, which he received on 16 January. The ceremony went ahead two days later in Westminster Abbey. Eight months after the wedding, Elizabeth was ready to give birth. It was no coincidence that she left London to deliver her child in Winchester.

The great hall is all that remains today of Winchester's once-imposing Norman castle. Hanging on its east wall, high out of reach, is a round table, reputed to have been the original used by King Arthur and his knights, when visiting the city. Freshly retouched, its bright coloured imagery include a seated king, a central union rose and radiating spokes in the Tudor colours of green and white, with places set for twenty-four knights. Modern radiocarbon dating has exposed the true age of the wood, placing in the thirteenth or fourteenth century, so the table is likely to have been created by Edward I or Edward III, both of whom held Arthurian-themed celebrations there. Prior to this discovery, the table's uncertain provenance contributed to the myth of Winchester's royal past, which was already well established by the time the Tudors arrived.

From the twelfth century, authors like Geoffrey of Monmouth, William of Malmesbury, Chretien de Troyes and Marie de France established Arthur as the hero of romances that were among the most widely read by the literate English aristocracy. Edward III's Order of the Garter, founded in 1348, was inspired by the round table oath and Henry VII's father-in-law, Edward IV, had felt a special affinity with King Arthur, aspiring to a chivalric court of jousting knights, a romance tale made real. Soon after claiming the throne in 1461, Edward IV commissioned genealogical trees tracing his descent back to 'Arthur returned from Avalon, the red dragon revived', and distributed them among his nobility. Hardyng's chronicle of 1463 located the scene of the king's adventures at Winchester, which he identified as a possible site of Camelot, writing that 'The rounde table at Wynchestere beganne, and ther it ende, and ther it hangeth yet.' Two decades later, John Lydgate's posthumously published *The Fall of Princes* included the prophecy that Arthur would return 'out of fayrye' and reign again, and William Caxton printed Malory's *Morte d'Arthur*, bringing Merlin's prophecy of the red king and white queen to the fore again. It was a story that suited England's monarchs in the late fifteenth century, and Henry VII allied it to his personal use of the Welsh red dragon in order to establish an ancestral authenticity for the new dynasty. As England's ancient capital, the reputed site of the fabled Camelot, Winchester was a romantic bastion of popular culture. In 1486, the city was carefully selected as a symbolic location to realign the new dynasty with its Welsh heritage and recreate a context for the iconography of the new regime. Henry wanted to endow his first-born son, the hope of his fledgling dynasty, with the strength and riches of national myth. It also provided continuity with the imagery of the Edwardian regime, as did the marriage to Elizabeth, which went some way to placate the Yorkists who had sided with Henry at Bosworth or had reconciled to his regime since.

By 1486, Winchester Castle was considered old and draughty, so Elizabeth was settled at the Prior's House, now renamed the Deanery, at St Swithin's Priory. This three-storey stone building, with its arched entrance portico, was used to house distinguished guests separately from the pilgrims lodged in the usual guest house. Winchester lay on one of the major highways of medieval England, and was a centre for pilgrimage housing around thirty Benedictine monks in 1500, who kept open house for visitors under the new Prior Thomas Silkested. There, Elizabeth's ladies would have gone about the business of readying a chamber for her lying-in, against a backdrop of monastic business, punctuated by bells and the sound of voices raised in prayer and chant. Among the women gathered to perform this office in September 1486 were the two grandmothers, Margaret Beaufort and Elizabeth Woodville who had arranged the match, as well as Elizabeth's sisters Anne and Cecily, whose youth would have limited their involvement. It is possible that Elizabeth was attended by her mother's favourite midwife, Marjory Cobbe, who had attended Elizabeth Woodville's final confinement only six years before. During the months of her pregnancy, the queen would have been attended by doctors and physicians, such as the Walter Lemster, to whom Henry granted £40 a year for life that February. Margaret Beaufort was responsible for arranging the details of the lying-in chamber, drawing up a set of ordinances that enshrined this intimate aspect of royal protocol. She was impressively thorough, from the number and colour of cushions in the room, to the ranks and duties of the women in assistance.

Prince Arthur was born between midnight and one in the morning on 20 September. His gender would have come as a relief to his parents, representing not just the arrival of an heir to the throne but the justification of their use of the myth. He was formally given his auspicious name four days later in Winchester Cathedral, to the sounds of celebratory gunshots and the ringing of bells. Prominent Yorkists were involved in the ceremony, the queen's sisters Cecily and Anne carrying the baby and the baptismal cloth respectively, and long-standing allies and servants like Lord Neville of Raby and Sir Richard Croft from Ludlow. Thomas Stanley was one of the godfathers and the dowager queen, Elizabeth Woodville, stood as godmother. John, Earl of Lincoln was definitely present and it is likely that Edward, Earl of Warwick was too. Later chroniclers stated that the child was named to 'honour the British race', describing the people 'rejoicing' in reaction to the child's name, whose choice made foreign princes 'tremble and quake', appearing to them 'terrible and formidable'. He was given the title of Duke of Cornwall and there were no indications that he was anything other than a strong, healthy baby.

On 26 October, the court arrived at Farnham in Surrey, where Arthur's household was to be established. Home to the bishops of Winchester and part of the Beaufort family inheritance, the palace sat alongside the castle, behind an imposing newly built red-brick gatehouse and was equipped with modern living quarters. The last bishop, William Waynflete, had died that August, allowing for the appointment of a new incumbent, Peter Courtenay, who agreed to relinquish his claim on the palace in favour of the prince. One thousand marks were allocated for the employment of a lady governess of the nursery, assisted by a dry nurse, wet nurse and various yeomen, grooms and others who saw to the practical running of the house. Elizabeth Darcy was appointed governess, with Elizabeth Gibbs as wet nurse and Alice Bywymbe, Agnes Hobbes and Evelyn Hobbes as rockers.[1] Most of those employed came from the Eltham Palace royal nursery of Edward's reign, which was continuing to cater for the needs of his younger children, three of his daughters being still under the age of 10. Similar rules and hours to those at Eltham and Ludlow would have been used, to ensure the security and smooth running of the establishment and the good behaviour of those connected with it. The king and queen left Arthur in his nursery and proceeded to Westminster.

To the modern reader, it seems brutal to separate a mother and child just weeks after the birth. Yet there were sound reasons for this, following fifteenth-century notions of pedagogy. Elizabeth, in particular, would have been a frequent visitor to her son's household, just as he would have been brought to court to see his parents at times of celebration and festivity. One interruption to his peaceful schedule came in March 1487, when news reached Henry of the imminent invasion of the Lincoln-Simnel forces. Fearful that his son and heir might prove a target for the rebels, the king sent word to Queen Elizabeth to collect Arthur and join him at Warwick Castle. The queen was then staying at Chertsey Abbey, around 20 miles away from her son, and hurried to the palace to collect him, arriving at Kenilworth on 29 May. From there, Henry set out to defeat the rebels, while Elizabeth waited with little Arthur. The little boy's future may have been very different, probably involving flight and exile, had the Battle of Stoke not gone in Tudor's favour. Once the threat had been crushed, Arthur would have returned to Farnham, although he may have been brought to Westminster to be part of the events surrounding his mother's coronation that November, partly for his own entertainment, partly to serve as an important symbol of dynastic success.

On 29 November 1489, the day after his sister Margaret was born, Arthur was created Knight of the Bath. The following February, he travelled by barge down the Thames to Westminster Palace, where he was invested as Prince of Wales and Earl of Chester, the ceremony conducted by the Mayor of London and the Spanish ambassadors, as his future marriage with Catherine of Aragon was already under negotiation. The boy was only 3 but he had been well prepared to make an impression commensurate with his position, riding a horse in public up to the gates of Westminster Hall. It was a taste of the formal ceremony that would be a feature of his future, with one concession to his youth; the chair of state was piled with cushions, but under the canopy, the cap with the gold circlet and the sword, ring, sceptre and rod, and the minstrels playing were as expected. Then, on 8 May 1491, at the age of 4½, Arthur was at St George's Chapel, in Windsor Castle, to be made a Knight of the Garter. Wardrobe accounts from this period indicate that he was dressed in satin, velvet, ermine and damask, and slept in a feather bed with a down-stuffed bolster and sheets of fine lawn and Holland cloth.[2] Gradually he made the transition from the female-dominated nursery to a more male establishment. Arthur's wet nurse was finally paid off in 1490, while Thomas Poyntz and Stephen Bereworth, the boy's doctor, were given salaries of £40 each, John Whytyng became his sewer, or server at table, John Almor his sergeant-at-arms, Thomas Fisher was yeoman of the cellar and Richard Howell became Marshall of the Household.

Arthur's formal education would have begun around the time he reached his fifth birthday, with a focus on the humanist tenets of classics, rhetoric, history, poetry, ethics, philosophy, music and science. His first tutor was John Rede, once a headmaster of Winchester College, then Bernard André, a blind French Augustinian friar, and finally the king's physician Thomas Linacre. Arthur was fluent in Latin and French, proficient at the lute under the tutelage of Giles Duwes, a skilful dancer and would come to learn by heart a number of texts by Cicero, Ovid, Homer, Livy and Virgil. In 1490, William Caxton dedicated his version of the *Aeneid* to the little prince. He was also proficient in archery, receiving a gift of a long bow, as recorded in the privy purse accounts of January 1492. Arthur received the most fashionable education of his time, incorporating newly discovered texts and a range of subjects under the Italian concept of the *uomo universale*, the universal man, or scholar, who might master whatever he turned his hand to. The difference between the upbringing of the previous generation, that of late medieval thinkers, and this new, Renaissance model, was exactly what Arthur would need to prepare him for kingship in the sixteenth century.

Rede and André had connections with a circle of humanists who were patronised by Arthur's grandmother, Margaret Beaufort. They included men who would shape English thinking at the turn of a new century: Thomas Linacre, who had been taught alongside the Medici children at Bologna; John Fisher, Margaret's chaplain and doctor of sacred theology; William Grocyn, lecturer in Greek at Oxford; William Lily, the grammarian who had been on pilgrimage to Jerusalem; John Colet, lecturer at Oxford and later Dean of St Paul's; and Thomas More, then a student at Lincoln's Inn. Erasmus described them at the end of the century, delighted at the climate of intellectual debate he had found in England:

> When I listen to my friend Colet, I seem to hear Plato himself. Who would not marvel at the perfection of encyclopaedic learning in Grocyn? What could be keener or nobler or nicer than Linacre's judgement? It is marvellous how thick upon the ground the harvest of ancient literature is here everywhere flowering forth.[3]

Yet André seems to have guarded his position as the prince's tutor jealously, openly criticising rivals like Linacre when he presented his latest work at court. Ultimately, the friar retained control over the prince until his majority. Although this was only possible with the permission of the king, the distance between Henry's court and Arthur's home meant that few other scholars were able to exert their influence. The friar collated and edited a number of texts for Arthur's education, among them St Augustine's *City of God*, and personally selected authors for his curriculum. André praised the intelligence of his pupil with a biblical comparison: 'that famous utterance of the Apostle Paul has been proved true of me: Apollo planted, I watered, God has given the increase.'

The prince's first exercises in power came in his rule over the Welsh Marches. He was created warden in May 1490, with the Earl of Surrey as his deputy and, from the following year, his name gave authority to peace commissions, to establish a greater sense of local allegiance to the future king. It was a nominal independence, with the boy as a figurehead of justice for the rule of his experienced servants, and all appointments were vetted in secret by his father, but it was a start. When Henry VII visited France in 1492, he followed the precedent set by Edward IV in 1475, and named his 5-year-old son as his Lieutenant and Keeper of England. In the spring of 1493, Arthur's household moved from Farnham to Ludlow, on the Welsh Marches, in the footsteps of his grandfather Edward IV. From then, his time was divided between Ludlow Castle and Tickenhill Palace in Bewdley, two royal properties that were around 20 miles apart. Yet Arthur was not rooted completely in this area. Records indicate that his movements included visits to Shrewsbury in 1494 and 1495, Oxford a number of times after 1495, Coventry and London in 1498, Chester in 1499 and other nearby locations. Despite his youth, Arthur increasingly sat in sessions of the peace, making his first appearance at Hereford Castle in April 1493, where proceedings are described as taking place in the presence of 'the most beloved first-born son of the said King, Arthur, Prince of Wales'.[4] It was an essential part of his training for future kingship to witness the processes and application of justice, to develop empathy tempered with a working knowledge of the law.

By all contemporary accounts, Arthur was a healthy, good-looking child. In September 1497, the Milanese ambassador, Raimondo de Soncino, described meeting the English royal family, among whom was 'the King's eldest son Arthur, Prince of Wales, about 11 years of age, but taller than his years would warrant, of remarkable beauty and grace and very ready in speaking Latin'.[5] Arthur also played a role in greeting the ambassador, engaging in a 'brief and familiar talk' with Soncino before they all went in to dinner. He was also present later, when the visitors met the queen, and they took formal leave of him before departing the court.[6] A portrait painted around 1500 presents the prince with a long, thin face and dark eyes, sensitive mouth and fashionably cut dark hair. He poses with a white rose between his fingers, dressed in a gown of cloth of gold lined with fur, over a red doublet with gold edging, a jewelled pendant of black stones set in gold and a black hat and jewel, from which hang three pearls. Painted in oil with gold leaf on a wooden panel, it is the only surviving portrait painted during the boy's lifetime, possibly commissioned in celebration of his marriage. An altarpiece depicting Henry's family which was painted a couple of years after Arthur's death, shows a youth with a somewhat generic face, the copy of his father's long dark hair and eyes, wide mouth and strong nose. Other contemporary images, in a Guild Book of Ordinances and at prayer in a window at Great Malvern Priory, are similarly generic and lacking in personal detail, and were even touched up in later years. A final image of Arthur from the 1520s depicts a more mature face, with strong nose and small mouth, the subject wearing a gold chain of office and a red hat with a pilgrim badge, his empty right hand open before him, where the previous portrait had held a flower. From these images, it seems likely that the 15-year-old Arthur was dark in colouring, with a longish, slender face and nose, thin lips and a sensitive expression; a young king-in-waiting wearing his learning and legacy as visibly as the marks of his status.

Since 1487, negotiations had been flying back and forth between England and Spain for Arthur's marriage to Catherine of Aragon. Finally, after the details had been arranged, a proxy wedding ceremony was held at nine in the morning on 19 May 1499 in the chapel at Tickenhill. Spanish ambassador de Puebla stood in for Catherine, repeating her vows and joining his right hand with that of Arthur, and accepted him as the princess's husband. Arthur replied in a 'loud and clear voice' that 'he was very much rejoiced to contract with Catherine ... in indissoluble marriage, not only in obedience to the Pope and King Henry, but also for his deep and sincere love for the Princess, his wife.' A papal dispensation had been acquired for Arthur to say his vows, as he was still four months off his thirteenth birthday. De Puebla was given a seat of honour at the banquet that followed and ate from the best dishes, to his great delight. From that moment forward, Catherine was officially styled 'Princess of Wales' but although she and Arthur were legally married, they were still in separate countries.

Promises might have been made, but there was still a possibility that the marriage would not take place. The threats posed by Perkin Warbeck and Edward, Earl of Warwick were sufficient for the Spanish to be concerned about the stability of the Tudor throne and the prince's youth could provide an excuse for Ferdinand and Isabella to renege upon their agreement. Thus, after the two prisoners in the Tower had been executed in November 1499, and Arthur had reached his fourteenth birthday the following September, the entire process was repeated. De Puebla stood in again during a second ceremony held at Ludlow on 22 November 1500. All that remained was for Catherine to come to England. While they waited, the young pair wrote to each other enthusiastically, even passionately. Some of the terms of endearment may have been fairly formulaic, taken from the Latin texts taught to Arthur by André, but they were sincerely meant. There is something touching about the young man's efforts to prove himself a lover. In October 1499, Arthur thanked Catherine for her 'sweet letters' in which he had 'easily perceived your entire love for me' and conveyed his own 'urgent desire' to see her. He complimented Catherine, saying that her letters 'written by [her] very own hand evoked her presence and even her embrace'. Taking an even more intimate tone, he continued, 'I cannot tell you what an earnest desire I feel to see your Highness, and how vexatious to me is this procrastination about your coming. Let it be hastened, that the love conceived between us and the wished-for joys may reap their proper fruit.' Sadly, Catherine's letters to Arthur have not survived.

II

Hindsight has created an imbalance when it comes to Arthur's historical reputation. His premature death has placed particular focus on the intimate aspects of his brief marriage, eclipsing other aspects of his life and character, potential and education. The one thing that people tend to know about Arthur, if they know anything, is that he died young. Yet as he was anticipating his wedding, through the spring and summer of 1501, it would have seemed to the prince that he was about to embark on the next step in his life's journey, encompassing parenthood, succession and kingship. Had it been so, the details of his wedding night with Catherine would never have been made public as they were in the late 1520s, with all the possibilities of their intimacy discussed in public. Instead, what happened between two teenagers became the subject of international debate and the cause of England's break with Rome, bringing centuries of tradition to an end. There is no question that Arthur's premature death had a huge impact upon the course of English history and redefinition of national identity in the sixteenth century.

In October 1501, Catherine finally landed in England. Henry and Arthur hurried to meet her, intercepting the Spaniards at Dogmersfield in Hampshire. At first, Catherine's household resisted, as it went against protocol, but Henry insisted they were now in his country, subject to his rules. Communication was difficult as the princess spoke no English and her hosts spoke no Spanish but they made themselves understood as best they could with the help of translators and Latin pronounced with different accents. That evening, Henry retired to dine, leaving Arthur with Catherine while the Spanish minstrels played and the young pair danced, but not together. Arthur partnered Lady Guildford while Catherine took the floor with some of her ladies. While the Spanish were prepared to bow to the English king's wishes and relax their rules over contact before the wedding ceremony, dancing together would not have been appropriate for the young couple, even though they were technically man and wife already. It may also have been that they did not yet know a dance they could perform together, that Catherine executed Spanish steps while Arthur performed an English favourite. There is every reason to suppose that Catherine and Arthur were pleased with each other. In fact, Arthur would write to Ferdinand and Isabella that he had 'never felt so much joy' in his entire life as when he 'beheld the sweet face of his bride' and that 'no woman in the world could be more agreeable to him.'

Catherine's entry into London a few days later was marked by magnificent pageantry that included the imagery of her own descent, coupled with that of her future husband. Arthur was positioned in Cheapside to watch her progress as she reached the fifth display, which was entitled 'The Temple of God', with the figure of the deity adorned in gems and pearls, seated on a throne surrounded by burning candles and singing angels. A huge red rose was borne aloft by heraldic beasts. Beside his father, mother and grandmother, Arthur watched his wife from 'a howys wheryn that tyme dwelled Wylliam Geffrey, haberdasher', standing in the windows, 'not in very opyn sight ... beholdynge the persones, their raise, ordre and behavynges of the hole companye, bothe of Englonde and of Spayne, as well of their apparell and horsis'.[7] Arthur was also present when King Henry hosted the Spanish party at Baynard's Castle the day before the wedding. This was a visit for business rather than pleasure, and Arthur sat and watched with his younger brother Henry as the Spanish presented the terms of the forthcoming match and gave the king Ferdinand's assurances of his daughter's virginity. The topic might be delicate, but it was also a matter of politics and state. The impression this made upon Arthur, aged 15, and Henry, aged 10, was one of an inescapable rite of passage. Women's good reputations were indispensable and the act of marriage marked their transition between innocence and sexual experience. It was a very clear line in the sand, drawn and valued by men, and the princess was the commodity over which they were bargaining.

The following day, Sunday 14 November, Catherine and Arthur were married in St Paul's Cathedral. Arthur had travelled there from his lodgings in the Great Wardrobe, just to the south of the cathedral and, dazzling in white satin, took his place at Catherine's side to repeat their wedding vows before the congregation. Henry VII intended that the young couple should be seen, so a raised wooden platform had been erected along the entire 350ft from the choir to the west door, standing 4ft high and 12ft wide. Covered in red cloth, it was railed along each side to keep onlookers at bay. Catherine and Arthur were literally to be centre stage, elevated over the heads of Londoners, in something like the culminating pageant of the recent days, but in the flesh instead of in representation. The agreement between England and Spain was read aloud, after which the princess was endowed with the titles and lands which Henry had bestowed on her as her settlement as his daughter-in-law. After they were formally pronounced man and wife, the pair turned to acknowledge the crowd, 'so the present multitude of people might see and behold their persons', and walked along the length of the platform, hand in hand. One observer described them as a 'lusty and amorous couple'. Catherine and Arthur then returned to the Archbishop's Palace, where the wedding feast was to be served to over 100 guests. The theme for the feast was 'all the delicacies, dainties and curious meats that might be purveyed or got within the whole realm of England', which were served up in three courses, of twelve, fifteen then eighteen dishes. The feasting continued for four or five hours.

Before the end of the feast, Catherine's ladies and the Earl of Oxford departed for Baynard's Castle, to make the necessary arrangements for the wedding night. A normal part of the ritual, the ceremony combined elements of the public and private, and physical consummation was essential to consolidate the vows spoken earlier by the couple in the cathedral, marking the final stage of the ceremony. The bed was inspected and tested by the earl, who sat on each side to ensure it was comfortable and that no concealed blades had been smuggled into the chamber. Catherine and Arthur travelled from the Bishop's Palace to the castle, where they were changed and prepared for bed, around eight in the evening. The princess was brought in first, dressed in her nightgown and laid 'reverently' in bed. Arthur stayed up longer, drinking and celebrating with his gentlemen, but finally they carried him in, singing and making merry, before, at last, the guests withdrew and the pair were left alone. They might have spent their entire lives being trained to endure the public gaze but, in private, how well equipped were they for the anticipated consummation of their marriage? To put it bluntly, the question that confounded England in the 1530s and has been wrangled over by historians ever since, is how likely is it that Catherine and Arthur had sex?

The next morning, Arthur appeared flushed and thirsty, 'good and sanguine', calling for a drink as he had spent the night 'in the midst of Spain' and that it was a 'good pastime to have a wife'. These words have to be understood in the context of political and masculine expectations, from the pageantry references, to the proof of virginity at Baynard's Castle, the bawdiness of his friends and the expectations on his shoulders that he would live up to his part in the most expensive and magnificent occasion of his life. Arthur's role to that point had been kept to a minimum. He had met Catherine briefly, in private, but otherwise had taken a backseat, beside his father, or overlooking events while the princess took centre stage. The public gaze had fallen on her throughout, as a foreigner and guest of honour, and even Arthur's presence at her side in St Paul's and at the wedding feast was designed to complement her, in matching white satin, rather than to eclipse her. Still, despite all the various ceremonies they had been through, the marriage was incomplete. Only Arthur could claim his bride in the physical, binding sense that would ensure the full, undisputed union of England and Spain, rendering the match indissoluble in the eyes of the Church. The nuptial night was the first time that the lead was handed over to the prince. This was his moment, with this single act to perform, when the traditional gender roles dictated the submission of Spain to conquering England. There must have been considerable pressure on him to perform.

Then there was the additional need for Arthur to prove himself a man. As a future king of England, a youth verging on the threshold of manhood, he could not be seen to fail this test. His duty was to achieve intercourse and definitions of his masculinity, his prowess and fitness to rule, rested upon his success or failure. Robust heterosexuality was considered an essential component of masculine health and previous kings whose sexuality was dubious, such as Catherine's great-uncle Henry IV of Spain, Edward II or the Lancastrians Richard II and Henry VI, had been perceived as weak and effeminate, unsuitable as monarchs. There was also the precedent of the prince's own conception, which had taken place on his parents' wedding night, or before, or soon afterwards. Arthur had absorbed the cult of his own identity, which his father had begun to weave since before his birth; the associations with the mythical warrior king, and by extension his advocate, the fecund Edward III; the symbols of fertility and flowering; the parallels with historical and biblical figures. His father had been an only child and the dynasty was in its infancy. Arthur had to complete the carefully constructed picture himself by passing the challenge of masculine sexuality, of successfully penetrating a woman and proving his ability to father sons. The marriage would not have gone ahead had he been too young, or weak, or if he had not yet undergone puberty, as some historians have speculated; it had already been delayed after the threshold age of 14 and Henry must have given the Spanish assurances of his son's normal physical development. Delivered from the hands of the young bucks at court, with their bawdy words ringing in his ears, the 15-year-old Arthur knew it was his job to claim the virginity that had been guaranteed by his father-in-law of Aragon. In the morning, his friends would have been looking for confirmation that he had.

Was he successful? Later, Catherine swore that they didn't have sex and she never wavered from this position all her life. The following morning, she was quiet and subdued, remaining with her ladies. In the depositions dating from the 1520s, the voice of Juan de Gamarra stands out. As a 12-year-old boy, he had slept in her antechamber on the wedding night, literally adjoining Catherine's bedroom, and stated that 'Prince Arthur got up very early, which surprised everyone a lot,' perhaps even before the princess herself woke; when he went into her room, he found Catherine's dresser and confidante, Francesca de Carceres, appearing sad and informing the others 'that nothing had passed between Prince Arthur and his wife, which surprised everyone and made them laugh at him'.[8] Hence the need for Arthur's boast. Catherine's first lady, Dona Elvira, was convinced that the princess was still as pure as she had been when she left her mother's womb, and she imparted this belief to Ferdinand, who did not doubt her. In addition, Catherine's doctor later deposed that Arthur had not been capable of the act, having been 'denied the strength necessary to know a woman, as if he was a cold piece of stone, because he was in the final stages of phthisis [tuberculosis]' and he had never before seen a man whose limbs were so thin. Convincing as this may sound, though, it is a testimony made in hindsight, by a man who treated the prince on his deathbed.

Arthur never stated implicitly that they had slept together, although his bawdy request for drink was designed to imply that consummation had taken place. This line could be taken at face value, or it might have been the bravado of a young man giving assurance that he had not failed in his duty, especially if he had failed, and could feel the disappointment of the Spaniards. His words must be taken in the context of political and gendered expectations. It was all part of the performance of the last few days, of the keeping-up of appearances and the appropriate behaviour of those who ruled. Arthur's request for drink, even though it related to something intimate, was a function of his public identity and did not necessarily bear relation to private truths. If consummation had not taken place, this did not make his words a lie, as he did not explicitly state that penetration had taken place. His chosen phrase 'in the midst of Spain', with its obvious physical implication, could equally refer metaphorically to Catherine's company, and her body as the symbolic representation of Spain. As the pageants had enforced, she was the embodiment and representative of Spain, as he was of England. The non-sexual experience of her physicality, including her appearance and clothing, her accent and language, was being used by Arthur as something of a metaphysical conceit, akin to those later used by John Donne, that had translated their bedchamber into a little enclave of Spain, where Arthur had to fulfil the role of diplomat. It implied sex but it also did not confirm it. Its bawdiness lay in its suggestion rather than its actuality. Arthur could hardly have behaved as Catherine did the following morning; he had to define himself differently, as polar opposite as masculinity was from femininity, as active rather than passive, as boastful and swaggering rather than quiet and subdued. If his gentlemen took his words to mean that Arthur had fulfilled his manly duties and confirmed his masculinity, then so much the better.

Between Catherine's later denial and Arthur's suggestion lies much grey area for interpretation. Of course, by the late 1520s, it was in Catherine's interests to say that the marriage had not be consummated, but it was also crucial to her in the spring of 1502, when the question first arose in a formal context. In addition to the events of the wedding night, a complete lack of consummation meant the pair would have never achieved full sex during the entire four-and-a-half-month span of their marriage. Understandably, this scenario is less credible simply because of the greater opportunities afforded the couple once they were established in their own household, but Catherine still maintained that she had shared a bed with Arthur on only seven occasions and he had never 'known' her. Arthur's gentleman Maurice St John contradicted this, claiming that they had slept together at Shrovetide, the day before Lent began, which fell on 19 February that year, after which 'the prince began to decay and was never so lusty in body and courage until his death.'[9] There was also the example of Catherine's elder brother, Juan, Prince of Asturias. Having been married at the age of 18, his death nine months later was probably from tuberculosis, but was judged by many at the time to have resulted from over-exertion in the marital bed. He left his young bride pregnant but she miscarried three months after being widowed, leaving the joint Spanish thrones of Castile and Aragon without a male heir, so that the inheritance passed to their son-in-law Philip I, and became part of the Holy Roman Empire.

Regardless of all the views expressed later by various 'witnesses', there were only two people in the bedchamber of the Prince and Princess of Wales that night. Only those two people knew what had passed between them, although it is possible that the inexperienced teenagers had actually come to very different conclusions about their degree of success. But plenty of other people have formed an opinion on it, including the chronicler Edward Hall, who was 4 years old at the time, although still able to state in the 1540s that 'this lusty prince and his beautifull bride were brought and ioyned together in one bed naked, and there dyd that acte, whiche to the performance and full consummacion of matrimony was moost requisite and expedient.'

So what really happened? It is not possible to know for certain, but nor is it necessary to accuse either the prince or princess of telling falsehoods. Historians have often reduced this delicate situation to two possible interpretations: either the couple did sleep together and Catherine lied about it, or they didn't and Arthur's boast was intended to mislead. However, a third option is possible. Amid the fumblings of two inexperienced but pressurised teenagers who did not share a common language, they might both have been right. Arthur may have believed that full intercourse had taken place while Catherine, arguing in the 1520s from a standpoint of sexual experience, knew that it had not. How might this have come about?

With the closing of the chamber door and the footsteps of the court receding, Catherine and Arthur were truly alone. Lying side by side in their perfumed sheets, with the fire burning in the grate, they both understood the significance of the occasion but, without hindsight, they also believed that there was no rush. They were still young and thought they had the next thirty or forty years together, hardly guessing that the metaphorical clock was already ticking for their short-lived union. Communication cannot have been easy; looks, smiles, touches and good will must have made up the shortfall of language between them. The exchange of words was not essential for intercourse to take place, but it would have helped establish an intimacy between two people who were virtual strangers. They must have been tired, and Arthur had been drinking, and they could not share what they had been through in the last few days and weeks. There is also a chance that as the date was a major saint's day, and a Sunday, the couple behaved like the good Catholics they were raised to be, and abstained. However, given the pressure on Arthur, it would seem more likely that consummation was attempted.

Incredible as it may seem to a modern reader, Arthur may have believed that he had acted sufficiently to relieve his bride of her virginity. To address a sensitive question directly, just how far was penetration required in order to constitute a successful consummation? There may have been some form of foreplay, or else Arthur may have achieved some shallow degree of penetration that was not sufficient to rupture her hymen, leaving her technically a virgin. It is also possible that on what must have been his first sexual encounter, Arthur experienced premature ejaculation upon, or soon after, penetration. Catherine's quietness the following morning might indicate the embarrassment and discomfort of a bungled effort at intercourse rather than complete non-consummation. In later years, when she was forced to defend her virgin state, she did so from a position of comparison with the robust lovemaking of her second husband. It is perfectly possible that Arthur thought he had experienced full sex, or at least taken his wife's virginity, while she thought he had not. The court took it for granted that he had. Catherine had no way of knowing that the question would ever be raised again.

III

Following festivities at Westminster and Richmond, the question of Arthur and Catherine's living arrangements had to be addressed. It was not the first time this issue had arisen, due to the youth of the couple. Back in 1500, before Catherine had come to England, Henry had decided that 'the prince will know his wife sexually on the day of the wedding and then separate himself from her for two or three years because it is said in some way the prince is frail.' This suggested a compromise, so that the match was legally binding but a full sexual relationship was delayed. 'The King told me', the Spanish ambassador wrote to Catherine's parents, 'that he wanted to have them [Arthur and Catherine] with him for the first three years so that the prince should mature in strength'. [10] Contemporary medical opinion was divided when it came to sexual relations between young newly-weds. While a physical relationship was considered beneficial in physical and emotional terms, the denial of natural urges leading to health problems and temptation, the timing was critical.

It was a common practice among aristocratic families for marriages to be made while the bride and groom were still underage, as Catherine and Arthur had experienced, but the exact moment of consummation could be delayed for several years after the pair had begun to live together. This contained risks, as the premature death of one of the parties prior to the physical act meant that the bereaved partner had no claim upon dowry payments or financial support. For weeks, the question of Arthur and Catherine's married life hung in the air. Then, eventually, against the advice of the Spanish and much of his Council, the king ruled that Catherine would accompany Arthur into Wales at once. They departed for Ludlow on 21 December, five days after the princess turned 16.

Arthur's business in the Welsh Marches must have been pressing indeed if the pair could not wait to celebrate Christmas in London, or for better weather to arrive. With Arthur riding on horseback and Catherine sitting in a litter, they spent three or four days covering the 130 miles to reach Bewdley, on the River Severn, described by Leland as 'so comely a man cannot imagine a town better'. They passed Christmas at Tickenhill Manor, set on a ridge overlooking the town, where Catherine would have had the chance to see the chapel where she had been married to Arthur by proxy in 1499. No doubt they observed the holy day there and dined in the 100ft-long hall on the south side of the house, which had been given new doorways and stone-tile windows and repaired with local timber in recent years. Nothing now remains of the old palace, which was set amid extensive gardens and hunting grounds, although Catherine and Arthur were unlikely to have had much time, or enough clement weather, to take advantage of the park. Given their rate of travel, they would only have needed an additional day or two to cover the 20 miles due west to Ludlow. Depending on how long they remained at Tickenhill, the pair may have arrived at their destination around New Year.

There was little time to enjoy a 'honeymoon' period. Arthur resumed his duties, meeting his wife for meals, but otherwise the prince's work required him to travel and undertake long days of work in the government of Wales. They did not have much time together to become acquainted, although Anthony Willoughby later remarked that they had slept together at Shrovetide, 19 February, and that he had frequently accompanied Arthur to his wife's chamber door at night. This stands in direct opposition to Catherine's affirmation that they shared a bed on only seven occasions throughout their four and a half months of marriage. At the end of March, Catherine and Arthur both fell ill. The prince's last public engagement was during the celebrations for Maundy Thursday on 24 March. He may have been distributing money to the poor, or even assisting in the traditional foot washing. It seems more than coincidence that both husband and wife succumbed at the same time, suggesting that they contracted a virus, perhaps because Arthur came into close bodily contact with the people on this last occasion. Unfortunately, no evidence remains to confirm whether other members of their household were affected, which would have been a likely outcome of this scenario. At the time, it was recorded that a 'great sickness' was in the area, which may have been the plague, or possibly the sweating sickness, a particularly virulent and dramatic illness that had arrived in England in 1485 and was known to kill within hours.

On the evening of Saturday 2 April, Prince Arthur died while Catherine languished in bed. He was 15½. Examining the body, the Spanish Dr Alcarez diagnosed his condition as 'tisis' or 'phthisis', pulmonary tuberculosis, which was common during this period, especially among children, and could become severe very quickly. Some of the symptoms were indeed similar to those of the sweating sickness. Yet if Arthur had been suffering from tuberculosis on a long-term basis, his weakness should have surfaced before this point, and the king and queen would not have consented to his marriage or his return to Ludlow. According to modern understanding, the disease is spread in the air by bacteria when people who have the active form of tuberculosis cough and sneeze. Arthur might have come into contact with an infected person during his work in the Welsh Marches, or picked it up at court, perhaps even from his father, who would be claimed by the same illness seven years later. Only one in ten cases progresses from latent to acute, triggering symptoms of coughing, fever, weight loss and sweating. It can then kill very rapidly. Catherine and Arthur did not both have tuberculosis, but if the prince was entering an acute phase of illness, during which he had been losing weight, he would have been too weak to fight off any virus from which an otherwise healthy person might recover. Thus, when both young people were infected with a virulent strain of sickness that March, perhaps as a result of his work on Maundy Thursday, Catherine was able to fight it off, but Arthur's recent decline left him too weak. This is a plausible explanation for their joint sickness and the difference in outcome, but there are no accounts of rapid decline in the boy in the spring months of 1502. To be fair, though, there are no surviving accounts of their time at Ludlow at all, so conclusive answers cannot be drawn. It is equally possible that the prince was suffering from some form of testicular cancer that also prevented him from consummating his marriage or an inherited illness that would also afflict his nephew Edward VI. All that can be stated with certainty is that Arthur died and Catherine survived.

The unknown author of *The Receyt of the Ladie Kateryne*, who had recently described all the vivid detail of the couple's wedding pageantry, had not expected to follow it so soon with the account of a funeral. Yet, book four of five concludes Arthur's brief moment in the spotlight with these details, enclosing his short life and ending a chapter of Catherine's. It paints a picture of the boy's last valiant battle, against 'a moost petifull disease and sikeness, that with so soore and great violens hedde battilid and driven in the singler partise of him inward; that cruell and fervent enemye of nature, the dedly corupcion, did utterly venquysshe and overcome the pure and frendfull blood without almoner of phisicall help and remedy'. The news was broken to Henry by his confessor early the following morning, Tuesday 5 April, and the king sent for his wife, so that they might 'take the Painefull sorrows together'.[11] After comforting each other, Elizabeth concealed her pain long enough to remind Henry that they still had healthy children and were still young enough to have more.

An account by John Writhe, Garter King at Arms, describes the preparations of Arthur's body in advance of his burial. First, the prince was seared and dressed in spices and other sweet stuff, so that his body would not leak, and was sewn into good black cloth with a white cross on top. Following Arthur's instructions, his bowels were removed to be buried in the little round Ludlow chapel of St Mary Magdalene. Arthur lay in his chamber under a table that was covered over with rich cloth of gold and bearing a cross and silver candlesticks and wax tapers. Four other large tapers were set to burn in his room. Writhe mentions his alms folk, who sat about the corpse day and night, holding torches and keeping vigil, possibly those whom he had attended on Maundy Thursday. His body remained there for three whole weeks, until St George's Day, 23 April, on the afternoon of which he was removed to the church. Arthur's yeomen of the chamber carried him into the Hall at Ludlow, draped in black cloth of gold, with a cross of white cloth of gold, and rested him on a trestle, where three bishops censed the body and sprinkled it with holy water. Then noblemen came to pay their respects, including the principal mourners, Arthur's chamberlain, and other members of his household. A canopy was carried over the corpse, with banners at every corner, depicting the Trinity, the Cross, Our Lady and St George, while a banner of Arthur's own arms was carried before him by Sir Griffiths ap Rhys. Before them were two Spaniards 'of the best degree' from Catherine's household, behind the pursuivants, who were officials from the College of Arms, then the churchmen, bishops, abbots and priors, parsons, priests and friars, flanked by eighty poor men in black mourning bearing torches.

Arthur was carried into the choir of the parish church of St Laurence, where he would lie for the next two nights. A dirge was sung for his soul and readings given by the bishops of Lincoln, Salisbury and Chester; the following day there were more masses, songs and offerings, then alms were given to the poor. Finally, Arthur was placed on a chariot drawn by six horses trapped in black cloth with escutcheons of gold. The vehicle was covered in black velvet, with a white cross of cloth of gold, banners at each corner and surrounded by mourners in black hoods. On St Mark's Day, 25 April, the procession left Ludlow for Tickenhill, in Bewdley, but the weather was so terrible, battering them with wind and rain, that the horses were replaced by oxen, to drag the hearse through the rutted streets. From there, they proceeded to Worcester in better weather, being met at the city gates and drawn through the streets by fresh horses, with dignitaries and churchmen on either side. The Norman Worcester Cathedral, formerly a priory, had been designated by Henry as his son's resting place. The following day, the ceremony proper began, with the Man at Arms riding a charger into the choir, carrying a poleaxe pointing downwards, followed by lords and officers who laid palls of cloth of gold tissue across the hearse. A sermon was read, more alms distributed, more incense waved and, amid much weeping, the members of Arthur's household broke their staffs of office and cast them down into the grave.

Arthur's chantry chapel lies on the south side of the high altar. It may have been completed as early as 1504, or as late as 1516, when it was blessed by the bishop. Inside it, his tomb was made from granite, and featured heraldic devices and overlooked by statues of saints and kings, including Henry VII and Edward IV under a fan ceiling and elaborate tracery. Now rubbed black with age, it would once have been painted and gilded and, perhaps, topped by an effigy of the young prince. The iconography inside the chantry highlights the purpose of such tombs to appeal to a wide loyalty base, prompted by allegiance to family badges, and thus encouraging prayer. Very few people along the Welsh Marches could have been ignorant of the meaning of the white rose of York or the ostrich feathers of the Prince of Wales. They would also have been moved by the French *fleur de lys*, the Beaufort portcullis and the Yorkist falcon and fetterlock, mixed in with new allegiances: the pomegranate of Catherine of Aragon and her mother Isabella's sheaf of arrows.

Arthur's household had been a court in waiting, anticipating a time when the youth would become king and they his leading men. From its small nucleus of regional loyalties and the Spanish marriage, an impressive individual should have emerged to rule England, educated along humanist lines and experienced in the ways of government, with a network of allegiances and a wife and children at his side. His death represented the loss of a future king and his reign, the loss of years of investment that had been made in his education, his guidance and in the prince as an individual. When Henry VII died, in April 1509, Arthur would have been 22 and married for eight years, potentially the father of several surviving children. The Tudor dynasty might have had a responsible, shrewd adult king and heirs to the throne devoted to the new learning and devout in their Catholicism. Arthur and Catherine would have been united by their shared destiny in steering England's course through the challenges of the sixteenth century, perhaps for three or four decades to come. Instead, years of uncertainty, unhappiness and penury awaited the widow. If ever a death changed the course of history, it was that of Arthur Tudor, Prince of Wales, the king England never had. While the true impact of his loss would not be felt for years, the immediate result was that it was his younger brother, Henry VIII, who took the path, the life, that had been Arthur's. It was Henry who succeeded their father in April 1509 and married his brother's widow Catherine of Aragon that June. He would go on to become England's most famous, and most notorious, king.

IV

Arthur's death heralded a new era of infectious disease in England. Along with the sweating sickness in 1485, England had seen a recurrence of the plague in 1479–80, reputedly the most virulent of the century. This was followed by another outbreak in 1499–1500 and again in 1509–1510. In January 1518, Henry VIII issued the first plague regulations. All infected homes had to be hung with a bale of hay, suspended beside the front door for at least forty days and those sufferers who dared to go out in public were to carry a white wand before them. A further peril emerged in 1514, with the first reference to smallpox in the country. Henry VIII had been ill that spring and, as Peter Martyr recorded in Spain, his physicians feared his fever would lead to an outbreak of 'variolae', derived from cow pox. Henry recovered but the disease still raged through London. On 30 June, Gerard de Pleine wrote from the city to Margaret of Savoy that it was responsible for the delay of the marriage between Princess Mary Tudor and Louis XII of France.[12] It was 1518 when the king's secretary Richard Pace told Wolsey that Henry was moving to Bisham Abbey to avoid the illness, 'for they do die in these parts in every place, not only of the small pokkes and mezils but of the great sickness.' Battles were no longer being fought on English soil but death was still a brutal reality, encountered in the streets and described in sermons or painted on the walls of churches. The sixteenth century was to see three great threats emerge to the health of England's aristocratic families. They might no longer be called upon to bear arms against their cousins, on bloody battlefields that claimed the lives of thousands of men, but they were vulnerable to the onslaught of illness, low fertility and the temper of the king. There was to be one more unexpected royal death before the century was very old.

Not long after the loss of Prince Arthur, Queen Elizabeth of York died in childbirth. Having comforted her husband with the idea of producing a new heir, she conceived quickly and was preparing to take to her chamber at Richmond as the new year of 1503 arrived. Elizabeth was approaching her thirty-seventh birthday, which made her very old for motherhood by the standards of the time, although it was by no means uncommon for women to bear children even into their early forties. However, something went wrong. Either Elizabeth miscalculated the date or the child arrived prematurely, but she was overtaken with pain and delivered her child on 2 February while she was staying at the Tower of London. The baby, a girl named Katherine, lived for only eight days, and Elizabeth followed her to the grave on 11 February, probably as the result of a post-partum infection.

The dead may have featured often in church art, prayer books, myths and stories, but there are few depictions of the process of burial outside accounts of royal interments. It could be glimpsed as one of seven images sometimes chosen by medieval artists in a series known as the Acts or Works of Mercy: feeding the hungry, clothing the naked, giving drink to the thirsty, sheltering travellers, freeing prisoners, comforting the sick and burying the dead. One interesting representation of the process of burial was created in a painted glass Acts of Mercy, in roundels in Leicester in around the year 1500. A body is shown, shrouded, tied at the legs, being lowered into a grave, with bones scattered around it. The priest stands by the grave, reading from a book held by another clergyman, sprinkling the body with holy water and touching it with the processional cross.

A widow stands to watch the burial and a benefactor holds a rosary and a lit candle. Such funerals might still have been followed by bellringing to drive away devils, prayers and feasting. One wake described in the Stonor papers involved the feeding of poor mourners with bread and cheese, while the gentlemen and priests ate roast mutton, veal, chicken and lamb. Further up the social ladder, guests were given two courses, including geese, pheasants, roast pigeon and other meats cooked in expensive spices. The funeral feast of John Trevelyan in 1492 cost 935*d*, while 1,482*d* (£6 3*s* 6*d*) was spent in wax alone to light the funeral of Lord Lisle, illegitimate son of Edward IV, in 1542.[13] A trend for aristocratic rites were set by the arrangements made for Elizabeth of York in 1503.

The first masses were said for the queen on 22 February in the little chapel of St Peter ad Vincula within the Tower walls. Then, her coffin was loaded onto a hearse fringed with black velvet, surmounted by a cross of white cloth of gold. Across the corners were laid white banners, to signify the nature of her death. It was topped by a carved effigy of the queen, dressed in robes of state over crimson satin, black and blue velvet, her long hair loose, her hands sparkling with gems, a rich crown upon her head and a sceptre in her hand. Preceded by 600 poor men, Elizabeth was carried in solemn estate from the Tower of London to Westminster Abbey, drawn by six horses in black velvet. Four gentlewomen ushers knelt on each corner of the hearse for the duration of the journey. The London streets were solemn, with local churches and landmarks wreathed in funeral colours. All along the route, the hearse was greeted and censed by leading dignitaries and prelates. Thirty-seven virgins, one for each year of her life, were dressed in white linen and wreaths of the Tudor colours, white and green, carrying lit candles, and the same number of torchbearers wore white hooded woollen gowns. More than 1,000 lights burned on the hearse, and the vaults, walls and furniture of the abbey was draped in black cloth and lit by more tapers. The guests were feasted afterwards in the queen's great chamber in Westminster Palace, the menu reflecting the fact that it was a fish day in the calendar, before a night vigil was kept over the former queen. Elizabeth was then buried temporarily in one of the side chapels until she joined her husband in the completed Lady

Chapel. Her funeral cost £2,832 7s 3d, one of the most expensive of her generation, even outstripping that of Henry himself.

Elizabeth's death had been unexpected. It left her no time to make arrangements for her immortal soul. On 16 July 1504, Henry VII made an indenture to this effect with William Warham, Archbishop of Canterbury; Richard Fox, Bishop of Winchester; John Islip, Bishop of Westminster Abbey; and the dean and chapters at St Paul's and of St Stephen's chapel in Westminster. Daily masses were to be said for the soul of the queen and her dead children, and the anniversary of her death, which was also her birthday, was to be kept throughout the king's lifetime. The entire religious community was to gather on 11 February in the choir at the abbey, or in the Lady Chapel once it was complete, where a requiem mass would be sung, bells would be rung to scare away the Devil and 100 tapers of new wax would be burned in her honour. Alms were to be distributed among the 'blind, lame, impotent and most needy'. The chapel, which had only just been begun, is perhaps the most elaborate survival of all the pre-Reformation memorial chapels, as is the bronze and black marble Renaissance tomb of Henry and Elizabeth, completed by Pietro Torrigiano. With its bronze medallions in copper gilt and cherubs supporting coats of arms, its statues of the saints and heraldic devices, it marked a new style of funerary architecture. Four candles were to burn permanently around it, with nine-foot tapers lit on special occasions. The chapel was consecrated on 19 February 1516.

The wills of the aristocracy early in the new century show just how much purgatory and prayer still mattered. In 1500, Joan, Viscountess Lisle requested that twenty-two torches be burned at her funeral, 300 shirts be provided for the poor and two 'honest and virtuous priests' pray for her soul for the space of three years. Sir William Lyttleton paid for prayers for his entire family for seven years and the annual obit of his death was held at Halesowen Monastery. In 1506, Eleanor, Lady Wyndham left a pair of silver chalices to the Augustinian friars at Norwich to buy their prayers for her, and paid for alms to be distributed on the occasions of her burial, her month's mind and year's mind. Edward Hastings left nothing to chance in November of the same year, when he required a priest to daily say a 'placebo, dirige and commendations, with mass of requiem, on the morrow … and other orisons and prayers as my executors shall appoint'.[14]

Katherine, Lady Hastings made her will on 22 November 1503. She was the daughter of Richard Neville, Earl of Salisbury and the niece of Cecily Neville, Duchess of York. Her second husband, William Hastings, had been executed by Richard III in 1483, but he had fathered her six children, all but one of them sons. Three of the boys had died young, leaving the family title to pass to Edward Hastings, born in 1466, who had himself fathered two sons by the time of his mother's death. Katherine would not live to see her grandson George marry Anne Stafford, a descendant of Humphrey and Anne Neville, but the pair produced eight children, five of whom were boys. Katherine's dynasty was established, but she needed to turn her attention to her soul in the autumn of 1503, as she passed her sixty-first birthday. The words of her will, more than mere convention, give an insight into the approach taken to death in the first part of the sixteenth century. Given her husband's unfortunate end, it is hardly surprising that she feared an unexpected death that would not allow her to prepare fully:

> I Katherine Hastings, widow, late the wife of William, Lord Hastings, having perfect memory and whole mind, considering that nothing is more certain than death, and therefore at all times to be ready unto death, and to look for the time of the coming of the same, in such wise that death steal not upon unprepared; whereunto is required not only disposition ghostly but also of such goods as God of his immeasurable goodness hath leant me the use and disposition of, intending, through his special grace, so to pass by these temporals and momentary goods, that I shall not lose eternal, make, ordain and declare this is my testament and last will.[15]

Catherine left her soul to God, to the Virgin Mary 'and to all the company of heaven', and her body to be buried in the Lady Chapel of her parish church at Ashby-de-la-Zouche, with a priest aid to pay for her soul and those of her parents and husband. St Helen's already had strong family connections, having been rebuilt from 1474 by Sir William, at the time that he was converting the nearby manor house into a castle. He may have intended to lie there himself, creating a special Hastings family chapel but, after his unexpected death, his body had been interred in St George's, Windsor. Catherine also asked that he pray for 'all Christian souls' and 'in special for those souls which I am most bounden to cause to be prayed for, for the space of three years next ensuing after my departing'. To the church in Ashby and the College at Newarke in Leicester, she left various vestments and religious artefacts, as well as lands and estates, in order to pay for a 'yearly obit' to be kept in the College for her immediate relatives 'for ever'. After that, she bequeathed her worldly goods. She died between January and March 1504.[16]

A similar approach was taken by another survivor of the turbulent wars of the previous century. Henry VII's stepfather Thomas, Lord Stanley, Earl of Derby had fathered eleven children but only seen three grow to maturity. He outlived his heir, George, who was reputedly the victim of a poisoning at a banquet, at the age of 43, which may have also claimed the life of his eldest son, so the Derby titles passed down to George's second son. Having been the lead mourner at the funeral of Queen Elizabeth the year before, Lord Stanley's health was rapidly failing by the time he came to write his will on 28 July 1504. He asked to be buried in the middle of the chapel, in the north aisle, in Burscough Priory in Lancashire, exercising as much power as he could, during life, to ensure that his plans were honoured after he had departed:

> ... of my ancestors foundation, where the bodies of my father, mother and other of my ancestors lay buried, having provided a tomb to be there placed, with the personages of myself and both my wives, for a perpetual remembrance to be prayed for, also I will that the personages which I have caused to be made for my father and mother, my grandfather and great-grandfather, shall be set in the arches within the chancel within that priory in the places provided for the same; and whereas I have before given to the said priory and convent great gifts of money, jewels and ornaments, and also done great reparations in the said priory, I nevertheless bequeath £20 to the intent that the said Prior and

convent shall be bound by their deed, sealed with their common seal, to me and my heirs, to cause one of the canons thereof to say mass in the said chapel for my soul, and for the soul of my Lady, my wife, after her decease, and for the soul of Eleanor, late my wife, and for the souls of my father, mother, ancestors, children, brethren and sisters … also for the souls of them who died in my or my father's service, and for the souls of all those I have in any wise offended, and for all Christian souls for evermore.[17]

Masses were to be said for Stanley in the parishes of Winwick and Werington for a year. He left bequests to various religious houses and paid 300 marks for the rent and toll of Werington Bridge, so it should be free for all people to cross it forever. Thomas Stanley died the day after signing his will. As with many of his peers, the elaborate instructions he left for the eternal commemoration of his soul only lasted as long as the monasteries; Burscough Priory was dissolved by his stepgrandson in 1536 and the Stanleys' chantry and tombs were lost.

The death of Henry VII in April 1509 was marked by the expected level of pomp and ceremony of a Catholic king of England. His symptoms indicate that he was in the final stages of acute tuberculosis. Having experienced mixed health for years, he had suffered from a range of respiratory problems which usually manifest as bad coughs, worsening in the spring. He was 'very ill' at Wanstead in 1503 and the following year at Eltham, before becoming dangerously unwell in October 1507, with what seems to have been tubercular symptoms. He recovered, only to fall ill again the following February, his condition exacerbated by failing eyesight and gout. The Spanish ambassador had reported in July 1508 that he was 'in the last stage of consumption', with fevers and coughing. Yet again the king had rallied for a brief respite but by 29 March 1509 Henry was forced to recognise that he was 'very ill and utterly without hope of recovery', leading him to confide in his servants that if 'it pleased God to send him a new life, they would find him a new changed man.'[18] Henry completed his thirty-seven page will on the last day of March. On Easter Sunday, 8 April, he crawled from his bed into his privy closet to receive the sacrament and on 16th, he issued a general pardon, after which he went into rapid decline. Two weeks later Henry began his final struggle, which lasted a little over twenty-four hours. A sketch was made of him on his death bed by Sir Thomas Wriothesley, Garter Knight at Arms, who recorded those waiting around his canopied bed, including clerics and physicians and those of noble blood. He died late at night on 21 April.

The king's magnificent Lady Chapel at Westminster was not finished at the time of his death, but this did not prevent Henry VII from being laid to rest there. His funeral took place on 9 May, when seven large horses in black velvet drew the chariot on which the coffin rested, covered with black cloth of gold. On top of it, Henry's effigy lay on golden cushions, dressed in his parliamentary robes, wearing the crown and carrying the orb and sceptre in its hands. Six hundred torches were carried behind him on the journey from Richmond to St George's Fields in Southwark. There, Henry's body was met by the Lords, Commons and religious figures all dressed in black and the procession travelled through the streets of London, over the bridge to St Paul's. First came the sword-bearer and vice chamberlain, followed by messengers, trumpeters and minstrels, then foreigners, ushers, chaplains and squires; after them were the aldermen and sheriffs, two heralds and Sir Edward Darrell, mounted on a horse trapped in black velvet, carrying the king's standard. But this was just the beginning. Behind them were Knights of the Bath, deans, councillors, justices, friars, canons, lords and barons. Then three knights bearing the king's helmet with crown, his harness and battle-axe, and his armour embroidered with the English arms; the Mayor of London carried his mace. Then came the hearse carrying the body, followed by the Duke of Buckingham and four earls, leading the Knights of the Garter, with Sir Thomas Brandon, Master of the Horse, leading the other gentlemen.

Henry's body stayed at St Paul's overnight, under a 'stately hearse made of wax' while sermons were read and masses performed, before heading along Fleet Street to Charing Cross, where it was censed, and on to Westminster. There, he was set in a hearse of lights as masses were said, after which the staves of office were broken and a 'sumptuous entertainment' was held in the palace. The portrait of Henry on Torrigiano's bronze cast, probably taken from his death mask, shows a man with high cheek bones and a gaunt face, his brows rounded above smallish eyes, a firm chin and flowing shoulder-length hair. The imposing tomb is a celebration and an artistic statement, a sign that the ruler fathered a dynasty, established peace and moved England into the Renaissance, away from the old-style transi tombs with their *memento mori* juxtaposition of life and death. Henry VII's final resting place marks the achievements of life, not the constant threat of death.

8

Henry Fitzroy, Duke of Somerset and Richmond (1519–36)

I

Arthur Tudor had only lived a little way into the sixteenth century. He had too brief a glimpse to get a sense of the new world that waited on the horizon. His humanist education had turned him from the French romances and Burgundian high culture of the Yorkists towards the scholarship of ancient Greece and Rome. Walking the splendid courtyards and corridors at Richmond Palace, he would have sensed the stirrings of the Renaissance, in the Italian carpets and tapestries, and the conversations of the scholars under the patronage of his grandmother. It was during the highlight of his young life, the wedding pageants of November 1501, that these influences came together, full of promise for the new century and his future reign. Yet that bud of cultural promise, which Arthur never lived to see bloom, was to come to life under the reign of his brother, in an unparalleled extravagance of riches and culture. On the jousting field, in court masques, at the Field of Cloth of Gold, and in his personal and religious iconoclasm, it was Henry VIII who stole the limelight that Arthur had vacated, who shaped a new identity for England, who was responsible for both meeting, and creating, the challenges of the sixteenth century. Primarily for Henry, this was about perpetuating his dynasty.

After fifteen years of marriage to Catherine of Aragon, Henry had to accept that his wife would never bear him the legitimate son he so desperately desired. Despite six pregnancies, stretching over nine years, the couple had produced only one surviving daughter, Princess Mary, born in 1516. What had begun as a devoted pairing, with strong physical attraction and compatibility, had been eroded by the pressure of miscarriage and infant death, so that the previously insignificant six-year age gap between the couple had become divisive. In 1525, the year that Catherine turned 40 and went through the menopause, Henry was still an energetic 34, fond of dancing, hunting and jousting, and able to father more heirs. As he investigated chapters of the Bible which suggested that marriage to a dead brother's wife would prove childless, Henry became ever more convinced that he had displeased God. Catherine had not given him a boy, so, he concluded, his marriage to her must be invalid. After all, Henry had already proved himself capable of fathering sons elsewhere. In 1525, he began to consider handing over his inheritance to his 6-year-old son, Henry Fitzroy, elevating him to an unprecedented position of influence in the Tudor court. The only problem, of course, was that Fitzroy was illegitimate.

Fitzroy was the result of a liaison Henry had with one of Catherine of Aragon's ladies in waiting. Elizabeth, or Bessie, Blount had been born around 1500 at Kinlet, in Shropshire, into a family that had affiliations with the household of Prince Arthur at Ludlow. It is highly likely that the Blounts visited the Prince and Princess of Wales there during their brief marriage, or that Arthur and Catherine paid them a visit when they were staying nearby at Tickenhill. It was common practice for young men and women of high rank to be placed in an aristocratic household, and Bessie's relatives drew on their connections to place her in the most lucrative of positions, under the protection of the queen herself. She was not the only young woman there, as a Mrs Stoner had been designated the 'mother of the maids' to oversee their conduct and training. In May 1513, she received her first year's wages, 100s, suggesting that she had formally entered court life at the age of 12.[1] Bessie was reputed to be very beautiful. In contemporary terms, her looks matched the Renaissance ideal of fair skin, blue eyes and golden hair. She was young, noble, accomplished and attractive. Henry's court was a heady place in the early years, the most exciting place for any young woman with social ambitions. It is not clear exactly when her relationship with Henry began, or how long it lasted. Writing a century later, Lord Herbert of Cherbury described the 'chains of love' that bound Henry to Bessie, 'which damsel in singing, dancing and in all goodly pastimes, exceeded all other, by the which goodly pastimes, she won the King's heart'. He went on to state that she bore him a son 'at last', which suggests the affair comprised of more than a single encounter. However, this owes much to romantic myth. All that can be stated as fact is that the pair slept together around October 1518, when their child was conceived.

Bessie disappeared from sight in the autumn of 1518. There was of course a stigma attached to unmarried mothers, and church records show that women who conceived outside of wedlock were required to ask for forgiveness in public and sometimes whipped in the marketplace for fornication. Private letters dating from the period also highlight the cases of pregnant wives whose morality was suspected, when they and their child were repudiated by the husband, although these are rare. In Bessie's case, though, there was no stigma attached to bearing the king's son. Henry's status gave her protection from the censure of society and the Church; in fact, the Church actively colluded to facilitate her lying-in. It seems that she was sent away from court less due to disapproval than discretion, as Queen Catherine had recently lost her sixth and final child.

Henry entrusted all the arrangements for his son's birth to his chief minister, the capable Thomas Wolsey. This was to establish a pattern of patronage that would last for the remainder of Wolsey's life, suggesting that he was a patron, sponsor, friend, even perhaps a godfather to Fitzroy. Bessie was taken to Essex, to the Augustinian Priory of St Laurence, at Blackmore, near Chelmsford. The prior, Thomas Goodwin, who had held his position since 1513, was someone Wolsey felt could be trusted to lodge the expectant mother in his own medieval moated house known as Jericho, close to the church. The priory was dissolved in 1524 but the nave still exists as part of the church, while the house was rebuilt or redeveloped into the private property that stands beside it today. Bessie gave birth to a healthy boy in the summer of 1519, in June or July. It was probably no coincidence that Henry stayed in Essex that summer, just 10 miles to the south-west at Havering atte Bowe, then at Beaulieu, 12 miles to the east, both of which were close enough to enable a discreet visit to his newborn son.

Henry Fitzroy's early years passed quietly. He may have been raised by his mother, who was married off to Gilbert Tailboys, whom she bore two other children in the 1520s. It is plausible that during these years, Fitzroy was part of their nursery at Kyme, in Lincolnshire, but there is also a chance that he was raised in the household of his half-sister, Princess Mary. In 1519, the 3-year-old Mary's household was rearranged and her old governess, Margaret Bryan, was replaced. Seventeen years later, in 1536, Margaret wrote in a letter that she had 'been a mother to the children his grace have had since'. At that point, Henry VIII had fathered only one other legitimate child – Elizabeth, by Anne Boleyn – but Margaret's use of the plural 'children' suggests the presence of at least one other. This can only have been Henry Fitzroy. Perhaps both options are correct, and he resided in Lincolnshire part of the time, while his royal blood facilitated regular visits to London, where he was under Margaret's care, and also a guest at Durham Place, the residence of his mentor, Thomas Wolsey. He received some formal education, as his later tutor would complain about the way he had been taught to speak Latin.

It was not until he reached his sixth birthday that little Henry received much official attention, and then he burst upon the Tudor scene with a glut of honours and titles. The timing was significant, for he had reached the age of transition, when young boys generally left their female-oriented nursery in favour of a male-run establishment, and had survived the dangerous, often fatal early years of childhood. Analyses of Tudor mortality indicate that if a child survived birth, the first year had the highest incidence of premature death, followed by a different set of threats encountered between the ages of 1 and 5. If children reached 5, they had a fairly good chance of making it into their teens, which were the next area of greatest peril.[2] It was also in this critical year, 1525, that Henry's father was coming to the realisation that he would have no more children by his first wife, Catherine of Aragon. She had not fallen pregnant since before Fitzroy's birth and, as her fortieth birthday approached, it appears that this was the year that she experienced her menopause.

By May that year, Henry was already planning to raise his son's profile. A note written to the king by Wolsey indicates that heraldic arms had been devised for the boy, featuring the white lion of Richmond and the silver yale of Somerset, flanking a central escutcheon that featured a castle and the heads of two bucks, representing Nottingham. The boy's status was revealed by the silver line scoring through the arms of England and France, denoting illegitimacy. This combination, along with the motto 'duty binds me', virtually interchangeable with that of former royals, indicates exactly what the king's intentions were. Soon, they would be revealed to the world.

The most important day in the young boy's life so far was 18 June 1525. It was quite plausibly his sixth birthday. It began early in the morning at Wolsey's Durham House, where Fitzroy and a company of other gentlemen took to barges for the trip to newly completed Bridewell Palace. There, he was conducted along a gallery that flanked the privy garden to the king's apartments on the second floor of the inner courtyard. Senior members of the court had gathered to witness the process by which Henry was to be ennobled; Wolsey was present, along with the other two dukes in the realm, Norfolk and Suffolk, the earls of Worcester, Northumberland and Shrewsbury, Sir Thomas Boleyn and representatives of the Church. Fitzroy was dressed in the robes of an earl and accompanied by the earls of Oxford and Arundel as he knelt before his father. Henry placed a girdle around his neck and Thomas More read aloud the patent that conferred the earldom of Nottingham upon the boy, with an annuity of £20.[3] After this, Fitzroy retired from the chamber and returned in the robes of a duke, with a procession of nobles carrying his train, sword, cap of estate and rod of gold. The same process was repeated, only this time Fitzroy was granted the dukedoms of Richmond and Somerset.[4] From that point forward, he would be referred to in official documentation as the 'right high and noble prince Henry, Duke of Richmond and Somerset'. A double dukedom in such circumstances was unprecedented.

This ennoblement of an illegitimate son had undeniable dynastic significance. The most recent precedent was the elevation of Henry II's son William Longsword to an earldom, way back at the end of the twelfth century. The conferring of such favour upon Fitzroy seems to suggest that, until the king fathered a surviving male child within a marriage, he was considering Fitzroy his heir. In certain circumstances, legitimacy could be conferred retrospectively, although this was unusual. It is interesting, therefore, that Henry VIII chose to give his son the Duchy of Somerset, traditionally held by the Beaufort family. This established a connection between the boy and his great-great-great-great-grandfather, John of Gaunt, whose four children had been legitimised despite being born before their parents' marriage. Nor had they initially been barred from inheriting the throne, as that all-important clause was added later, and might equally have been revoked by an Act of Parliament. But this was not all. In addition to his earldom and double dukedom, Fitzroy was made Captain of the Town and Castle of Berwick upon Tweed, Keeper of the City and Castle of Carlisle, Warden General of the Scottish Marshes, High Steward of the Bishopric of Durham, High Steward of the Liberties of the Archbishop of York and Lord High Admiral of England.

A few other children of royal blood were elevated at the same time as Fitzroy that summer, perhaps with the intention to create ties of affinity, a future support network, as was frequently done when legitimate heirs went through a rite of passage. There was Henry Courtenay, Earl of Devonshire, then in his twenties, a grandson of Edward IV through his daughter Katherine, who was given the title Marquis of Exeter. Henry Brandon, son of Henry's sister Mary and Charles, Duke of Suffolk, became Earl of Lincoln, taking John de la Pole's old title, despite the fact that he was only 2. The slightly older Sir Thomas Manners, Lord Roos, the great nephew of Edward IV, took the former title of Edmund, Earl of Rutland, while the rising diplomatic star of the court, Thomas Boleyn, became Viscount Rochford.[5]

Fitzroy's elevation in status demanded a household worthy of a duke. His ordinances and expenses were drawn up on 24 July, giving a glimpse into the fabric of the boy's daily life, his food and meals, his pastimes and expectations. Over the course of forty-two days in June and July, Henry's establishment cost a total of just over £523. Almost £12 was claimed by the bakehouse and pastry, £36 for the buttery, £53 for the slaughterhouse, £52 for the poultry, £15 for the grocer and £118 for the chandlery and saucer. He also had to shoulder some of the cost of his own ennoblement, paying out £33 for his installation and £35 for board and wages for his servants at Windsor and Hampton Court. The writing and sealing of his patents of creation was undertaken by a Master Pexsall, for which he received £13 6s 8d. Henry also received a new pair of virginals at 40s.[6]

It was important that the boy looked the part, and the same went for his home and those in his household. Just over £12 was spent on a 'vestment' of purple velvet and cloth of gold, with a cross of crimson tissue, which must have featured in the ceremonies of 18 June. Henry's footmen were kitted out in blue and yellow doublets at a cost of £32, while the liveries for his councillors, gentlemen and servants ran to £513. The horses in Henry's stable were decked out in black velvet with gilt reins, copper buckles and gold and silk buttons. Wolsey had given him a litter to travel in, which was garnished in cloth of silver. For his chapel, two new altar cloths were delivered, made of blue bawdkyn, lined with green buckram and fringed with silk. Fitzroy's wardrobe expenses of £1,193 did not fall far behind those of Princess Mary, who required £1,600 for the same period.[7]

The king also set out what and when his important son should be eating. The menu for dinner and supper might include green geese, roast capons or veal, swan or partridge, half a lamb or kid, pigeons and wildfowl, with custard, tart or fruit. The first main meal of the day was taken around mid- to late morning, and cost around 20s, and a more substantial supper (35s) following around four or five in the afternoon. Different recommendations were made for different times of the year, first divided between Michaelmas, at the end of September, to Shrovetide in February, as well as a specific fast diet for Lent, Fridays and Saturdays. This included salt and fresh salmon, cod, turbot, shrimps and ling, as might be expected, but also baked meats and butter, at a cost of 45s a day. Spices for a day cost 20d and wax and white lights 8d. Specific requirements were set down for Fitzroy's staff, each of whom was allotted a number of dishes according to rank. His chancellor, chamberlain and others of similar standing might dine on two courses of roast veal or goose, venison and wine at 6s per day, while his yeomen had one serving of beef, baked meats and ale; the grooms were not even permitted baked meats. Senior members of his court were provided with three and a half yards of cloth, costing 8d a yard, for their clothing; grooms and pages received three yards of lower-quality material, which cost only 3s 4d.[8] The accounts tell us that the boy had two cloths of estate, that one of his four chairs was decorated with a cloth of gold, that he had four large and twenty small carpets, and a scarlet counterpoint and eight pillows on his bed.[9]

Fitzroy's household were dressed in blue, yellow and white, emblazoned with his badge of a half-lion bursting out of a Tudor rose, edged in gold. Living away from both his parents, those who served, advised and taught him on a daily basis were the closest thing the boy had to a family. In many ways, this presents a convincing parallel to the experience of a Prince of Wales in peacetime, with Henry being raised in a separate establishment, apart from any half-siblings or close relatives, in preparation for his future role, just as Edward V and Prince Arthur had been. Many of those appointed to his household were already Wolsey's men, and it was he who would oversee the establishment, from a distance. In the boy's closest circle were Brian Higdon, Dean of York from 1516 to 1539, head of his council; Thomas Magnus, Archdeacon of East Riding, Canon of Windsor from 1520, surveyor and General Receiver; Sir William Bulmore, Lieutenant of the East March, steward of his household; Sir Godfrey Fulgeham or Foljambe, esquire of the king's body in 1513, his treasurer; Sir Thomas Tempest, a serjeant at law who was the household controller; William Parr was the Chamberlain and Richard Page his Vice Chamberlain. Henry's first formal tutor was John Palsgrave, who had also taught the king's sister, Mary, while he received lessons in music and dancing from William Saunders. Sir Thomas Fairfax was his serjeant at law, George Lawson was cofferer, Sir William Eure and William Frankeleyn, Archdeacon of Durham were among his councillors, Walter Luke was general attorney, Dr Tate his almoner, Richard Cotton the clerk comptroller and his Master of the Horse was Edward Seymour. He had a nurse, Anne Partridge, who received 50s a quarter for her wages and was permitted a maid of her own.[10] With these appointments, everything was in place for the boy to begin his life as a great magnate.

II

With these important decisions made, Fitzroy said goodbye to his father at Hampton Court and began the long journey to his new home. He was not sent to Ludlow, where the education of a Prince of Wales traditionally took place. That was reserved for Henry's only legitimate child to date, Princess Mary, who set off for the Welsh Borders around the same time as Fitzroy went north, to the castle of Sheriff Hutton. The journey is documented in detail, as the king was anxious to see how his son would be received outside London circles. Their first stop was at the home of Sir William Jekyll at Stoke Newington in Middlesex, which they left on 26 July for the residence of Lady Maud Parr in Northampton, 70 miles away. There he was 'marvellously well intreated and had good cheer', and was gifted a 'grey, ambling nag'.[11] At Northampton, Fitzroy's household bade farewell to their main escort, which returned to London, then they travelled east through Buntingford and Shengay before they reached Huntingdon, Cambridgeshire. There, a Dr Hall was waiting to greet them outside the town and 'the honest men of the town presented unto his grace, four great pikes and four tenches.'[12] While staying at Huntingdon, perhaps in the castle, Fitzroy received the gifts of 'swans, cranes and other wild fowl' from the nearby Abbot of Ramsey. After resting at Huntingdon, the party headed north, staying at the home of a George Kirkham on 31 July, before reaching Collyweston Place, the former home of Fitzroy's great-grandmother, Margaret Beaufort, to whom he was now connected through the Duchy of Somerset.

Part of a letter written by members of Fitzroy's council to Wolsey from Collyweston on 2 August relates that 'on the way he killed a buck himself in Clyff Park, where David Cecil made him good cheer'. The boy preferred not to ride in the litter that had been provided for him by Wolsey: he 'rode nott in his horse litter, but only … a three or four myles … but ever sythens his grace hathe ryden upon his hobye [pony] and hathe been very well at ease'.[13] Henry was also enjoying good health, being 'in better case and more lusty of his boddy than his grace was at first taking of his journey'. To be sure that this would continue, the boy's council requested that Wolsey remembered to 'send a phisician unto my lords grace, for the preservation of his person'.[14] Collyweston was now Henry's own property, and while he stayed there for a week, he received more presents of wildfowl for his table, from the abbots of Peterborough and Crowland. They were back on the road again on 7 August, passing through Grantham and Marton Abbey, before they arrived in the city of York, just over 100 miles north of the Beaufort property. At York they were joined by John Uvedale, a clerk in the signet office, whom Wolsey had appointed as the boy's secretary. Fitzroy stayed in the city for eleven days before embarking on the final 10 miles of his journey, accompanied by a delegate of local dignitaries, reaching the castle of Sheriff Hutton on 29 August.[15]

What Fitzroy saw when he approached his new home was a large castle set in an impressive park which had reverted to the crown upon the death of the Duke of Norfolk in 1524. It was described by the antiquarian John Leland in the 1540s as being 'well maintained' and comprising a base court containing the offices of the establishment, before the castle entrance, which did not have a ditch or moat, but stood on high ground. The front face of the building had three great towers, the central one being the gatehouse. Within, in the second 'area' of the castle, Leland counted five or six towers, with impressive stairs leading up to the great hall. The hall itself, and the rest of the building, were so splendid that he considered there to be 'no house in the North so like princely lodgings'.[16] Presumably it had changed little, or only for the better, since Richard III had lodged Edward, Earl of Warwick and

Elizabeth of York there in the 1480s, or since the poet John Skelton had praised its beautiful grounds while staying as a guest of the Duke of Norfolk.

Over the next few months, details emerged about Fitzroy's residency at the castle. Primarily, his main concern was to continue with his formal education, under the guidance of John Palsgrave, who claimed that he had never had a pupil equal to the duke, 'no man, rich or poor, had ever better wit'.[17] The draft of a letter the tutor wrote to the king promises that 'according to my saying to you in the gallery at Hampton Court, I do my uttermost best to cause him to love learning and to be merry at it, in so much that without any manner of fear or compulsion he hath already a great furtherance in the principles grammatical both Greek and Latin.' He also reported the boy's tendency to lisp, which he put this down to his age: 'I trust now at the changing of his teeth to amend that default, but much might have been done thereunto at the beginning.'[18] Palsgrave was also in contact with Sir Thomas More, discussing with him his decisions regarding the boy's syllabus. A draft letter recounts Henry's progress:

> Has already, however, taught him the principles of grammar, both in Greek and Latin, and made him read the First Eclogue of Virgil, 'and two of the first scenes of Adelphorum, which he can pronounce right prettily; but I find Quintilian and Erasmus true, for the barbarous tongue of him that taught him his matins is and hath been a great hindrance to me.

Councillor William Frankeleyn reported to Wolsey that:

> my lord of Richmond is a chylde of excellent wisdom and towardness; and, for his good and quyk capacity, retentive memorie, vertuous inclinasion to all honour, humanity and goodness, I think hard it wolbe to fynde any creature lyving of twise his age able of worthy to be compared to him. How his grace used himself in dispeaching mr almoner and with what gravitie and good maner he desyred to be reccommendid unto the Kingis highness, the quene and your grace, I doubt not but the said mr almoner will advertyse your grace at his coming.[19]

Frankeleyn added that he was to attend a local court of Oyer and Terminer the following day in Pontefract before beginning a survey of the boy's lands at Sheriff Hutton.[20] With the business of local government out of the way, the survey revealed some necessary repairs to the place, prompting £234 to be paid to a Robert Forest for carrying out improvements to the walls, towers and roof, sweeping the chimneys and replacing the gates.[21] Local dignitaries visited the castle to pay their respects: 'all the noble men and other worshipful men of all these north counties daily resorted to his lordship in great number', and Henry was 'as highly esteemed in honour as ever was any young prince in these parts'. Wolsey could hardly overlook the parallel that Henry's council was drawing with the Yorkist princes.

As was the practice among the households of noblemen, a number of other boys were included in Fitzroy's entourage and shared his lessons. There was his chamberlain's 12-year-old nephew, William Parr, whose sister would become Henry VIII's last wife, along with Bessie Blount's young brothers, George and Henry. Palsgrave's letters highlight the downside of this arrangement, as some members of the household were actively anti-intellectual, believing that 'learning is a great hindrance to a nobleman' and 'call[ing] upon [Henry] to bring his mind from learning, some to hear cry at a hare, some to kill a buck with his bow, sometime with greyhounds and sometime with buckhounds ... some to see a flight with a hawk, some to ride a horse'.[22] Palsgrave's was a thankless task and his annual salary of £13 6s 8d was insufficient for his needs.

Palsgrave's correspondence reveals that Fitzroy's mother was also involved in the boy's education. One surviving letter establishes that Bessie Blount, now married to Gilbert Tailboys, was taking more of an active interest in his life than historians have previously suspected. The tutor thanked her for her 'favourable letter' and feared he would not 'abide' longer, or continue in his position 'if her Ladyship were not good to him'. His frank response is a mixture of report and plea, complaint and praise, illustrating the difficulties of his position:

Has suffered greatly since coming to Yorkshire, both from poverty and calumny. Six sundry articles have been contrived against him, in some of which her Ladyship was as guilty as he. It is but a sorry promotion, having foregone, in less than a twelvemonth, half what he has had in all his life, and got more trouble to defend his poor honesty than ever honest man had. Is determined, however, not 'to be a knowyn thereof to no creature' but her Ladyship, but to persevere. Would not have mentioned it even to her, but that she might 'substantially provide that the especial gifts of grace which God hath given unto my lord of Richmond's grace, far above that which you yourself could think, be not by malicious and evil-disposed persons corrupted.' 'But, Madam, to be plain with you, on my conscience my lord of Richmond is of as good a nature, as much inclined to all manner virtuous and honorable inclinations, as any babes living. Now is my room undoubted great about him; for the King's grace said unto me, in the presence of Master Parre and Master Page, 'I deliver,' quod he, "unto you three, my worldly jewel; you twain to have the guiding of his body, and thou, Palsgrave, to bring him up in virtue and learning."' If, therefore, there be not faith and honesty in him, the King is much deceived in him, and the child's morals are in danger; but if others contrive matters against him in his presence, as though he were guilty, 'the babes shall begin to despise me or ever he know me.' Begs her to come hither, and inquire the truth for herself. All these despites arise from his poverty. Need not remind her how many bishops would be glad to grant her advowsons. Has fallen into a sore tertian fever.[23]

Henry's description of his son as 'my worldly jewel' is a telling metaphor which underlines the boy's personal and dynastic potential in the 1520s. As for the boy's mother, Bessie does not appear to have been at court during this time, and if she was resident on her husband's estates at South Kyme, Lincolnshire, she would have been 100 miles south of Sheriff Hutton and just 80 miles from Pontefract. Both were within visiting distance, but no record survives to suggest whether she made the journey.

The household was preparing for Fitzroy's first Christmas season in his new home. William Amyas had been dispatched to London to order New

Year's gifts for the boy to give to the king and queen, his sister Mary, the dukes of Norfolk and Suffolk and the marquises of Exeter and Dorset. Gifts were dispatched from court in return, including a gilt ewer with a star and the royal arms upon the cover from the king and a garter of crown gold from Wolsey.[24] On Christmas day, the Council at Sheriff Hutton wrote to Wolsey that 'your honourable young and tender godsonne my lord of Richemounde is at this present time … in good and prosperous helthe and as towardly a yong prince as has even been seen in our tyme.'[25] The boy had humbly asked, while the letter was being composed, for his godfather's daily blessing and 'the contynuance of your gracious favour towards him'.[26] Expense accounts of that year include payments for players and minstrels who, no doubt, were busy at Sheriff Hutton that Christmas.

In 1526, Dr Richard Croke replaced Palsgrave as Fitzroy's tutor and tensions began to arise between him and members of the Council. Croke had studied with Erasmus in Paris, and taught Greek at the universities of Leipzig and Cambridge, becoming a doctor of divinity at the latter. He also complained that Fitzroy was being encouraged to neglect his work in favour of outdoor pursuits, and that the boys were being influenced against him (Croke), insulting him and openly calling him rogue, fool and bastard.[27] When Croke threatened to discipline Fitzroy, the pupil replied that if he was beaten, he would beat Croke in return. The new tutor wrote to Henry VIII on 1 February 1527, complaining about 'misreports against himself' and stating that the clerk comptroller Sir George Cotton was committing fraud, incurring additional expenses by 'entertaining friends and servants above their allowance. In fact, Wolsey's carefully planned regime was being ignored while Fitzroy spent more time with Cotton than with Croke, being entertained by fools singing bawdy songs instead of studying.[28] He added that William Parr, Fitzroy's chamberlain, had been absent for sixty-six weeks 'and when present has seldom given attendance, but spent his time in hawking and hunting'.[29]

Croke begged Wolsey to send direction to the Council regarding the amount of time the boy should spend at his lessons and that he should not be interrupted, and also that he should not be required by Cotton to write letters after dinner 'to the dulling of his wits, spirits and memory, and no little hurt of his head, stomach and body'.[30] One letter Fitzroy did write that March was to his father, 'too show him his progress in writing and to ask the King's blessing and pardon for having so long forborne to write'. Perhaps in response to the disharmony around his tutor, the duke told his father he would 'endeavour to obtain learning and virtue correspondent to his advancement'.[31] He also found time to correspond with Wolsey, insisting that 'no creature living is more bound to his favour than he'.[32]

The following Christmas, Fitzroy's household was at Pontefract. The Council informed Wolsey that he had 'kept a right honourable Christmas' and that 'numbers of worshipful persons have come to visit him.' By 14 January, he had resumed his studies, and William Saunders was proving to be 'very diligent in teaching [him] singing and playing on the virginals'.[33] On the same day, Henry wrote to thank his father for his New Year's gift. That February, an examination into the duke's household, perhaps in response to Richard Croke's criticisms, prompted a downscaling, the Council deciding that the 'best means to lessen the charge of ... Richmond's household' was 'to discharge a number of his servants and diminish the wages of others'. Eighteen members of the household were given their leave, 'some for offences and others as superfluous' in the hope that the duke 'may be able to live on the lands and revenues assigned him by the King, amounting to upwards of £4,000'.[34] They had now completed 'good and formal books of [the] household' and all was 'in marvellous good order'.

Early in 1527, Fitzroy took the step of making contact with King James V of Scotland. The boys were cousins, as James was the son of Henry VIII's elder sister Margaret, born in 1512, making him 14 to Fitzroy's 8. James had inherited the throne at the age of seventeen months, after the death of his father at Flodden Field. Their exchange highlights not only their close blood relation but also the possibility for their futures, as two powerful rulers. Even if Fitzroy's chances of being named England's heir were slim, he could still expect to play a significant political role during the reign of his sister Mary, probably in the north and along the borders. Establishing friendly relations with James was thus a wise diplomatic move. Perhaps at some future point, Henry might even require James's support. On 11 February 1527, Fitzroy wrote to James from Pontefract Castle, having understood that the young Scottish king desired 'three or four couple of hounds for hunting the fox' and was sending him 'ten couple that he has tried', along with Nicholas Eton, his yeoman of the hunt, who was to remain in Scotland a month 'to show the mode of hunting'.[35] James thanked his cousin for 'his honest present' and sent him in return 'two brace of hounds for deer and smaller beasts', along with the promise of 'some of the best red hawks in the realm' if Fitzroy took pleasure in hawking.[36] James also wrote to thank Thomas Magnus, the Receiver General at Sheriff Hutton, for making 'the acquentence … betuix us and our tender cousin the duk of Richemonde'.[37] In turn, Magnus recounted the friendship to Wolsey and hoped that 'peace would be promoted among the Lords by him, and by the Queen [Margaret] being with her son'.[38]

The question of Fitzroy's marriage arose the same year. Henry was considering marrying his daughter Mary to the Emperor Charles V. The emperor was already married, to Isabella of Portugal, but her health was frail and he was already looking at the options available to him should be become a widower: his 'wife expects to be confined in June, but she is so weak that the doctors fear she will die, and if so, he wishes to marry the princess Mary, as his people urged him to marry his present wife and not the Princess, as the latter was so young'. While he was thinking about matches, Charles offered the daughter of his sister Eleanor of Austria 'to the Duke of Richmond, with a dowry of 300,000 or 400,000 ducats'. This was the wealthy Infanta Maria, born in 1521, her father's only heir to the Kingdom of Portugal. According to ambassadors Lee and Ghinucci, there was good reason to believe that Fitzroy's future prospects would be impressive:

> he proposed to give the Duke of Richmond 'who is near of his blood and of excellent qualities, and is already furnished to keep the state of a great prince, and yet may be easily by the King's means exalted to higher things,' to some noble princess of near blood to the Emperor, to strengthen the bond between them.

The emperor also hinted that he might bestow the Duchy of Milan upon Fitzroy, a scheme which pleased Wolsey greatly. Writing to the English ambassadors in Spain in September 1527, he added a postscript in code, asking them to 'call upon the matter of the Duke of Richmont's marriage to the dowghter of Portingale and the gyfte of the duchy of Mylayn in contemplacion of the same marriage, setting forth in suche wise and such matter as the French ambassadors take no jealousy or suspicion thereby'.[39] But the Milanese duchy from the emperor never materialised and nor was Charles in a position to remarry. Isabel of Portugal bore him a son, Philip, that May, and went on to have five more pregnancies.

Another attractive candidate on the marriage market was Catherine de Medici, known as the 'Pope's niece', who had been born in April 1519, making her just months older than Fitzroy. A rich heiress after the death of her parents, Catherine's hand was sought by the Scottish and French, raising her value in the eyes of Henry VIII, as well as offering some Italian Renaissance glamour. This potential match emerges from a letter written to Wolsey by John Russell in Rome, who had been urging the pope that if he 'would marry her to have good alliance, we knew where he should bestow her better than any that is yet rehearsed, upon a duchy in England that might spend as much as two as the best of them'.[40] It was around this time that a rumour emerged that the king was considering making Fitzroy King of Ireland, raising his status sufficiently to overshadow the taint of illegitimacy that might mar the chances of such an important match. It may be that his intention was to influence the pope, to whom Henry just sent a substantial gift of 30,000 crowns,[41] but the Irish plan was never taken to fruition.

Life in Fitzroy's household continued as before. In December 1527, the Earl of Northumberland wrote to Wolsey after visiting the boy at Pontefract, where he was 'so well received that his dulled wit cannot disclose how much he was gratified with the Duke's good qualities'.[42] A month later, Fitzroy wrote to his father that he was giving 'his whole mind to such sciences and feats of learning as he is informed stand with Henry's pleasure', and requested a harness for his exercise in arms 'according to his learning in Julius Caesar, in which he hoped to prosper as well as he had done in other learnings'.[43] He also felt able to make a request of the king regarding one of his servants, in April 1528, asking for the referral of his old chaplain Sir William Swallow to the living of Fremyngton in Devonshire, which was in Richmond's gift, but required the king's favour to conclude.[44]

In May, Fitzroy and his household were staying at Pontefract Castle when outbreaks of the sweating sickness were recorded in the town. William Parr wrote to Wolsey that, thankfully, the young duke was in good health, but that 'there bee six persones lately disseassed within the lordship of Pountefrete … and that many young childrene bee sicke of the pokkes nere thereabouts'. The Council had agreed to remove their charge to 'Ledestone', a house belonging to the prior of Pontefract, 3 miles away from the castle. This was Ledston Hall, or the manor that stood on the present site of the later hall. The oldest part of the building dates to the eleventh century with a thirteenth-century chapel dedicated to St Thomas. It was here that Fitzroy retreated from an illness that understandably terrified the king, after it had claimed the life of his elder brother. Parr went on to describe the symptoms of the dead, saying they were 'takene with a great cold, and after that strikene into a fervent heat and sweting, whereupon their righte myendes were takne from theym and soo died'. The chamberlain pleaded for a doctor to be sent to them, asking the king to consider 'what great daunger it is for my said lorde in this tyme of such straunge infirmyties to bee dititute of a phisicion'.[45] Initially, Henry's own doctor, Sir William Butts, had been assigned to the boy, and he would attend him later in life, but he was clearly not present at Ledston. Thomas Magnus reported to the king that the boy was attended by only five people, in great comfort, free of sickness.[46] Henry himself had retired from court and was living in the countryside at Wolsey's manor of Tittenhanger, in Hertfordshire, following the death of one of his closest friends at court, Sir William Compton.

Fitzroy's precautionary move to Ledston was a sensible one. That July, he wrote to thank his father for letters and the 'goodly apparel' he had sent and promised to 'apply [him]self to learning and proceed in virtue'.[47] Among these gifts were a golden unicorn horn (a narwhal tooth) set with pearls and turquoise and a gold collar with seven white enamel roses.[48] By October, the household had returned to Sheriff Hutton, where Magnus informed Wolsey that 'my Lord of Richmond is in good health and merry.' The boy also wrote to his father that he had 'paste this last sommere withoute any perelle or daunger off the ragious swete that hath reigned in these partis … and myche the better I truste with the help off suche preservatives as your highnes did sende unto me'.[49] He had recently paid a visit for one night to the Duke of Northumberland, 'who pressed him to come and see his house at Topcliff, and [Henry] conducted himself more like a man than a child of his tender age'.[50] Soon afterwards, the Earl and Countess of Westmorland visited Sheriff Hutton. The Fourth Earl, Ralph Neville, was a relation of Fitzroy's great-grandmother, Cecily Neville of Raby, and this connection underpinned the couple's decision to leave their young son Henry, aged 3, to reside at Sheriff Hutton. The accounts for March 1529 indicate that a chain and garter of crown gold were made for Fitzroy, weighing twenty ounces and costing £3, along with three gold links for which the goldsmith was paid £8. This may have been a sign that his life was about to change.

III

In 1529, Henry Fitzroy was recalled from the north to his father's court. He left on 16 June, a date which is likely to have been around his tenth birthday. His return was scarcely remarked upon because of the immense upheaval that overshadowed it, the news concerning what had been his father's two closest relationships. Firstly, the king had reached the decision that his marriage to Catherine of Aragon was no longer viable since, after six pregnancies, she had only produced a single daughter and had now passed the age of childbearing. Henry had fallen in love with Anne Boleyn, the daughter of the ambassador to France and the Low Countries, Viscount Rochford, Sir Thomas Boleyn. For the last two years, while Fitzroy had been in the north, Henry had been attempting to dissolve his marriage through papal intervention and the judgement of the European universities. At the end of May 1529, a long-awaited court was opened at Blackfriars, presided over by cardinals Campeggio and Wolsey, which the king hoped would pronounce the union invalid. One result of this would be the potential birth of a legitimate male heir to Henry and Anne, which would considerably affect Fitzroy's status and future.

However, the court failed to deliver and a scapegoat for the king's frustrations was found in Thomas Wolsey. Having alienated Anne Boleyn, the cardinal was accused of deliberately prolonging the proceedings and serving the needs of the pope over those of the king. He was removed from office and surrendered much of the wealth and properties he had accrued through years of service, before fleeing to York, where he retained the position of archdeacon. This was a fundamental change for Fitzroy, whose entire life until that point had fallen under his godfather's remit, from practical arrangements and patronage to fatherly guidance and protection. Henry probably decided that this was a good time for the boy to leave his childhood arrangements behind and take a more active role in politics. On 22 June, he had been appointed Lord Lieutenant of Ireland, governing at a distance over a body of three men drawn from the Irish Privy Council. It was a title that the king himself had held at the age of 3, another indicator that Henry intended his son to follow his path unless he had a legitimate heir. Then, on 9 August, the young duke was summoned to his father's fifth Parliament, which came to be known as the Reformation Parliament, scheduled to sit that autumn. Another important reason for the king to disband of Fitzroy's household and bring him to court at such a volatile time, must have been to remove the boy from Wolsey's control. It may also have been designed to demonstrate the king's ability to bear healthy male sons while God had denied them to Catherine. Thus, Fitzroy was an argument Henry hoped to deploy to prove the invalidity of a match made with the wife of his dead brother, Arthur.

On 3 November, the Reformation Parliament met at Blackfriars, removing to Westminster the following day on account of the plague in the city. Richmond's name is not included in the roll of initial attendees, although his former treasurer William Parr and his stepfather Gilbert

Tailboys attended. Exactly what role the boy played in the proceedings, or if he attended at all, is unclear. His proximity to his father, and the death of Wolsey, means that the supply of letters dries up and few insights into his life survive from this period. Instead, he is included in the rolls on official occasions, such as the Order of the Garter celebrations at Windsor the following April. That month the royal accounts record 20s paid to Guillaum, the king's fletcher, 'for arrows for my lord of Richmond', and 40s paid to his nurse.[51] The Venetian ambassador commented that the duke was 'a youth of great promise so much does he resemble his father'. French ambassador Jaoquim de Vaux went further and provided a description of Fitzroy at his father's court:

> The Duke of Richmond is here, a most handsome, urbane, and learned young gentleman, very dear to the King on account of his figure, discretion, and good manners. He has been summoned by the King from York, where he has been living nearly five years. He is certainly a wonderful lad for his age. He commends himself most humbly to your Majesty, saying he wishes to be a good Frenchman, and to make himself the servant of the Dauphin.[52]

Fitzroy may well have been a guest at Greenwich over the Christmas period of 1529, or at New Year, when his father gifted him a two-handled cup with a cover, engraved with flowers and serpents, two little gilt pots and a great, flat standing cup.[53] He also received gifts from others after his arrival in London, especially of horses, which were shrewd gestures of loyalty to a young man likely to play a significant part in England's future.

Briefly, another path was considered for Fitzroy. Wolsey privately admitted to Cardinal Campeggio that the king was considering a marriage between the boy and his half-sister Mary. The medieval Church would not have considered this as scandalous as it appears today. Sex between half-siblings, even full siblings for purposes of procreation only, was considered preferable to fornication between two unrelated individuals. Dispensations could be obtained, although these could not protect against possible health problems inherited by their children. Pope Clement was even prepared to issue the necessary paperwork, if it would secure the Tudor succession and prevent England from breaking with Rome. But such a match was not an ideal solution and perhaps speaks more of Henry's despair at the lack of progress towards an annulment, than any real intention. The scheme was quickly dropped; it may have been a suggestion of Wolsey's as it appears to have died with his career.

A further point in the struggle between Catholic beliefs about the afterlife and the reformed faith was marked in 1529 by the publication of Thomas More's *Supplication of the Souls*. Written in response to Simon Fish's *Supplication of the Beggars,* it purports to speak with the voices of souls in purgatory, who argue against Fish's rejection of its existence and pleads for prayers and pity for the dead. In emotive terms, it opens with a vivid description of the torments of limbo and a reminder of those who had been lost, who now felt abandoned:

> In most piteous wise continually calleth and crieth upon your devout charity and most tender pity for help, comfort and relief , your late acquaintance, kindred, spouses, companions, play-fellows and friends and no your humble and unacquainted and half-forgotten suppliants poor prisoners of God, the sely (helpless) souls in purgatory, here abiding and enduring the grievous pains and hot cleansing fire that fretteth and burneth out the rusty and filthy spots of our sin, till the mercy of Almighty God, the rather by your good and charitable means vouchsafe to deliver us hence.

Until now, declared the souls, they had been remembered by kind people, 'recommended unto God and ease, helped and relieved' through private prayers, daily masses and 'other ghostly suffrages'. But since there had lately 'sprungen up certain seditious people' who laboured to destroy them and deprive them of their comfort, the souls pleaded with the living to read More's tract 'as an wholesome treacle at your heart against the deadly poison of their pestilent persuasion that would bring you in that error to ween there were no purgatory'. Those who rejected the notion, stated More, had been deceived by the Devil. In the coming years, the scholar would clash with Henry VIII over his break with Rome and eventually lose his head for refusing to swear the 1534 Act of Supremacy placing Henry at the head of the new Church of England.

Fitzroy's stepfather Gilbert Tailboys died on 15 April 1530, becoming one of those 'helpless souls' requiring the prayers of the living. He left no known will, which suggests that his end was unexpected and he ran out of time. It may well have been that, at the age of 32 or 33, he suffered an accident, poisoning or the sudden onset of illness. Tailboys was buried near the pulpit of Kyme Church, in Lincolnshire, but no tomb survives and he is now remembered by a stone slab erected in 1905. It was a unique time to die, on the cusp of a new era in which centuries of beliefs were about to swept away in favour of new approaches. Those drawing up their last testaments and considering how to bestow their worldly goods faced critical questions about the destinations of their souls in the light of the debate highlighted in texts like those of Fish and More. Wills written during the 1520s and early years of the 1530s capture something of this transitional mood. William Cousyn asked his brother in 1522 to 'bury me as he shall thinke best', with twenty poor men carrying torches and £10 to be distributed as alms, although he wanted 'no month's mind' except one memorial within fifteen days. Thomas Rydowte was still leaving sums of money to local churches in the Bath area in 1524, to be dedicated to certain saints, while four years later, priest Richard Wollman left detailed instructions for poor children and prisoners to say a dirge and priests to sing for seven years at the grave of his mother. The will of John Hakehad, Canon of Wells Cathedral, drawn up in 1530, gave quite matter-of-fact directions for his pall-bearers to be paid and that the residents of his tenements were to 'provide for my soul'. Others thought more to benefit the living than to persuade them to recall them in prayer: in 1538, Thomas Starkey entrusted his body to be buried 'at the discretion of the curate', leaving his father £40 'in part of recompense of his great cost and charges upon my bringing up in good learning', and his books to the children of a Dr Wootton, 'as he thinks profitable to their learning', the rest going to Magdalene College, Cambridge. Through the 1530s, some wills still left payments for the celebration of 'month's minds' and for prayers for a period of five or seven years, indicating that this religious transition was not uniform, but depended upon personal belief and social standing.[54]

A report of a London funeral from 1523 survives, in the accounts of the Society of Drapers. Sir William Roche, an alderman of the city, was buried on 15 September and the description of his burial and the feast afterwards are so detailed as to allow a thorough glimpse into the nature of grief and memorial at this point in time:

The right worshipfull sir William Roche knight and alderman, decessyd betwene ix. and x. of the clock before none. On whose soule Jh'u have mercye. Amen. He was buryed the xv[th] daye of this instant moneth of September at afternone, in this wise. First, ij. branchys of whyte wax were borne before the priests and clerks in surplesys singyng. Then a standard of his crest, which was the red roobuck's hedd, with gylt hornes, havyng also ij. winges, the one of gold, the other verde. Thereafter certayne mourners; then a pynion of his arms, and his cote armour, borne by the herald, which arys was a cheker of warren of sylver and azure, a bull passaunt goules, with hornes of sylver, and iij. roches, also sylver, being all sett in a felde of gold. Then the corps borne next after the cote armure, by certayne clerks, and iiij. of the assystans of the Drapers, viz. Mr. Warner, Mr. Blower, Mr. Spencer, and Mr. Tull, who went in their livery and hoods about the said corps. Ther followyd the corse Mr. John Roche his sone, as chief mourner, alone; and after hym ij. couples of mourners more. Then the sword-bearer and my lord maire in black. Then the aldermen and sheriffs after them, and the whole livory of this felowshippe, in order. Then the ladys and gentylwomen, as the aldermen's wyfes and others, which, after dirige, cam home to his house and dranke, where they had spice-brede and comfetts, wyne, ale, and beere.

On the morrow, the mourners went again in order to the church, where they had a collacion made by sir Stephen. After which collacion the herald appointed the chief mourners, in order, to offer up the target, sword, and helmet, to the priest; and after they offered in order, and also my lord mayor, the aldermen, the livery, and others, which offering went to the poor. Then the whole communion was ministered. After which done, the herald again going before, there followed him the banner-bearers, and offered the banners also;

and then, in order, again the mourners, my lord mayor, and others, returned to the house of the said Mr. Roche, where they dined all, save the livery of this fellowship, which dined in the Drapers' Hall, by reason he had given them towards the same vjl. xiijs. iiijd. which was bestowed by John Quarles and William Berwyck, stewards for the same, the xvj. day of September, in eight mess of meat, as follows: First, brawn and mustard, boiled capon, swan roast, capon and custard. The second course, pidgeons and tarts, bread, wine, ale, and beer. And my lady Roche, of her gentylnes, sent moreover four gallons of French wine, and also a box of wafers and a bottell of hippocras.[55]

Gilbert Tailboys's death brought Bessie Blount back to court, where she would have had regular contact with her son. Perhaps she observed a period of mourning, but was definitely re-established by the New Year of 1532, when she was included on the list of the king's gifts as the recipient of a gilt goblet with a cover. It is very interesting that Henry did not consider marriage to Bessie at this point. Now that she was free, and he was intending to remarry regardless of papal disapproval, a marriage between them could have been the first step to legitimising Henry Fitzroy. This would have followed the precedent of the Beaufort family, whose Somerset dukedom Fitzroy now bore, and could have allowed the king to accept the boy as his heir. Legally, it could have been achieved with an Act of Parliament, modelled on that of 1390, and all Henry's concerns about the succession would have been resolved. A member of the emperor's household, Loys de Heylwigen, was convinced that this was Henry's intention, stating with confidence that the king was repudiating Catherine in order to 'legitimate by subsequent marriage a bastard son of his'.[56] Yet he was wrong. Henry did not choose this option. He was in love with Anne Boleyn and convinced that she would give him a son once they were married. Perhaps he thought he had already done enough for Fitzroy, and that there was no way Anne could fail in her maternal duty. Perhaps he did not want to even consider that possibility. Either way, Fitzroy's opportunity passed.

Fitzroy lost another father figure in 1530. After he had disappointed the king in his marital plans, Cardinal Wolsey's fall was rapid. Stripped of his offices, he was summoned to trial in London from his sanctuary in the north. It must have been a harsh lesson for the 11-year-old boy to see the decline of the man who had been his confidant and patron, who had arranged all the details of his life and household, who represented power, faith and authority; yet there was never really a choice about his feelings. He may have regretted the loss of Wolsey but it was the will of his father and, as such, could only be the boy's will too. By bringing his son close at the time of the cardinal's banishment, Henry was ensuring that the ties of family and loyalty to the throne overrode any emotional ties. Fitzroy would not see Wolsey again, as he never made it to London, dying at Leicester on 29 November 1530, and thus avoiding the trial and executioner's block awaiting him at his journey's end. It may be that the trauma of his final days exacerbated an existing illness. The suggestions by Elizabethan chronicler Edward Hall that Wolsey took his own life would have been unthinkable to the cardinal. Henry VIII and Anne Boleyn celebrated his death by watching a masque depicting Wolsey being dragged down into the mouth of hell. The role of Henry Fitzroy's mentor and godfather would soon be taken by another of the key figures of his father's court.

At court, the king's great affair rumbled on. Young Henry was living the life of a Tudor prince, based largely at Windsor Castle, but he also took over Wolsey's Durham Place and later had the use of Baynard's Castle and Coldharbour House, two other impressive royal residences on the Thames. He would also have been a guest at his father's palaces and spent time at his country retreat of Tonge, near Sittingbourne, where he is likely to have occupied the castle. Of the latter, only part of the moat survives, but it had once been owned by his great-great-grandmother Cecily, Duchess of York. Fitzroy's residency is further suggested by the grant of the adjoining almshouses to William Butts, the duke's physician. In May 1531, a man by the name of Arthur was paid 20s for a lute for Fitzroy and the boy received the usual golden and gilt trinkets and goblets from his father at New Year.[57] Early in 1532, he was suffering from some undiagnosed illness which required the services of a physician, who was compensated 40s for his trouble. His education continued, although it is possible that Richard Croke had by now been replaced by George Folbury, a Cambridge preacher, at least until March 1531, when he was granted a position in North Yorkshire, perhaps as a reward for his services.[58] Fitzroy's wardrobe was also updated, to include cloth of gold and silver, velvet and silk, cut into hats, gowns, cloaks and doublets trimmed with fur and sewn with gold buttons in the shape of flowers, triangles and sundials.[59]

By 1532, King Henry and Queen Catherine were living apart and the king was determined to marry Anne Boleyn. Richmond accompanied them on their journey to France that autumn, as part of a concord with Francis I, which would give Anne a degree of international recognition as a potential queen of England. The young duke, then aged 13, was allotted an entourage of forty men, as befitted his status.[60] The only other men in the kingdom who shared his stature were Thomas Howard, Duke of Norfolk and Fitzroy's uncle by marriage, Charles Brandon, Duke of Suffolk. It was at this time that Norfolk stepped into the position that Wolsey had vacated, becoming a friend and mentor to the young man, and encouraging his friendship with Norfolk's son Henry, Earl of Surrey, who was two or three years the boy's senior. Howard was then almost 60 and an ambitious, prominent figure at court, uncle to Henry's new love, Anne Boleyn. He had risen to be Lord Treasurer, Earl Marshal and the king's chief minister after the fall of Wolsey. He also had another intention in mind, observing to the imperial ambassador back in 1529 that 'the King wishes the Duke to marry one of my daughters'. Arrangements for the match were finalised in 1531, when the pair were formally engaged and after this point, Norfolk considered Fitzroy to be his son-in-law.

Fitzroy set sail for France with his father on 11 October 1532. It was his first experience of a sea crossing and of the world beyond English shores, although their base for the visit, Calais, was still in English hands. Yet it is not clear whether he was included in the initial party when Henry rode to meet Francis alone at Boulogne, leaving Anne behind. The account of the ambassador Carlo Capello, in the Venetian papers, has Richmond among the list of lords to greet the French king on 21 October:

According to the advices received their Majesties met on the 21st, at the distance of a league and a half from Calais. The most Christian King was accompanied by the Cardinal of Lorraine, the Lord Steward Montmorency, Monsr. di St. Pol, Monsr. de Guise, Monsr. de Pontier, and other lords and gentlemen, some 1,800 in number, who came processionally, all most richly clad, the meanest wearing black velvet. The King of England was with the Dukes of Norfolk, Suffolk, and Richmond, the Bishops, and others numbering 800 horse, all in embroidered coats, some of velvet and others of cloth.[61]

It is impossible to know now whether this was certain, or an assumption, as other sources deny the duke's presence on that occasion. He was definitely there to mark his father's return from Calais, riding out to meet the two kings 'with a great company of noble men … and saluting the French King, embraced him in a most honourable and courteous manner'.[62] An eyewitness recorded that 'the King's son is very handsome and accomplished'[63] and, briefly, it was almost as if the illegitimacy did not matter. The duke took part in the festivities that followed, including a special event for the Order of the Garter, during which he was seated at Francis's side, and enjoyed the entertainments and feasts that ran over the following weeks. On one day alone:

the most Christian King sent to the English King an entire suit of white velvet, very costly, with embroidery; and the most Christian King clad himself in a similar suit; and dressed thus alike they heard mass. The other greetings such as banquets and entertainments, were very exquisite, and replete with every demonstration of honour.[64]

During that time, a scheme was hatched between the two kings whereby Fitzroy would remain behind after the English departed and spend some time at the French court, for the purposes of his education but also 'for the greater security of the matters between' the two countries, as a kind of noble hostage, a guarantee of good relations. Another way of looking at it might be to consider Fitzroy in a diplomatic role or, as the Venetian ambassador Zuam Venier added, Henry 'gave, as servant to the most Christian King, his natural son'.[65] It was reported elsewhere that 'the King of England yesterday gave unto the King his bastard son, who is a young child of fifteen or sixteen years, and the same day he made him a present of six horses.'[66] Fitzroy was 13 at the time, and this move might have been considered valuable for a brief period to provide him with the sort of social and cultural polish that Anne Boleyn had acquired during her time at the French court. It would also conveniently sideline him in time for the anticipated male heir Anne had promised to deliver. She and Henry consummated their relationship at this time, either in France or at Dover upon their return; it is likely that they went through a secret marriage service after landing in England, on 14 November.

Francis had three sons of his own, similar in age to the duke, whose education and company the boy might be expected to share. The Dauphin Francis was then 14, but had spent years as a hostage in his father's place after the French defeat at Pavia, which left the boy sombre and serious, a budding scholar with a preference for dressing in black. His next brother Henri, just three or four months older than Fitzroy, had shared that captivity, but seemed a more robust character. Negotiations were taking place for him to marry Catherine de Medici, the Pope's niece, who had previously been considered as a wife for Fitzroy. The youngest of the three was Charles, who was then only 10. It was even suggested that this might be some sort of exchange; Capello related that 'the Duke of Orléans, the second son of the most Christian King, will come to England with King Henry, whose son, the Duke of Richmond, will remain with King Francis'.[67] As it transpired, though, Henri of Valois did not go to England.

Francis took his leave of Henry on 29 October and the English king set sail for England soon after. Around the same time, Fitzroy left Calais accompanied by the Earl of Surrey and a sizeable entourage. He was welcomed at the French court, finding the country congenial, and received gifts along the way and settled in well with the Valois princes, although Surrey was enjoying himself less, as the duke's almoner Richard Tate wrote from Paris on 11 December:

My lords of Richmond and Surrey have been well welcomed in their journey
toward the French court, with presents of wine and other gentle offers. My lord
of Richmond has been in good health, and finds the country 'very natural unto
him.' Surrey has suffered from an ague which he had before he left Calais, but
it is hoped the worst is past. On arriving at the Court, which was at Chantely,
the Great Master's house, the King embraced my lord, and made him great
cheer, 'saying that he thought himself now to have four sons, and exty[med]
him no less.' After the Daulphin [sic] and his brethren and all the noblemen had
embraced him, he was taken into the King's privy chamber, where the King
told him he should always be as one of his chamber. In Paris he has lodging in
the Dauphin's own lodging, and sups with him and his brethren.[68]

It seems that France suited Fitzroy. In January 1533, the Dauphin hosted
a tournament in which Henry took part and the Dauphin's governor
commented that he was 'being nurtured with the King's children'.[69]
Perhaps in response to the English king's Order of the Garter ceremony
the previous autumn, Francis I planned to celebrate St George's day 1533
at Fontainbleau. The day before, the Venetian Marin Guistinian recorded
that 'an English herald, bearing the habits of the Order which the King
of England conferred on the Lord Steward and the Admiral at Boulogne
when the conference was held, arrived at this Court.' Francis had planned
elaborate entertainments for the occasion and, said Guistinian, it would be
'attended by the Duke of Richmond, the English King's natural son, who
has the same order'.[70] Perhaps this was an indication that Fitzroy had won
the French king's favour, as he accompanied Francis south on progress that
summer. While the Dauphin and his brothers travelled with the queen,
the duke and Surrey stayed with the king as they passed through Lyons,
Toulouse and Montpellier, greeted by pageants and gifts along the route.
While they were away, Anne Boleyn was crowned Queen of England
and prepared to enter her confinement to deliver the son that would
replace Fitzroy.

That July, Fitzroy's 'father-in-law', the Duke of Norfolk, arrived in
France, to ask Francis to support Henry VIII against the pope. He was

accompanied by his nephew, George Boleyn, brother of the new queen. The French royal family were waiting in Riom, in the Auvergne, from where Richmond and Surrey rode out over a mile to meet Norfolk. From there, the court moved on to Mountfarran, from where Anthony Browne wrote to Thomas Cromwell, giving details about the preparations for the town but, disappointingly, did not mention Fitzroy. However, the duke would have witnessed the magnificent reception of the king by:

> citizens on horseback, and 300 footmen with artillery, clothed in jerkins of cloth of gold, or orange velvet or satin. The religious met him in the town, with the sacrament and a procession. The streets were gravelled, and the sides hung with verdure, and covered with linen, with the arms of the King, Queen, and Dauphin. In divers places there were fair pageants, and the streets were furnished with torches and trumpets blown.[71]

Yet while they were enjoying the diversions, news arrived that the pope had pronounced in favour of Henry VIII's marriage to Catherine, ruling that Anne Boleyn's imminent child would be illegitimate. Henry recalled George Boleyn and urged Norfolk to persuade Francis to oppose the pope, but the French king refused, so Henry recalled Norfolk, Richmond and Surrey. The official excuse was that Fitzroy had just celebrated his fourteenth birthday, and so was required to return to England in order to be married to Norfolk's daughter Mary. Their departure was confirmed by the Chronicle of Calais, which related that 'the Duke of Richmond, bastard sonne to King Henry VIII, and the erle of Surrey, came to Caleys out of France, where they had bene almost xii months.' This took place on 25 September, meaning that the news had probably already arrived in France that Anne's promised son had turned out to be a girl. Though the new queen had proven herself capable of bearing a live child, and hoped to deliver more, it was still a blow to Henry. There was no guarantee of any future pregnancy or child of either gender. After everything that Henry had done in the last seven years to secure himself a legitimate male heir, Fitzroy was still his only son. And yet, he still seemed to be the king's best hope for the succession. To cement his future even further, on 26 November, Henry Fitzroy and Mary Howard were married at Hampton Court.

IV

The duke's new wife was the same age as him, having also been born in 1519. She was reputed to be very beautiful, but a sketch of her by Holbein is disappointingly unfinished, giving her merely the ghost of features, lightly drawn in a pale face. The eyes are cast down, the mouth small and expression demure, the forehead is wide and the chin somewhat pointed. Beneath the black hat with its matching feather, a little of her red-gold hair is visible and the collar of her chemise covers her throat and neck. There is little to denote any personality beyond the conventions of the time. She was also intelligent, as her involvement with the Devonshire manuscript reveals. Playing a role in Anne Boleyn's court, Mary was one of three women who collected poetry in the manuscript, including extracts of famous works, translations and new compositions. For a king's son, few details survive about the wedding or any subsequent festivities that were held to mark the occasion. Ambassador Chapuys only remarks on the fact that it was taking place. Nor does it seem that the pair consummated their match, according to the debate that arose upon Fitzroy's death, after which she was denied the dower lands to which she would otherwise have been entitled.

The young couple were both aged 14 and it may be that King Henry was concerned that early sexual activity might weaken his son's health. He may have been thinking of Arthur, and genuinely believed that his brother had slept with Catherine and suffered as a result. Ironically, it was the Duke of Norfolk who, upon Henry's investigation into the royal marriage, had volunteered the information that he had 'known' his wife at the age of 15. It may also have been that Henry was keeping his options open when it came to the boy's marriage. England's current situation was difficult, poised on the verge of irrevocable change, he having made an implacable enemy out of Catherine of Aragon's nephew, the Holy Roman Emperor. Anne Boleyn was strongly in favour of the Howard marriage. Mary was, in fact, her cousin, so it was a convenience that reflected the times. If it remained unconsummated, there was always the option of undoing it later, leaving Fitzroy free to marry a European princess when the situation had calmed down. For the time being, the duke remained at Windsor with his brother-in-law Surrey. The latter's later poems capture a romantic idyll of young men growing to maturity together amid the beautiful surroundings of the castle:

> ... proude Windsore, where I in lust and joy
> With a Kynges sonne my childish yeres did passe
> In greater feasts than Priam's sonnes of Troy ...
> The stately seats, the ladies bright of hewe
> The daunces short, long tales of great delight ...
> On foaming horse with swords and friendly hearts
> With chere as though one should another whelm
> Where we have fought and chased oft with darts ...
> In active games of nimbleness and strength
> Where we did strain, trained with swarms of youth
> Our tender limbs that yet shot up in length ...
> The wild forest, the clothed holts with green
> The reins availed and swift y-breathed horse
> With cry of hounds and merry blast between
> When we did chase the fearful hart of foree ...
> The secret thoughts, imparted with such trust
> The wanton talke, the divers change of play
> The friendship swore, eche promise kept so just
> Wherewith we passed the winter nights away.[72]

The possibility also arose of sending Fitzroy out to Ireland, to rule the country in person as its Lieutenant, but the situation there was becoming volatile. In 1534, the country erupted in full-scale rebellion and Henry's minister Thomas Cromwell blamed the chaos on the fact that the duke had not been sent there sooner, writing that 'had he allowed him to go to Ireland eight months ago, as he was told to do, nothing of what has since happened would have taken place.'[73] Ultimately, though, it was too dangerous to risk sending the king's only son and Sir William Skeffington was sent instead that October to deal with the rebels.

Fitzroy's life continued much as it had been into the New Year, when he gave his father a great spoon of gold weighing more than four ounces, and received silver gilt pots in return, as well as a silver salt cellar and a ring from his new stepmother. On 15 January, he attended Parliament at Westminster and, five days later, voted in a chapter of the garter. In fact, he made regular appearances that spring, and was among those listed as present when the session was prorogued on 30 March.[74] That May, Fitzroy was back at Windsor for the Order of the Garter ceremonies, although this time he took the role usually played by the king, even though his father was present:'

A chapter of the Order of the Garter was held at Greenwich on St. George's day 26 Hen. VIII., the King and divers nobles being present. It was decided to hold the feast at Windsor on 17 May, the Sovereign's place being supplied by the Duke of Richmond assisted by the Duke of Norfolk.[75]

The Black Book of the Garter contains an illustration of a St George's Day procession dating to around 1534. Fitzroy is glimpsed on the extreme right, ahead of the king, as if just about to march from view. Dressed in the red and blue garter robes, he appears in profile, with red-gold hair like his father. The only other surviving image of the duke was painted around the same time by the same artist, the Fleming Lucas Horenbout, who was based at the Tudor court from the mid-1520s. It is a traditionally circular miniature on a bright blue background, showing a youth with heavy-lidded eyes, long nose and pursed red mouth. Fitzroy is in a state of undress, his shirt collar open and his hair concealed by a decorative cap, a curiously personal and intimate depiction of the king's son in *déshabillé*.

By the spring of 1534, Anne Boleyn had conceived again and, with her 'goodly belly' visible to all, the king was anticipating the delivery of a son. Again, this would mean a change in Fitzroy's status, as his strength lay in being his father's only male child. But then, with the arrival of summer, the pregnancy seems to have gone away, without mention at court, suggesting that that queen was either mistaken or had miscarried. Fitzroy did not go with them on their summer progress, preferring instead to pass those months at his manor of Canford in Dorset. Part of the inheritance of the Duchy of Lancaster, the manor had been developed under John of Gaunt in the fourteenth century, to include an impressive kitchen range and chapel. Standing in a beautiful park beside the River Stour, it also encompassed the Norman church of St Augustine, where the duke would have worshipped. Fitzroy may also have visited other estates in his possession before being recalled to court that November. His status, and his knowledge of France, may have contributed towards the king's choice to have Fitzroy host a feast on St Andrew's Day for the visiting French admiral Philippe de Chabot. The event was sandwiched between two other entertainments given by Norfolk and Henry VIII himself, establishing the duke as very much a significant player in the royal family and in this powerful aristocratic triumvirate.[76]

The year 1535 saw Richmond continuing to play the host at court. At Westminster in January, he voted to elect James V of Scotland as a Knight of the Garter[77] and, the following month, he was given the responsibility of looking after the imperial ambassador Chapuys, who relates that 'all the lords were in Council, and dined at Cromwell's house, except the Duke of Richmond who remained to entertain me. My men were also retained to dine, and great cheer shown them. All which was done merely to increase the jealousy of the French.'[78] That May, the young duke undertook a more sinister duty, attending the executions of Carthusian monks who refused to accept the religious changes Henry was beginning to institute in England. Fitzroy was at Tyburn with Norfolk, Thomas and George Boleyn and other lords, 'quite near the sufferers', which must have been a grisly spectacle but also, perhaps, an important rite of passage for a young man who might be involved in the future dispensation of justice.[79]

Throughout that summer, the question of the king's heir remained unanswered. After miscarrying her second child, Anne had not yet fallen pregnant again and, according to rumour, her uncle the Duke of Norfolk was hoping the situation would allow him to 'get the rule into his own hands', by his status as Fitzroy's father-in-law, and by marrying another of his sons to the Princess Elizabeth:

> The Duke of Norfolk, according to the Admiral, affirms that he would sooner die than see any change as regards the King or the new Queen; which is not unlike what the writer has heard in other ways of Norfolk, viz., that this breaking off might reasonably have been expected, matters depending very much on his dexterity, and the affairs of England being commonly managed more than barbarously. For he, being one of the greatest men in the kingdom, and having sons, and the Duke of Richmond for his son-in-law, might hope one day to have that daughter for one of his sons, or, if disorders ensued, to get the rule into his own hands.[80]

Fitzroy may or may not have been aware of his father-in-law's schemes but he is very unlikely to have backed any action against his father, to whom he owed everything. Yet it was one thing to seek to exploit disorder during Henry VIII's lifetime and quite another if Norfolk attempted it after the king's death. In that scenario, if the inheritance was to become a battlefield between Fitzroy, Mary and Elizabeth, the question of the youth's kingship would take on a very different aspect. He presented the most attractive solution to the inheritance dilemma, which always favoured a male over a female, and had taken a role in politics and local government, as well as being intelligent, athletic and 'a goodly young lord, and a toward, in many qualities and feats'. He was also of age, reaching his fourteenth birthday in the summer of 1533, the age when his cousin James V of Scotland had been declared capable of rule. In short, Fitzroy was the ideal son for Henry VIII, save for the circumstances of his birth. He was shaping up well as a potential king and this was recognised by leading members of the court. For the meantime, though, life continued as normal. Fitzroy was in Sheffield in July, from where he wrote to Cromwell that he lacked 'park [and] game' for his friends and requested that the king intervene to offer him the use of more royal grounds.[81] When he returned to court that autumn, Anne Boleyn was again pregnant.

In October 1535, Fitzroy's household moved to his estate at Tonge, near Sittingbourne, in Kent. Through the summer and into autumn, it had been based in Lewes, probably in the priory's manor house, known as the 'Lord's Place', which Henry VIII would later give to his fourth wife, Anne of Cleves. From there, they had gone north to Sheffield, before pausing in Godstone in Surrey, and then on to Kent. Tonge was originally a small village, now vanished, centred around the manor house and church of St Giles, with a poor hospital called St James, Puckeshall and almshouses. The manor had belonged to Cecily Neville, having come into the York family through the Mortimer line and being subsumed into the Crown's wealth upon the kingship of Henry's great-grandfather, Edward IV. Apart from Fitzroy's kitchen records, another surviving detail that links him to the place is the gift of the almshouses to the king's physician Sir William Butts, who had been appointed to care for the duke's health. There is no evidence at all to place Richmond at Tonge at any particular time but, as his household had moved there, it seems likely that he anticipated visiting in the summer of 1536. As it transpired, though, the king would visit Kent alone.

Events early in the new year brought the question of Fitzroy's potential kingship to the fore in a dramatic and pressing way. January saw the usual celebrations at court, and the king presented his son with a silver gilt bowl with a star at the bottom, engraved with the boy's arms, a standing bowl with the figure of a small boy holding spear and shield bearing a French inscription and a jug with handles like serpents featuring the initials H and A topped with a crown. In the second week of the year, news arrived from Kimbolton Castle. Henry's first wife and queen, Catherine of Aragon, had died at the age of 50, meaning that there was no longer any legal impediment to Henry's union with Anne Boleyn. It also meant that the pope could no longer insist that the king return to Catherine. Henry was relieved, stating, 'God be praised that we are free from all suspicion of war' and reputedly dressed in yellow with a feather in his cap. This may have been an act of deference, as yellow was a traditional Spanish colour of mourning, but it was also symbolic of his freedom, in the removal of a burden that had long troubled his conscience. Anne celebrated too, declaring that now she was finally queen. Ironically, though, this moment may have been bittersweet for her, as she was intelligent enough to realise that the death of her rival would make her own position more fragile. Catherine was given the funeral of a widowed Princess of Wales, rather than that of a Queen of England. At Peterborough Cathedral, she was laid to rest amid solemn Catholic rites, her way lit by torches, her body borne under a canopy with ladies riding behind on palfreys draped in black and others in chariots, to a tomb that her friend the imperial ambassador considered to be too far from the altar. In retrospect, this seems to be the first in a series of events that year which would force the king to confront his own mortality.

On 24 January, Henry had an accident while jousting in the tilt yard at Greenwich. Unseated by his opponent's lance, dressed in full armour, he fell heavily and was pinned under his horse, so that onlookers 'thought it a miracle he was not killed'. He lay unconscious for two hours, during which the members of his council urgently debated who would succeed him – the 2-year-old Elizabeth, the 19-year-old Mary, who had been declared illegitimate, or the 16-year-old Fitzroy. Under duress in some cases, councillors had sworn an oath to uphold the first Act of Succession, passed in 1534. Failure to do so bore the penalty of death in the cases of Cardinal John Fisher and Sir Thomas More. By that oath, England would have bypassed Mary and Henry for the sake of a 2-year-old girl whose mother was relatively unpopular with the people. Then again, in the event of the king's death, such allegiances and oaths would become invalid. Norfolk at least was poised to exploit the ensuing disorder. Henry recovered but, five days later, Anne Boleyn miscarried her child, after around three and a half months' gestation, which had the appearance of a male. Once again, the precious legitimate prince had eluded the king. Once again, this worked to Richmond's advantage.

On 2 May 1536 Anne was arrested on charges of adultery, incest and for conspiring the king's death. Henry Fitzroy was not one of the peers summoned to sit in judgement at the trial of his stepmother on 15 May. He did attend her execution at the Tower of London on 19 May, perhaps by choice, perhaps as the king's representative; perhaps he was there with his father-in-law, Norfolk, who had been quick to distance himself from his errant relations. Richmond's position regarding his stepmother was a delicate one. Having learned the lesson of Wolsey's fall, he is likely to have reacted pragmatically to the scandalous revelations and loss of a queen who had bestowed him with thoughtful gifts at New Year. Yet no indication survives of any warmth between them, any personal relationship, and Henry's existence may have been felt as an unintentional rebuke to Anne each time she miscarried. As part of Norfolk's family, the young duke was equally part of the Boleyn faction but also removed from it by his greater loyalty to his father. Just as Norfolk shrewdly and swiftly embraced the king's cause, Fitzroy also washed his hands of Anne. It would not have been difficult. His father's actions made it easy. She was simply removed, tried and executed within a matter of weeks. Her stepson's life would have been untouched by this turn of events, save for the reminder of his father's ultimate justice and the sense of a danger narrowly avoided. He likely went to her execution with little sentiment, more as an essential part of his legal training.

Anne had been readying herself for death since the early hours of the morning, trying to calm herself sufficiently and accept her fate, in the interests of her soul. Before dawn, she had summoned the Constable of the Tower, Sir William Kingston, to hear mass with her and to be her witness as she swore on the Holy Sacraments that she had never betrayed the king. Kingston wrote to Cromwell the same day:

> she wylle declare herself to be a good woman for alle men, bot for the Kynge, at the our of her death, for this mornynge she sent for me that I myght be with her at such time as she received the good Lord, to the intent I shuld here her speak as towchyng her innocence always to be clere; and in the writing of this she sent for me. And at my comynge she sayd, 'Mr. Kyngston, I hear say I shall not die before noon, and I am very sorry therefore, for I thought to be dede by this time, and past my payne.' I told her it shuld be no payne, it was so

subtle. And then she said, 'I heard say the executor was very good, and I have a little neck,' and put her hand about it, laughing heartily. I have sene many men and also women executed, and all thay have bene in great sorrow, and to my knowledge this lady has much joy and pleasure in dethe. Sir, her almoner is continually with her, and has bene since ii. of the clock after midnight.[83]

An account of the scaffold speeches of George and Anne Boleyn has survived in the Viennese archives, giving an illustration of the way the condemned used their final platform as another way to smooth their path through death and approach it willingly. The fact of their innocence in this case, upon which most modern historians now agree, was irrelevant by this point. What mattered now was the way they conducted themselves in the final days and hours as they passed though the Valley of Shadows with the Devil close at hand, hoping to gain their soul if they showed unchristian behaviour. George's speech was composed, dignified and conventional: the scaffold was not the place for recriminations or emotions. He took the opportunity to seize this last chance and present himself as an example by which others may learn:

> He made a very catholic address to the people, saying he had not come thither to preach, but to serve as a mirror and example, acknowledging his sins against God and the King, and declaring he need not recite the causes why he was condemned, as it could give no pleasure to hear them. He first desired mercy and pardon of God, and afterwards of the King and all others whom he might have offended, and hoped that men would not follow the vanities of the world and the flatteries of the Court, which had brought him to that shameful end. He said if he had followed the teachings of the Gospel, which he had often read, he would not have fallen into this danger, for a good doer was far better than a good reader. In the end, he pardoned those who had condemned him to death, and asked the people to pray for his soul.[84]

In contrast, if Chapuys's account is to be believed, Anne made an effort to reconcile herself to her fate but she was still in shock and emotional at the end:

The said Queen (unjustly called) finally was beheaded upon a scaffold within the Tower with open gates. She was brought by the captain upon the said scaffold, and four young ladies followed her. She looked frequently behind her, and when she got upon the scaffold was very much exhausted and amazed. She begged leave to speak to the people, promising to say nothing but what was good. The captain gave her leave, and she began to raise her eyes to Heaven, and cry mercy to God and to the King for the offence she had done, desiring the people always to pray to God for the King, for he was a good, gentle, gracious, and amiable prince. She was then stripped of her short mantle furred with ermines, and afterwards took off her hood, which was of English make, herself. A young lady presented her with a linen cap, with which she covered her hair, and she knelt down, fastening her clothes about her feet, and one of the said ladies bandaged her eyes.[85]

There would be no magnificent tomb for Anne Boleyn. She did not even fare as well as Catherine of Aragon, who had been stripped of her queenship to be buried with the rites due to a widowed Princess of Wales in Peterborough Cathedral. Anne's severed head and body were wrapped in a white cloth and placed in a plain elm coffin. She was buried under the stone slabs of the chancel in an unmarked grave.

The charge against Anne that she had 'conspired the death of the King and another prince',[86] could have only have been referring to Fitzroy. Henry clearly believed that she had intended harm to his son, and to Princess Elizabeth, which gave rise to a scene recorded by Chapuys for the Emperor Charles V. The ambassador wrote that upon the same evening Anne was arrested, when:

the Duke of Richmond went to say Good night to his father, and ask his blessing after the English custom, the King began to weep, saying that he and his sister, meaning the Princess, were greatly bound to God for having escaped the hands of that accursed whore, who had determined to poison them; from which it is clear that the King knew something about it.[87]

This emotional outburst demonstrates that Henry's fear was real, whether or not it was unfounded, but also highlights aspects of the father-son relationship. The formality of Fitzroy's goodnight request for a blessing also has the hallmarks of intimacy and privilege, and sounds like it was a regular occurrence, a custom between them when staying in the same building. Henry's tears were safe within this private space, alone with his son, although privacy at the Tudor court was always relative and, as the existence of Chapuys's letter proves, even the most private moments had witnesses. Whether or not Fitzroy believed the charges against his stepmother cannot be ascertained given the lack of surviving evidence. However, if his father the king believed it, then to all intents and purposes, it became the truth. All accounts suggest that Richmond was a dutiful, obedient and grateful son: his father's enemy was his enemy.

Once again, the events of May 1536 manoeuvred Fitzroy into a strong position to inherit the English throne. Archbishop Thomas Cranmer, who had unmade the king's marriage to Catherine of Aragon, now declared Henry's marriage to Anne invalid, meaning that Princess Elizabeth was illegitimate. There were even rumours that she was not Henry's child at all, but the product of Anne's illicit affair with the courtier Sir Henry Norris. This gave rise to the unusual situation in which all three of Henry VIII's children were considered illegitimate, levelling the playing field, which could only be to the advantage of a male who had come of age. In the early summer of 1536, Fitzroy looked like the leading candidate. On 6 June, ambassador Chapuys reported a statement made before the king by the Earl of Sussex, Robert Radcliffe in the Privy Council, to the effect that 'considering that the Princess was a bastard, as well as the Duke of Richmond, it was advisable to prefer the male to the female, to the succession to the crown.'[88] Chapuys reported that the king did not contradict him. Perhaps it was a sign of his increasing proximity to the throne that Fitzroy was now set up in his own establishment at the royal property of Baynard's Castle, instead of the home of the Bishop of Norwich, which he had been using as a London base since 1534. It also meant that the youth was approaching the age when he might live independently with his wife and father a family of his own.

Henry had not given up hope of fathering a son within a legitimate marriage and he did not waste any time in this respect. On the day of Anne's execution, Cranmer issued a dispensation allowing Henry and Jane Seymour to marry, without banns, despite the fact that they were related in the third degree of affinity. The following day they were engaged. The wedding took place on 30 May. As Chapuys has it, the king intended to set aside his existing children in favour of any born to him of his new marriage. When 'speaking with Mistress Jane Semel [*sic*] of their future marriage, the latter suggested that the Princess should be replaced in her former position; and the King told her she was a fool, and ought to solicit the advancement of the children they would have between them, and not any others.'[89] But at that point, any sons borne by Jane Seymour were purely theoretical. The following month, Henry celebrated his forty-fifth birthday and, while he was still not as overweight as he would become in the next few years, he frequently experienced poor health. He had now been trying to father sons for twenty-seven years and his record was not good.

It was with this dilemma in mind that Henry passed the second Act of Succession that June. With no legitimate children, the Act gave the king permission to nominate his own successor in his own time. The implications for Fitzroy were obvious, but this was not a statement of intent, merely representing his inclusion in the running. Nevertheless, this was the closest the boy had ever come to inheriting the English throne. Of course, any children the king fathered by Jane, or subsequent wives, would take precedence, but the chances of this appeared slim. For a few brief weeks in June 1536, the possibility of Fitzroy becoming King Henry IX was very real. Then, before the end of the next month, the youth's health began to fail and, suddenly and unexpectedly, his life was cut short.

V

The young duke's fatal illness appears to have come on suddenly. In mid-May, he was included on a list compiled by Thomas Wriothesley for new appointments, receiving the position of Chamberlain of Chester and North Wales, and petitioning for another post for his servant. It seems unlikely that he would have been granted such a role if he had been seriously ill at the time. Three weeks later, on 8 June, Fitzroy was well enough to appear at the state opening of Henry VIII's sixth Parliament, walking just ahead of his father, whose cap he ceremoniously carried, as the lords processed from York Place to Westminster. The first mention of his poor health arises in a letter dated 8 July, and this condition already appeared serious: ambassador Chapuys wrote to Emperor Charles V of the likelihood of Princess Mary being named as her father's heir, 'especially failing the Duke of Richmond, who, in the judgment of physicians is consumptive and incurable'.[90] Ten days later, John Hussee reported to Lord Lisle that 'my Lord of Richmond is very sick'[91] and in his letter of 23 July, Chapuys recorded that the king was 'mortified ... because he has no hope that the Duke of Richmond can live long, whom he certainly intended to make his successor and, but for his illness, would have got him declared so by parliament'.[92]

No details survive about Fitzroy's symptoms or condition, but by mid-July it was apparent to those around him that his illness would swiftly prove fatal. Later, councillors of Richmond's half-brother Edward VI recalled the duke's death when the young king lay on his death bed, and at least once commented that Edward's illness was 'the same as that which killed the late ... Richmond'.[93] Only fifteen days separated the first report of Fitzroy's illness and his death. This suggests that, even if he had underlying symptoms, they had not been considered life-threatening until this last brief period, when they became acute, or else were exacerbated by an additional complication. If, as Chapuys believed, the duke was suffering from tuberculosis, a lung infection might have sped his demise in an era without antibiotics. This might have developed in a matter of days, as the king's absence from court suggests that his son's death was unexpected or sudden. In fact, Henry was at the royal manor of Milton Regis, near Sittingbourne, just 3 miles down the road from Richmond's manor at Tonge. It may have been that they intended to travel into Kent together, or that Fitzroy had intended to depart later and meet up with his father, but in the end he was too ill to make the journey. He remained at St James's Palace, which the king was in the process of completing.

It was Chapuys again who recorded, on 23 July, that 'I have just this moment heard that the Duke of Richmond died this morning; not a bad thing for the interests of the Princess'.[94] A Dr Ortiz reported to the empress that the king 'had determined to name his bastard son, the Duke of Richmond, but he died on 22 July',[95] although he was not in England, so may not have got the date right. It seems reasonable to assume that Fitzroy died on the night of 22–23 July, perhaps in the small hours. Henry was still in Kent when the news reached him, as is clear from a letter written later by Norfolk, which states, 'I was never at Dover with his highness since my lord of Richmond died, but at that time, of whose death word came to Sittingbourne.'[96] The king's reaction to the news went unrecorded but this in itself may be of significance. The king maintained such a complete and profound silence that Norfolk was forced to step in and make arrangements for Fitzroy's burial. Henry's state of mind is best suggested by the fact that he apparently failed to clarify his intentions on this matter to Norfolk, and criticised his choices bitterly after the fact.

Richmond was laid to rest in the traditional location of the Howard dynasty, Thetford Abbey, in Norfolk. The duke later stated that the king had insisted that the youth's body be 'conveyed secretly in a closed cart', so he had given instructions for this to be carried out. There were only two mourners, Fitzroy's governor George Cotton and his brother Richard Cotton, the comptroller of the duke's household, who were responsible for accompanying the coffin to the abbey. Chapuys relates that on 3 August, 'after being dead eight days, [Fitzroy] has been secretly carried in a wagon [*charette*], covered with straw, without any company except two persons clothed in green, who followed at a distance, into Norfolk, where the Duke his father-in-law will have him buried.'[97] This puts his removal from London on 31 July and, with time allowed for the proper rites and travelling, the funeral would have taken place a few days later. Norfolk's concern about the king's anger is apparent from his letter of 5 August to Thomas Cromwell:

> This night at 8 o'clock came letters from my friends and servants about London, all agreeing in one tale, that the King was displeased with me because my lord of Richmond was not buried honorably. The King wished the body conveyed secretly in a closed cart to Thedford, 'and at my suit thither,' and so buried; accordingly I ordered both the Cottons to have the body wrapped in lead and a close cart provided, but it was not done, nor was the body conveyed very secretly. I trust the King will not blame me undeservedly.[98]

Writing from 'Kenynghale Lodge', at ten o'clock at night, Norfolk was clearly affected by the loss, and the news of the king's displeasure, admitting to Cromwell that the letter was composed 'with the hand of him that is full, full, full of choler and agony'.[99]

Richmond was not to rest in peace for very long. Thetford Abbey was one of the last religious institutions to be dissolved during Henry VIII's scheme to close the monasteries. It was forced to submit in 1540, just four years after Richmond's death, so his remains were moved almost 40 miles to the church of St Michael the Archangel at Framlingham in Suffolk. The monument now standing in the church may be the original, brought from the abbey, or else was commissioned at the time of the removal, in which case it might have been produced to the king's specifications. It stands 9ft long, 5ft wide and 5ft high, with friezes depicting scenes, prophets and people from the Old Testament. Four images stand at the corners, each supporting a 'trophy of the passion' and Richmond's arms feature with a garter and impaled with those of his wife. Large and imposing, the tomb in Framlingham may not be exactly what Norfolk planned, but comes close to showing the monumental carving and scale desirable for a potential king of England. Most incongruous is its location in a small parish church, where it seems oversized. Built on a scale for prominence in a major abbey, Fitzroy's surviving memorial must be imagined within its intended context.

The life of Henry VIII's son ended unexpectedly in his eighteenth year. As his father's potential heir, the impact of this was dynastic and political, but exactly what effect his absence would have remained unseen for another two decades. For the time being, Fitzroy's death was an intense personal loss for the king, a wonderful opportunity lost, just as he was starting to appreciate its potential. On an immediate, practical level, the duke left behind a household to be disbanded and it is ironic that only in death do we get a really detailed insight into what it was like to live as the king's son. Only two days later, an inventory was made of Fitzroy's goods by a John Gostwick, probably after the news arrived at Tonge.

Henry had been in possession of a wardrobe fit for a future king, the fabrics and colours leaving no one in any doubt about his status and suggestive of his possible role to come. The full inventory of his clothing, which survives in the Harleian MS 1419, includes a crimson damask gown embroidered all over with gold, with seven buttons of gold; a gown of black velvet embroidered with a border of Venice gold lined with black velvet and Bruges satin; a gown of purple velvet edged with Venice gold and lined with yellow satin; a gown of purple satin tinsel and a gown of incarnate (red) damask trimmed with a small fringe. Richmond also possessed the ceremonial gowns of his office. In his wardrobe was his garter gown of purple velvet, the garter itself made of Venice gold, along with a kirtle of crimson velvet with a hood and a scarlet robe, with matching kirtle and hood. When he went riding, the duke had a coat of green satin with a silver fringe and a selection of coats made of green and black taffeta, of white, black and red velvet, and black and yellow satin. His doublets were of red or black velvet, and red, yellow or blue satin, edged with velvet, or Venice silver or gold. He had hose in matching colours and he owned furs of sable and black lamb.[100]

Some of Richmond's possessions were exquisite. At table, he might cut his meat with a rich dagger, trimmed and garnished with silver and gilt, while wearing a black velvet bonnet set with a gold brooch that featured a face, four rubies and twenty-six gold buttons. Spread out before him might have been silver dishes and spoons, a gold basin to hold salt decorated with a dragon and pearls, gilt cups decorated with eagles and roses, gold spoons with roses and pomegranates left over from the reign of Catherine of Aragon and another salt cellar reputedly made from a unicorn's horn. When he dressed for state occasions, Fitzroy had a selection of gold jewellery to adorn himself with. He owned a number of garters and collars set with rubies and diamonds, bracelets and rings set with gems, a gold necklet featuring seven white enamelled roses and a small chain of Paris work, enamelled black. When he prayed, he might have used some of the many gilt and gold chalices and censers, being sprinkled with holy water from a gilt pot engraved with roses and the Beaufort portcullis. He owned crosses featuring the images of the Virgin Mary and a whole host of saints, huge gilt altar candlesticks, communion cups decorated with flowers, serpents and feathers. While out hunting, the duke might have used his gilt wood knife with its shiny buckle and scabbard of green velvet, or worn one of five pairs of boots or three pairs of spurs. When he slept, it was under a tester, or canopy, of cloth of old, green tinsel and crimson velvet, with curtains of twenty panels made from red and yellow sarcanet, and cushions of cloth of gold, quilted and tasselled.[101]

Richmond was not given one of the elaborate transi, or *memento mori*, tombs showing his carved remains underneath, the skin taut across his ribs and his mouth gaping in agony. By the time he died, these were passing out of fashion in favour of more simple monuments. Size still mattered, though: the Howard family monoliths were as solid and dense as former tombs had been. Wrapped in elaborate tracery and they displayed biblical, heraldic and dynastic imagery more than personal commemoration. *Memento mori* memorials were also very much the choice at this time of an individual of mature years, contemplating their final days and their passage to heaven, and designing their own tombs. Frequently they had the wealth and leisure to dedicate to them. While such carvings were intended as harsh reminders about the reality and inevitability of death, it is rare to see them depicting the cadavers of young people or children. Premature death needed no such illustration. When the young were depicted on Tudor tombs, they tended to be plump, in the prime of life, as if they had merely fallen asleep. For all the proximity of death, the association of decay and youth still went against human instinct, which felt that its proper sphere should be old age. Yet Richmond's wardrobe accounts can be set beside his square white tomb, almost as a memorial to his life, an alternative cadaver speaking of lost grandeur and opportunity. His velvets and cloths of gold, no longer required, are more poignant as a *memento mori* for the sudden, unexpected juxtaposition of life and death.

On the same day as the inventory of Richmond's possessions was compiled, another document raised questions about the futures of the staff in his household. Appearing to originate from Tonge, and perhaps also authored by John Gostwick, the document asked how long the staff would remain in post and if some might be taken into the king's guard. Others wanted to know what liveries of black cloth they were to receive for mourning and whether their fees and entitlements would be continued or matched. The duke's governor, George Cotton, was in receipt of an annual salary of £20 while his brother Richard, as steward, received £16 13s 4d.[102] There were twenty-one gentleman yeomen and grooms, of whom eleven were married, and the yeomen of the chamber followed a similar pattern. Then there were other servants, stable workers, kitchen staff, laundry workers, estate keepers, clerks, secretaries and all the other offices that comprised the household of a king's son. Just as with Arthur Tudor and, to a different extent, Edward of Westminster, the royal heir's household was a symbol of hope. It attracted the service and loyalty of men who saw it as a potential lifelong connection, an investment in an individual whose fortunes were expected to rise, carrying their servants with them. It was a household in waiting, established solely around the existence of an individual prince. When that prince died, the household was broken up almost at once, and sometimes the servants found a place with other family members or patrons, or sometimes with other rising stars at court. In some cases it must have been a struggle. The Cotton brothers were fortunate enough to find favour with the king, George being knighted on 19 October and receiving the grant of Combermere in Shropshire, while Richard found a new role under Cromwell, supplying the royal troops who had been sent north to deal with the rebel uprising known as the Pilgrimage of Grace. After the birth of Prince Edward, a new opportunity arose for which the Cottons' experience with Richmond proved excellent preparation. Richard became cofferer and comptroller in the new prince's household in 1538, while George was his vice chamberlain.[103]

In a strange twist of fate, the tragedy that had befallen the English king was mirrored, just weeks later, in France. As Henry VIII had lost a potential heir, so the King of France suffered a similar bereavement in the August of 1536, only this heir was his eldest legitimate son. During Fitzroy and Surrey's 1532–33 sojourn in France, the English king's son had lived closely with the Valois royal family, including the Dauphin, Francis. The young man, reputedly very beautiful, was around sixteen months older than Fitzroy and the decorations for his christening had been designed by Leonardo da Vinci. He had briefly been engaged to Henry's daughter Mary, and great things were expected of him, before events on the international stage had changed his character. Sombre and serious after his period of incarceration by the emperor, his health had never really recovered from the years spent in the damp, dark cell in Madrid. Just three years after Fitzroy left France, the Dauphin died on 10 August 1536, at the age of 18. It was not even three weeks after Fitzroy's passing and, likely, of the same cause. His contemporaries blamed poison, as he had been taken ill after requesting a glass of water following a tennis game. His secretary, Montecuccoli, who had brought him the drink, was an Italian promoted by Francis's sister-in-law, Catherine de Medici, and thus an easy target. He confessed to poisoning under torture and, although he later retracted, suffered a traitor's death. Other contemporary evidence suggested his poor health since his imprisonment led him to develop tuberculosis.

The deaths of Henry Fitzroy and the Dauphin Francis, as well as those of Arthur Tudor and, in 1553, Henry VIII's second son, Edward VI, help define the nature, spread, symptoms and diagnosis of tuberculosis in the first half of the sixteenth century. Then referred to as phthisis, and later as consumption, the illness has become something of a default option, the usual explanation given by historians for the unexplained deaths of young people whose symptoms might broadly fit. In many cases, there is good reason for this, as contemporary doctors sometimes identified the illness, such as with Arthur at Ludlow in 1502, and Chapuys's reported diagnosis of Richmond. Yet diagnosis and fact do not always correlate when it comes to historical medicine, so the question must remain open, qualified by lack of evidence. Of all these young men claimed by disease, it seems most likely that Edward VI died of tuberculosis, or an infection complicating it, or arising from it, given the reports of him coughing up black and yellow sputum. However, the Tudor family in particular were to suffer more than their fair share of similar deaths, especially among youths of a certain age. Arthur and Edward VI were both 15 and Richmond 17. Despite this apparent family connection, tuberculosis is not a hereditary illness. It is transmitted by infection, the bacillus mycobacterium tuberculosis passed from one individual to another through speaking, coughing or sneezing. Yet heredity may have played a part. There may have been certain inherited defects or weaknesses in the family that made the young Tudor men more susceptible to infection, such as poor immune systems or weak lungs. Something in Henry VII's genes may have contributed to the vulnerability of his eldest son and grandsons in the face of an untreatable disease.

Tuberculosis can be difficult to diagnose, especially if it never develops from the latent to the acute phase. Frequent or close contact with other sufferers creates a higher risk of infection and someone with untreated acute tuberculosis can infect an estimated ten, fifteen or more people a year through physical proximity.[104] At the end of his life, it was clear that Henry VII was suffering from the illness, with his repeated lung trouble and infections. Earlier bouts of ill health suggest that he might have been struggling with it for years. When it came to treating the sick, Tudor notions of medicine might also have contributed to the spread of the disease, given doctors' tendency to seal off invalids in hot, dark rooms when the effectiveness of ventilation is a factor for the survival of the bacillus. Tuberculosis usually affects the lungs and often shows no symptoms, lying latent, with only around 10 per cent of cases becoming acute and proving fatal. Symptoms include coughing and chest pains, also weight loss, fever and fatigue, which might be mistaken for other causes. In 15 to 20 per cent of cases, particularly among the young, the illness can sometimes spread from the lungs to other organs. Only those in the acute phase can spread the illness and, without treatment, the death rate for active cases is 66 per cent.[105]

Some indication of just how virulent the disease could be, prior to the discovery of a treatment, is found in data collated by the Office of National Statistics, which record deaths in Britain from the condition throughout the twentieth century. In 1918, 46,200 people died from the illness, falling to 29,800 in 1928 and 21,900 in 1938. After a cure was discovered in the mid-1940s, the death rate dropped off even more dramatically, claiming 15,600 lives in 1948 and just 2,950 in 1958. By 2008, the condition claimed only 339 deaths, a drop of more than 100 per cent.[106] In this context, it is easy to see how the chances of surviving tuberculosis in the medieval and Tudor period were very slim, if the immune system was already weakened and given potentially prolonged exposure to acutely infected individuals. As Richmond's half-brother was to illustrate, repeated illness could wreak havoc on a susceptible young body, once again snatching away the chance of a potentially glorious life and reign.

What sort of king might Henry Fitzroy have made? From all contemporary descriptions, he seems to have been a young man very much in his father's model; handsome and red-haired, intelligent and well-read but preferring sport, fond of chivalry and romance, if Surrey's poetry is to be believed. The correspondence regarding his childhood establishment at Sheriff Hutton also gives glimpses of a boy who could be assertive, possibly even strong-willed, although he might be too easily distracted. This all sounds very much like a young Henry VIII, happy to leave the boring details of business to Wolsey while he hunted and danced.

There would have been no difficult minority under Fitzroy, had he succeeded in 1547, and the smooth transition of power would have been effected by his established ties of loyalty with some of the most powerful figures at court, as well as his friendships with the kings of Scotland and France. Furthermore, he might even have been better prepared to rule than his father, whose teenage years under Henry VII had been sheltered, with little effort made to prepare the young man for kingship. Although Fitzroy had not been raised for kingship, just like his father during the life of Prince Arthur, he had been raised as the king's only son. He had experience in the process of ruling in the north, witnessing justice and interceding on behalf of his allies. He had been frequently at court, taking part in rituals like the garter ceremonies but also taking a regular seat in Parliament. More recently, he had understood the changing nature of religion in the country, sitting in the reformation council, representing Henry at the executions of Carthusian monks who refused the submit to the royal will, and he had been a witness to the removal of a queen. All this had taught him valuable lessons in the absolute authority of the Crown and the methods for ensuring its continuity. Yet his was likely to have been a peaceful rule. Where his father had gone to war with France and Spain, Fitzroy's existing friendships would have allowed for greater harmony with Francis I and the new Dauphin, Henri, who was just three months his elder, and with his cousin James V. Having been raised in the 1520s, in the era before the Dissolution of the Monasteries and the break with Rome, it is impossible to know whether Richmond would have leaned more towards his early experiences of religion, or allowed his father's settlements of the 1530s to stand, or even whether he would have pushed for greater reform. He would certainly have been of an age to resist pressure from councillors who hoped to take the country further down the route of Protestantism, had he not wished to do so. Richmond's fertility was untried, but he had a young wife who was apparently healthy and would outlive him by two decades. It is not implausible that Mary might have borne at least one son while the pair were in their prime. Even the stigma of illegitimacy might have been overcome, as Henry ruled in the second Act of Succession. Fitzroy might have become a great king, like his father, but perhaps even better. Everything seemed to be moving in that direction in the early summer of 1536. As events transpired, though, the pendulum of fate was to swing the other way.

9

King Edward VI (1537–53)

I

The world into which the future Edward VI was born had changed completely from that of his predecessors. In the space of a generation, England had been wrenched, by force of law and violence, away from its medieval, Catholic mindset towards a far more modern way of thinking. The children born in the 1520s and '30s found themselves to be pioneers in a Renaissance world, where centuries-old traditions and ways of worship had been rejected in favour of a new faith, but the changes were still new enough to require definition and shape in order to become habits. While the Renaissance had forged new identities, the dramatic iconoclasm of the Reformation was still evolving. England no longer followed the dictates of a distant pope in the sacked city of Rome, its subjects owed their whole allegiance to their king. And Henry VIII had proved himself to be godlike in his kingship, restructuring his world to fit his needs. The issues of education, of life and death, and how the self and the nation were to be defined, were now under debate and there were some who still wanted to push the religious reforms further. In 1537, against this backdrop of change, the long-awaited fruit of Henry VIII's labour arrived in the shape of a legitimate son. Fifteen months after he had lost Henry Fitzroy, the boy he had been preparing to name as his heir, the king's dynastic ambitions were finally achieved.

Henry VIII's transition from his second to his third wife had been swiftly accomplished. Eleven days after the death of Anne Boleyn, he had been married to Jane Seymour in a quiet ceremony at Whitehall. Just like Anne, the new queen was a maid of honour to her predecessor, but Jane's mild, quiet compliance stood in stark contrast to the passion and fire of Henry's previous queens. The daughter of Sir John Seymour of Wulf Hall in Wiltshire, she was in her late twenties when she attracted the king's attention and their swift, secret wedding at Whitehall was followed, five days later, by her public proclamation as queen. Nine months later Jane fell pregnant and she had retreated to Hampton Court to enter her confinement by September. The sweating sickness was rife again and, given his experiences with illness, the king was understandably concerned. Norfolk wrote to Cromwell on 11 October that 'the death is extremely sore in London' and had also reached 'other places near Hampton Court' so that the king went to Esher, to reduce traffic around the queen. Precautions were being taken about admission to the palace, with a recognition that certain age groups were more likely to spread infection, and it was ruled that 'no young folks may come within the gates'. Norfolk asked Cromwell for guidance about approaching the king, as he did not wish to come to him 'out of any contagious air'.[1]

As Norfolk wrote, Jane was already in labour. She reputedly endured almost two days of struggling with the delivery before finally giving birth to a son in the early hours of 12 October. It was the day before St Edward's day, and the boy was given the saint's name, perhaps because of his mother's old-style Catholic devotion, perhaps also in reference to the king's grandfather. All the king's previous sons, including those short-lived ones by Catherine of Aragon, had been given the name Henry, so this marked a departure. The king might have hoped it would break an unfortunate cycle. The queen wrote to Cromwell, informing him of the birth of her son 'conceived in lawful matrimony'[2] and guns were fired from the Tower of London. Plans went ahead for the boy's christening, with careful precautions regarding the widespread sickness. Lord Maltravers wrote from Croydon that the king was 'not willing that the writer should come to Court at present from fear of the infection'[3] and the mayor and sheriffs were to forbid 'the access of persons to the court ... without special letters from the King ... on account of the plague'. The number of people given access to the court was not to exceed six in the company of a duke, four for an earl, three for a baron and so on.[4]

The christening took place at Hampton Court on 15 October, when the baby was three days old. To celebrate the occasion, Te Deums were sung in Westminster Abbey and other churches across the country 'and great fires [were lit] in every street, and [there was] goodly banqueting and triumphing cheer with shooting of guns all day and night, and messengers were sent to all the estates and cities of the realm, to whom were given great gifts'.[5] There was a long and dignified procession into the chapel, with gentlemen, knights, bishops and abbots preceding councillors, lords, royal household and ambassadors then came the Earl of Sussex bearing two covered basins, Wiltshire holding a taper of wax and the Earl of Essex carrying the golden bowl containing salt. Princess Elizabeth, at just 4 years old, bore the baby's chrisom, or baptismal cloth, and the wife of the Marquis of Exeter carried the child under a canopy. Princess Mary, aged 21, was a godmother and walked behind the canopy, her train carried by Lady Kingston.[6] After he was named, and given the titles of Duke of Cornwall and Earl of Chester, tapers were lit, the baby was returned to his mother and spices, wafers and spiced wine were served to the guests.

Jane did not live to enjoy her new motherhood. The Earl of Rutland reported that on the afternoon of 23 October, she had suffered 'an natural laxe', or bleed, after which she appeared to improve a little. However, all through that night she was 'very sick' so that her confessor was summoned and, by eight the following morning, he was preparing to administer the last rites.[7] Prayers were ordered for her recovery and, as Sir Thomas Palmer hoped, 'if good prayers can save her, she is not like to die, for never lady was so much plained [lamented for] with every man, rich and poor'.[8] Anticipating the worst, Norfolk 'sorrowfully' wrote to Cromwell, asking him 'to be here tomorrow early to comfort our good master, for as our mistress there is no likelihood of her life, the more pity, and I fear she shall not be on lyve at the time ye shall read this'.[9] Jane died of infection, or complications arising from the birth, on 24 October. John Hutton's letter to Cromwell expressed the death of other hopes in the queen's demise: 'we hoped her grace should have brought forth more fruit, but the power of God ought to be esteemed all for the best.'[10] On the same day, the king wrote to Francis I of his mixed emotions:

> I have so cordially received the congratulations, which, by this bearer and by your letters, you have made me for the son which it has pleased God to give me, that I desire nothing more than an occasion by the success of your good desires to make the like. Notwithstanding, Divine Providence has mingled my joy with the bitterness of the death of her who brought me this happiness.[11]

However, life had to continue, except that now Henry had his legitimate son. Two weeks later, on 3 November, Sir John Wallop wrote to Lord Lisle that 'the King is in good health and merry as a widower may be, the Prince also'.[12]

The funeral arrangements for Jane Seymour were the first in the royal family after the religious reforms of the mid-1530s. Catherine of Aragon had been buried as a widowed Princess of Wales in Peterborough Cathedral while Anne Boleyn's remains had been laid to rest in the chapel of St Peter ad Vincula, the traditional site for the burials of important figures executed on Tower Green. Jane died in the estate of a queen but, more so, a queen who had recently delivered Henry the legitimate son he had longed for. She was also the first queen to have died with that status since Henry's mother, Elizabeth of York and, like her, it had been a death shortly after childbirth. Therefore, her funeral on 12 November was a model of the most honourable practices of the moment. Although he had been critical of the way Norfolk had dealt with the burial of Henry Fitzroy, the king entrusted the duke and Sir William Paulet with the arrangements, as he took the traditional route of retiring 'to a solitary place to pass his sorrows'.[13] Norfolk sought out the accounts of Elizabeth of York's funeral in 1503, although he was probably an eyewitness to that occasion, having been 30 at the time of her death. The honours that had been given to Elizabeth were now bestowed on her daughter-in-law, with a slight twist to take account for the religious changes.

Jane's body was prepared by the wax chandler, who removed her entrails 'with searing, balming, spicing, and trammeling in cloth' before passing her on to the plumber, who leaded, soldered and chested her. Her organs were interred in the chapel while her body was laid under a hearse and surrounded by twenty-one lit tapers and a crowd of waiting women who 'put off their rich apparel, doing on their mourning habit and white kerchers hanging over their heads and shoulders'.[14] In contrast, the queen's effigy was dressed in cloth of gold and jewels. The chapel, chamber and galleries were hung with black cloth and decorated with images. A constant watch was kept over Jane's remains, ensured by a relay of mourners from the court and the chief clergymen of the land taking it in turns to conduct the mass. Finally, after twelve days in state, the queen was placed upon a chariot drawn by six horses and borne in a procession led by men with black staves and 200 poor wearing the queen's badge. Jane's final journey took her the 15 miles from Hampton Court to Windsor, followed by five chariots of her waiting women and almoners distributing money along the way. Dirges were sung upon her arrival, as she was conducted into St George's Abbey along a route lined with hangings more masses were said and watch was kept overnight. She was buried the following morning, and a feast was provided in Windsor Castle for the mourners. Jane was also commemorated in London, with dirges sung, 1,200 masses said and bells rung in St Paul's Cathedral, also by Norfolk's doing.[15]

There would be no chantry chapel for Jane and no fund set up to guarantee her swift passage through purgatory. In 1529, Henry VIII had passed an act forbidding payments for masses for the dead and his ban on the building of any more chantries was only eight years away. One of the last to be completed was that of Richard Fox at Winchester in 1528, featuring a cadaver tomb that showed the skeletal bishop with his head back and mouth open, appearing to writhe in agony. However, it is significant that, during this in-between stage, masses were still said for Jane's soul. This would be banned during the reign of her son. Jane was placed in a vault under the quire, at the eastern end of the chapel under the choir stalls. She did not receive a formal tomb, but this was intended to be a temporary measure, as Henry planned to be laid to rest beside her, in a dynastic move to emphasise the heritage and legitimacy of their son. When drafting his will in 1546, Henry asked to be placed with her, halfway between the altar and the sovereign's garter stall, until a more permanent tomb was created for them both. Once the tomb had been completed, he intended them to be moved into a separate chapel in the east of the church, imagining that this would take place fairly soon, as the tomb was 'almost made'.

Yet the tomb which Henry intended for himself and his wife to lie under in eternal rest, was not his. Just as he had 'appropriated' the possessions and properties of his chief minister, Cardinal Wolsey, he had also stolen the man's tomb. Back in 1518, Henry had planned a magnificent joint tomb for himself and Catherine of Aragon, made by the Italian Pietro Torrigiano, who had created the representation of the king's parents in bronze, in Westminster's Lady Chapel. Following this example, the king's sarcophagus was to be made of white marble and black touchstone, except it was to be a quarter bigger than that of his father. However, Torrigiano left England the following year, so Henry had to seek inspiration elsewhere. He turned, in 1527, to Jacopo Sansovino, who planned him a structure made from 'oriental stones' with life-size statues of Henry on horseback and Jane in gold, set amid white marble pillars, gilded angels and 143 saints, prophets and other figures. The details for this tomb were included in a manuscript seen by the seventeenth-century antiquarian John Speed, but have since been lost. For some reason, the project never came to fruition and, two decades later, Henry was still casting about for a suitable tomb. He found one, abandoned before completion, in the stonemasons' Westminster workshops.

Back in 1524, Wolsey had commissioned another Italian Renaissance sculptor, Benedetto de Rovenzanno, to create him a memorial, and the marble base, pillars and statues were well underway by the time of the minister's fall five years later. The tomb is a perfect symbol of the changes that Henry had instigated, rejecting the late medieval desire to control the manner of one's remembrance after death, and also just how far Henry had unleashed forces of religious reform that even he had not anticipated. It is ironic that Henry did not get to enjoy this tomb either, and remains under a simple marble slab, set into the floor. Also, despite all his noisy iconoclasm, Henry could not ultimately relinquish the Catholic faith into which he had been born. As well as requisitioning Wolsey's tomb, he left instructions for an altar to be constructed in his memorial chapel, topped by a canopy of angels, where daily masses were to be said for his soul and for Jane's. There were to be statues of children and apostles carrying candles, as well as 9ft-tall free-standing candles. The entire area was to be enclosed in bronze and black marble walls, which all sounds rather like a chantry chapel. Rovenzanno and his assistant worked on the tomb from 1530 to 1536, by which point the effigy of the king had been cast and polished, and on into the 1540s, until the artist returned to Italy. After that, Henry employed Giovanni Portinari during December 1543, paying him £37 9s 2d for copper and his labour.[16] It was incomplete at the time of Henry's death and, despite the directions in his son's will, was never finished. The tomb was broken up and sold to raise funds during the civil war, a century after the king's death.[17]

But at the time of Edward's birth in October 1537, his father's death was still a decade away. Henry might have been plunged into deepest mourning, dressing in black for three months, but provision needed to be made for the young life he had created; his son, the prince, England's future king. Whatever grief Henry might be feeling was offset by the existence of this legitimate prince, this new chance after the loss of Fitzroy, and Henry would spend his final years obsessing over the details to get it right. Edward's first household was run by Lady Margaret Bryan, who had also been governess to the king's three other children. She had been looking after Princess Elizabeth, but then stepped in to oversee Edward's infancy, following the king's detailed instructions about the standards of cleanliness and behaviour in the household. Edward was thriving and, 'our Lord be thanked, is in good health, and sucketh like a child of his puissance'.[18] Leland stated that his wet nurse was a Clara Domo but Holbein painted a portrait of a Margaret Clement (née Giggs) which was mislabelled as 'Mother Jak', a woman who was also reputed to be nursing the prince. There were four rockers and the lady mistress was Blanche Herbert, née Milborne, who later joined Princess Elizabeth's household as Blanche Parry. Edward's elder sister Mary was also a regular visitor to his nursery, travelling by barge along the river from her base at Richmond to Hampton Court, where her visits prompted payments to the prince's minstrels.[19]

Soon, male appointments were made to Edward's household too, as befitted his age and status. In March 1538, Sir William Sidney was appointed as his Chamberlain, Sir John Cornwallis as Steward, Richard Cotton vice chamberlain and Edward Cornwallis groom porter of the house.[20] Sidney was a veteran of the Tudor court, having fought at Flodden, been appointed Squire to the Body for Henry VIII, accompanied him to France and fought under his brother-in-law, Charles Brandon. Sir John Cornwallis had served in Brittany. Their instructions included the need to take 'alle diligent and honest heed, caution and foresight' to avoid 'all practises and evil enterprises which might be devised against his grace or the danger of his person'. It was Sidney's job to have the 'keeping, oversight, care and cure' of 'his majesty and the whole realm's most precious jewel' and see that 'all dangers and all adversaries of malicious persons and casual harms shall be vigilantly foreseen and avoided'. He was to observe that good order was kept in the household, admitting no strangers and permitting no one except the appointed officials to be in the prince's company to have access to his chamber, or to touch his person or cradle. Only those with a special token or express permission from the king should be admitted and no one under the position of a knight. Even then, they should only be allowed to kiss his hand. The household officials were to ensure that 'good, sufficient and large' quantities of all kinds of bread, meat and drink, eggs and butter were prepared for the prince and that his linen and clothing were to be 'purely washed, clean dried, kept, brushed and reserved cleanly ... without any intermeddling' by other persons with no place there. All new purchases, whether it be clothing, wool, linen, silk or gold, was to be 'newe wasshed, bifore his grace shall wear any of the same' and should be brushed, made clean, aired and the fire and perfumed thoroughly so the prince should have 'no harm or displeasure'.[21]

Crucially, the prince's new servants were to 'advoyde alle infection and daungier of pestilence and contagious diseases' by preventing any members of the household who were in direct contact with Edward from travelling to London or other towns during the summer months or other peak times of contagion. If such a journey were essential, they should obtain a licence to visit but, upon their return, refrain from entering the boy's presence for several days, until they could be pronounced clear of infection. If anyone in the household should unexpectedly fall ill, they were to be removed from the premises immediately. Henry was also concerned about the boys employed in places like the scullery and cellar, kitchen and woodyard, who 'without any respect go to and fro, and be not warre [aware] of the daungers of infection and do often times resort into suspect places'. Therefore, none was to be admitted into the house. The king may have had his brother Arthur in mind when he set down rules concerning another potential source of illness. It was traditional for poor people to wait at the gates of aristocratic properties asking for alms, so to keep them at a distance Henry ruled that a place should be appointed for them to gather, a good distance away. Any who ventured closer to the house should be grievously punished as an example to others.

The conduct of the prince's servants was of great significance. He was not to be served with anything to eat or drink, except that which was fed to everyone, allowing no one to meddle with it, and it was to be tested carefully from time to time.[22] The king was clearly not prepared to take any chances after the losses he had experienced.

And yet, it was Henry's health that was to cause concern in May 1538. As the French ambassador Castillon reported, it was the habit of the king's physicians to keep open the fistula on his leg, to allow it to drain. Early in the month, it closed over for ten or twelve days, meaning that 'the humours which had no outlet were like to have stifled him.' He was in severe danger, unable to speak and turning 'black in the face'. It sent the lords into turmoil, contemplating his demise, Castillon believing 'there would be much folly' with 'one party ... for the young Prince and the other for Madame Mary'.[23] Fortunately, Henry recovered completely and, just three days after the ambassador had composed his letter, went to visit Edward, whose household had moved from Hampton Court to Hunsdon House in Hertfordshire. Despite his full recovery, this episode served to confirm the dangerous combination of the king's volatile health and the prince's extreme youth.

II

Edward was to spend much of his childhood on the Hunsdon estate. It had formerly been in the possession of the Duke of Norfolk's father, but passed to the Crown on his death in 1525. Henry VIII had then developed the property, creating royal apartments and an estate including a moat. In February 1534 the 'master surveyor of the King's works at Hunsdon' reported on the newly installed 'parelles' of freestone for the chimneys in the:

> King's watching chamber, palett chamber, privy chamber, and in the other chamber beneath the same; for lime, plaster, "rigge tyles," corner tiles, paving tiles and plain tiles; for timber, and for wood bought by the acre; for wainscoats, laths, pails, tile pins, hooks, hinges, locks, clasps, keys … new glass bought of Galyon Hone and "sett with symond," which cost the King £2,900.[24]

Hunsdon was also where Henry had fled to escape the sweating sickness in the 1520s, so it was clearly considered a healthy and secluded place. It is shown in a portrait of Edward, painted early in his reign, glimpsed in the distance through a window. That month, possibly on the occasion of this visit, Henry was observed holding Edward 'dallying with him in his arms … and so holding him in a window to the sight and great comfort of the people'.

By 30 June, the prince's household had moved to Havering Palace, or Havering atte Bower in Essex. It was from there that Margaret Bryan wrote to Cromwell, promising to dress the child well for a forthcoming engagement, even though her resources were 'very bare'. She explained that Edward's best coat was 'tinsel and that he shall have on at that time. He hath never a good jewel to set in his cap'. She was also able to report that the prince was 'in good health and merry' and that he currently had four teeth, 'three full out and the fourth appearing'.[25] Perhaps Edward was to be readied for the visit of some of the king's council that September, including Thomas Audley and the Earl of Oxford. On the eighth of the month, they thanked the king for 'their licence to visit my lord Prince' and agreed that they never saw 'so goodly a child of his age, so merry, so pleasant, so good and loving countenance and so earnest an eye as it were a sage judgement towards every person that repaireth to his Grace'. Edward had grown, losing some of his baby fat; he could stand and 'would walk if they let him'.[26] However, Audley recommended that he be not allowed to push himself too far too fast, 'considering that his Grace is yet tender ... he should not strain himself, as his courage would serve him, till he come above a year of age.'[27] In October, Sybille Penne, Sidney's sister-in-law, was appointed as Edward's dry nurse, suggesting that he was weaned around this time. Sidney wrote to Cromwell, thanking him for the appointment and stating that he would not have recommended her if he was not 'right well assured of her good demeanor, ableness, honesty and truth' and she would show 'no want of diligence nor scarcity of goodwill' in accomplishing her work.[28] By the end of the year, George Owen had been appointed as the prince's doctor, and would remain so until the boy's death.

Havering was considered a good house for the summer, but too cold for the winter, so the prince and his establishment returned to Hunsdon for the season. They celebrated Christmas and the New Year there, and the prince received gifts from his family and his father's council. Lady Mary gave him an embroidered coat of crimson satin, Lady Elizabeth a cambric shirt she had made with her own hands, while the Earl of Essex gave him a gold bell and whistle, two oxen and twenty mutton, Southampton gave him a bonnet and others sent cups and bowls of silver and gilt, more meat.[29] That March, Margaret Bryan wrote to Henry from Hunsdon to report that 'My Lord Prince is in good health and merry. Would to

God the King and your Lordship had seen him last night. The minstrels played, and his Grace danced and played so wantonly that he could not stand still.'[30] Around this time, Edward was also visited by ambassadors from Cleves, when Henry was negotiating his fourth marriage, but burst into tears at the sight of the strange gentlemen.[31]

It was also around this time that the first portrait of Edward appears. Painted by Hans Holbein in 1539, it shows the prince as a chubby toddler with bulbous cheeks, sitting upright and looking directly towards the viewer, although his gaze is slightly dropped. He has a large, broad head, like a childish version of his father, with a prominent small chin, a square jaw and rosebud lips. His nose is the same as Holbein's depiction of Henry VIII's in 1538 and his eyes appear dark and a little drooping under fair, scanty brows. A little fair hair appears on his forehead, trimmed into a fringe or scraped back under his cap. He is dressed in an outfit of red and gold, his bonnet gold with dark stripes and white lining sitting beneath a red velvet hat stitched with golden beads and topped with a white feather. His red doublet is piped with gold, nipped in at the waist and a mantle, or longer sleeves, falls back to reveal full sleeves in gold, embroidered with black, the white frilly of his chemise showing. He stands behind a bench draped in green velvet, his chubby right hand raised and a golden rattle, resembling a sceptre, clasped in his left. A Latin text inscribed on a scroll below exhorts him to become his father's equal, or else to surpass him. The impression, despite his youth, is one of dignity, majesty and solidity.

The prince's health was of critical importance. All the accounts of Edward's young years repeat that he was a healthy child. The exception to this was a bout of quartan fever at the age of 4, a kind of malaria that recurs every three days. Returning from visiting the north in autumn 1541, Henry was deeply concerned and summoned 'all the physicians of the country to advise'; 'after long consultation', they agreed that the fever would endanger the prince, one of them adding in secret to the French ambassador that 'the Prince was so fat and unhealthy as to be unlikely to live long'.[32] For around ten days, Edward's life was despaired of, but then he began to rally and grew stronger. Dr Butts was dispatched to nurse the boy, who quickly grew impatient with the invalid diet he was prescribed, demanding meat instead of the broths and soups he was brought. In contrast, the king was so fearful of losing his only surviving son that he was unable to eat, being 'sad and disinclined for feasting' until the boy improved. It may be, though, that this illness recurred at this point, or created some weakness in his immune system, that prompted the doctors to fear in April 1542 that he would not enjoy a long life.

In 1536, Thomas Elyot's *Castell of Health* laid out some very specific guidelines for diet and exercise. The Renaissance belief that the four Galenic humours governed the body dictated the kind of food that should be consumed, depending upon the time of year. In the winter, which Elyot defined as between 12 December and 9 March, 'rheums and moisture' were on the increase, meaning a greater risk of colds and illnesses, which should be balanced with the moderate use of hot meat and drink and the abundant consumption of wine. From the start of March until the end of April, with the onset of spring, sharp juices should be taken, while from April until June, sweet tastes were better for the health, and so on. Elyot also commented that 'some children and young men, either by debility of nature, or some accidental cause, as sickness or much study, happen to gather humours phlegmatic or melancholy in the places of digestion so that concoction, or digestion, is weak in them.' This acknowledgement of the frailty of male youth was accompanied by the recommendation that they follow the diet of old men and respect their own balance of humours, eating hot foods if their temperament was cold, or wet foods if it was dry. Elyot recommended that boys should eat three meals a day until the age of 11, with an interval of four hours between breakfast and dinner and six between dinner and supper. They should not drink too much, as drink could drown the meat they ate and engender too much phlegm. There were also important rules to be followed about the order in which meats were eaten, the importance of sleep, the nature of exercise and when it should be taken.[33] It seems unlikely, given the importance of Edward's health, that those in charge of his care did not follow the latest beliefs about nutrition, although Elyot's attempts to place medical knowledge in the hands of those without an understanding of Greek may have been scorned by the court doctors. However, his writings were to prove very popular.

In addition, Elyot identified further maladies and weaknesses that were specific to gender and age groups. During their early infancy, children were particularly susceptible to vomiting, coughs, sores in the mouth, inflammation of the navel, moisture in the ears and fearfulness. When they started to cut their first teeth, fevers and cramps might accompany pain in the jaws and as they grew a little older, the dangers of worms in the belly and swellings under the chin might arise, along with the measles and small pox. It is also very interesting that Elyot saw the age of 14 and the middle to late teens to be a dangerous time for young men. They were prey to all kinds of fevers; pleurisy, the spitting and vomiting of blood, inflammation of the lungs, diseases of the sides, lethargies, frenzies, hot sicknesses and choleric passions.[34] Some of these are clearly medically based and accord with information given by twenty-first-century institutions about the risks for the 14–19 age range, including asthma, bronchitis and tuberculosis, brain and nervous conditions, cancers, blood disorders and hereditary illness.[35] Yet others may also straddle emotional and mental conditions, with 'hot sicknesses' and 'choleric passions' capturing a wider truth about the dangers of adolescence as a young man in both eras. While the 'teenage angst' of later times was not a recognised phenomenon in the sixteenth century, young people were biologically the same as today and experienced physical and hormonal changes that could bring about dramatic emotions. For the Tudors, these would have been manifest and interpreted in different ways, perhaps masked by the physicality of jousting or battle, or diagnosed as melancholy. The times are too different to draw direct parallels, but Elyot's work is one of the first indicators that the teenage years were considered potentially dangerous for young men.

It is no wonder, therefore, that the dedication of those who cared for Edward during these years was well rewarded. Sybille Penne was mentioned in the royal accounts at the end of March 1541, 'in consideration of her services in the nurture and education of Prince Edward,' receiving the Manor of Beamonde, Bucks, and rectory of Little Myssenden, Bucks, *Burcester;* manor or farm called Aufrikkes in Little Myssenden, Godstow; rectory of Penne, Bucks, and two cottages in

Penne, Chacombe; with advowsons of the churches of Little Myssenden and Penne.[36] The following July, George Carleton was given properties, lands and fishing rights in Cambridgeshire for his services to Prince Edward, as well as 'half the messuage called the Unicorn in Cheapside, London, lands in Cambridge and Ely, and 40 acres of marsh in the fen end of Wysbyche',[37] while Elizabeth Mustchamp, widow, a servant to Prince Edward was granted an annuity of £6 13s 4d for life.[38] In May 1543, Sir William Sydney, 'the King's servant' and Dame Agnes his wife were awarded the rents on leases belonging to St Swithin's Cathedral, Winchester, in 'consideration of [their] services to the prince,'[39] while Lady Margaret Bryan was given an annuity of £20.

One of Edward's first friends during these early years was Jane Dormer, later the Duchess of Feria. She was a frequent visitor to Edward's household, being a granddaughter of William Sidney, borne by the Sidneys' eldest daughter Mary, who had married William Dormer, a servant of Cromwell. Younger than Edward by three months, Jane was encouraged to play with the prince, who seemed to have become genuinely fond of her, calling her 'my Jane'. They read together, played and danced, 'and such like pastimes, answerable to their spirits and innocency of years'. Jane described him as being 'of great towardness to all virtuous parts and princely qualities, a marvellous sweet child, of very mild and generous condition'. Reputedly, when he beat her at cards, Edward laughed that 'now Jane, your King is gone, I shall be good enough for you.'[40]

Things changed for Edward in 1543. Firstly, his position changed at the age of 6, which he reached that October. He was no longer considered an infant who could live in an all-female sphere, but had entered the next phase of life, requiring new clothes, a new household and influences, even a new regime. On a personal level, though, with the king's last two marriages, to Anne of Cleves and Catherine Howard, proving to be disasters, it was with some relief that all Henry's children welcomed a new stepmother, Catherine Parr. Twice widowed already, Catherine had been a member of Princess Mary's household, just as her mother Maud had served Henry's first wife, Catherine of Aragon. Born around 1513, when the Spanish queen was at the height of her power and popularity, it is quite likely that she had been named after the queen, or was even perhaps her goddaughter. Catherine Parr's influence upon the king was to be a positive one. She encouraged him to reunite his children and welcomed them at court. She was also an educated, intelligent woman, dedicated to the reformed cause that Edward would embrace. It may even have been her influence that set him on that path. In December 1543, they all spent Christmas together at Whitehall and, the following spring, Edward's sisters were restored to their place in the succession after their brother, although he would later choose to ignore this.

The remodelling of Edward's household introduced him to new figures and new influences. Among his early tutors were Roger Ascham, one of the best Greek scholars of his day, who taught the prince calligraphy; Edmund Grindal, who wrote that the boy was 'wonderfully advanced of his years'; Richard Cox his almoner, whom Ascham considered to be 'the best schoolmaster of his time';[41] and John Belmaine, his tutor in French. He also received instruction from Randolph, a German, and Anthony Cooke, a humanist scholar whom the prince described as speaking 'weighingly'.[42] He was taught to play the lute by Philip van Wilder and showed typical Renaissance interest in the world by making a collection of globes and maps. Later, in 1544, Sir John Cheke would be confirmed as Edward's tutor to teach him 'of tongues, of the scripture, of philosophy and all liberal sciences'. Ascham described this appointment as 'full of hope, comfort and solace to all true hearts in England', which prayed daily that the prince would surpass his tutor in 'learning and knowledge, following his father in wisdom and felicity, [and] may so set out and maintain God's word, to the abolishment of all papistry, the confusion of all heresy that thereby he, feared of his enemies, loved of all his subjects may bring to his own glory, immortal fame and memory, to this realm wealth, honour and felicity, to true and unfeigned religion, perpetual peace, concord and felicity'.[43] John Cheke wrote that 'with God's blessing he will prove such a King, as neither to yield to Josiah in the maintenance of the true religion, nor to Solomon in the management of the estate, nor to David in the encouragement of godliness.' Edward was being raised in an environment of Protestant humanism.

Following the usual tradition for royal heirs, a number of young men were appointed to Edward's household, to 'be attendant upon [him] as by example of good education, as well in nurture as in good learning [who] might the more fairly induce him to profit in his learning'.[44] Chief among them was Barnaby Fitzpatrick, around two years older than the prince, who had been sent to England by his Irish father as a guarantee of peace between the two countries. Fitzpatrick was the prince's lifelong friend and whipping boy, receiving the corporal punishments that Edward earned, yet which were deemed inappropriate to be meted out to one of such rank. The pair continued to correspond after Fitzpatrick returned to Ireland at the end of 1552 and, by the following summer, four young men were resident at court as Edward's companions. There was Thomas Howard, son of Henry Fitzroy's closest friend Henry, Earl of Surrey; and Giles Paulet, a younger son of the Marquis of Winchester John, Lord Lumley, to whom Edward restored the titles of his executed father; and James Blount, Sixth Lord Mountjoy, later an ardent Protestant and alchemist.

When Blount's father contemplated his mortality in 1544, he left a striking memorial for his family, to remind them to always be mindful of their duty and of the possibility of imminent death. Charles Blount, the Fifth Lord Mountjoy had been tutored by John Palsgrave, whose former pupils had included Henry Fitzroy, and by the antiquarian John Leland and humanist scholar John Luis Vives. A secret Catholic, he gave shelter to the controversial priest Richard Whitford, who lived under his roof from 1539 to 1542, and tutored his children, although James would later shake off this influence in favour of the new faith. As he was about to embark for France with Henry VIII at the end of April 1544, he drew up a will with a very specific request, that, in case he was killed abroad, a stone be laid over his grave, 'with the following epitaph thereon, for a monument to my children to continue and keep themselves worthy of so much honour as to be called hereafter to die for their Master and Country':

Willingly have I sought
And willingly have I found

> The fatal end that wrought
> Me hither, as duty bound.
>
> Discharg'd I am of that I ought
> To my country by honest wounde
> My soul departed, Christ hath bought
> The end of man is ground.[45]

Charles Blount returned in one piece from France, but he may have contracted there the illness that led to his death on 10 October that year. His son James, the contemporary of Prince Edward, lived on until 1582, when the title passed, in turn, to his eldest son.

By March 1543, Edward was being described as 'the goodliest child in the world'[46] in a letter from the Privy Council to Duke of Suffolk. An undated miniature of him in profile can be identified as dating from the years 1543–46, although the attribution to Hans Holbein has been challenged. Edward is seen looking to the left, against a blue-grey circular background. He appears to be about 8 years old, and has changed considerably since Holbein's depiction of him as an infant, his features having more of an adult cast. His profile is delicate, the eyes watchful, the nose pointed and sensitively drawn, with the lips closed in a thoughtful pout. The prominent chin is still visible but his cheeks have hollowed out and his face is pale. His hair appears to be a light brown, with little hint of his father's red, close-cropped where it appears under the brim of his black hat, which is embellished with jewels and topped, as before, with a flamboyant white feather. He wears a pale red tunic with a high collar and a black cloak trimmed with fur. The overall impression is delicate and a little melancholic.

It was at this point that his father's thoughts turned to the boy's future marriage. Despite the connection established between Henry Fitzroy and James V, relations with Scotland had soured and, the previous December, the Scottish king had died shortly after a terrible defeat by Henry's troops at the battle of Solway Moss. He left a week-old daughter, Mary, whose hand Henry now sought for his young son. He hoped that the union would obtain 'for his son and their posterity, a root of foundation of perpetual honour' and promised that the pair would be 'so provided for as he could hardly desire better'.[47] According to agreement reached with the Scots ambassadors, the new queen was to remain in her native land, under the care of the lords appointed by Parliament, but 'for her education, instruction, safe and wholesome nurriture [nourishment] the King may appoint English folk about her.' Six Scottish barons and two bishops were to be hostages in England to guarantee her delivery, which would take place at the age of 8 or 10 'at the furthest', and the marriage would be solemnised when she reached the age of 12. This would take place at the end of 1554, when Edward would be 17.[48] The Treaty of Greenwich was signed on 1 July 1543 and the prospect of the two countries united under one crown seemed like a distinct possibility.

In autumn 1543, Edward stayed at Ashridge House, which had recently been the Convent of Bonhommes, while the king stayed at nearby Ampthill. The convent had been founded in a former manor house in Hertfordshire, which housed a phial of reputed holy blood. The house had been large enough for Edward I and his court to spend Christmas 1290 there, but it was considerably enlarged by the Black Prince in the 1360s. Having been surrendered to the Crown in November 1539, it reverted to use as a private house. Disappointing news came, though, when the Scots repudiated the marriage treaty that December, just six months after the signing of the agreement at Greenwich. Worse still, they renewed their former alliance with France, betrothing the young Queen Mary to the grandson of Francis I, also named Francis, who was the son of Henry Fitzroy's ally and contemporary, the Dauphin Henri. Mary and Francis would marry in 1558 and would reign in France for eighteen months before his premature death at the age of 16. Another young royal male dead in his teens, Francis II suffered from prolonged ill health, including spasming and fainting, but finally succumbed to an ear infection, which may have been meningitis or mastoiditis, which developed into an abscess. The French royal physician suggested alleviating his suffering by trepanning his skull, but this was rejected as too dangerous, and the short-lived king died in December 1560.

Back in 1543, Henry VIII was furious at the Scottish rejection and began an aggressive campaign against Mary's kingdom, known to history as the 'rough wooing', during which he dispatched Edward Seymour to raze Edinburgh to the ground. He also turned his wrath against France and, despite his increasing girth, poor health and lack of mobility, he began to plan a campaign against Francis I. The following July, he established a regency under his sixth wife, Catherine Parr, to rule during his absence. She was to be advised by the king's council and Prince Edward was to remove to Hampton Court under the care of his chamberlain, Sir Richard Page, along with William Sidney, Cox and Cheke as almoner-tutors and Jasper Horsey as chief gentleman of his privy chamber.[49] The cost of Edward's household at Hampton Court during the three months of his father's absence was £2,000, while that of the queen was £5,000.[50] At the end of July 1544, after Henry's departure, the queen wrote to him to report that 'the Prince and the rest of the King's children are in good health.'[51] The same year, under the influence of who brought all his children together, Henry passed the Third Act of Succession, which restored princesses Mary and Elizabeth to the throne and lay down plans for a potential minority government for Edward.

At the end of 1544, Edward pushed against the boundaries of his tutor, Richard Cox. Although Cox was able to report that his pupil was 'a vessel apt to receive all goodness and learning, witty, sharp and pleasant',[52] was also confident that he was above the discipline of his master. This brings to mind the occasion when Henry Fitzroy demonstrated a similar rebellion, around the same age, at Sheriff Hutton. Cox described how Edward's stubbornness, which he refers to as 'Captain Will', provoked the tutor to lose his temper, giving the boy 'such a wound that he knew not what to do'. Startling as this sounds to a modern reader, it appears to have been a turning point. Edward learned his lesson, and Cox never heard from 'Captain Will' again. Nor does the tutor seem to have incurred any wrath from the king as a result: discipline was considered part of his duty. Exactly what the 'wound' was, or how well Edward recovered, is not recorded.

Inventories of Henry VIII's goods made in 1547–48 recorded a number of items that help illuminate the daily life of Prince Edward. Based at Hampton Court, Durham House and other country residences like Hertford and Hunsdon, Edward's possessions pertained to his schooling, including a personal writing desk covered in black velvet, embroidered with the letter E, and another with green velvet, in which were stored writing implements. He also had wooden slabs for writing on, a set of chessmen in a black coffer, bells for hawks, astronomical instruments, an hourglass, a puppet, a box topped with a horse and rider, papers relating to his mother, a red box with 'sorcery' equipment, bells for hawks and two pairs of glasses.[53] The inventory also creates a sense of the rich environment that Edward grew up in, among his father's moveable goods: the paintings, musical instruments, tapestries, maps, venetian glass, books, jewellery and chapel items. Edward might have been a child, subject to his tutor's discipline, but he was a king in waiting.

There seems little reason to doubt Jane Dormer's comments that Edward was fond of his sister Mary, who was 21 years his elder and, perhaps, something of a mother figure. On 11 January 1546, he wrote to her from Hunsdon, hoping she did not think that his failure to write meant that she had been forgotten. On the contrary, he wrote that 'affection ever holds the chief place in my heart both for you and my dearest mother.' He hoped to see her soon, to be able to tell her 'in truth how much and how greatly I esteem you'.[54] That May he wrote again, pleased to hear that she had recovered from an illness and exclaiming that he loved her greatly, even though he wrote infrequently, just as he loved his best clothes the most although he hardly wore them. He also wrote to their stepmother, Queen Catherine Parr, about concerns he had for Mary, asking the queen to preserve her 'from all the wiles and enchantments of the evil one, and beseech her to no longer attend foreign dances and merriments which do not become a most Christian princess'.[55]

Early in 1546, Cox reported that Edward, aged 9, was 'of such towardness in learning, godliness, gentleness and all honest qualities', that he was considered 'a singular gift sent of God and an imp worthy of such a father'. By this point, Cox added he had learned four books of

Cato and knew the Bible, Vives, Aesop and 'Latin-making'.[56] That August, as Henry was concluding his peace with France, Edward received the ambassador Monsieur de Morette, who later wrote that he had rejoiced 'very much to have seen my lord prince's grace, of whose praises he cannot speak enough'.[57] By the autumn, the boy was at Hatfield House, studying French according to a letter from Cox to the king's secretary, William Paget. A second letter expressed Cox's hopes that the prince would meet his father's expectations. Edward was also praised by William Thomas, later clerk of the Council, who depicted him in a dialogue entitled *Peregrine*:

> If ye knew the towardness of that young Prince, your heart would melt to hear him named, and your stomach abhor the malice of them that would him ill; the beautiest creature that lived under sun, the wittiest, the most amiable and the gentlest thing of all the world. Such a spirit of capacity, learning the things taught him by his schoolmasters, that it is a wonder to hear say. And finally he hath such a grace of porte and gesture in gravity which he commeth in to any presence, that it should seem he were already a father and yet passeth he not the age of ten years. A thing undoubtedly much rather seen than to be believed.[58]

Though all were in agreement that Edward was 'toward' or advanced beyond his years, he had still not reached the age of majority. At the end of December 1546, Henry's health failing and he summoned his council in order to consider the terms of his will. In an attempt to prevent any one faction from gaining too much power, the king had appointed sixteen executors to oversee his will, in which Edward took precedence over his sisters by virtue of his gender and his legitimacy. Either Henry never saw the final changes to his will or else he was too ill to approve them; the last draft was 'signed' by his dry stamp, allowing for the possibility that certain changes were made as he lay incapacitated, or even after his death, which occurred in the early hours of the morning on 28 January 1547. As had been the case with his father, Henry VIII's death was kept secret for a few days to allow for the smooth transition of power.

There were parallels with Edward VI's situation and the accession of Edward V in 1483, but the new king's uncle was no Richard III. Upon hearing news of Henry's death, Edward Seymour rode to his nephew at Hertford and carried him to his sister Elizabeth at Enfield to secure his person. It was there that he broke the news of their father's death to the children and the terms of his will. The crown was to go to Edward, followed by Mary then Elizabeth and, if they should die without issue, it would pass to the Grey and Suffolk families, descendants of Henry's second sister, Mary, Duchess of Suffolk. The issue of Henry's elder sister, Margaret, who had married James IV of Scotland, were excluded from succession, although Margaret's great-granddaughter, Mary Queen of Scots, would continue to assert her superior claim to the English throne.

Despite having broken with Rome and rejected centuries-old beliefs about the afterlife, Henry's final words leave no doubt that he was still a firm believer in the rituals of the Catholic Church. He expressed hope that his words would be acceptable to God, repented of his sins and bequeathed his soul in the traditional way, although his imperious tone shows that he expected his will to be done, even in the afterlife:

> We do instantly require and desire the blessed Virgin Mary, his mother, with all the whole company of heaven, continually to pray for us, and with us, whiles we live in this world, and in the time of passing out of the same, that we may the sooner attain everlasting life after our departure out of this transitory life, which we do hope and claim by Christ's passion and word. We also will and specially desire and require that where and whensoever it shall please God to call us out of this world transitory to his infinite mercy and grace … that our executors, as soon as conveniently they may, shall cause all divine service accustomed for dead folk to be celebrated for us in the next and most proper place.[59]

The services of placebo and dirge were to be 'devoutly done, observed and solemnly kept' with the poor prompted to pray for the 'offences and wealth of his soul'. The Dean and Canon of Westminster, and their successors forever, were to appoint two priests to say eternal masses for his soul and four solemn obits should be kept for him in the college at Windsor.[60] It is deeply ironic that Henry set in motion the chain of events that would come to fruition in the year of his death, preventing the fulfilment of his final wishes.

From Enfield, Edward was conveyed to London, as related by a record in the College of Arms:

> Upon Monday next following they accompanied his highness in goodly order from his place of Enfield to his tower of London, to which he came about three of the clock in the afternoon of the same day, where all the nobility of his realm were ready to receive him, to their great joy and comfort. And at his approaching near unto the same was great shot of ordinance in all places there about as well out of the Tower and out of the ships.[61]

His noble escort conducted him to his rooms, which had been 'richly hung and garnished with rich cloth of arras and clothes of estate' which befitted a king. The following day, the Council assembled in the king's presence under the lead of his uncle, Edward Seymour, Lord Hertford. After doing homage to the young king, they elected Seymour Lord Protector and elevated him to the position of Duke of Somerset, a title which had formerly belonged to Henry Fitzroy. This seems to have been done according to the boy's wishes, as he justified this to the Council by their blood relationship, simply stating it was because he was 'the King's uncle on his mother's side'.

Henry VIII's coffin had lain in the chapel at Whitehall Palace since 2 February 1547, between burning tapers and banners depicting saints in gold thread. An account in the College of Arms describes how masses and observances were continually made around his body, over which watch was kept, day and night. Above him stretched a canopy in rich cloth of gold with a valance of black silk and fringe of black and gold silk. Later, the coffin was placed under a pall of gold, studded with precious stones, and there were more masses and dirges and requests to 'pray for the soul of the high and mighty prince, our late sovereign lord and

King'. On 7 February, 21,000 Londoners packed into Leadenhall and the churchyard of St Michael, at Cornhill, to be issued with alms of a silver groat each as encouragement to pray for the king's soul. It seemed very much as if the king had retreated considerably from his former religious hard line. Henry had left detailed instructions regarding the location of his burial in St George's Chapel, Windsor:

> Our last Will and Testament, doe will and ordaine, that our bodie be buried and enterred in the quire of our College of Windsor, midway between the stalls, and the high altar; and there be made and set, as soon as convenientlie maie be donne after our descease, by our executors, at our costs and charges (if it be not donne by us in our life time), an honourable tombe for our bones to rest in, which is well onward and almost made therefore already, with a fair grate about it, in which we will also, the bones of our true and loving wife Queen Jane be put also.[62]

Early on the morning of 14 February 1547, a 4 mile-long procession of 1,000 horsemen and followers gathered at Charing Cross. There, they awaited the arrival of the king's immense hearse, which was due to depart from Whitehall Palace. The gilded chariot was seven storeys high and featured an effigy of the monarch, carved, painted and dressed to appear as Henry had in life. It had probably been produced by Nicholas Bellin of Modena, who was the latest Italian hired to work on the king's tomb.[63] A Spanish visitor who witnessed the moment related how the effigy 'looked exactly like that of the King himself and he seemed just as if he were alive'. It wore robes of crimson velvet, furred with miniver and powdered with ermine and a red satin doublet embroidered with gold. On its head was a black satin nightcap set with precious stones, on top of which sat 'a crown imperial of inestimable value', while a collar of the garter was placed around its neck and a garter on its leg. Its legs were encased in scarlet hose and its feet had been fitted with slippers of crimson velvet. The hands were covered in gloves and diamond rings had been placed on the fingers, while gold bracelets set with stones and pearls encircled the arms. The effigy carried the sceptre in its right hand and the orb in its left; an armorial sword lay at its side. The event required almost 33,000 yards of black cloth and over 8,000 yards of black silk, purchased from London merchants at a cost of £12,000.[64] It clothed the mourners, draped the church and was hung in the chapels, making a solemn swathe of death across the English countryside.

From Westminster, the mourners travelled slowly west, covering a distance of 11 miles before stopping for the night at Syon Abbey, which had been the wealthiest convent at the time of the Dissolution, but was now in the possession of the new Lord Protector. It was here, overnight, that a macabre event reputedly occurred during: Henry's coffin burst open and leaked fluids that were eagerly licked up by a dog.[65] Whether this is true, or belongs to the legends and prophecies that attached themselves to the 'mouldworp', it is a visceral illustration of the humbling processes of death and serves as a powerful *memento mori*. The next morning, the procession set off again, along roads that had been repaved and stripped of their overhanging trees to allow the hearse to pass, bridges that had seen emergency repairs and towns where the streets were swept and the inhabitants railed off. After a journey of 15 miles more, they arrived at Windsor. Along the route from the castle bridge to the door of the chapel, the crowds were held back by wooden railings draped in black and bearing the king's arms.

The service of interment took place the following day, 16 February. Henry had specified that the requiem mass be read in Latin by the Catholic Bishop Stephen Gardiner and that a sum of 1,000 marks was to be distributed among the poor with instructions that they were to pray for his soul. One eyewitness account related the final symbolic act by which the king's household was disbanded:

> … with their staves and rods in their hands … first the lord great master and after him, the lord chamberlain and all the rest, brake their staves in shivers upon their heads and cast them after the corpse into the pit with exceeding sorrow and heaviness, not without grievous sighs and tears … then the trumpets sounded with great melody and courage, to the comfort of all them that were present.[66]

Then the titles and right of Edward VI were pronounced and repeated three times. Henry VIII was dead and buried, and his 9-year old son was king. On 8 and 12 February, gold and gems were issued from the Westminster jewel house, to be made into a crown for the boy. [67]

Just eight weeks after the death of Henry VIII, his closest rival, Francis I of France, also died. They had competed in the arena of international politics and wrestled at the Field of the Cloth of Gold, vying to outdo one another in clothing and jewels. They had also been at war, taking advantage of each other's weaknesses, making and breaking alliances with their mutual rival the emperor, steering their way through the tumultuous sixteenth century. But while Henry had broken with Rome, Francis had remained staunchly Catholic and, on the afternoon of 31 March 1547, he died in that faith, at Rambouillet, halfway through a journey he proved unable to complete. Just as with Henry, years of extravagant living had caught up with the king, but unlike his English counterpart, Francis was suffering from syphilis. This may have accounted for his death, although a contemporary Swiss doctor suggests that his right lung was diseased, while a second physician, Saint-Mauris, described the king's kidneys as 'wasted, his entrails decayed, this throat cankered and a lung affected'. [68]

Francis's son, the new King Henri II, ordered a joint interment for his father, beside his two elder brothers, the Dauphin Francis and Charles, Duke of Orléans, whom he had outlived. Their bodies were exhumed and brought from Tournon and Beauvais to accompany the old king to Notre-Dame, in Paris. Following the English tradition, an effigy of Francis was created, based on his death mask. It wore state robes, an imperial crown and the collar of St Michael about its neck. On pillows to either side lay the sceptre and hand of justice, and a canopy was stretched overhead, illuminated by four candles. For the eleven days that the effigy lay in state, it was served continually with meals and drink, which were laid before it on a fully dressed table, with attendants, before being removed untouched. Then the effigy and coffin were drawn by a wagon and six horses to Notre-Dame and placed in the choir, alongside the coffins of his sons, while the usual masses and prayers were recited, and the king's household broke their wands to throw into the grave. Henri II commissioned a magnificent *memento mori* tomb for his father, designed by Philibert de L'Orme, a master Renaissance mason. It comprised a Roman triumphal arch and an arcaded area for the sarcophagus, with kneeling mourners and the figure of the king, with tableaux depicting his feats in battle. His heart was placed inside a white marble urn decorated with representations of architecture, painting, sculpture and geometry, astronomy, song, music and poetry.[69] Underneath the arch, Francis and his first queen, Claude, are graphically depicted as life-sized naked corpses. The French king's tomb, created in this religiously pivotal year, shows just how much funereal fashions in England had undergone a transformation.

III

On 19 February, Edward followed the traditional route on horseback from the Tower to the Palace of Westminster, where the streets had been gravelled and railed. Riding under a canopy alongside the Lord Protector, Edward had been dressed in a gown of cloth of silver embroidered with damask gold, with a girdle of white velvet wrought with Venice silver, garnished with rubies, diamonds and true lovers' knots made from pearls. He wore a matching white velvet doublet and cap, also with gems and embroidery. His horse was trapped in crimson satin, embroidered with pearls and damask gold. Aldermen and guildsmen lined the route, and priests and clerks stood at intervals with crosses and censors, while the houses were draped with arras tapestries, cloth of gold and silver, streamers and banners. Pageants had been prepared along the route and the king paused to hear speeches and songs, stopping for a long time outside St Paul's to watch a Spanish rope-dancer. At Fenchurch Street, a scaffold had been erected and draped with tapestries, containing a choir and musicians, while the conduit in Cornhill ran with wine. Two children and two figures dressed as Valentine in moss and ivy, and Wild Urson with a yew club, delivered speeches to the king.[70] Four more children represented Grace, Nature, Fortune and Charity, along with the figures of Sapience (wisdom) and the seven Liberal Sciences (grammar, logic, arithmetic, rhetoric, geometry, astronomy and music), who bestowed brief blessings upon the king. There followed a dumb show, or tableau, of Edward's parentage, through the symbolic creatures of Jane Seymour's phoenix and Henry VIII's lion giving way to the young lion representing Edward.[71] Further along the route he was met by Jason and the Golden Fleece and St George, before arriving at Westminster.

Edward's coronation took place in the Abbey on Sunday 20 February. Due to his age, a shorter version of the traditional ceremony was used, lest the 'tedious length of the same … should weary and be hurtsome peradventure to the King's majesty, being yet of tender age'.[72] Edward arrived between ten and eleven o'clock to take his place in the coronation chair, where Archbishop Cranmer proclaimed him a second Josiah and urged him to continue the reformation of the Church of England, with 'idolatry destroyed, the tyranny of the Bishops of Rome banished from you subjects and images removed'. After being anointed, he was transferred to a lighter chair, dressed with cloth of tissue and carried by four gentlemen ushers to the four corners of the platform, to display him to the congregation, who shouted their acceptance of him.[73] He wore the crown of King Edward the Confessor, then the imperial crown, then the one which had been made specially for him. After the service, Edward sat crowned at the head of a feast in Westminster Hall and, over the next two days, in a gallery to watch the jousting.[74] After that, he took up residence at Whitehall, Greenwich and St James's, with Hampton Court reserved as his summer retreat. That Easter, Edward was at Greenwich, as the record of his religious offerings shows and, by Whitsun, he was back at Westminster.

One of the first matters of Edward's reign was war with the Scots, in continuation of his father's 'rough wooing'. Lord Protector Somerset led an English army to a decisive victory on 10 September at the Battle of Pinkie Cleugh and Edward wrote to his 'dearest uncle' a week later from Oatlands Palace:

> Dearest uncle, by your letters and report of the messenger, we have at good
> length understanded, to our great comfort, the good success it hath pleased
> God to grant us against the Scots by your good courage and wise foresight,
> for the which and other the benefits of God heaped upon us … so do we give
> unto you, good uncle, our most harty thanks.[75]

Unexpectedly, though, Edward soon found himself in a difficult position
with his other Seymour uncle, Thomas, and his stepmother. Catherine
Parr had attended his coronation, then retired to the country, to Old
Manor at Chelsea. There, she had married Thomas Seymour in secret
that May, with whom she had been in love prior to her marriage to
Henry VIII. The Council was not informed, as the pair rightly judged it
would have withheld approval, but the truth of the matter soon came to
light. Edward was angry to learn of the match, seeming so disrespectful to
his father, but he allowed the charismatic Thomas to influence him, even
going so far as to permit him to dictate a letter to Catherine, the day after
he had written thanking the Lord Protector, giving the impression that
he had actively encouraged the marriage to take place. The match could
have caused potential problems for Edward, depending on the time scale
as, if Catherine conceived quickly, or gave birth prematurely, there may
have been doubts about whether the child had been fathered by the late
king.[76] On 25 June, he wrote to her from St James's Palace:

> Ye shal not need to fear any grief to come, or to suspect lack of any need, seeing
> that he, being my uncle, is of so good a nature that he will not be troublesome
> any mean unto you; and I of that mind that of divers just causes I must favour
> you … And I will so provide for you both, that hereafter, if any grief befall, I
> shall be a sufficient succour in your godly or praisable enterprises.[77]

It is an awkward letter to read, giving the reader pause to consider how
far, at 9 years old, Edward was able to exercise his own will against the
influence of powerful men he trusted. The following year, he would give
evidence against Thomas Seymour, admitting that 'the Lord Admiral came
to me in the time of the last parliament at Westminster and desired me to

write a thing for him … he said it was none ill thing, it is for the queen's majesty.'[78] The situation became more complicated as the young king was caught up in the rivalry between the two Seymour brothers, and Thomas attempted to ingratiate himself with the boy through expensive gifts and money, encouraging him to be independent. Eventually, he attempted to pressure Edward into signing a bill to make Thomas his personal governor and to persuade him that he did not require a Lord Protector. Tensions came to a head when Thomas was arrested on the night of 16 January 1549, attempting to break into the king's apartments at Hampton Court, during which he shot one of the king's dogs. Convicted of treason, he was executed that March but the uneasy balance between the young king's independence and the will of his advisors was to continue for the rest of his short reign.

Edward had been educated to be sympathetic to the Protestant movement, but the religious reforms introduced in the early years of his reign, when he was aged 9–11, were more extreme than anything his father had achieved. Jane Dormer, an ardent Catholic, refused to believe that Edward had been in favour of these changes, or that he had fully understood their implications. She stated that:

> mischievous and heretical governors, contrary to his father's will, abused his tender age: who, ruling to effect their own ends notoriously injured the natural good inclinations of this gentle and noble prince. For, when he was King, in passing by the ruins of goodly monasteries, he demanded, what buildings were those? It was answered that they were religious houses, dissolved and demolished by order of the King his father, for abuses. He replied: 'could not my father punish the offenders and suffer so goodly buildings to stand, being so great an ornament to this kingdom and put in by better men, that might have governed and inhabited them?'[79]

When Jane wrote of Edward's affection for his sister Mary, this also encompassed sympathy for her Catholicism; of his questioning of her regarding her faith and his exhortation to be patient in the face of his ministers' strictures, crying and 'grieving matters could not be according to her will and desire' and that when he was older he would 'remedy all'.[80]

Did the 9-year-old Edward dream up the 1547 injunctions pushed through Parliament by Edward Seymour? Did the child who wished the monasteries had been put into more competent hands order that bells should be removed from church towers, rood screens and lofts dismantled, images of saints whitewashed over, icons and statues removed, shrines destroyed, chalices melted down, processions, ashes and palms forbidden, the dissolution of chantry chapels and the notion of purgatory condemned? Eighteen years had passed since Simon Fish had published *A Supplication for the Beggars*, rejecting the existence of purgatory and prayers for the dead, because he argued that neither was mentioned in the Bible. Fish had been arrested and condemned in London, although he died of the plague before he could be executed, yet his theories predated the changes in English approaches to memorials that now become law. Starting in 1547, at least 2,374 chantries were dissolved and the bequests in wills for prayers for the dead and their memorials ceased to be honoured. Far from being a permanent memorial for the eternal life of the soul, the honouring of the dead was as short-lived as the physical structures they had erected. What had once been believed to be carved in stone, was demolished nationwide in a few short years. To use the example of one major English city, in Bristol alone, there had been thirty-five permanent chantries and thirty-three chantry priests in 1547, along with another twenty-two temporary memorials for the lighting of candles and recitation of masses and obits.[81] An entire system of belief regarding one of the major uncertainties of life, the experience of the soul after death, was being dismantled.

Just how far did this dramatic change reflect the national mood? Historians continue to disagree about the beliefs of the English in the 1530s and '40s, if it is even possible to discover a uniform belief across class, age and place. While A.G. Dickens believes that most people no longer believed in purgatory, rendering the need for masses obsolete. Eamon Duffy sees the demolition of chantries more as an imposition upon congregations forced to dance to the royal tune. It remains a moot point whether the changes of 1547 were catching up with a wider sea change in beliefs or an attempt to impose new rules upon a people who were forced to follow, sometimes reluctantly. The former scenario makes it more likely that Edward could accept the need for regulation at 9 years old; the latter implies that he was more of a religious radical, or that his uncle was. The fact that the introduction of the Book of Common Prayer in 1549 sparked a mass rebellion in Devon and Cornwall indicates the slow travel of change across the country. But Duffy's detailed study of the Devonian parish of Morebath, through the accounts of parish priest Christopher Trychay, exposes a deep hostility to the changes that supports the notion that they were being imposed from the top down, rather than chasing and seeking to clarify an existing mood.[82] The revolt was more than just a rejection of the new prayer book, it called for the undoing of much of the recent legislation, and a return to the high Catholicism of masses in Latin, prayers for purgatory, chantry chapels, icons, saints and statues, palms and ashes, and the literal translation of the bread and wine into the body and blood of Christ.[83] Nor was the unrest confined to the south-west, spreading into the Midlands, through Oxfordshire, Berkshire, Buckinghamshire and Northamptonshire. The Lord Protector dispatched armies to deal with the rebels and prominent leaders, including the vicars of local churches, were hung from their steeples.[84] At the same time, rebellion broke out under Robert Kett in Norfolk, against the enclosure of common land, which was also severely dealt with. Within three years of Henry VIII's death, the mood in his son's kingdom was rebellious.

And yet, there is evidence that Edward was closely involved in religious matters and keen to learn more about the reforms. A new preaching place was erected in the privy gardens at Whitehall and Edward frequently accompanied his tutor John Cheke and the Lord Protector to attend sermons given there by the Protestant royal chaplain Hugh Latimer. On 29 June 1548, the king listened to Stephen Gardiner, Bishop of Winchester preach about the recent changes in religion. Edward sat and made notes, especially regarding any aspects that touched upon kingship. Then, in August 1549, at the age of 11, Edward composed and wrote his own thoughts against papacy, entitled *A Small Treatise against the Primacy of the Pope*, which is explicit and extreme in its condemnation, particularly mentioning idolatry:

It is true the Pope is primate of the church, but it is not the divine or catholic church but the diabolical one ... the bishop of Rome is like a wolf amongst sheep, eating and devouring the poor sheep of Christ; and when they are hid by fear, he takes the voice of a sheep to betray and devour them.

... the Bishop of Rome lies notoriously if, in nothing else, but in his pretending to be the head of the Christian church, and having the keys of heaven. [But] when the Pope is dead and none hath the keys, whence it must follow, that the pope being dead, heaven's gates are closed.

... Behold how he is filled and puffed up with pride and vanity. Behold how large and fair a name and title he takes, though he be a venomous serpent, calling himself the most holy father whereas he is a detestable thief and contaminated with all uncleanness.

All others exercise their tyranny against bodies, but this wolf and tyrant exercises his tyranny over the souls of men, constraining the poor and simple lambs of God to forsake their faith, whereby they are saved, to follow his abominable traditions and diabolical precepts; which if they refuse to obey, to wit, adoring images and offering to his idols and devils, he burns, racks and torments them, or forces them to a costly recantation.[85]

A note on the manuscript in a contemporary hand, perhaps that of Edward's French tutor Jean Belmain, a radical Calvinist, records that the work was entirely that of the king, and a rough draft of the treatise shows corrections in another hand. His sources were the books at his disposal and conversations with figures such as Belmain, Latimer, Gardiner and the Bishop of Rochester, Nicholas Ridley. Edward was astute and, in 1550, pointed out that the oath John Hooper was about to swear to become Bishop of Gloucester was still the same as had been used by Henry VIII, containing references to the worship of saints and their powers of intercession with God.[84]

Early in 1551, Edward was addressed in the Erasmian Martin Bucer's *De Regno Christi*, presented to him as a new year's treaty, full of advice and guidance. Bucer urged him to 'restore for [his] peoples the blessed kingdom of the son of God', to purge the church of 'dead wood, thorns and brambles', that might obscure the word of God and 'the impiety and injustice of dissipated men who might corrupt others'. He must also be willing to 'countenance dangers, exile and death itself' on this dangerous mission to help create this kingdom of God upon Earth.[87] In that same year, the French theologian Jean Calvin also addressed the young king, urging him to purge the English clergy of corruption. Three months later, he dedicated his commentaries upon Isaiah to Edward, adding that the young king should let nothing distract him from his important task.[88] Under these influences, as well as those among the circle of his educators, and in the context of the recent acts of reform, Edward's identity as a religious reformer, as a leading Protestant monarch, was gaining ground. European leaders of the reformed faith had every reason to look to England as a friend in the wake of the Catholic Counter-Reformation that had been launched by Pope Paul III. The Council of Trent, which sat at intervals between 1545 and 1563, was attempting to restore the old Latin mass, the worship of saints and idols, the prayers for the dead and various other practices considered heresies in the eyes of the Protestants. No doubt this act did nothing but fuel a young king keen to be seen as a champion of religious idealism.

An unattributed painting entitled *Edward VI and the Pope: An Allegory of the Reformation* seeks to personify the young king as the spirit of religious change. While the exact dating of its composition is unclear, placed by experts in a range spanning the years 1547 to the 1570s, it was produced by someone who had lived through Edward's reign, perhaps an eyewitness at court. It may even date precisely to the boy's lifetime, a piece of contemporary propaganda. The young king is central, seated on a throne upon a dais beneath a gold canopy of estate. His feet rest upon a gold cushion, beside which an open book bears the text 'the word of the Lord endureth forever.' Below it, the pope is being crushed, a message upon his chest reads 'all flesh is grass' and ribbons around him bear other messages: 'feigned holiness', 'idolatory' and 'superstition'. To Edward's right, his father sits up in his death bed, pointing to his son as his legal and spiritual successor; to his left, around a table stand an array of councillors, including the Lord Protector; Edward Seymour, who stands at his side; Thomas Cranmer, Archbishop of Canterbury; John Russell, the Lord Privy Seal;

and William Paget, Comptroller of the King's Household. An additional figure may be John Dudley, Earl of Warwick or Thomas Seymour, as it bears some facial resemblance to the Protector. Other courtiers and clerics face them on the other side of the table. The top right-hand corner of the painting contains an inserted scene, either a picture within a picture, or a scene out of the window, showing acts of iconoclasm. Amidst it all, Edward smiles sweetly, almost knowingly, looking like a very young child in his habitual feathered hat and red robes furred with ermine. This work may have been commissioned to represent the changes taking place at the time, but for all its iconography and structure, it does not represent a powerful king. Edward is a tiny cherub set amid chaos, a ceremonial figure that represents the continuity of the dynasty, failing to convince as the progenitor of the action around him. It seems more likely, as Margaret Aston has asserted, that this painting was produced later, drawing multiple elements together as a record of the Protestant Reformation. It acknowledges Edward's reign and his councillors for taking a dramatic step down a path that was to become the mainstream in the reign of his sister Elizabeth.

IV

In October 1549, Edward, Duke of Somerset was deposed as Lord Protector. The Council blamed his inflexibility and narrow-mindedness for the uprisings earlier in the year and prepared to challenge him under the leadership of John Dudley, Earl of Warwick. Somerset took King Edward and escaped to Windsor Castle, possibly against the boy's will, as he was kept under 'watch and ward', and believed himself in prison. He also developed a bad cold as the result of being moved at night. When London threatened to rise against him, Seymour prompted Edward to write a letter asking for an end to hostilities and promising that the Protector would submit to a process of arbitration, but the Council replied that it had appointed Somerset and that he had no power independently of it. Finally, the Earl of Warwick arrived and arrested Somerset, returning

King Edward to the safety of Richmond Palace. A list of twenty-nine articles was drawn up against the former Protector and he was accused of offences which, as Edward himself wrote, included 'ambition, vainglory, entering into rash wars', negligence, enriching himself from the royal coffers, following his own opinion and doing 'all by his own opinion'.[89] Somerset was replaced by John Dudley, Earl of Warwick and held in the Tower until 6 February 1550, when he was released with a fine of £10,000. Although he was later permitted a brief return to the Council, he was executed early in 1552 for conspiring to overthrow Warwick. His death was recorded, by the London diarist Henry Machyn, as taking place soon after eight in the morning, before a 'great company' that included the king's guard and sheriffs, who removed his body to the quire of St Peter ad Vincula.[90]

Edward's new protector, John Dudley, came from a family with a chequered past. His father, Edmund, had been the chief financial minister of Henry VII, responsible for raising his unpopular taxes and executed as a scapegoat as soon as Henry VIII came to the throne. His son had served as Vice Admiral and Lord Admiral during Prince Edward's childhood, fought in Scotland and France, and become close to the old king before his death. He was part of the religious reform party, an excellent soldier and administrator, and had fathered a family of thirteen.

On 4 June 1550, Edward attended the wedding of Dudley's fourth surviving son, the 18-year-old Robert, who was married to Amy Robsart at Sheen Palace. Thoughts also turned to potential brides for the young king, who would soon be approaching the significant milestone of his thirteenth birthday. When the French ambassador arrived to discuss a marriage treaty with Princess Elizabeth of Valois, Edward impressed the visitors by playing the lute. He took them hunting with hounds, they watched him at target practice and coursing in Hyde Park, and entertained them at several dinners. Elizabeth was the daughter of the new King of France, Henri II, and had been born in April 1545, so any potential marriage would not be taking place for another seven or eight years. Coincidentally, the 5-year-old princess shared a chamber with her sister-in-law, the young Mary, Queen of Scots, aged 8 in 1550, who had once been intended as Edward's bride. He also proved a gracious host when Mary's mother, Marie of Guise, visited him at Hampton Court and Westminster in November 1550.

A portrait of Edward at this point by William Scrots shows him as a serious, thin-faced young man with a long jaw line and pouting mouth, pointed chin and ear and a largish nose. With his hair close-cropped again under the black hat and white plume, it is clear to see how the subject has evolved from the unidentified round miniature of a few years before. His red-gold clothing with the high collar creates a further echo. Scrots makes the king look very much an adolescent in this head and shoulders work, but a second, full-length image he created around the same time leaves little doubt of the boy's kingship. Standing before a gold curtain embroidered with black and a blue-grey pillar set with coloured marble, Edward appears every inch the king. The visual references to the smaller portrait can be found again in details of his clothing, in the same black jewelled hat and feather and in the close-cropped hair, now with a reddish sheen which echoes the colours of the background. But Edward has undergone a dramatic change of clothing, appearing in black with gold trimming, the broad shoulders and codpiece of his father, referencing the old king's silhouette as he stands facing the viewer. His legs are parted, encased in black hose and shoes, giving an impression of strength and virility, and while his right hand clasps a pair of gloves, his left rests upon the hilt of a dagger, separate from the sword that also hangs nearby. The pointed chin and ear remain the same but the dark eyes are now fixed and the small mouth is resolute. This portrait gives the impression that Edward has come of age, and indeed he almost had, as he entered his fourteenth year. A couple of alternative versions also survive, perhaps created by artists in Scrots's workshop; one shows Edward in the same location and position, although this time his black and gold outfit has been exchanged for a reddish-brown ensemble with black and gold edging, while another has a garter around the left knee and the order's blue ribbon around his neck. The fact that they derived from the same master is clear from a payment of fifty marks given to Scrots in 1552 for the creation of 'three great tables', or full-length portraits.[91]

Yet for all the grandeur of his portraits, in 1551 there came a timely reminder of the mortality of young men. The sweating sickness had broken out again that summer and, on 9 July, Edward wrote that:

> at this time came the sweat into London, which was more vehement than the old sweat. For if one took cold he died within 3 hours, and if he escaped it held him but 9 hours, or 10 at the most. Also if he slept … as he should be very desirous to do, then he raved, and should die raving.

Edward's two friends Henry and Charles Brandon were among those so quickly lost. The sons of his uncle the Duke of Suffolk by his fourth wife, they had been raised in his household and educated alongside him. Their childish doodles appear on the side of some pieces of Edward's work.[92] Henry was born in September 1535 and had inherited the title on the death of his father a decade later, while Charles was born two or three years later. Both boys were painted by Holbein on bright blue miniature roundels, at the ages of 5 and 3. Henry wears a cap with a feather like that of the king, leaning on his left arm upon the edge of a tilting table, as if unwilling to sit still. He looks plaintively at the viewer, with clear eyes and resolute mouth, while his younger brother appears angelic, almost surprised under his bell of gold hair. On the occasion of his coronation in 1547, Edward had created both boys Knights of the Bath and their futures at his side seemed assured. During the summer of 1551, though, the pair had been at St John's College, Cambridge, and as the sweat raced through the city they tried to escape by heading for the Bishop of Lincoln's Palace at Buckden, around 20 miles away. It was too late though, as the infection had set in and both boys died, on the same day, 14 July, within an hour of each other. They were aged 15 and around 13. The deaths of Charles and Henry represented a major blow to the Brandon dynasty, as two previous sons born to their father had also died in childhood. A month's mind was held for them on 22 September.

The 1551 outbreak of the sweat was especially bad. Henry Machyn's diary reports that between 7 and 20 July, the illness claimed 938 lives in London. The following year, Dr John Caius, president of the Royal

College of Physicians and attendant upon the king, wrote a treatise entitled *A Book or Council against the Disease Commonly Called the Sweat or Sweating Sickness.* The illness's lack of discrimination between social classes and its rapid acceleration was particularly commented upon, as its victims might be dancing at court at nine o'clock and dead by eleven. However, the dancing at court that Christmas resulted only in mirth and pleasure, rather than mortality.

At the end of 1551, Edward was involved in the seasonal pageantry at court, both performing in and directing the revels.[93] He had always enjoyed tumblers, jesters and players, and in 1552 he had even managed to offend the imperial ambassador – who had come to him on behalf of Princess Mary to discuss her right to hear mass – by moving to one side in order to see the players. Henry Machyn's diary records a 'great triumph' at Greenwich in May 1551, which the king and his company, dressed all in black, won against the Earl of Hertford, Edward Seymour, whose company all wore yellow, running at the ring and fighting with swords in a tournament.[94] Details like this are a reminder that, underneath all the religious reforms and political rivalry of his reign, Edward was still a child. An educated, devout, intelligent child, perhaps, but still young enough to be distracted by pleasure, and still healthy enough to indulge his sense of fun. Although he was frequently ill, wearing glasses for his poor vision and suffering a debilitating episode of illness in October 1550, he was still a keen sportsman. His regular enjoyment of tennis, bowling, riding and especially archery, his avid watching of tilting and jousting, during which he 'skirmished' in 1550 and participated fully in 1551,[95] belie the impression of a sickly child. Rather than being signals of an unhealthy constitution, making his premature death inevitable, his illnesses were isolated incidents that may have had a cumulative effect towards the end of his life. Through the spring of 1551, he led a challenge mounted by sixteen gentlemen to any who wished to try their hand at running at base, shooting and running at the ring, and won on 1 April. He exercised himself in the use of arms which, the imperial ambassador recorded, he enjoyed 'heartily'. He also enjoyed playing cards, chess, dice and games of chance, revelled in the gifts of falcons and greyhounds, danced and took part in masques. As he reached his fourteenth birthday in October 1551, it must have seemed that this youth combined a new religious zeal with the playfulness of his father. Edward was shaping into a significant Tudor king.

Then tragedy struck. On 2 April 1552, Edward fell ill with a combination of measles and smallpox. Ten days later, he wrote to his friend Barnaby Fitzpatrick, who was then in France, with typically English understatement, that 'we have a little been troubled with the smallpox ... but now we have shaken it quite away.'[96] Sixteen days later, the imperial ambassador described him as 'cheerful' and by mid-May he was able to ride from Greenwich Park to Blackheath, where he shot and rode at the ring. Edward seems to have made a full and speedy recovery and that summer he planned a lengthy royal progress, although the route took into account known outbreaks of infectious disease. He outlined his route for Barnaby, which included visits to Guildford in Surrey, Petworth in Sussex, and Chichester and Portsmouth on the south coast, among other places. He also reported that 'at this time, the most part of England (thanks be to God) is clear of any dangerous or infectious sickness.' The sweat or plague had raged 'only in Bristol and in the country near about'.[97] Yet this was to be the last time the king would enjoy a period of consistent good health.

That October, after his return to London, Edward met the Italian physician and astrologer Hieronymus Cardano, a Renaissance polymath who developed influential theories in mathematics, mechanics, biology and astronomy. Cardano concluded that the king was partially deaf and short-sighted. He was 'of a stature somewhat below the middle height, pale faced with grey eyes', and 'carried himself like an old man', with projecting shoulder blades and a 'bad habit of body than a sufferer of fixed diseases'.[98] If those were his only problems at the time, this atypical period of good health was not to last long. Within weeks, the king's diary falls silent, the final entry being made at Westminster Palace. By the following month, Edward was seriously ill again, perhaps with the first stages of the disease that would kill him seven months later. Measles is notorious for suppressing the immune system so although he had apparently recovered from the infection in April, it may have left him vulnerable. His health provided a dramatic contrast at court with the celebrations that had taken place just a year before, when he had dressed up to take part in a play. Henry Machyn recorded that on 12 December, Edward 'removed from Westminster unto Greenwich to keep Christmas' and if he did appoint a Lord of Misrule for his 'goodly pastime' as the merchant surmised, it was in an attempt to raise his spirits.[99]

When the new year arrived, Edward was still suffering from a fever and a cough that did not respond to treatment. The imperial ambassador commented that his pain seemed to come from a 'compression of the organs on the right side' which left him unable to draw breath. Soon, he was confined to his bed with a feverish cold. The account of the Italian Giulio Raviglio Rosso, writing in 1558, gives details of Edward's health that spring:

> On the first of February … the catarrh increased in Edward, and the misery began to harm him further [so] the visiting Duke [of Warwick] … wished to comprehend the true opinion, that the two physicians had regarding his life, and therefore he called two, who had attended continuously upon the person of his Majesty, and to those he added four others of the greatest experts in the realm and made them swear an oath of loyalty … he wished to understand from them all if the illness was consumption , if [it was] mortal and how much time they judged that he might be able to survive; the which consulting themselves together concluded that the King was consumptive, the infirmity mortal but that nevertheless they were sure he would live until the next September.[100]

But the physicians were to be proven wrong. In March, Edward had recovered enough to take the air in the park and on 11 April, he made the journey by boat to Greenwich. Machyn was on hand again to record his movements. When the king passed by the Tower, there was 'a great shot of guns and chambers and all the ships shot of guns … a great number'.[101] Yet despite the solitude at Greenwich, which the physicians had hoped would do the king some good, Edward was still coughing up sputum mixed with blood.

The king's isolation was giving rise to rumours and conflicting reports: on 7 May, Warwick asserted that the doctors anticipated that Edward would make a full recovery but, five days later, the imperial ambassador wrote that the same physicians believed him to be suffering from a suppurating tumour of the lung. He had a fever and a cough, and his belly, head and feet were swollen and covered in ulcers. Two weeks later Schefyre reported that the king 'does not sleep except when he be stuffed with drugs, which doctors call opiates, the sputum which he brings up is black, fetid and full of carbon, it smells beyond measure'. Warwick's apparent optimism may have been diplomatic, as the contrast between the two accounts can hardly have been the result of misunderstanding. It also contradicts his behaviour around the French ambassadors in mid-April, who perceived 'even from the Duke's own words, how little prospect there remained of the King's recovery'.[102] Princess Mary had clearly received a positive report, as she wrote on 16 May to congratulate her brother on recovering from a 'rheum cold', but the ambassador was being regularly updated by John Banister, a medical student whose father held a position in the king's household. Edward's final public engagement came on 17 May, when he met the French ambassadors, despite the fact that he was still coughing and feeling weak.

At this point he could no longer ignore his state but had to accept he was dying. He reputedly said to John Cheke that he was glad to die, perhaps as a release from the pain, but such a sentiment would also have been consistent with his faith: to embrace, even to welcome death and make a good end. But this was not just a personal journey; the boy took seriously his duties as a Protestant king with the spiritual welfare of his subjects in his hands, recalling the words of Bucer and Calvin, and the comparison Cranmer had made between himself and Josiah. In such a context, his final actions make perfect sense. On 21 May he wrote a 'devise' to add to his existing will, ruling his Catholic sister Mary out of the succession in favour of his Protestant cousin Lady Jane Grey. This went against the terms of Henry VIII's will, but it only had power to determine that king's immediate successor; Edward VI had the equal right to decide to pass the throne to whomever he chose. However, Mary's claim was stronger than Jane's, and the decision was clearly made to ensure religious continuity. There is also a clear preference for the country to be ruled by a man:

My devise for the Succession.

1. For lack of issue of my body ... coming of the issue female, as I have after declared to the Lady Frances' heirs males, such issue to the Lady Jane's heirs males, To the Lady Katerins heirs males, To the Lady Mary's heirs males, To the heirs males of the daughters which she shall have hereafter. Then to the Lady Margarets heirs males. For lack of such issue, to the heirs males of the Lady Jane's daughters. To the heirs males of the Lady Katerins daughters, and so forth til yow come to the Lady Margarets' daughters' heirs males.

2. If after my death theire male be entred into 18 yere old, then he to have the hole rule and gouernauce therof.

3. But if he be under 18, then his mother to be governres til he entre 18 yere old, But to doe nothing without the advice and agreement of 6 parcel of a counsel to be pointed by my last will to the nombre of 20.

4. If the mother die before they entre into 18 the realme to be governed by the counsel Provided that after he be 14 yere al great matters of importaunce be opened to him.

5. If I died without issue, and there were none heire male, then the Lady Fraunces to be governres. For lack of her, the eldest daughters, and for lack of them the Lady Margaret to be governres after as is aforesaid, til sume heire male be borne, and then the mother of that child to be governres.

6. And if during the rule of the goveernres ther die 4 of the counsel, then shal she by her letters call an assemble of the counsel within on month following and chose 4 more, wherin she shall have three voices. But after her death the 16 shall chose among themselves til the heir come to 14 yeare olde, and then he by their advice shal chose them.[103]

Soon after this, Edward was confined to his bed, suffering terrible agonies which announced that his end was near. In these final weeks, his symptoms escalated considerably, so that on 10 June, his doctors gave him only three days to live. He was unable to eat, racked by fever, flat on his back as his legs swelled. When his ulcers burst or he coughed up sputum, it gave off a terrible stench. Nine days later, he was still hanging on, although his demise was expected at any moment. The ambassador reported that his hair and nails were falling out and that he could hardly breathe and never moved. Among his loyal attendants at the end was Sir Henry Sidney, the son of his former chamberlain, whom he must have known almost his entire life. Sidney related that while he was still able to speak, the king prayed for God to deliver England from popery and hoped that the succession of Lady Jane Grey would prevent the country from lapsing into Catholicism. Somehow, he lasted until the start of June and, even more improbably, appeared at a window to dispel rumours that he was already dead.

As imperial ambassador Jehan Scheyfve recorded for the emperor on 4 July:

> As for the King, his condition is still as I reported to your Majesty on the 27th of last month, though since then he has shown himself at a window at Greenwich, where many saw him, but so thin and wasted that all men said he was doomed, and that he was only shown because the people were murmuring and saying he was already dead, and in order that his death, when it should occur, might the more easily be concealed. The people believed that the King was to show himself again last Sunday, the 2nd of the month, and a great crowd went to see, but they were told it should be done the following day. A large gathering then assembled, but a gentleman of the Bed-chamber came out and told them that the air was too chill. As far as I am able to ascertain, Sire, the King is very ill to-day and cannot last long. He will die suddenly, and no one can foretell whether he will live an hour longer, notwithstanding his having been shown to the people, for that was done against the physicians' advice. It seems there is at present about the King a certain woman who professes to understand medicine, and is administering certain restoratives, though not independently of the physicians.[104]

As Scheyfve notes, the king the witnesses saw on that day was thin and frail, only confirming that he would soon be gone. Edward died in Sidney's arms on 6 July, at around eight in the evening, surrendering his soul with 'great sweetness' and asking God to have mercy on him and take his spirit. Edward endured a longer, more drawn-out death than his uncle Arthur or his half-brother Henry Fitzroy, the former having little warning, the latter declining over the course of two or three weeks. It is often assumed that all three died of the same disease, but if this is the case, the nature of Edward's death suggests that he experienced other complications, or that his illness affected him differently, resulting in months of ill health.

It was probably tuberculosis that killed Edward. Other suggestions have included lung disease and septicaemia. Jennifer Loach[105] diagnoses a suppurating pulmonary infection after his cold developed into acute bilateral bronchopneumonia, causing abscesses to form in the lungs. This would have resulted in Edward coughing up coloured sputum, mixed with blood, as well as suffering fever and weight loss, leading to a poisoning of his other organs. The swelling in his lower body could be indicative of kidney failure. Concurring with the imperial ambassador, Christopher Skidmore[106] favours tuberculosis, which Edward contracted after the measles and smallpox he experienced in 1552, lowering his immunity. Machyn recorded in his diary that Edward had been 'poisoned, as everybody says', and had gone 'where now, thanks be to God there be many of the false traitors brought to their end' and prayed that 'more shall follow as they may be spied out.'[107] But the notion of poison was not given credence at court by those who had witnessed the king's health over the course of his life.

Edward's body was opened, embalmed and placed upon a catafalque in Westminster Abbey, without candles, surrounded by a guard of twelve men. He was interred in the Lady Chapel at Westminster on 8 August. His sister Mary did not impose her Catholicism upon the ceremony, but allowed proceedings to follow the changes he had introduced, under the guidance of Sir Gilbert Dethick, the Garter Knight at Arms.[108] However, she could not prevent herself from ordering masses to be said for the boy's soul. The procession was led by singing children, the king's officers and household bearing banners and the chariot carrying the hearse, draped in cloth of gold. An effigy of Edward lay on top of the latter, dressed in robes of estate, a coat embroidered in gold and a crown, carrying the orb and sceptre. The heralds bore standards depicting a dragon and a white greyhound, followed by the king's heraldic devices and achievements, including his helmet and crest, his target, garter and sword, 'gorgeous and rich'. The chief mourners followed, mostly gentlemen of the king's chamber, dressed alike in mantles of cloth of gold lined with white satin. Edward was buried in the east side of the Lady Chapel, under a brass altar and a canopy supported by pillars and capitals, although this has since been destroyed.[109] Henry Machyn witnessed the occasion. He wrote that the 'greatest moan' was made for him, that was 'ever heard of or seen, both of all sorts of people, weeping and lamenting'.[110]

Obviously, Edward's death had a devastating impact upon England as a newly reformed nation and, specifically, upon a number of individuals. Had the young king lived, his religious policy continuing under Northumberland and other like-minded servants, there would have been no hiatus of the mid-1550s and no burning of Protestant martyrs. Had he even survived another decade, assuming that Mary would still have died in 1558, he would have outlived his eldest sister and made a smoother transition to power for Queen Elizabeth. Had he fathered a son, perhaps by a princess of France, or by one of his own cousins, the sixteenth century would have looked remarkably different. Of course, all this is just idle speculation, a rewriting of events that cannot be rewritten. Only in alternative fiction can real people be 'saved' from the realities of their own fates and returned to the stage to enjoy a parallel reality. And yet, it is possible for the historian to examine what happened as a result of an individual's death, what filled the space they vacated in political, dynastic and religious terms. Edward's loss opened up a void that allowed the Catholic Counter-Reformation in England a brief window of opportunity and established an unprecedented period of religious conflict. The young king was powerless to prevent his own death, but he did attempt to take steps to control his country, through the succession, after he had gone. In the event, he failed, but his failure was short-lived.

The sympathetic heir Edward had been seeking in 1553 was to be his second sister, Elizabeth, who established a more tolerant approach upon her accession in 1558.

In 1554, Peter Martyr dedicated his *Commentaries on the Epistles to the Romans* to Edward's former tutor Sir Anthony Cooke, lamenting the king's loss; 'it is a griefe unto me to thinke that that most noble wit, most sacred brest and incredible piety of that famous King Edward the VI of that name, your most dear pupil is so suddenly taken from us.' Yet he also thanked Cooke for his pains, for 'your worthy office which you faithfully and with great renown executed in the Christian public wealth, in instructing Edward, that most holy King ... whose wit, goodness and religion and other virtues heroical ... can never be praised according to their desert'.[111]

Religious changes by the end of Edward's reign had made England a far more Protestant country, having followed the example of Luther's teachings in banning images in churches and the veneration of saints. These moves also completed the process that had been evolving since the 1520s, with the rejection of chantry chapels and beliefs in purgatory and the afterlife, bringing about a revolution in the way people thought about death. Pre-Reformation Catholics had believed that life was merely an interlude before the everlasting bliss of death. Good deeds and a good death would influence this process, but the moment of death itself, or the process of dying, was a test, a dark valley of shadows through which the soul had to pass; a battlefield where the Devil would be waiting to make one last, determined assault upon the individual. After that, a different struggle ensued as purgatory led either to hell or heaven, whose outcome the soul no longer had any power to influence, but might be aided by the prayers and masses of the living. Some might already have been destined to achieve heaven, but the damnation of sinners was by no means guaranteed, and the power of salvation was in God's gift. The Protestant belief removed this stage of limbo, with the immediate passage of the soul to heaven or hell, depending upon whether the individual was one of Luther's predestined, one of those who had sought God.

The detailed churchwardens' records from one London parish across this period helps illustrate a change in the methods for honouring the dead. The church of St Mary at Hill was originally built on Lovat Lane, in Billingsgate, in the fourteenth century. It had a late medieval north aisle and steeple, completed between 1490 and 1497, and contained four chapels, to St Stephen, St Katherine, St Anne and St Christopher. The abbot's former kitchen was demolished to make way for the new south aisle, which was ready for use by 1501. The church was destroyed in the great fire of 1666 but its records survived; these relate payments made for rents, expenses and the maintenance of the church and its many chantry chapels.

The records from the late fifteenth century are consistent with the practice of Catholicism and the usual memorials to the dead. Throughout this period, there are a handful of wealthy benefactors whose bequests ensured they were remembered. Between Michaelmas 1483 and Michaelmas 1485, 3s 4d was paid daily to the priests and clerks for keeping the obit of John Bradmer on 25 November; 6s 10d was paid for the obit of John Weston on 19 April; and the obit of Richard Goselin was observed on 1 December, for a payment of 4s 1d and an offering and bread and ale for the priest and clerks. Five chantry chapels were recorded in this cycle of accounts. John Bedaham's chantry saw his obit kept twice on 14 May for 8s 10d, as well as £13 6s 8d to the priest, 6s 8d as a bequest to the churchwarden, £5 11s to three poor men every Sunday and 18s for oil to keep Bedaham's lamp burning. There were also chantries with regular obits kept for a John Causton, Rose Wrytell and a Mr Nasing. The costs of William Cambridge's chantry chapel amounted to 44s 8d, including 8s 8d for the keeping of his obit twice annually, 13s and 4d as a bequest from the Cambridge family to the Mayor of London and 3s 4d to the sword-bearer who accompanied the mayor.[112]

The church accounts also include an exhaustive list of pre-Reformation furniture, with altar leaves, hanging and stones, square banners, banner staves and banners for the rood loft. There were branches of iron and brass; candlesticks; canopies and chalices; figures of the virgin, St Thomas and St Nicholas; painted glass; holy water sprinklers; a monstrance for the sacrament; silver pax and pyx; the great rood screen with images of St Mary and St John; streamers; tablets; tapers; and veils for Lent. Such features, along with the names of Bedaham, Cambridge, Causton, Wrytll,

Nasing, Bradmer, Weston and Goselin, recur through each session of the accounts until the end of the 1540s. In 1547–48, when the first Edwardian reforms were pushed through, all mention of chantry chapels disappears and there are indications that the fabric of the church was changing: 13s 4d was paid for the dismantling of the rood loft, taking down the iron work and the tabernacle over the vestry door. In 1548–49, the church purchased two copies of the new Book of Common Prayer at a cost of 7s 6d and sold the gilt of three images for 12s; 1549–50 also saw the sale of old prayer books, chalice, pyx, silver bell and twelve ounces of silver, altar stones and tables, raising a total of £1 5s 7d. This would have helped cover the 22s 6d paid for the taking down of the high altar and paving of the quire.[113]

The details of burial services also changed as a result of England's shifting religious climate. Those dying in the Catholic faith were sprinkled with holy water and censed, before being wished God speed upon their journey to Abraham's bosom. A priest would have been present in the chamber, holding a cross before the bed and placing a piece of communion bread in the mouth of the dying. In 1549, the cross and bread, the sprinkling and censing were removed, but the soul continued to be wished a speedy journey until 1552. At Willesborough, Kent, mourners at the funeral of Mother Cosen in 1560 were criticised for carrying crosses in the funeral procession to the church.[114] It had been customary for the priest to come out of the church and meet the dead upon their entry into the churchyard, or 'at the church stile', to conduct them into the building. This also changed: the coffin was now brought inside, up to the altar, where the priest was waiting.

The London diarist Henry Machyn, who recorded many of the events of Edward's reign, is particularly interesting on the question of death and funeral rites. Although little else is known about him, he was a merchant who supplied funeral trappings and his diary takes a particular interest in the ceremonies accompanying the final journeys of prominent citizens, but also of less well-known figures. He comments upon the burial of Sir William Locke, late alderman and sheriff, laid to rest at St Thomas's on 27 August 1550, with sixty poor men in mourning gowns and white staffs, after which the mourners ate a 'great dinner'. On 18 October, Machyn records that they buried Judge Hynde in St Dunstan's, in the presence of other judges and serjeants, with clerks singing and the dead man's heraldic devices. There was 'much ado there for him' and a 'great deal of money and of meat and drink and gowns to the poor'.[115]

At the end of November 1550, he recorded three more deaths. First to be buried, on the 19th of the month, was Lady Jude, wife of Andrew Jude, former Mayor of London. She was laid to rest in the parish of St Helen in Bishopsgate Street, and church and street were hung with black and the poor issued with gowns. Five days later, it was the 'noble captain Sir James Wilford', who was carried from the place of his death at the Crutched Friars near Tower Hill, to St Bartholomew's beside St Anthony's, with many mourners, to be buried in the same tomb as his great-uncle of the same name. The funeral was attended by the worshipful company of clerks, indicating the profession of the deceased, and the sermon was preached by the reformed friar Myles Coverdale. Finally, on the last day of the month, the diarist records the burial of 'Christopher Machyn, merchant-tailor, in the parish of St James and the brother of Henry Machyn'. The company of merchant tailors were present, the clerks sang and a preacher called Maidwell gave the sermon.[116]

Wills from these years indicate the religious and practical concerns of the dying in the immediate aftermath of Edward's reforms. Christopher Barker was an officer in the College of Arms who had served Charles Brandon, Duke of Suffolk and accompanied King Henry VIII to France in 1513. By the time he came to make his will on 31 December 1549, he must have been at least 60, and had helped arranged the christening of Prince Edward and the funerals of Jane Seymour, Henry VIII and Edward himself. Perhaps it was his long experience in this field that dictated his choices regarding his own resting place. He followed the Catholic tradition of expressing 'a pious hope that his soul may be received into Abraham's bosom', which recalls the hope that a small number of individuals would bypass purgatory and be received at once in heaven. Then he directed that his 'wretched corpse and carcas' be buried in a vault he had prepared in the chapel beside St Faith's church.

He had been a member of the vintner's company since 1521, and master between 1540 and 1543, and now left it the reversion of his tenements in Lime Street, while his third wife Edith received his freehold lands and tenements in Essex and Middlesex, and in Wanstead, West Ham and Barking.[117] Christopher Barker died just four days after making his will, on 4 January 1550, in Paternoster Road. He was buried in St Faith's Under St Paul's but any tomb he may have had was destroyed in the great fire of 1666.

Some will makers were minimal in their funerary requirements while others still left bequests for the beautification of local churches, to influence the living for their prayers. Geographical distance from London might have been a factor in the slow dissemination of change. The city draper Jasper Allen, writing his will on 4 November 1548, requested that he be buried 'without any pomp or pride of vain glory' and that thirteen sermons were to be preached on as many Sundays next after his burial, to be paid at the rate of 6s 8d each. He also left bequests of money, clothes, and coals to the new hospital lately founded by King Henry VIII, to various prisons and for redemption of prisoners, to poor householders in the parish of St Nicholas and others.[118] Five months later and 100 miles to the west, Edmund Winter was dying in the diocese of Bath and Wells. He also invoked Abraham, leaving his soul 'to the mercy of Almighty God trusting to have the everlasting fruition of his Kingdom with Abraham, Isaac and Jacob'. When the widowed Elizabeth Fitzjames of Temple Combe made her will in 1550, she left eight pence to every householder in the villages of Combe and Horsington 'so that they take pains to go with my corpse to see it buried' and ordered that pennies be given out at the funeral itself. Also in Somerset, when Nicholas Jobbyn was preparing to die in 1552, he stated his wish to be buried by the pulpit in the church of St Mary of Stalles and paid 40s for 'the making or setting up of the name of Jesus in goodly colours upon the high front or wainscott in Stalles Church and these texts written after the best manner in the same font: *in nomine Jesu, omne genu flectatat celestrium, terrestrium et infernorum* [at the name of Jesus, every knee should bow in heaven, on earth and under the earth] both in English and Latin that all men may see to read it'.[119]

No doubt responses to these changes were not consistent. They would have depended upon individual faith, but also factors like age, wealth, health and geographical location. While some embraced change, happily rejecting the old tenets of purgatory and prayers for the dead, others clung to them in horror at the heresy that threatened to jeopardise their souls. It must have been the case, however, that some were left confused by the rapid changes of the 1540s and 1550s, which would see an utter rejection of Catholicism before its complete, albeit brief, restoration. A percentage of those who died during this period must have been uncertain about their ultimate fate, trusting to God and clinging even more fervently to what they had believed to be the truth. Powerful faith and inconsistent policy would engender an era of religious martyrdoms.

10

Guildford Dudley (1535–54)

I

Guildford Dudley is a difficult historical phenomenon to pin down. His fame rests on the events of a few weeks in the summer of 1553, but these came about in circumstances so unpredictable, so unusual, that everything about his life which precedes them is simply a blank. Guildford has an approximate birthdate; we can guess where he may have been born and raised; a couple of details survive about the education of his siblings. Beyond that, as a member of a large family, intended for some minor role at court, administrating a country estate or some aspect of royal service, he would have left a slender trace of dates: birth, marriage, parentage, promotion, inheritance, service and death. There are no biographical anecdotes about his character or achievements, his ambitions or efforts. Of course, he most certainly did live a full life before the summer of 1553, probably a life typical for a boy of his time, spent in lessons, sports and duty to his king and parents. He just did so in a way that went unrecorded. He was not his father's heir, or even the spare heir. As the seventh or eighth son born in the family, he was unlikely to inherit much or to distinguish himself, let alone aim at the throne. Nor does any evidence survive to suggest that he was talented in any particular field – but nor does such evidence survive for his brother Robert, who was to become one of the leading statesmen of Elizabeth's reign. Guildford's fame was accidental.

It was the result of being in a certain place at a certain time, of being the only unmarried son of the Duke of Northumberland in June 1553. His premature death was equally surprising. Just when it seemed that he might have been saved, events beyond his control hastened his end. He may not have fought in battle but he was as much a casualty of dynastic conflict for the throne as Edmund of York in 1460 and Edward, Prince of Wales in 1471. If anything, certain circumstances of his fate parallel the experience of Edward V: both were raised to kingship as a result of their parentage, unable to play an active part in their fates and awaited their end in the Tower. Both were lost kings of England, lost lives and lost opportunities.

For the members of the reformed faith, Edward VI's death put the spiritual welfare of England in peril. By 1553, the Book of Common Prayer had been established for three years and the colourful panoply of Catholicism dismantled. Churches looked different inside, methods of worship had changed, as had important rites of passage like christenings, marriage and funerals. The old stone altars had been broken up and taken away, to be replaced by a more low-key wooden table, and the glittering candles and jewels of saints' shrines no longer attracted the prayers of the infirm, asking for their intercession with God. Since Henry VIII had begun to dissolve the monasteries in the 1530s, a new generation of men had taken positions of power, raised in the new religion, reading the works of prominent European Protestants and pushing through reform with Edward VI's approval. But the terms of Henry VIII's will named Edward's successor as his elder sister, Mary, whose ardent Catholicism had led her into conflict with her brother. It was partly to prevent these recent religious reforms from being undone that Guildford Dudley's brief moment in the limelight came about.

Following the execution of Edmund Dudley in 1510, the family had slowly improved their fortunes. Edmund's son John had become the ward of Sir Edward Guildford, of Halden in Kent, and grown up in his household, later marrying Guildford's daughter Jane. Named after his mother's side of the family, Guildford was the second youngest surviving son of his parents' thirteen children, arriving at some point in 1535. The family's bases of Dudley Castle in the West Midlands and Ely Place in London would have defined his childhood, which passed in the usual occupations of sons of the aristocracy: in sports and physical training and an education based on the classical tenets, with a Protestant slant. He would have shared lessons with the brothers who were closest to him in age: John, who arrived in around 1527, Ambrose in 1530, Henry in 1531 and Robert in 1532. He would have benefited from the building works that took place to modernise Dudley Castle in the 1540s and enjoyed hunting, shooting and riding in the surrounding countryside. When they visited London, it would have been to stay in the large and impressive palace of the bishops of Ely in Holborn, of which an eighteenth-century map shows an entrance gate and courtyard beside a walled garden, leading through to a great hall surrounded by service rooms, then a cloister around a quadrangle, joined on to St Etheldreda's chapel, which overlooked fields. Little else is known about Guildford's early years apart from the fact that he was described in Grafton's chronicle as a 'comely, virtuous and goodly gentleman'.

In 1552, when he was around 17, Guildford's father, the Earl of Warwick, now Duke of Northumberland, had suggested Lady Margaret Clifford as a potential bride for his son. This would have been a good match for Guildford, as Margaret was a direct descendant of Henry VII, being his great-granddaughter through the line of Princess Mary, also Queen of France, and Charles Brandon, Duke of Suffolk. Mary had borne two sons who died prematurely and two daughters, Frances and Eleanor. Frances had married Henry Grey, Marquis of Dorset and borne three girls, while Eleanor married Henry Clifford, Earl of Cumberland whom she gave two boys, who also died young, and a single daughter, Margaret. She was 12 in 1552. On 4 July, the Council wrote to both Northumberland and Clifford, encouraging them to 'grow some good end concerning the marriage between the Lord Guildford and his daughter'.[1] Edward VI had thought it a good match and encouraged Northumberland, but the bride's family objected.[2] This failed attempt indicates that the duke was more interested in making a good match for his son than in the royal succession, as the three unmarried Grey sisters had a senior claim to that of Margaret, and yet Northumberland initially preferred the Clifford marriage. Dudley's three older sons were already married, indicating that the duke was keen o, and Guildford had reached the salient age, so his alliance did not come out of the blue.

The question of Northumberland's motives has long exercised historians, who have painted him as many things from ruthlessly ambitious to cautiously reactive. In April 1553, when Edward VI's condition worsened, Northumberland's actions seemed to suggest that he saw Princess Mary as her brother's successor. He maintained a regular communication with her about the king's health and restored her full status, title and arms as a princess of England, which her father had denied her in the 1530s. Mary had every reason to believe that the duke would be loyal to her cause once the death of her brother left the way open for her succession. The duke found a bride for his unmarried son the same month, and the imperial ambassador recorded that 'during the last few days, the Duke has found means to ally and bind his son, my Lord Guildford, to the Duke of Suffolk's eldest daughter.'[3] On 28 April, the betrothal of Guildford Dudley and Lady Jane Grey was announced at court, and received the approval of king and Council.

And yet the bride herself was reluctant. Having been born in late 1536 or early 1537, Jane was then 16, an ardent Protestant devoted to her studies. She had received a humanist education, studying Latin, Greek, Hebrew and Italian, which was still rare for aristocratic women, although it was gaining ground in certain circles. She had also lived for a time, in 1547–48, in the household of Catherine Parr, known for her reformist influence, and had served as chief mourner at her funeral in September 1548. The dramatist Nicholas Udall relates in his translation of Erasmus's *Paraphrase on the Four Gospels* that 'a great number of noble women in that time in England were given to the study of human sciences and strange tongues.'[4] A visiting Roger Ascham famously discovered Jane at the family home of Bradgate Park, in Leicestershire, reading alone while the others had gone hunting. Giulio Raviglio Rosso adds that violence and persuasion were brought to bear upon the girl: 'urged by the mother, and beat by the father, she was required to content herself.'[5]

Guildford was not the first husband suggested for her. In 1541 the French ambassador had proposed that she marry Charles, Duke of

Orléans, the third son of Francis I, which would have placed her in the line of succession to the French throne, but the young man died of the plague in 1545. In 1551 another union was raised, closer to home. Edward Seymour, Duke of Somerset saw Jane as a potential bride for his eldest son Edward, Earl of Hertford, the king's cousin. This idea may have been abandoned as a result of Somerset's fall from grace, but his son went on to conduct a secret marriage with Jane's cousin, Catherine Grey, which resulted in their imprisonment in the Tower. Even at 16, Jane did not seem ready to become a wife or, perhaps, specifically the wife of Guildford, as she responded by 'strongly deprecating such marriage'.[6]

The match seems to have been the work of the two fathers. Henry Grey was in favour, and his wife's cherished hopes that Jane might marry Edward VI were clearly now impossible. But Frances was close to her cousin Princess Mary and unwilling to usurp her place in the succession. Another family friend, William Parr, Marquis of Northampton, lent his support to the union of Jane and Guildford, although probably more for personal reasons of his own. Parr's first marriage had been declared invalid and he eventually married his long-term mistress, Elisabeth Brooke, finally setting up home with her in 1551, but the couple feared that if Mary came to throne and restored the old Catholic ways, their marriage would be considered invalid. Indeed, they were right to fear this, as Mary did later declare the marriage bigamous and ordered them to separate. Elisabeth was forced to live on the charity of friends and William was ordered to return to his first wife; if he lived again with Elisabeth he would be executed for bigamy. Foreseeing this eventuality in 1553, the pair urged Northumberland and Grey forward in their mission.

No fan of Northumberland, Giulio Raviglio Rosso takes up the narrative with his own interpretation of the duke's motives:

The Duke having understood the judgment of the physicians, and finding himself with that great authority which he had in the city, immediately designed, any time that it might please God to call Edward to Himself, to seek to raise himself to be master in that realm, as the evidence itself showed clearly thereafter, focusing more sharply on that objective, where his own unjust desire lay, than on any part of his duty, which was very great. And with this intention he determined to give his ... son to the first born of the Duke of Suffolk, named Jane.[7]

It may be that ambition drove the duke, who had been in a position of unparalleled power in recent years. As Jane's father-in-law, he would be able to control her and retain the position that he was almost certain to lose under Mary, as historian Nicola Tallis believes.[8] Eric Ives caricatures the usual 'script', the subsequent historical interpretations of Northumberland's role, with the lines 'enter Mephistopheles ... dragging with him the teenage Jane Grey whom he has forced to marry his son Guildford.' Around the duke was a 'gaggle of noble sycophants cowed into supporting him' until the people rose up to prevent his 'machinations' and 'Jane and Guildford, innocent victims, go to the Tower and death.'[9] However, the duke's recent illness in 1552–53 and his slowness in acting to quash Mary when she attempted to assert her claim have been interpreted by others, including Derek Wilson, as evidence that he would have been happy to relinquish the reins of power and retreat into a quiet retirement.[10] It may well have been ambition, though, which drove Jane's father. Robert Wingfield comments that 'the timid and trustful duke therefore hoped to gain a scarcely imaginable haul of immense wealth and greater honour of his house from this match, and readily followed Northumberland's wishes.'[11]

Yet Rosso was also of the opinion that the former illegitimacy of princesses Mary and Elizabeth was an important concern, even though they had been restored to their places by Henry VIII's third Act of Succession in 1544. Their inheritance, according to Rosso's account of Northumberland's arguments, would create disorder in the realm. The question of their faith appears briefly at the end and reminds us that it is difficult to know how far the duke was a realist, or an idealist, when it came to religion:

> ... this occasion might be a good device for conducting at last his scheme by those means, and ways, that he carried out thereafter: of which the first, that he used, was, that the infirmity continuing in the King, and the illness worsening more every hour, the Duke persuaded him to make a will, putting it to him as a

matter conscience before the eyes, that, when it might please God to call him to Himself, it was an honest thing, and very proper, that he might leave some order to that realm, so that in the future quiet could continue to exist, as it had done in the years passed, and pointing out to him the damage, that the said realm would suffer, whatever time he might leave of it to those heirs either Mary or Elizabeth, his sisters; because the one herself, and the other were declared bastards by state Parliament; and for the relatives of them, which they would possibly have to make with foreigners, as well as on account of religion.[12]

Exactly what Guildford made of this is unknown. No record survives of his being reluctant, as it does with Jane, but the information surviving about his life, let alone his thoughts and feelings, is almost prohibitively thin. Presumably he was raised as an obedient and dutiful son and it would have been his duty to marry the woman his father chose for him. Jane was a good match. He was marrying into the royal family. She was educated and intelligent; she was a Protestant and, reputedly, beautiful, if rather short. An anonymous witness who saw her in the Tower of the London that summer described her as 'a beautiful young woman, pretty and endowed with intelligence, educated and well-dressed', while chronicler Richard Grafton, who knew her, stated that she was a 'fair lady whom nature had so not only beautified, but God also had endowed with singular gifts'.[13] On paper, Guildford appears to have had no cause for complaint, but paper does not take into account the vagaries of the human heart. And yet, had Guildford already been in love, or chosen his own sweetheart, he may have had cause to hope for a marriage of affection, or a 'carnal' marriage as it was then known, just as his parents had enjoyed. John and Jane Dudley had married for love and had permitted their son Robert to wed Amy Robsart for the same reason in 1550. Had there been an existing preference on Guildford's side, they may have been sympathetic, but that is assuming this was a normal marriage, under normal circumstances. The dynastic and religious problems arising in the summer of 1553 were anything other than 'normal,' if such a thing can be defined. As Edward VI lay dying, he urged his Council to honour his change to the succession to prevent a national lapse into Catholicism, and the Duke of Northumberland was Edward's loyal servant. Whether the duke planted the seed of the idea in the king's mind, or was responding to Edward's initiative, will probably never be known.

On 25 May 1553, the Feast of the Holy Spirit, three weddings were held in the chapel of Durham Place, an impressive former bishops' seat on the Strand, which Northumberland had recently acquired. In 1380 the building had maintained twelve chaplains to celebrate divine service and a contemporary description of it includes a vaulted chamber under the chapel, a solar by the chapel entrance and two separate chambers within the vestibule of the chapel itself. There was also a large garden, of about two acres, extending down to the River Thames, which was no doubt utilised for the wedding celebrations. The great hall abutted the river, and was described around 1592 as 'stately and high, supported with loftie marble pillers. It standeth upon the Thamise very pleasantly'. As recently as April 1551, Durham Place had lodged the French ambassador, when it was well provisioned and 'richly hanged … and had at his cominge ready sett in the court of the same, for a present from the Kinges Maiestie, certeine fatt oxen, calves, sheepe, lambes and all manner of wyld foule of every sorte, a certain [number] all alive, and also of all manner of freshe fyshe of the best that might be gotten, with wyne allso in his cellar'.[14]

The day was a significant Dudley-Grey affair, with two pairs of siblings getting married. As well as Guildford marrying Jane, both his and Jane's sister were also wed. Catherine Dudley was the youngest of Northumberland's children and possibly still underage when she was united to Henry Hastings, Earl of Huntingdon. A clause in the will of Jane Dudley, who died in 1555, suggests that Catherine was under 12, allowing for the match to be dissolved 'if it so chance that my Lord Hastings do refuse her or she him'.[15] Hastings was then around 17 and had been educated alongside Edward VI. The pair did not repudiate each other in the end, but lived together as man and wife from at least 1559, inheriting the Huntingdon title, although they remained childless. The third couple to marry at Durham House on that summer day in 1553 were Catherine Grey and Henry, Lord Herbert, heir to the Earl of Pembroke. Catherine was definitely 12, nearly 13, having been born in August 1540 and Henry was perhaps a year or two older. Their marriage was not made permanent, though, being dissolved the following year by Pembroke after the Dudley family had fallen from favour. In something of a marital coup, the third Grey daughter, Mary, was also betrothed on this occasion, to a distant relative, Arthur Grey, Lord Grey de Wilton.

King Edward was unable to attend the wedding because of his failing health but he sent Guildford and Jane wedding gifts including cloth of gold, silver, purple, black, crimson and white fabric, a collar of great pearls and enamelled flowers, thirteen table diamonds set in gold, enamelled black, a gold girdle and many other jewelled ornaments.[16] The king also gave permission for Northumberland's brother, Sir Andrew Dudley, his Master of the Wardrobe, to organise the wedding clothes. Jane wore a purple wedding dress with gold and silver brocade, embroidered with pearls and diamonds, her hair hanging loose. Frances, the mother of the bride, was provided with a 'loose gown of black velvet, embroidered', while Guildford's mother Jane was also given clothes and jewels, as was the Marchioness of Northampton, Elisabeth Brooke, second wife of William Parr, who had supported the match.[17] But some of the clothing had a macabre heritage, having been forfeited to the king by Edward Seymour, Duke of Somerset, who had gone to his death in the Tower seventeen months before.

There were jousts, games and two masques, one for men and one for women, accompanied by feasting in the great hall. Rosso recorded that it was a 'very splendid, and royal, wedding, with a large gathering of people, and of the principal [people] of the realm', among whom the Venetian and French ambassadors were guests. The only sour note was the severe food poisoning experienced by Guildford and a few others after a cook made a mistake when preparing a salad, 'plucking one leaf for another'.[18] He appears to have still been ill in the middle of June. Even if he had not been unwell, it may have been decided that the wedding was not to be consummated at once on account of the couple's tender age. Jane's biographer, Nicola Tallis, believes that the pair did share a bed during this time, however, to ensure that the match was legally binding.[19]

Guildford and Jane remained together at Durham Place, which was now the main Dudley residence in London. It was probably there that Northumberland informed them about the change in Edward's will and his choice of Jane as queen. This is likely to have happened soon after the king drafted the new document on 21 June and although she had been aware of her former position in the succession, the sudden promotion above her cousins and aunts was unexpected. As she later deposed, the news 'caught me quite unaware' and 'very deeply upset me'.[20] Jane wished to leave Durham Place and go to her mother but she was forbidden from doing so. Soon afterwards she fell ill and was given permission to go to Old Manor, Chelsea, now owned by Northumberland, where she had formerly spent happy months living with Catherine Parr. What role Guildford played in this is unclear. It is unlikely that we will ever know whether he was his father's instrument or if he felt any degree of compassion for Jane. Did they have a personal connection? Had intimacy established a friendship between them? Or did Guildford see her as his ticket to the throne? The truth probably includes elements of all these possibilities. In the absence of contradictory evidence, it seems that Guildford is likely to have followed the example set by his older brothers. The Northumberland–Suffolk coup was a family affair, drawing in John, Henry, Ambrose and Robert Dudley, who would stand by their father and suffer imprisonment with him.

On 4 July, the imperial ambassador Jehan Scheyfve wrote to the emperor to explain the current situation. He had heard that 'the King of England has made a will, appointing as true heir to the Crown, after his death, Suffolk's eldest daughter, who has married my Lord Guilford, son of the Duke of Northumberland.' Naturally leaning towards support of the Catholic Church and Princess Mary, the emperor's cousin, Scheyfve was concerned to hear that 'the Princess has been expressly excluded on religious grounds and because she is asserted to have disobeyed the King and his Council, and infringed the decrees of Parliament.' Mary had been popular with the English people for decades, as had her mother, Catherine of Aragon, whose cruel treatment by Henry VIII had not been forgotten. The ambassador captured the various rumours that were flying about the court, that the Duke of Suffolk, Jane's father, was to succeed and that Mary was to be reclassified as a bastard, although Northumberland had recently restored her to her former legitimate position. He believed that the Council had agreed to the changes in Edward's will 'rather out of fear than for any other reason' and that it had 'demurred and made many difficulties before consenting'. He implied that Mary's exclusion had been achieved by bribery, that Edward was leaving legacies of thousands of pounds to ensure compliance, which Northumberland was supplementing with gifts of his own.

On the same day, 4 July, princesses Mary and Elizabeth had both been summoned to court by Edward's Council, supposedly to comfort their brother during his last illness. Scheyfve feared that the Council would seize Mary as soon as Edward died, and so she had been warned to retreat from her present residence at Hunsdon and establish herself in the countryside, at Framlingham Castle in Suffolk. Framlingham was 60 miles from London, well-fortified, among an established Catholic support base and close enough to the coast in case the princess needed to flee the country. Six warships were awaiting Mary's instructions, two at Leigh and four at Woolwich.[21] However, the ambassador was concerned that Northumberland was also arming himself to be prepared for a challenge to the changes in the king's will:

> The Duke of Northumberland has 500 men wearing his livery, the Duke of Suffolk 300 and the other councillors numbers proportionate to their rank and importance; and they have bought up all the arms and armour in the kingdom, not only enough for their own use, but all they could find for sale, in order to keep it out of the hands of the Princess' friends. The result is that every one is murmuring against Northumberland, saying he is a great tyrant, that he has poisoned the King, and wishes to plunge the kingdom into disturbances and hand it over to the French.[22]

In addition, Scheyfve reported that pressure was being exerted upon the clerics in the Council who could prove sympathetic to Mary and her faith: 'The preachers and priests have once more been made to sign certain articles, and they are told that unless they abide by them they shall be deprived of their benefices and pensions, and imprisoned and chastised in exemplary fashion into the bargain.'[23] But the duke had yet to make a move: 'Northumberland is still behaving courteously towards the Princess, as if nothing were about to happen.'[24]

The French ambassadors Jehan de Montmorency and Jacques de Marnix added their voices to Scheyfvre's on 7 July. They were as yet unaware that Edward had died, but speculated that Northumberland might be responsible for administering poison to the king:

> We have heard that the King has been caused to make a will by which he has appointed heir to the Crown the eldest daughter of the late Duke of Suffolk, who has been married to my Lord Guilford, younger son of the Duke of Northumberland ... He has reinforced the watch in London and at the Tower, and has sought to justify his ambition to get the Crown for his son, by prevailing upon the King and most of the Council to act in such a manner that he may not incur the same blame as if he had grasped the Crown himself, and may avoid the suspicion, which is hanging over him, of having poisoned the King, or caused him to be poisoned.[25]

Exactly what frantic discussions took place behind closed doors in the Council chamber during Edward's last hours cannot be known beyond what survives in the form of the king's own device for the succession. Until Edward passed away, both sides carefully watched each other and waited.

II

When Edward did die, on 6 July, the news was kept a secret. It was not a very well-kept secret, though, and at least one messenger slipped out of the palace to ride and inform Princess Mary. The king's death had been so long anticipated, and prefaced by so much speculation, that those close to the court did not take long to work out that it had finally happened.

While writing their joint letter to the emperor on the following day, the imperial and French ambassadors noted:

> While we were writing the above, the Lord Admiral of England, accompanied by the Treasurer and the Earl of Shrewsbury, took over the command of the Tower of London. This would seem to confirm the news of the King's death, as also the fact that the Council have met in an unwonted place, into which the secretaries were not admitted. Several persons have been sent off in divers directions, it is believed to close the passages. Three or four warships have sailed towards the mouth of the Thames.[26]

Two days later, the ambassadors informed the emperor that 'the Council concealed from us the fact of the King's death, which is nonetheless true and generally known,' in order to 'gain time' to have Jane 'sworn and accepted as Queen, as the late King's will directs'.[27] By extension, if Jane was queen, Guildford was king, or consort, and his subsequent efforts to be recognised as such suggest that this was not as unwelcome to him as it was to his wife. On 9 July, the archers of the guard swore the oath of loyalty to Jane and were informed that:

> the Lady Mary, was not fit to succeed because of the divorce that had separated her father, King Henry, from her mother, Queen Catherine … Lady Mary was unable to administer the kingdom, being a woman and of the old religion; and mutations and changes might take place that would cause the ruin of the country.[28]

This gender-based motivation for the new device for the succession was echoed in events that took place between Jane and Guildford in the following days.

On 9 July, Jane was summoned from Old Manor at Chelsea, to Northumberland's house of Syon, formerly the abbey. There she was greeted and banqueted, and found the Council awaiting her, probably the duke and Guildford too, joining forces to persuade her to accept the throne and briefing her about the coming days.[29] The following afternoon, attended by a 'noble train of both sexes',[30] Guildford accompanied Jane by boat to the Tower, perhaps with apprehension, perhaps excitement, as the crown was almost within his reach. At around four or five o'clock, they made a ceremonial entrance, 'with accustomed pomp',[31] and were greeted by Northumberland, the Council, the Tower's constables and prominent citizens. Jane's train was carried by her mother and, Machyn adds, all the guns were set off and there was a great report of the trumpets. Guildford walked alongside her, his cap in his hand. The extravagant descriptions of the pair, reputed to have been recorded by the Genovese merchant Baptista Spinola, who claimed to have been close enough to see the freckles on Jane's face, frequently repeated in accounts of her life were, in fact, a work of fiction created by an historical novelist in 1909.[32]

A proclamation was issued on Jane's behalf, stating her new queenship in accordance to the will of Edward VI. Criers on the street corners 'published an order given under the Great Seal of England, … which, by the new Queen's authority', repeated the bastardy of Mary and Elizabeth and the fears of a foreign alliance. 'However', added Scheyfvre, 'no one present showed any sign of rejoicing, and no one cried: "Long live the Queen!" except the herald who made the proclamation and a few archers who followed him.'[33] An apprentice named Gilbert Potter was brave, or foolish, enough to cry out in response that Mary was the rightful queen, for which he lost his ears.[34] On the same day, the ambassadors were formally briefed 'that the new King and Queen are to be proclaimed this very day in the Tower of London and at Westminster; and we have heard that the Council have quite decided not to allow the Lady Mary to succeed'.[35]

The crown was conveyed to Jane's apartments from the jewel house for her to try on, upon which William Paulet said that she 'could take it without fear and that another also should be made, to crown [her] husband'.[36] Jane had not expected this, and it raised a source of contention between herself and her young husband. One of the driving forces behind Edward VI's alterations to his will, and to religion, was the fear of handing the country over to the rule of a woman, Mary or Elizabeth, who might then make a foreign marriage. England would then come under the control of a prince of France or Spain, and the country would lose its autonomy and, depending upon the queen's choice of husband, its new religious stance might be compromised, even undone. Yet there was no male heir in the immediate line of descent from Mary, Duchess of Suffolk, as only daughters had survived. Edward had made provision for the inheritance of male heirs borne by Jane and her sisters, but the need was more immediate.

To Northumberland, the perfect solution had presented itself in the importation, by marriage, of a young aristocratic English man who had already reached adulthood. Hence Guildford's union with Jane was as much about preventing the threat of a foreign king, as it was about religion and his father's ambition. Clearly, he had been privy to the intentions of Edward's device but his wife had not. Jane does not seem to have realised this until she tried the crown, and her reluctance was to prove a stumbling block. She informed Guildford that if he was to become king, it would be by an Act of Parliament; in the interim, she offered him the Duchy of Clarence. As the ambassadors related to the emperor:

> Guilford tried to induce his wife to cede her right to the Crown to him, so that he might not only be consort and administrator [*administrateur*], but king in person, intending to have himself confirmed as such by Parliament. But she refused to do so, and gave him the title of Duke of Clarence, which is reserved for the younger son of the king. He already had himself addressed as 'Your Grace' and 'Your Excellency,' sat at the head of the Council board, and was served alone.[37]

Guildford was caught in a difficult position between his parents and his wife. Determined to assert the majesty he felt was his due, according to the ambassadors, he dined in state, alone, and attempted to preside over Council meetings. Their report is based on rumour, though, as they were not present in the Tower and did not have access to Guildford or his immediate circle. Scheyfvre spoke little English and was dependent upon reports from other ambassadors and merchants. Their value lies in recording the chaotic mood of the moment, as contemporaries in London watching events unfold. The extent to which Jane's refusal angered Guildford's mother is clear from her order that he should desist from sleeping with her until she complied, and urged him to return to Syon House.[38] Whether of out affection, pique or level-headed loyalty to the path upon which they were now embarked, Jane intervened to prevent his departure. How Guildford really responded to the situation is unknown. He must have been briefed by his father about what to do in the coming days, before Northumberland and his other sons departed for Norfolk, in an attempt to apprehend Princess Mary.

In Northumberland's absence, his plans crumbled. His prestigious talent had been to be the co-ordinating glue, driving and uniting all elements and, although Jane had been proclaimed queen, and oaths of loyalty sworn, this proved insufficient once he had left. Yet the duke had no choice: Mary had assembled a significant number of troops in East Anglia and sent a letter to London declaring her queenship. Supremely able as he was, Northumberland's plot crumbled because he could not be in two places at once and lacked a second-in-command of equal calibre. As Cardinal Commendone noted, Jane's father, the Duke of Suffolk, was 'not held as a man of great valour and therefore lacked authority'.[39] Northumberland was aware of the risk he was taking, foreshadowing his own downfall at the final Council dinner, and told his colleagues that 'if we thought that through malice, conspiracy or dissension leave us, your friends, in the briars and betray us, we could as well sundry ways foresee and provide for our safeguards as any of you by betraying us can do for yours.' His life, that of his family and his army, and the continuance of the reformed religion they had fought for, now depended upon the 'constant hearts, abandoning all malice and envy' of the Council and he warned them that God would not acquit them of 'the sacred and holy oath of allegiance made freely by you to this virtuous lady … who by your and our enticement is rather of force placed therein than by her own seeking and request'.[40] He had taken a huge gamble and knew he was now dependent upon the support of the men he left behind. It was a valiant effort: he could hardly have said more, but it did not prove to be enough.

Between 19 and 20 July, the Council moved against Northumberland. On the 19th, it issued a letter to Lord Rich bearing signatures by sixteen leading councillors, asking him to remain loyal to Queen Jane, but on the following day, it met at Baynard's Castle and declared in Mary's favour. The motivation appears to have been recognition of Mary's claim over Jane's but also the conviction that Northumberland had acted out of self-interest, 'which moved the Duke to seize the Crown of England in order to transfer it to his own house',[41] as the ambassadors wrote to the emperor's son, Prince Philip, who would become Mary's husband. Scheyfvre also reported that the duke's unpopularity was to blame and that it was generally believed that he was responsible for the late king's death:

> he took into consideration his extreme unpopularity in this realm, and decided to kill the late King Edward, as every one supposes and the course of the malady demonstrates. It is generally said that he poisoned the King, and whether it was that the poison was not intended to act at once, but only gradually, or whether the King's constitution was too weak to resist, in any case his hair and nails fell off, he as it were dried up, and died between eight and nine on the evening of the 6th instant.[42]

As soon as Jane's father heard of the Council's defection, he left the Tower, having been persuaded by his daughter to remain in London, broadcasting 'I am but one man,' and declared in favour of Queen Mary. Then he returned to the Tower and entered his daughter's chamber while she was at dinner, sitting under a canopy of state, and tore the hangings down. Jane and Guildford found their status change dramatically. They now became prisoners and were removed from the royal apartments, to the gentlemen gaoler's lodgings in Jane's case and the Bell Tower for Guildford. Jane's mother and ladies in waiting were permitted to return home, which they did at once, but Suffolk found himself confined under lock and key.

Seeing that the tide had turned against him, Northumberland had no choice but to accept the Council's word, although he was keen to stress that all his actions had been fulfilled with their express permission, and he had the Great Seal upon his documents as evidence:

And although the Duke, wherever he had passed, had caused my Lady and the lords who supported her to be declared traitors to the Crown, and had burnt two villages belonging to the said lords, yet when he had seen and considered the Council's letters he summoned the Earl of Huntingdon, the Admiral, my Lord Grey and others of his chief followers, and declared to them loudly that all he had done up to that time had been enacted with the authority, consent and knowledge of the Council, in proof of which he had documents sealed with the Great Seal of England. However, as the Council had changed their minds, he did not wish to differ from or combat their decisions, supposing that they had been moved by good reasons and considerations; so for his part he intended to follow their advice and conform, and he begged the lords, who had been called together, to do the same. This they decided to do, and the Duke in person then stood by the herald who made the proclamation, crying out three times in a loud voice that my Lady Mary was Queen of England.[43]

On 25 July, when Northumberland returned to London empty handed, he was arrested and sent to the Tower. Abandoned by all their London supporters, there was nothing for Guildford and Jane to do but pray for clemency after Mary's now-inevitable arrival.

The new Tudor queen entered London around seven on the evening of 3 August. The city and its leading dignitaries, most of whom had sworn allegiance to Jane the previous week, turned out to greet her. She passed through Aldgate, where streamers had been hung and the length of the street from Leadenhall to the Tower was laid with fresh gravel.[44] The city guilds displayed their banners in prominent support, trumpets sounded, the guns of the Tower were fired and the mayor handed her the sceptre 'in token of loyalty and homage'.[45] Mary looked in a gown of purple velvet, the kirtle thick with gold embroidery, and pearls and precious stones around her neck and upon her head. She paused at the gateway of the Tower to be greeted by its officials and to meet with the Council.

Inside the Tower, Guildford would have guessed the meaning of the cannons being fired. He may even have seen part of the proceedings. The

Bell Tower was situated in the south-west corner of the complex, on the Thames side, right by the entrance by which Mary would have arrived. To the east, its windows would have given views over Tower Green and the site of executions, where Guildford must have anticipated his actions would soon lead him. Constructed in the late twelfth century, the Bell Tower was a squat, solid thick-walled addition to the Tower complex, topped by the curfew bell that was sounded each night to prompt the inhabitants to return to their quarters. Guildford may have been aware that the Bell Tower had been the place of incarceration for the martyrs Thomas More and John Fisher, whose last days had been spent in excruciating discomfort before their execution in the year of his birth. A few days later, he was joined there by his brother Robert, while Northumberland and the other Dudley siblings, Henry and Ambrose, were incarcerated in other locations nearby. There, they waited for the axe to fall.

It fell first for Northumberland. He was summoned to trial in Westminster Hall on 18 August, and faced a panel of judges who, until recently, had been his colleagues on the Council, and the very men who had betrayed him. He repeated his statement of capitulation, asserting that he had acted on the Council's authority, ratified by the Great Seal, but it was not enough to save him. He was to be made a scapegoat for the more extreme religious reforms of recent years, accused of not just attempting to usurp the line of succession but of 'seducing'[46] Edward into heresy. Recognising that his fate was inevitable, the duke issued a plea for his sons, insisting that 'they went by my commandment, who am their father, and not of their own free wills'. Scheyfve's account lists the formal proceedings and ceremony of the occasion:

The old Duke of Norfolk, Earl Marshal of England, stood to represent the Queen as President of the Court. He was seated on a seat with a dossal, adorned with a pall and royal mantle, raised upon a high scaffolding. On his right sat the Lord High Treasurer, the Earl of Arundel, and several Lords of the Council and peers. On his left were: the Lord Privy Seal, the Earl of Shrewsbury, the old Chancellor, Cobham, Paget, and several others …

The Duke was then brought in, under safe escort, preceded by one carrying the axe of justice, and stood before his judges. The recorder read out his deposition and confession from among the documents of the trial, and asked if he maintained all that was stated therein, so that judgment might be given according to custom … The Duke raised his hand in sign of taking his oath; then he fell on his knees and appealed to the Queen for mercy, saying that all he had done was by the advice, consent and command of the Council; he confessed the occasion of it and reiterated his confession. He proffered three requests: one that the Queen's Councillors and judges should intercede with her to obtain grace and pardon for him; the second that certain Councillors might be deputed to hear certain matters he wished to declare; the third that time might be granted to him to reconcile himself with God and the execution of the sentence deferred for a few days. Thereupon the Duke of Norfolk, without consulting the judges or commissioners or taking their votes or advice – as indeed there was no need, as the Duke made a full confession – pronounced sentence against him; by which he was condemned to be hanged, his heart to be drawn from his body and flung against his face, and quartered.[47]

Condemned alongside Northumberland were his eldest son John Dudley and William Parr, Marquis of Northampton, who had encouraged the marriage. The executions of the duke and his eldest son were set for the morning of 21 August. They had time to prepare for their fate, to recant their sins and resign themselves, therefore making the good death that was considered so critical. This was one of the requests Northumberland made at his trial and, in the wake of what followed, indicates the genuine nature of his religious faith in the light of pressure that might be exerted upon him in his final days.

What is perhaps most controversial, and confusing, about Northumberland's entire career, is what happened in the last twenty-four hours of his life. Taken from his cell before eight o'clock on the appointed day, he was not led to the scaffold on Tower Green as he had been expecting, but instead taken into the small church of St Peter ad Vincula nearby. This was a new church, rebuilt by Henry VIII in 1519–20 but its short history had already identified it as place of sudden death, having received the headless corpses of Anne Boleyn, Catherine Howard, Thomas More, John Fisher, Thomas Cromwell and others. There, the duke and his eldest son knelt to receive communion in the fully restored Catholic rites. Following this, Northumberland publicly recanted:

> Truly, I profess here before you all that I have received the sacrament according to the true Catholic faith, and the plagues that is upon the realm and upon us now is that we have erred from the faith these sixteen years. And this I profess unto you all from the bottom of my heart.[48]

How the historian should interpret the duke's actions lies within the context of contemporary beliefs in the afterlife. There have been many reactions to his end, ranging from sympathy to condemnation, but the duke cannot be judged out of the context of time which produced texts such as *Artis Moriendi*. Some have speculated that he had no choice. Perhaps he was indeed a devoted Protestant who had urged through extreme religious reform in recent years, and made this concession to the new queen in the hope of buying clemency for his sons, or in the belief that he might later have the opportunity to make a private revocation for the benefit of his soul. If this is the case, his gamble paid off, as the sentence of execution passed on his heir, John Dudley, was never carried out and all his other sons, save for Guildford, were released. Or perhaps he had in fact secretly harboured Catholic sympathies and his career at the side of Edward VI was driven by ambition and hypocrisy, although this seems unlikely. The recantation was certainly an act required by Mary as the final humiliation of the man who attempted to depose her, but was also a way of resetting the religious dial, in her attempt to return the country to its pre-Reformation worship. What better way to convince her subjects of their heresy than a full and frank recantation by the architect of change? Having established at his trial that the duke was entirely to blame for the state of the country's heresy, the queen required him to reject all his former actions.

This also ensured that the Protestant faction would not be able honour the duke as a religious martyr. Even at the last minute, he may have been hoping that his sentence would be commuted, and was writing letters to prominent members of the Council, pleading with them to influence the new queen in his favour. Taking Catholic Communion which, after all, he would have done frequently during his younger years, may have been a price he was prepared to pay for his freedom. He may not have known on 21 August that this was not the bargain. Perhaps Mary had not even made up her mind at that point. Some have concluded that Northumberland was playing a canny game to the end, just as many of his contemporaries would do, paying public lip service for the sake of his sons, while holding his true faith in his heart, trusting God to understand the reason for his actions.

However, the most plausible explanation for the duke's failure to challenge Mary's order to recant can be found in the notion of the good death. Northumberland had had time to come to terms with the fact that he was about to die. He was a dead man walking and he knew it. His eyes were upon the heavens, no longer concerned with the problems and quarrels of mortal life. As scaffold speeches of the era confirm, the usual practice was to die fully accepting the authority of the reigning monarch, even when that monarch was wrong. Anne Boleyn had urged the crowds to loyalty to Henry VIII, and stated that he had enacted justice upon her in his God-given wisdom, even though she was almost certainly innocent of the crimes of which she had been convicted. A full acceptance of Mary's authority was necessary for the duke's soul to be at peace. To die with such a serious unresolved conflict, fighting against the monarch who was God's anointed, would jeopardise his salvation. The duke must have accepted that it was God's will that Mary became queen, and that to oppose her wishes would have been treason and heresy. It was rather too little, too late, but it was his attempt to counter his resistance to what had turned out to be Divine Will. In the context of his devout belief in God and the importance of making a good death, his actions make perfect sense.

But this was not all. Northumberland had the opportunity to make amends to those he had wronged in life:

> The Duke recanted, and summoned the two sons of the late Duke of Somerset to come before him; he asked their pardon for the injury he had done to their father, the Protector of England, and confessed that he had wrongly and falsely procured his death. He did the same with several others against whom he had exercised revenge.[49]

Then, the imperial ambassador related:

> he confessed and received the holy sacrament, heard mass devoutly and performed all the customary acts of devotion according to the ancient religion, declaring loudly before those who were in the Tower that since he had forsaken God and the Church to follow the new religion he had done no good, and his actions had been unfortunate. He confessed publicly that he had continued in error for three or four years, and went so far as to approve the authority of the Roman Church, using words that avowed the said authority.[50]

Schefyre did not see Northumberland's actions as heresy, but rather as gestures made in a genuine desire to help his country:

> The Duke's Christian death has been misinterpreted and denounced by the heretics, who say he did as he did out of hypocrisy, in the belief that he might incline the Queen to show him mercy. But small attention is paid to the sayings of heretics and misguided men, and the truth is generally accepted and recognised, namely that the Catholic manner in which he and his accomplices ended their lives, together with their final profession of faith and recantation will assist religious affairs here, and promote them.[51]

On the following morning, 22 August 1553, John Dudley, Duke of Northumberland went to his execution on Tower Green. His final speech echoed the comments he had made the day before, for the same reasons, asserting Mary's divine right to rule, even calling it 'miraculous':

> He repeated the same words on the scaffold, loudly, before the people. He recommended them to obey the Queen, whom he called good and virtuous, saying that she had attained the throne miraculously, by reason of her true right by inheritance, and that therein he acknowledged the hand of God. He exhorted noblemen and people to obedience; and declared that he had received no instigation or persuasion to make the profession, but was moved thereto by his own desire, calling to witness God and his confessor, who had ever heard the same from him. He added that a warning should be taken from

the condition of Germany, where rebellion and troubles had followed upon the loss of faith and true religion. He made the sign of the cross, and kissed it [the crucifix] before his death.[52]

There can be no doubt, according to the standards of his time, that even though Northumberland was executed, he made a good death. His body was interred in the chapel where he had received the body and blood of Christ just twenty-four hours before.

Schefyre could not resist adding a little anecdote about the circular nature of history in the Dudley dynasty:

> We have been told that the scaffolding on which the Duke was beheaded was first put up for his father, who lost his head at the same place and on the same day forty-five years ago, for similar crimes and ambition, having attempted to exclude the late King Henry VIII from the Crown and usurp it, after concealing for five or six days the death of the late King Henry VII for that purpose.[53]

Jane and Guildford were indicted on 12 August but they had to endure a two-month wait to hear their fates. In their quarters in the Tower, they would have been aware of the duke's execution, hearing the guns announce his death, perhaps even witnessing the fall of the axe from their windows. They may also have been informed about the circumstances of his recantation and perhaps understood why he had done it, perhaps not. Their trials, and those of their immediate circle, were fixed for 13 November, leaving two months of anticipation and agony, which was also an opportunity for them to prepare their souls for death. When the day arrived, they found that a deliberate choice had been made to deny them any privacy, so they embarked upon the demeaning journey through the streets of London, before the very crowds they had hoped would cheer for their coronations a few months before. The procession was headed by an officer carrying a great axe with the blade turned away from the accused, to denote their innocence until the verdict had been passed. He was followed by the former Archbishop of Canterbury, Thomas Cranmer, whom Mary had loathed for years, for having pronounced against her mother's marriage, and had wasted no time in ordering his arrest. Guildford came next, under heavy guard, followed by Jane, dressed in black, a Bible in her hands, after which came the other Dudley brothers. Their destination was the imposing fifteenth-century Guildhall, a symbol of legal and political power which had witnessed the trials and condemnations of the former queen, Catherine Howard, and her reputed lovers; the Protestant martyr Anne Askew; Henry Howard, Earl of Surrey and other prominent figures. Cranmer and the Dudley brothers were pronounced guilty and sentenced to be hung, drawn and quartered, while Jane was to be 'burned alive on Tower Hill or beheaded as the Queen should please'.[54]

And yet, it seemed that Mary was willing to show leniency to Guildford and Jane, considering them victims of a plot arranged by Northumberland. They returned to the Tower but no date was set for their execution and, as the weeks passed, Jane was permitted to walk within the gardens. Perhaps Guildford was even permitted to see her, as he was able to write a message to her father in Jane's prayer book: 'your loving and obedient son wishes unto your grace long life in this world with as much joy and comfort as I wish to myself, and in the world to come joy everlasting.'[55] As the new year of 1554 dawned, the pair must have entertained a degree of hope that they might be permitted to live. William Parr, Marquis of Northampton had also been released, and would live until 1571. They had every right to hope; they may well have been pardoned and permitted to live in obscurity, or Guildford could have found a place at Elizabeth's court. Even the ambassadors were convinced that there was no need for Jane to die:

As to Jane of Suffolk, if for the reasons she gave you, or for others, she does not wish to inflict the pain of death upon her, let her at least consider whether it would not be well to keep her in some safe place where she could be watched and guarded so that there should be no fear of her attempting to trouble the kingdom.[56]

Within weeks, though, Mary's marital plans put an end to their hopes.

III

On 15 January 1554, the official announcement was made that the queen would be married to Prince Philip, son and heir of the emperor. It was exactly what many of her subjects had feared. The predictions made by Edward and Northumberland in the early summer of 1553 were coming to pass: the dismantling of all the religious reforms and a return to Catholicism, followed by marriage to a foreign prince whose influence would reduce England to a mere annexe of another country. As early as the previous August, the emperor had foreseen the dangers of this and advised that the matter be delayed a little:

> As to the Queen's marriage, as we know by your letters that her inclinations are for a foreign alliance, it would perhaps be better to forego this point for the present, as they [the English] are resenting her actions with regard to religion. If we were to pursue the matter now, evil-minded people might take advantage of it to maintain that the Duke of Northumberland's objections were well-founded.[57]

Even the following January was to prove too soon, but Mary was 37 and keen to wed. During the negotiations, the first signs came of a worrying deference that England's queen was expected to show to her foreign husband. The Council informed the imperial ambassador that it did not advise her to sign the nuptial agreement 'before His Highness had done so, for custom prescribes that the husband shall speak first, not the wife'.[58] In a similar vein, Simon Renaud believed that 'the Queen, being a woman, cannot penetrate their knavish tricks nor weigh matters of state.'[59] It was precisely this kind of protocol that led to concern among Mary's subjects, which soon spread to rebellion. As early as 18 January, Simon Renaud wrote to the emperor concerning a case that highlighted the fear of Spaniards in the west of England. He related that a certain Peter Carew had assembled a group of gentlemen in Exeter to sign a letter to the queen. It stated that they did not wish Philip to disembark in the West Country because they believed that the 'Spaniards would wish to do as they pleased and violate their daughters'. Instead of enduring this, they preferred to 'choose death'. Carew excused himself by saying that he 'had been induced to believe that the Spaniards were coming in arms to England to oppress the people'.[60] But he was not the only one. And so, said Renaud, 'the revolt and commotion ... begun'.[61]

The most dangerous and organised rebellion arose in Kent. Thomas Wyatt, the son of the poet, published a proclamation at Maidstone, near his home of Allington Castle, to the effect that 'liberty and commonwealth' were being threatened by the queen's 'determinate pleasure to marry with a stranger'. The ambassadors reported that 'Wyatt is fortifying himself to the best of his ability in a house of his in Kent, laying in stores, munitions and arquebuses', but they were not convinced by his professed motives: 'although the rebels are taking the foreign match as a pretext, their real objects are religion and to favour Elizabeth, which were the aims of Carew also, and it is said that the rising is spreading.'[62] They championed the young Edward Courtenay, Earl of Devon, a great-grandson of Edward IV, as a replacement monarch, and planned to marry him to Princess Elizabeth, to continue an English, Protestant rule. The queen summoned her sister to court and dispatched the old Duke of Norfolk, Henry Fitzroy's father-in-law, now aged around 80, to put down the rebels. Norfolk found himself outnumbered and, embarrassingly, many of his men defected to Wyatt. Another strategy was required. Instead, the royal troops sat back and waited, allowing the rebels to reach London before encircling them and capturing their leader.

According to the ambassadors, this rebellion left the queen distressed and unhappy, not just because of the threat to her own person, but because it necessitated a suspension of her marriage plans. Worse for Jane and Guildford, it emerged that her father, the Duke of Suffolk, had given his support to the anti-Spanish faction. He was found, early in February, hiding on his estates, while his brother Thomas was apprehended in a hollow tree, his presence sniffed out by a dog.[63] This effectively signed death warrants for them all. Sitting passively in the Tower, waiting and praying as events unfolded outside but powerless to influence them, the pair's fate was sealed. The decision to order their executions, taken by the queen at the start of February, may have the feel of a knee-jerk reaction, but Mary clearly considered it essential for the security of her realm and marriage.

The executions of Jane and Guildford were scheduled to take place on the same day, 9 February, but they were given a brief reprieve in which Mary intended that Jane should convert to the Catholic faith. This would appear to support the queen's previous intention towards Northumberland, and her insistence that he took mass before his death. To encourage Jane to her way of thinking, Mary sent her chaplain John Feckenham to visit her in her apartments, and she spent many of her final hours with him. Feckenham was then almost 40, a staunch Catholic who had been a monk at Evesham Abbey until its dissolution in 1540. He had been sent to the Tower by Archbishop Cranmer for resistance to reform around 1549, and there he had pursued reflection and study, so that he was frequently required to take part in theological disputes. *The Literary Remains of Lady Jane Grey*,[64] published in 1825, contains an account of a dialogue between Jane and Feckenham recording the process of questioning he employed in a final effort to save her soul. He asked her what was required of a Christian; whether faith alone was justification for salvation; what was the purpose of good works; what was the nature of communion; and how many sacraments were there. His persuasion failed but Jane respected him and something of a brief friendship flourished, so that she allowed him to accompany her to the scaffold.

The day before her execution, Jane wrote to her sister Catherine, giving an insight into the way in which she was preparing for death. She sent Catherine her own copy of the New Testament in Greek, which she described as 'not outwardly trimmed with gold or the curious embroidery of the artfulest needles, yet inwardly it is worth more than all the precious mines which the vast world can boast of.' It was the Lord's 'last will', Jane explained, 'which he bequeathed unto us wretches and wretched sinners, which shall lead you to the path of eternal joy'. If Catherine read the book, she wrote, it would 'bring you to an immortal and everlasting life', teach her to live 'and learn you to die'. In a comment upon their dynastic failure, she added that the book would bring her sister 'greater felicity than you should have gained possession of our woeful father's lands, for as if God had prospered him, you should have inherited his honours and manors'. Jane urged Catherine to 'live to die, that you by death may purchase eternal life and trust not that the tenderness of your age shall lengthen your life.' At 16, Jane's faith helped her come to terms with the executioner's act as the will of her God. In order to do the same, Catherine was to 'defy the world, defy the devil, and despise the flesh and delight yourself only with the Lord ... desire with St Paul to be dissolved and be with Christ, with whom, even in death there is life.'[65]

Jane warned her sister about being unprepared when death stole up unexpected. Instead, she should 'be like the good servant and even at midnight be waking, lest when death cometh and stealeth upon you, like a thief in the night, you be found with the servants of darkness sleeping'. Regarding her own death, Jane urged her sister to rejoice that she would be 'delivered of this corruption, and put on incorruption', for she was assured that 'for losing of a mortal life, win one that is immortal, joyful and everlasting'. Catherine should never deny God's truth, or He would 'by vengeance make short what you by your soul's loss would prolong'. By remaining true to Him, she would be welcomed into an 'uncircumscribed comfort and to his own glory'.[66]

To her father, Jane wrote more bitterly, opening with 'it had pleased God to hasten my death by you, by whom my life should rather have been lengthened', yet she gave thanks for it and accounted herself blessed. She 'washed my hands with the innocence of my fact, my guiltless blood may cry before the Lord, Mercy to the Lord!' Although her father may be sorrowful at her death, she assured him that there was 'nothing that can be more welcome than from this vale of misery to pire to that heavenly throne of all joy and pleasure'.[67]

In their final days, it is likely that Guildford was preparing himself for death in a similar vein. Yet it is anecdotes about Jane's piety that survive, not his, so it is difficult to ascertain the strength of his faith. The fact that his mind may not have been wholly fixed upon the eternal, and his difference of approach, are revealed by his request to see Jane one last time on 11 February. Jane refused the meeting, saying that it 'would only ... increase their misery and pain, it was better to put it off ... as they would meet shortly elsewhere, and live bound by indissoluble ties'.[68] No doubt Guildford also believed in their imminent reunion, but he still felt the need of earthly comfort on the day before his death. It is impossible to deduce whether there was any affection between the young married couple. They had been united too briefly, and against the bride's wishes, to develop any real depth of feeling, although their shared fate might have bred mutual compassion. The few indicators of an emotional connection may equally point to convention: Guildford's mother's insistence that he refuse to sleep with her as a punishment, and Jane's own choice of her husband's name for a baby she was to be godmother to. When Jane wrote a letter to Mary in August 1553, explaining how she had ended up claiming the crown, she described herself as 'a wife who loves her husband'.[69] It may have all happened too quickly for any sense of romance; far more likely is a sense of destinies irrevocably united, of two inexperienced young people who had joined forces in a venture that had failed.

Guildford was the first to die. He was taken to Tower Hill at around ten o'clock in the morning. There was a crowd and he shook hands with many well-wishers, including John Throckmorton, who had links to the Grey family by marriage and whose brother was involved in the Wyatt rebellion, and Sir Anthony Browne, who had stayed out of the succession crisis. After this, Guildford was handed over to Thomas Offley, the sheriff in charge of his execution. Jane is said to have watched the process from a window.[70] Guildford had no 'ghostly father' with him, but made a short speech, which does not survive, before kneeling and asking the people to pray for him, 'holding up his eyes and hands to God many times'.[71] He was killed by a single blow of the axe. Richard Grafton related that 'even those that never before the time of his execution saw him, did with lamentable tears bewail his death.'[72] His body was placed in a wooden box on a cart which, according to the Grafton Chronicle, was seen by Jane on her way outside, the 'dead carcas, lying in a car in straw was again brought into the Tower, which miserable sight was to her a double sorrow and grief'.[73] Another account has Jane declaring, 'Oh Guildford, Guildford!' through her window. Guildford was interred in the chapel of St Peter ad Vincula.

Jane was then led out to the green beside the White Tower. The anonymous *Chronicle of Queen Jane and of Two Years of Queen Mary* includes the speech she delivered moments before her death:

Good people, I am come hither to die, and by a law I am condemned to the same. The fact, indeed, against the Queen's highness was unlawful, and the consenting thereunto by me: but touching the procurement and desire thereof by me or on my behalf, I do wash my hands thereof in innocency, before God, and the face of you, good Christian people, this day. I pray you all, good Christian people, to bear me witness that I die a true Christian woman, and that I look to be saved by none other means but only by the mercy of God in the merits of the blood of his only son Jesus Christ: and I confess, when I did know the word of God I neglected the same, I loved myself and the world, and therefore this plague or punishment is happily and worthily happened unto me for my sins. And I thank God of his goodness that he has given me a time and respite to repent. And now, good people, I pray you to assist me with your prayers.[74]

Jane then concluded by reciting Psalm 51 and asking forgiveness for her executioner. Feckenham was on hand to guide her as she was blindfolded and fumbled for the block. Eleven days later her father shared her fate.

Over the coming months, Guildford's brothers John, Henry, Ambrose and Robert remained as prisoners in the Beauchamp Tower and certain carvings on the wall appear to relate to their period of confinement. The word 'IANE' may have been carved by Guildford, or equally by his father, the Duke of Northumberland as he faced separation from Jane Guildford, whom he had married for love thirty years before. That the duke was present, and carved upon the walls, is evident from the Warwick device of the bear and ragged staff set in a border of roses, acorns and lilies, above the name IOHN DVDLI.[75] The widowed Duchess of Northumberland and her son-in-law Henry Sidney made constant efforts to ingratiate themselves with Queen Mary, and the brothers were finally released in October 1554. John Dudley died almost at once after arriving at Sidney's home of Penshurst Place, Henry was killed at the Battle of St Quentin in 1557, Ambrose survived the battle and outlived them all, while Robert went on to become the notorious favourite of Queen Elizabeth I, after she succeeded her sister in 1558.

The Dudley dynasty was dealt a blow by the death of Guildford and, soon afterwards, those of John and Henry. Northumberland had fathered thirteen children, of whom six had died in infancy. Of the seven who survived to adulthood, only two became parents. Mary, who married Sir Henry Sidney, bore seven children, among them the poet Sir Philip Sidney. Robert Dudley had an illegitimate son by his mistress Douglas Sheffield, and a legitimate one by his second wife, Lettice Knollys. On the shoulders of this child, Robert, Lord Denbigh, rested the hopes of the Dudley line but, after the boy died at the age of 3, that branch of the family became extinct. The Sidney family fared little better, but Northumberland's bloodline continued through the union of Henry and Mary Dudley. Of the seven children born to them, three reached adulthood and although only one son became a father, he had a family of eleven, of which four were boys. These great-grandsons of John Dudley took his genes into the seventeenth century.

It is almost impossible to answer the question of what sort of king Guildford Dudley might have made. The slender evidence of his life has not revealed his character or intentions, but the circumstances of his succession allow for two general assumptions. Firstly, he was still a young man, who had been placed on the throne by his father. In 1553, Northumberland was 48 or 49, an experienced statesman who might anticipate being of active service for at least another decade, health permitting. Guildford and Jane were educated, and Jane certainly had strength of character, but they are unlikely to have cast off the duke's influence in at least the first few years of their reign. They would have needed Northumberland's guidance through a period of apprenticeship, while they learned the ropes of government. This suggests a period of governmental continuity, with many of the Council members existing under Edward VI remaining in place. Secondly, Guildford had been raised in the reformed faith, so the acts passed in recent years would not have been challenged or revoked. From what little indicators remain regarding his relationship with Jane, the seeds of potential conflict might be seen in the uncomfortable question of Guildford's status, as duke or as king. Yet this might have been due to the speed of change, the fact that everything had come about so quickly, that such details had yet to be ironed out. The idea of Guildford's kingship certainly came as a surprise to Jane but she did raise the possibility of elevating him through an Act of Parliament. If the ambassadors are to be believed, Guildford had a sense of his own position and a determination to achieve it, maintaining his majesty and dining in state, but the validity of their single account of this cannot be taken for granted. The couple might have been able to overcome this question easily, or else it might indicate a deeper, cultural rift, as arose under Queen Mary, with the expected subjection of the wife to the husband. The intimate struggles of a private life which Guildford and Jane never lived, cannot provide answers about their potential success as rulers. All that remains a certainty is the fact of their premature deaths.

Including Guildford and Jane in his book of Protestant martyrs, John Foxe had no doubt as to Jane's reluctance to claim the throne or the couple's manipulation at the hands of their parents. To Foxe, they were 'innocents ... such as by just law and faithful witnesses can never be proved to have offended by themselves'. By the terms of Jane's final speech, she would have disagreed. Did Guildford share the depths of her devotion? Was he as willing to embrace death for his transgressions in life? Did he accept his death as God's will, or did he long to escape the confines of the Tower and fight another day? There is not enough evidence for us to know.

The result of Northumberland's failure to secure Jane and Guildford on the throne was the return of Catholicism. The final will to be cited in this book dates from May 1556, in the middle of this Counter-Reformation, at the height of the Marian burnings of Protestants. Edward, Lord Hastings came from a family whose history had been affected by the turbulence of the Wars of the Roses. His great-great-grandfather had been unexpectedly dragged out of a council meeting by Richard III in 1483 and immediately executed, but his grandfather Edward and father George had restored the family fortunes under the Tudors. Edward was the fourth son among eight siblings, born in 1521. He was a devout Catholic and flourished under the reign of Mary but, after her death, he was imprisoned for hearing mass. When he wrote his will on 10 May, he did not know he had another fifteen years left, but the terms and details of his testament return us to wills of the 1440s, connecting with the faith of former generations and underlining the cyclical nature of history.

Hastings left £20 to be distributed among the poor at his burial and 40s for a preacher, to preach for three consecutive Sundays afterwards. He also requested that four marks were to be distributed among the poor of his parish every Good Friday for three years. To his church, St Giles of Stoke Poges in Buckinghamshire, he left a cope, a vestment and a pair of altar cloths, each bearing his arms, and he left funds for maintenance of the local roads and for prisoners and scholars. The details he set down for the creation of his tomb hark back to an earlier time: he wanted 'a chapel of stone, with an altar therein, adjoining to the church' where his parents lay. Within it, his executors should build a stone tomb 'with the images of my said mother and father in stone', their arms upon it and a vault below, where he was to lie, with a 'plate of copper, double-gilt ... to represent my image in harness, with the garter, and a memorial in writing of me, with my arms, to be placed upright on the wall of that chapel'. He requested that five chambers should be built, with fires; four for the poor and one for a chantry priest, and requested that his nephew maintain a priest who was to sing for his soul and those of his parents and brother. Within a few years, though, Hastings was to see everything change again so that chantry chapels were never reintroduced. Some became grammar schools while others were sold as houses.

IV

Guildford and Jane's story has captured the imagination of artists and historians since their deaths. The fact that their stories were so closely linked, and that far more biographical material survived about Jane, has both helped and hindered Guildford's memory. Had he not been married to her, it is unlikely that his name would have become so well known, yet by virtue of his position in relation to her, he is forever overshadowed. Jane was given a voice early, speaking out in Elizabethan ballads to denounce Mary I's popery and becoming the subject of Thomas Chaloner's 1579 'Elegy on the Death of Lady Jane Grey', in which Guildford does not receive even a single mention. He finally makes it into a play of 1607, by Webster and Dekker, although the focus of *The Famous History of Sir Thomas Wyat* is not upon him and Jane, but on its eponymous hero. Possibly based on an earlier play, Jane and Guildford are presented as a loving couple manipulated by the ambition of others, for which they pay the ultimate price. In the first act, Jane tells Guildford that she already enjoys a kingdom, having him, while he replies that she must become queen. The play has Jane die before Guildford, who is confronted by the sight of her head and, he describes its beauty in somewhat Hamletesque style (which is known to have been performed the same year, 1607):

> Do malefactors, look
> Thus when they die a ruddy lip
> A clear reflecting eye
> Cheeks purer than the maiden orient pearl
> That sprinkles bashfulness through the clouds
> Her innocence has given her this look
> The like for me to show so well being dead
> How willingly would Guildford lose his head.[76]

In 1694, Restoration dramatist John Banks used Jane's story to promote his post-revolution anti-Catholic message. In *Innocent Usurper* or *The Death of Lady Jane Gray, a Tragedy*, he gives Guildford quite a different role, making him threaten suicide unless his wife accepts the throne. He comes, passionate and fresh from his wedding night:

> What have I felt! what Ravishing Delight!
> What Mines of Pleasure hast thou found this Night!
> What Mysteries of Love without a Name!
> What quenching Cordials, and what killing Flame!
> Soft like a Babe she laid me in her Bosom,
> Whilst all the night I revell'd in her Arms.
> In Dreams of Love, I've done the like before,
> But always wak'd till now, cheated and poor.

He is enthusiastic to think of his wife becoming queen and himself:

> A Crown! where e'er she goes she is the Queen,
> And makes her Presence still the Court of Love,
> Cupids, like Subjects, waiting on her looks,
> Crowns in her Eyes, and Scepters in her Smiles.
> She, like the Golden World, in Bed did lie,
> Like Conquering Alexander, I lay by;
> And what in Ages he cou'd scarce inthrall,
> Won in a Night, and Crown'd me King of all.

But her refusal prompts him to threaten suicide, in order to save his father's honour:

> Ha! Then I'll search amongst the Stars, or dive
> To th' bottom, where this Merciless Virtue grows—
> Farewel, O most Belov'd! And yet most Cruel!
> Farewel to those false Dreams of Crowns by Day,
> And Heav'n by Night; Farewel to Love for ever.
> Perhaps when I am Dead, she'll take the Crown;
> Then of necessity, this way's the best,
> To save a Father's Life, and be at rest.[77]

Jane prevents him from falling upon his sword and reluctantly agrees to accept the crown. At the end of the play, far from refusing Guildford one last audience, Jane practically had to be torn away from him, illustrating that it is essentially a play about star-crossed lovers than the realities of the Tudor dynastic conflict.

Jane's reputation really took off in the eighteenth century, her learning, innocence and sacrifice making her a heroine of the Enlightenment, and she featured in works by dramatist Nicholas Rowe, historians Gilbert Burnet and Oliver Goldsmith, and philosophers David Hume and William Goodwin. Jane's story became something of a favoured tale of the Victorians, presenting an ideal of womanhood as she stumbles, blindfolded, feeling for the block. She is artist Paul Delaroche's spotless virgin, kneeling in white, her hair spilling about her, prepared for sacrifice. She is the regal lady in brown, holding her prayer book, in the recently discovered Streatham portrait, thought to date from the 1590s. She is Frederick Pickersgill's pre-Raphaelite heroine in green and gold, reading the first of five huge books piled up in a window seat while the hunt takes place outside. She is kneeling, preparing for her execution in George Whiting Flagg's of 1835. She is also the subject of an engraving by W. Holl, looking not unlike Queen Victoria in her youth, with a string of pearls across her headdress. She was the subject of operas by Nicola Vaccai in 1836, Antonio d'Antoni in 1848, Timoteo Pasini in 1853, Giuseppe Menghetti in 1859 and Henri Busser in 1891. And, due to his connection with her, Guildford was carried along for the ride.

No actual likeness of Guildford survives. It is in the nineteenth century that images of him started to emerge. In 1827, romantic genre artist Charles Robert Leslie exhibited *Lady Jane Grey Prevailed Upon to Accept the Crown* at the Royal Academy. The painting implies that she capitulated under Guildford's influence, placing him by her side, one arm behind her, while the other gestures at papers held by the waiting councillors. He is a typical youth of his moment in time, with something of Shelley about his features, wide and solid in black velvet and a crimson drape. Jane looks up to him in trusting adoration, small and vulnerable in her virginal white gown. Another portrait of the same time places Guildford alone against a silver surround, part of a series in the House of Lords. Created during Pugin's restoration of Parliament, it is acknowledged to be a copy of a portrait of a young man dating from the 1580s, but represents a more regal interpretation of Guildford. One more nineteenth-century portrait exists of him in the National Trust collection at Tyntesfield House in Somerset. Whether based on a lost original or a work of the artist's imagination, it shows a slightly hesitant-looking youth, one hand on the hilt of his sword as he stares off into the distance. His features are regular, the eyes dark and the nose prominent, the hair appearing fair under hat and feather, which are much in the style of Edward VI's headgear. Guildford wears a black and silver striped doublet with a double red edging, furs and gold sleeves, but it is the depiction of an innocent victim rather than an aspiring monarch. In art, as in biographical material, he has always been overshadowed by Jane. But there is something fitting that, just as he was allied to her cause in life, so that union persists for five centuries in death. The pair barely knew each other, sharing only a few short weeks, yet their historical and artistic reputations will be forever intertwined.

It was this romantic aspect of Jane and Guildford's posthumous love story that gave rise to the 1986 film *Lady Jane*, starring Helena Bonham-Carter and Carey Elwes. The pair initially resist the match, before accepting it as a dynastic arrangement, only to fall deeply in love and suffer the tragedy of separation and execution. There is no doubt that their stories, in real life, provide an excellent narrative arc, which accounts for the frequency with which artists have used it, seduced by its romance. Yet, despite all this attention, the real Guildford remains something of a mystery:

Guilford: So then we will.

Jane: Yes, we will.

Guilford: We'll fly.

Jane: We'll fly.

Guilford: Away, beyond their reach.

Jane: So far …

Guilford: Their touch can't tarnish us, and at last, we will be …

Jane: Nothing …

Guilford: Nobody …

Jane: Each other's.

Guilford: Only this time, forever.[78]

11

Death and the Heir
(1450–1550)

In 1562 Peter Bruegel the Elder completed his huge oil painting entitled *The Triumph of Death*. It shows a panoramic landscape overrun by skeletons, all traces of humanity and civilisation destroyed; fires burn, ships are wrecked, trees rot, creatures lie dying, the skies darken with smoke and the tolling of bells marks the end of the world. In this apocalyptic vision, death is the great leveller, taking rich and poor alike. A king and a cardinal feature among the dozens of bodies strewn across the canvas, cheek by jowl alongside servants and peasants. A few piteous human pleasures are parodied: one skeleton takes a woman in an embrace, a jester hides and the games of chance, chess and cards, have been scattered. Stylistically, art has come a long way from the fresco of *The Three Living and the Three Dead* at St Andrews, Wickhampton. The *mise-en-scène* of Bruegel's painting highlights the immense cultural change that had taken place between the creation of the two works but it touches the same themes as the church image: the fear of unexpected and unavoidable death; the need to take steps during life to ensure that the soul was prepared. While medieval culture often depicted death with a wry, dark humour, recognising the earthly world as a battlefield for the soul, the reality was a very real preoccupation with the manner of death, which manifest itself in an individual's behaviour, patronage, their will, bequests and gifts, as well as in art, literature and ecclesiastical architecture. As markers for this era, these two very different paintings encompass the paradox of change and and may serve as symbols, even chronological brackets, for the ten young men featured in this book.

The century spanning 1450–1550 was a time of great change, from the end of the Hundred Years' War through to the succession of England's first ruling queen. In 1450, it was still a medieval, Catholic country, crammed full with religious houses and shrines overflowing with relics and jewels, a world where the Lancastrian kings still claimed their right to rule France and alternated their dynastic feuds with pilgrimage and piety. The nobility founded elaborate chantries, where lights flickered in remembrance of their souls; the dying left great sums to the Church to ensure that a multitude of prayers would hasten their path through purgatory. Their bequests paid for the repair of church buildings and furnishings, for alms to the poor, for verses to be painted on church walls and for the construction of magnificent tombs featuring effigies of themselves in prayer. In effect, before the Reformation, the rich man could buy his way into heaven. Just over 100 years later, by the time of Edward VI's death, England had broken with Rome and established its own national church. Centuries of social ritual and the prevailing culture had been redefined by the Renaissance and the Reformation. The Bible was translated into English and a new Book of Common Prayer was made available in all churches, whose rood lofts and statues had been dismantled. The wealthy might have taken up residence in the old monastic houses but anybody who could read could open a Bible, and all those who were conscious could listen and interpret it for themselves. The ultimate goal of Christianity, the salvation of the soul, had become more widely accessible across the social spectrum. Save for the brief interlude of Mary's reign, England had become a Protestant realm. Yet, despite this national sea change, the constants of life and death remained. Medicine could no more save a boy dying in 1553 than it could in 1484 and the struggle for the throne still resulted in violent death in 1554, just as it had in 1460. The rites of passage defining the cycle of life might be administered differently, but the inevitability of death was the same.

These 100 years were a dangerous time to be a young aristocratic male. They witnessed the flower of English manhood being slaughtered on the battlefield, a child king murdered in the Tower, youths languishing with untreatable illness and the axe falling upon claimants to the throne. During the Wars of the Roses, noble youths ran the risk of being killed in the conflict between the houses of York and Lancaster; in a pitched battle, like John, Earl of Lincoln, or in flight from one, like Edmund, Earl of Rutland. Death might also follow in the form of the executioner in the battle's immediate aftermath, as happened to Edward, Prince of Wales in 1471. Sometimes, as in the case of Edward, Earl of Warwick, this end came years later, simply because of his parentage. After those wars subsided, the greatest killer of young men of royal blood was disease, which remained largely untreatable. With the arrival of the sixteenth century, the sweating sickness, the plague and tuberculosis offered more to fear than defeat in battle. Their royal status and the health precautions taken for Edward of Middleham, Prince Arthur, Henry Fitzroy and Edward VI were not sufficient to protect them from what was perceived to be God's will. Thus, although this work straddles the divide between avoidable and unavoidable death, exploring the time-specific circumstances of each, these ten individuals are connected by the very fact that they died in youth. The manner of death's coming, and the spiritual state of its victim, were to prove of infinitesimal importance to those concerned, and their subsequent historical reputation, but the simple fact of death, the absence of existence, was an unarguable line in the sand. Their hearts stopped beating. What this book has attempted to analyse is the effect of the sudden disappearance of an individual and its impact upon their dynastic line, within the context of changing beliefs about death.

These ten young men experienced one of four kinds of death. They lost their lives in battle, by execution, through illness or, in the case of Edward V, probably by murder. In almost every case, they had advance warning of their end, or its likelihood: Edward of Westminster and John of Lincoln were well aware of the potential dangers of battle and would have taken Holy Communion or at least prayed and confessed their sins beforehand. Edward of Warwick and Guildford Dudley knew they were to be executed and had time to seek out the services of a priest and come to terms with their end. Henry Fitzroy and Edward VI were aware of their declining health and could prepare accordingly. And, while the circumstances of Edward of Middleham's death are unclear, his adult carers would more than likely have seen signs that prompted them to seek prayers for their charge. The illness of Prince Arthur was more unexpected and developed quickly, but it is likely that he remained sufficiently conscious to recognise the approach of death and have the chaplain of Ludlow Chapel to visit him. The two exceptions are Edmund, Earl of Rutland and Edward V, whose deaths were sudden. When leaving Sandal Castle on 30 December 1460, Edmund was not anticipating coming under attack from the Lancastrian forces. His final flight towards the chantry chapel on Wakefield Bridge indicates not just a bid for sanctuary, but the recognition of a critical symbol, the hope to attain spiritual salvation. The actions of his brothers in 1476, reburying him in a chapel of his own and, no doubt, ordering prayers and memorials, were hoped to help his chances of passing through purgatory, had he been lingering there sixteen years later. The reason why the death of Edward V in 1483 proved so shocking to his contemporaries went beyond his age and status. If we accept the version of events in which the young king was smothered in his sleep, then his murderers robbed him of the opportunity to make a good death. Death in sin, or in sleep, was deeply feared at the time, leaving the soul vulnerable to be stolen by the Devil. This can explain the artistic depictions of the princes as angelic, often with a book, offering the hope that they had said their prayers before bedtime.

Illness was a constant threat to life throughout the medieval and early modern period, between the two great plague years of 1348 and 1665. It could come on suddenly, killing within hours, like the dreaded sweat, or one of the many bubonic resurgences seen every few years. John Lydgate's fifteenth-century advice on avoiding the plague was partly emotional – to avoid sorrow and heaviness, and to remain glad – and partly practical – to flee wicked airs and infected places, to drink good wine and only eat wholesome meat, to smell sweet things and keep clear of black mists. He also recommended the avoidance of brothels and baths, as 'the exchange of humours in such places causes great harm'.[1] A century later, Sir Thomas Elyot was advising that those of a sanguine and choleric temperament were more likely to be infected with the pestilence than those who were phlegmatic or melancholy. He prescribed keeping out of the sun, advised against sitting too close to the fire and consuming hot herbs, prescribing many sharp, tart flavours like vinegars and capers. However, he agreed with Lydgate that the best remedy of all was to 'flee from the place corrupted' and not to receive any guests or deliveries into the house. He concluded his advice by putting his trust in the power of God above man's reason or counsel.[2] After all, putting one's trust in God was all that could really be done in the face of such threats as the plague, pox or sweat, which spread through this period unchecked with such devastating consequences. The sweating sickness disappeared as unexpectedly as it had appeared, and its exact nature and origins remain a mystery. It is likely to have contributed to the death of Arthur, Prince of Wales as the Tudor dynasty was in its infancy, and saw off the last males of the Brandon line in its final outbreak of 1551.

Illness also claimed the lives of young and potential kings elsewhere in Europe, including Juan, Prince of Asturias, aged 19 in 1497; Francis, Dauphin of France, aged 18 in 1536; and Francis II of France, aged 16 in 1560. Another similarly devastating loss would befall England in 1592, with the death of Henry, Prince of Wales, the eldest son and heir of James I, at the age of 18. As a consequence, the throne passed to his sickly younger brother, who became Charles I. Death was also an occupational hazard of royalty in Scotland at this time, as a glance at the Stewarts in the fifteenth and sixteenth centuries proves. James I was murdered at 42; James II was murdered at 29; James III died in battle at 36; James IV was killed at Flodden at 40; James V died at 30, heartbroken after the Scottish defeat of Solway Moss; Mary, Queen of Scots was executed; and her second husband, Henry, Lord Darnley, died in suspicious circumstances.

Sudden death was the most feared of all, even more than lingering illness and execution, which at least gave warning and allowed time for preparation. The coroners' inquests in the Middlesex rolls of 1549 highlight the strange and brutal circumstances that overcame individuals unexpectedly, and regularly, fuelling this fear and giving rise to a state of mental readiness to encounter death, in whatever form it may take. As Lady Jane Grey advised her sister, her contemporaries should never take their eye off the Devil, or relax their guard against constant threats. In January 1549, a Philip Powley died unexpectedly in Newgate gaol of a 'divine visitation', while in March a Robert Mason was attacked upon King's Bridge and received two stab wounds to the head. In April 1550, Peter Applegard died of the pestilence in a hospice while Anthony Skedall was killed by a blow to the head from a staff in May. Ralph Croft was dispatched by a sword in June, John Christian was stabbed with a dagger in August while in the same month, William Wreyke had his neck broken by an assailant. Stabbings or other mortal wounds were inflicted monthly within the Middlesex district.[3] The 'Everyday Life and Fatal Hazard in Sixteenth-Century England' project, run by Stephen Gunn and Tomasz Gromelski, documents a range of odd and unusual premature deaths, from collapsing scaffolding to a pig bite which became infected, collapsing pits and accidental strangulation by a belt, jokes gone wrong and falls from trees by boys attempting to rob birds' nests. One man stumbled in a rutted road and was stabbed by the dagger he wore at his belt, another was pulled into a spindle, a third fell on rocks during a game and others died of cold or fell into rivers while attempting to cross. Others died by falling downstairs, crushed under carts, falling down wells, hit by flying hammers, polevaulting to take a short cut, attacked by stags and crushed by a falling flitch of bacon.[4] The bizarre and domestic nature of many of these unfortunate ends, and there are many, must have given death the grim appearance of a joker, waiting to pounce in even the most innocuous of circumstances.

Illness, violence and death were not the only threat to the medieval and Tudor aristocracy. Fertility could be a major problem, and a proportion of adult males failed to father families, or else produced only illegitimate offspring. The genetic line might pass through the descendants of daughters in the family, to the benefit of other dynastic branches, but the titles of their parents became extinct. One Tudor family which illustrates the fragility of male survival and inheritance is the Radcliffes.

John Radcliffe, the Ninth Baron Fitzwalter, born in 1452, had married Margaret Whetewell and fathered six children in the 1480s, of which only one was a boy. John was beheaded in Calais in 1496 for supporting Perkin Warbeck but his son, Robert, found favour at the court of the young Henry VIII, marrying the sister of the Duke of Buckingham. This was the point at which the family line might have waned, if Robert had succumbed to the terrible new sweating sickness, or been killed in a joust, or claimed by another illness or accident. When the line rested on the shoulders of one individual, such random events could easily eclipse dynastic fortunes, resulting in the passing of titles and lands sideways, to cousins, or even out of the family altogether. However, Robert turned the fortunes of the Radcliffes around, by marrying three times and fathering seven children, five of whom were boys. It seemed, by the late 1530s, that he had provided sufficient heirs to continue the dynasty. Yet of those five boys, three failed to produce offspring: one died in infancy and while the two others reached adulthood and were married, both died without leaving an heir of either gender. That left Robert's two eldest sons, by his first wife. The first, Henry, fathered two boys. The eldest, Thomas, died without issue but his brother, also Henry, produced a son, who married twice and outlived his four children. Robert's second son, Humphrey, also had two sons; the first died young and the second married twice but produced no surviving heir. Thus, in 1629, within three generations of Robert's efforts to expand his family, his line of the Radcliffes was extinct. Their titles passed to a cousin.

The story of the Radcliffes yields some important data about a family who were not directly engaged in warfare, or responsible for the royal inheritance. They were, in many ways, a typical aristocratic family of the era, as far as such a thing existed. Between the birth of Robert in 1483 and the death of his great-grandson in 1629, at least fourteen direct descendants of Robert were born. Of these, eleven were males, which was a very promising ratio, but of those eleven, six, perhaps seven, failed to father children of either gender, often despite being married. This raises the question of fertility within the family as several of these heirs were married more than once, placing the focus specifically upon the males.

When it came to the offspring of Robert's mother, quite a different story emerges. Elizabeth Radcliffe, née Stafford, had three siblings. Her younger brother Henry had no issue and her sister Anne bore eight children, but her eldest brother, Edward, had four children who went on to produce forty-five offspring between them. It is difficult to say what led some family lines to multiply while others dwindled but, with the help of modern science, we can guess that it must have been a combination of health, age, gynaecological issues, sperm motility and opportunity.

Another family, that of Henry VIII's close companion and brother-in-law Charles Brandon, provides an even more extreme example of the dwindling of male genes. Tracing the male line from Sir William Brandon, born in 1456, a striking imbalance emerges between the survival of boys and girls. William fathered three legitimate children with his wife Elizabeth Bruyn. The eldest, William, died before 1500, in his mid- or late teens; the youngest was a girl, and the middle child was Charles Brandon, born in around 1484. Charles was married four times. His first match was declared invalid, without issue, and the second provided him with two daughters. After that, Charles married Mary Tudor, dowager Queen of France, sister of Henry VIII, and she bore him four children. The eldest, a boy named Henry, lived from 1516 to 1522, but inspired the name of his sibling, also named Henry, who was born the year after his namesake's death. Yet this second Henry did not survive either, dying at the age of 10 or 11 in 1534. Charles and Mary's two daughters fared no better when it came to producing boys. Frances produced three daughters, the eldest of whom was Lady Jane Grey, while Eleanor Brandon had a girl and two boys, both of whom died in infancy. Following Mary's death, Charles remarried for a final time. His fourth wife gave him two sons: Henry, born 1535, and Charles, born in 1537. When both boys died of the sweating sickness in 1551, their father's dukedom of Suffolk became extinct. Henry Machyn reported at their month's mind that 'yt was grett pity of [their] dethe, and it had plesyd God, of so noble a stock they were, for ther is no more left of them.'[5] Of the seventeen live births resulting from the paternity of Sir William Brandon, nine were female. Of the eight males in the family line, seven died before reaching adulthood.

Similar statistics indicate the dynastic difficulties of the Tudors. Of the twenty-three live births of two generations engendered by Henry VII, eleven were male and only two – Henry VIII and James V of Scotland – produced offspring. While Henry VII fathered seven, perhaps eight, children, at least three died in infancy and only Margaret, Henry and Mary became parents. While Henry's struggles to father a son have already been covered, and Mary was only survived by daughters, the offspring of his sister Margaret also illustrate this difficulty. Of the six children born to her by James IV of Scotland, only a single boy survived. This stands in contrast with more fertile or fecund contemporaries, like the Devereux family. John Devereux, born in 1463, became a parent in the 1480s, like Henry VII. His two surviving legitimate offspring were Walter and Anne. Anne went on to produce four boys and four girls of her own. Walter, who inherited the title of Baron Ferrers of Chartley, and became First Viscount Hereford, married twice and fathered five children. After three generations, a total of forty-eight children survived to adulthood and, of the thirty-nine whose gender is known, twenty were male. While some dynasties, like the Tudors, Radcliffes and Brandons, inexplicably dwindled in numbers through illness, accident and failure to reproduce, others like the Devereux multiplied and thrived, carrying their genes and inheritance into the seventeenth century.

Although they were involved in a deadly feud with the Neville family, and took part in many of the key battles of the Wars of the Roses, the branch of the Percys descended from Henry Hotspur proved to be successful progenitors who avoided death during youth. Hotspur died in 1403 at the Battle of Shrewsbury, but through the next three generations of his direct descendants there were forty-eight live births, divided equally so that exactly half were male and half were female. Another fifteenth-century success story when it came to fertility and fecundity, were the Woodvilles, who became notorious among their enemies for the number of their offspring. Richard, Earl Rivers and Jacquetta Woodville had a family of fourteen, all but one of whom reached adulthood. This yielded them twenty-five legitimate grandchildren of whom eleven were boys, which appears to offer good odds for the continuity of their line. However, these grandchildren were all borne by the Woodvilles' daughters, and none of their sons had issue except for one illegitimate child. Moreover, six male members of the family were killed by their opponents: Richard was executed with his son John in 1469; his eldest son Anthony and his grandson Richard Grey were executed in 1483 and his two other grandsons died in the Tower. As a result, the Earl Rivers title became extinct upon the death of his last surviving son, Richard, in 1491. Fecundity was not a problem for the Woodvilles, but the survival of their men was.

Other dukedoms that became extinct during this period through lack of surviving male heirs were those of Bedford (Jasper Tudor, 1495), Buckingham (Edward Stafford, 1521), Clarence (Edward Plantagenet, 1499), Exeter (Henry Holland, 1475), Gloucester (Richard III, 1485) Northumberland (John Dudley, 1553) and Richmond (Henry Fitzroy, 1536). However, although the Wars of the Roses and illnesses like tuberculosis did kill off some of the English aristocracy, others survived. Research indicates[6] that in each generation through around a quarter of the nobility died leaving no male heir. This was a loss for those branches of the family tree, but it was also an opportunity for others to step into their shoes and inherit their titles or estates, moving into the positions they had vacated, as George, Duke of Clarence had upon the death of his elder brother Edmund, Duke of Rutland. Whenever a death occurred, a new career was waiting to develop and newly created noble families benefited. This book, therefore, has been focused on the 'opportunity cost' of ten individuals; the chance passing to the next in line and what was made of that chance. This movement creates the cyclical model of the English aristocracy, in a state of constant attack by violence and illness, but also in constant renewal through the elevation of new blood and the processes of inheritance and reward.

The questions raised about the premature ends of young aristocratic males in this period also invite comparisons across time. England is no longer fighting a civil war and medical understanding has developed beyond measure, but there may well be a wider phenomenon of males dying young, something inherent, either cultural or biological, that transcends the specific circumstances of time and place. A number of worldwide studies about the causes of death in young males in the twenty-first century reveals a constant trend. The Center for Disease Control and Prevention in the US records that the number one cause of death among white males in the 15–19 bracket[7] in 2013 was 'unintentional injuries'. These accidents accounted for 43.7 per cent of all deaths. It was the same in the 20–24 age range, where an even larger 50.3 per cent were claimed in this way. The second cause of death for both age groups was suicide. Homicide claimed 8.5 per cent of the late teens and 8 per cent in the 20–24 range, while cancer accounted for 6 per cent and 3.7 per cent respectively and heart disease for 2.6 per cent and 2.7 per cent. Other causes included birth defects, influenza, stroke and septicaemia. The figures for 2004 and 2006–11 tell the same story.[8] The Australian Institute of Health and Welfare recorded 1,203 deaths among young people aged 15–24, of which 820, or 68 per cent, were males. More than three quarters of these mortalities were considered avoidable; again, accidental or unintentional death. The leading causes were injury and poisoning, which includes accidental poisoning by drug overdose. Next, suicide accounted for a quarter, and accidents in vehicles another quarter, with violent assault the fourth main cause.[9] The Office for National Statistics in the UK found that for young men aged 5–19, the main cause of death in 2009 was transport accidents, followed by suicide and homicide. After that came lymphoid cancer, congenital defects, cerebral palsy, brain cancer, bronchitis, bone cancer and meningitis. Among the 20–34 age group, three main causes stood out far more than the others: suicide, accidental poisoning and accidents. The statistics also state that, worldwide, men under the age of 25 are three times more likely to die in transport accidents than young women.[10] The World Health Organization, which covers all continents, listed the deaths of 1.3 million adolescents in 2012. The key causes were road accidents, suicide, violence and respiratory disease.

What emerges from these modern statistics is the high significance of violence and accidents claiming the lives of young men. In twenty-first-century terms, this might translate into a range of incidents from car crashes to assaults, falls or unintentional overdoses. This raises the question of risk-taking behaviour as a cultural rite of passage for young men, then and now: while today's youths might attempt to prove themselves by driving too fast, fighting or overindulging in abusive substances, their fifteenth-century counterparts would have come of age by proving themselves in battle. Risk-taking behaviour among young men is a culturally recognised aspect of the modern world, and adolescence is considered a period of turbulent change and transition. Writing on this topic in the Forum for Qualitative Social Research, Elaine Sharland states that 'most commentators agree that this is a period in which major transitions are to be negotiated, both in the internal self, and with the expectations of the external world.'[11] This pedagogical realization might be the product of a specific moment in time but it is not exclusive to it. Recognition can be found in Elyot's *Castell of Health* (1536) that the age of 14 was important in terms of rites of passage, with specific dietary advice included for the recognised frailties of boys before they attained that age, after which they might follow the general guidelines laid down for male health. Young aristocratic males five centuries ago did not experience the 'teenage' years in the same way as their modern counterparts but the comparison is not completely anachronistic, as they certainly recognised the transitional phases of life and understood that there were certain rites of passage to pass through in order to gain social acceptance. For medieval and Tudor boys, these included reaching the age of legal majority, the inheritance of estates, getting married, taking a position in the legal courts or a post in the royal service, or proving oneself battle. This was embedded in their cognitive development as much as it was a cultural construct. While the focus upon developing as an 'individual' is a modern concept which these ten young men would not have recognized, their emphasis was upon dynasty and duty. To be of service to their family and sovereign, to do their duty to God, they sought to attain certain goals to reach the place for which they believed their birth had destined them.

What can be stated for certain is that the largest cause of premature death in young men today is accident or violence, and that of the ten young medieval and Tudor men studied in this work, six died by violence. A smaller percentage of young men die of illnesses like tuberculosis or pulmonary disease in the modern world, due to the understanding, diagnosis and treatment of such conditions. It is to be expected that these illnesses could claim a higher proportion of our historical case studies, which they did, accounting for four out of the ten deaths.

In the period 1450–1550, young women died too. They have been conspicuously absent from this book because they deserve a separate study of their own. Their experiences of mortality were similar in some ways to those of young men but also vastly different in others. The ways in which they met death were as specifically gendered as was those of their brothers and husbands in battle. One of the main killers of women in their late teens and twenties was childbirth and injuries or infections arising from it. Just as susceptible to disease as the men, women's relation to illness and death was different in a legal and social sense. In their roles as daughters, wives and mothers, they were the vessels that carried men's heirs, physically responsible for delivering the next generation, but it was the male line through which the titles and estates usually passed. This meant that their loss left a different imprint upon families and dynasties: the question of death and the heiress, or death and the mother, would require a separate book of its own. Such a book about the significant aristocratic women dying young in this period might include Mary of York, the second daughter of Edward IV, who passed away in 1482 at the age of 14, although her loss was essentially personal, without dynastic implications. It would certainly include Catherine Howard, who lost her head for reputed adultery and Jane Grey, telling a similar story to that of Guildford. For such a work to find sufficient women, the age bracket would need to be widened to include those dying in their late twenties, a few years older than John de la Pole, and Edward, Earl of Warwick, who, at the age of 24, were the eldest of the ten youths included in this volume. This would allow for the inclusion of Isabel Neville, Duchess of Clarence, Warwick's mother, who died aged 25, and Anne Neville, Queen of England and mother of Edward of Middleham, who died aged 28, both of whom appear to have died from some wasting illness like tuberculosis. There would also be Jane Seymour, Henry VIII's third queen, mother of Edward VI, whose death at 28 prevented the arrival of any royal siblings, whose existence would have changed the course of English royal history. What the aristocratic family trees of England show that, during this period, setting aside childbirth, women did not die young in the same numbers as their male counterparts did. The fact that Arthur died in 1502 and Catherine survived, is a story in itself.

Edmund, Earl of Rutland; Edward of Westminster, Prince of Wales; Edward V; Edward of Middleham, Prince of Wales; Edward, Earl of Warwick; John, Earl of Lincoln; Arthur Tudor, Prince of Wales; Henry Fitzroy, Duke of Richmond and Somerset; Edward VI; and Guildford Dudley. In the biographies of these ten young men it is possible to glimpse the paths they might have taken, the promise they might have fulfilled. But beyond the hour of their death, all is speculation. A surprising number of young men in positions of power met an untimely, premature end during this century and the focus of this book has been the evidence of their lives and the effects of their death. As ten trajectories cut short, the impact of their loss was felt in dynastic, family, political and religious terms. Rather than musing on what 'might have been', the observation of what was, of what did come to pass, provides an interesting insight into the opportunity-seeking behaviour of the court and the English aristocracy. Sometimes eagerly, sometimes with reluctance, their positions were filled by someone waiting in line, who benefited in terms of finances or power, or who breathed a sigh of relief and survived thanks to another's death.

In the cases of Edward of Westminster and Edward of Middleham, death brought a particular family line to an end. Henry VI had no more sons to continue the fight for his cause, nor any daughters to marry to powerful foreigners who might invade England and restore the Lancastrian line. The direct descent that came from Edward III, through John of Gaunt, Henry IV and Henry V, came to an end on the battlefield at Tewkesbury. The result of this was that Edward IV was able to regain his throne and reign for another twelve years. Upon the death of Edward of Middleham, the position of his father, Richard III, became a little less stable, as it removed the possibility of future challenges to anyone wishing to topple him from the throne. Had Richard left a surviving legitimate son in 1485, the disparate Yorkist threats of his reign might have united under a more significant leader, posing a real challenge to Henry VII. Edward of Middleham's death meant that there were no direct legitimate descendants of Richard III and the dubious honour of being his heir passed to John, Earl of Lincoln, prompting his challenge to the Tudors in 1487, and his resulting death.

In some cases, premature death meant the replacement of one ruler by another. Although he had never been formally crowned, the 12-year-old Edward V inherited the throne upon the death of his father on 9 April 1483. As his father's eldest son, with the right conferred upon him in Edward IV's will and as consequence of his investment as Prince of Wales and the oaths of the nobility, he was accepted in April as the country's next legitimate king. No public challenge was raised until June, during which month he was still using the royal seal. The result of his disappearance, and his assumed death, was that the throne was taken by Richard III, ushering in a new phase of Yorkist history. In some cases, the death of an individual was to the advantage of their siblings: George, Duke of Clarence stepped into the shoes of his elder brother Edmund; Henry VIII succeeded where Arthur had not; and even Margaret Pole, Countess of Salisbury later received part of the inheritance denied to her brother Edward, Earl of Warwick.

Sometimes death ensured continuity, where there would otherwise have been change. The loss of John, Earl of Lincoln in battle, and the execution of Edward, Earl of Warwick preserved the regime of Henry VII in the 1490s. By contrast, premature death could lead to chaos: Edward VI's untimely end created a succession crisis in which the expected line of descent was temporarily bypassed, projecting Guildford Dudley briefly to power by virtue of his marriage. Just as Edward VI's death created the opportunity for Guildford, death allowed greater security for the continuance of Mary I's regime. Another result of the deaths of Edward VI and Guildford, after the lost opportunity of the Wyatt rebellion, was the national reversion to Catholicism and rejection of recent ecclesiastical reforms.

It is impossible to 'undo' these deaths and see subsequent history as independent from them. Each of them changed history by living and by dying. The existence of each of these ten young men is worth remembering for what they did achieve and represent, for the part they did play in medieval and Tudor politics, and as symbols for the eternal shadow in the mind of their contemporaries regarding the power of death. Just as in 1443, and the birth of Edmund, Earl of Rutland, through to the execution of Guildford Dudley in 1554, life was a continual paradox of struggle and opportunity, of celebration and failure, of fighting to improve the lot of the dynasty and of personal struggle against enemies and illness. The deaths of aristocratic heirs in the medieval and Tudor periods are metonymic for the eternal struggle of mankind, and the fact that, after it has been lost, life goes on.

> Here is the reste of all your businesse,
> Here is the porte of peace and restfulnes
> to them that stondeth in stormes of disease,
> only refuge to wretches in distrese,
> and all comforte of myschefe and mis-ease.[12]

Notes

INTRODUCTION

1 Binski.
2 Gottfried.
3 Houlbrooke.
4 Corpus of Middle English Prose and Verse, http://quod.lib.umich.edu/c/
  cme/EEWills/1:54?rgn=div1;view=toc
5 Kent Archaeological Society, http://www.kentarchaeology.org.uk/Research/
  Libr/Wills/Bk58/034.htm
6 Corpus of Middle English Prose and Verse, http://quod.lib.umich.edu/c/
  cme/EEWills/1:56?rgn=div1;view=fulltext

1 EDMUND, EARL OF RUTLAND (1443–60)

1 Gristwood.
2 Licence.
3 Kleineke.
4 Bentley.
5 Ibid.
6 Ibid.
7 *Calendar of Close Rolls* (CCR), *Henry VI Volume VI.*
8 Ibid.
9 *Calendar of Patent Rolls* (CPR) *38 Henry VI.*
10 Ibid.
11 Roskell.
12 Dockray and Knowles, *The Battle of Wakefield.*
13 Ibid.
14 Haigh.

15 *Calendar of Charter Rolls, Volume VI, 1427-1516*

16 *Calendar of Close Rolls (CCR), Edward IV Volume 1, 1461–1468*

17 Ibid.

18 *Calendar of Patent Rolls 2, Edward IV.*

19 *Calendar of Patent Rolls 3, Edward IV.*

20 O'Flanagan.

21 Burke.

2   EDWARD OF WESTMINSTER, PRINCE OF WALES (1453–71)

1 Haswell.

2 Ibid.

3 Griffiths.

4 Ibid.

5 Hookham.

6 Ibid.

7 *Rotuli Parliamentorum Volume V*, pp. 288–89.

8 Hookham.

9 Griffiths.

10 Lewis.

11 Ibid.

12 Griffiths.

13 *State Letters and Papers of Milan 1385–1618*, 26.

14 Lewis.

15 Haswell.

16 Ibid.

17 Fortescue, *De Laudibus Legum Angliae.*

18 Ibid.

19 Ibid.

20 Ibid.

21 Ibid.

22 Ibid

23 Griffiths.

24 Lowe.

25 Griffiths.

26 Baluze MS., 9037, 7, art. 173, Bibliothèque Nationale, Paris, Holograph.

27 SLP Milan 150, 151.

28 Milan 183.

29 Milan 184.

30 Milan 189.

31 Milan 191.

32 Milan 192, 193.

33   Milan 217.

34   Anonymous, *Historie of the Arrivall of Edward IV*.

35   Fabyan.

36   Anonymous, *A Chronicle of the First Thirteen Years of the Reign of King Edward IV*.

3   KING EDWARD V (1470–83?)

1   For more discussion on this, *see* Licence.

2   More.

3   Anonymous, *Ingulph's Chronicle*.

4   Hicks.

5   CPR November 1472.

6   Hicks.

7   Ibid.

8   Ibid.

9   See Licence.

10   Hicks.

11   Mancini.

12   Croyland.

13   Ibid.

14   Mancini.

15   Ibid.

16   Ibid.

17   Dockray and Hammond, *Richard III*.

18   Nichols, *Grants etc from the Crown*.

19   Mancini.

20   Ibid.

21   Croyland.

22   Nichols, *Testament Vetusta*.

23   Ibid.

24   Ibid.

25   Ibid.

4   EDWARD OF MIDDLEHAM, PRINCE OF WALES (1473?–84)

1   CPR April 1477.

2   CPR February 1478.

3   Idley.

4   Ibid.

5   Ibid.

6   CPR July 1483.

7   Hilton.

8   Hall, *Hall's Chronicle.*

9   British Library Harley MS 433 f. 26v, translation from the Latin printed in Horrox and Hammond, vol. 1, p. 83.

10   http://bradscholars.brad.ac.uk:8080/bitstream/handle/10454/818/ Towton03-Preprint.pdf?sequence=1&isAllowed=y

11   Rickman.

12   Davis.

13   http://www.towton.org.uk/wp-content/uploads/rally_to_the_cross.pdf

14   Croyland.

5 JOHN DE LA POLE, EARL OF LINCOLN (1462/4?–87)

1   Clark.

2   Oxford Dictionary of National Biography online.

3   Ibid.

4   CPR Edward IV Vol. I, 1461–1468.

5   Ibid.

6   Ibid.

7   Ibid.

8   CCR Edward IV Vol. I, 1461–1468.

9   Ibid.

10   CPR Edward IV Vol. II July 1471.

11   Burgess.

12   Gairdner.

13   Ibid.

14   Oxford Dictionary of National Biography online.

15   Ibid.

16   Weightman.

17   Ibid.

18   Bacon.

19   Weightman.

20   Ashdown-Hill.

21   Bacon.

22   Weightman.

23   Bacon.

24   Rotuli Parliamentorum, Vol. VI, 1783.

25   Ibid.

26   Napier.

27   Oxford Dictionary of National Biography online.

28   Napier.

29 Oxford Dictionary of National Biography online.
30 MacGibbon.

6 EDWARD, EARL OF WARWICK (1475–99)

1 Oxford Dictionary of National Biography.
2 Jackson.
3 Rotuli Parliamentorum, Volume 6, 1783.
4 Bennett.
5 Hall.
6 Underwood and Jones.
7 Ibid.
8 Wroe.
9 Arthurson.
10 Ibid.
11 Wroe.
12 For more discussion on this, *see* Licence.
13 Wroe.
14 Ibid.
15 Ibid.
16 Arthurson.
17 CSP Spain Vol. 1, 98.
18 Comper.
19 CSP Spain Vol. 1, 249.
20 CSP Venice Vol. 5, 525.

7 ARTHUR TUDOR, PRINCE OF WALES (1486–1502)

1 Cunningham.
2 Ibid.
3 Erasmus.
4 Cunningham.
5 SLP Milan Vol. 1, 539.
6 Ibid.
7 Kipling.
8 Tremlett.
9 Ibid.
10 SLP Spain Vol. 1.
11 Kipling.
12 Creighton.
13 Daniell.
14 Nichols, *Testament Vetusta*.

15 Ibid.
16 Ibid.
17 Ibid.
18 Hutchinson.

8 HENRY FITZROY, DUKE OF SOMERSET AND RICHMOND (1519–36)

1   SLP Henry VIII Vol. 4, 1461.
2   Stone.
3   SLP Henry VIII Vol. 4, 1431.
4   Ibid.
5   SLP Henry VIII Vol. 4, 1512.
6   Ibid.
7   SLP Henry VIII Vol. 4, 1513.
8   SLP Henry VIII Vol. 4, 1514.
9   SLP Henry VIII Vol. 4, 1515.
10 Murphy.
11 Ibid.
12 SLP Henry VIII Vol. 4, 1540.
13 Weller.
14 Ibid.
15 Ibid.
16 Ibid.
17 Murphy.
18 SLP Henry VIII Vol. 4, 5806.
19 Weller.
20 SLP Henry VIII Vol. 5, 1690.
21 Weller.
22 SLP Henry VIII Vol. 4, 5806.
23 SLP Henry VIII Vol. 4, 5807.
24 Weller.
25 Ibid.
26 Ibid.
27 Murphy.
28 Ibid.
29 Henry VIII Vol. 5, 1947.
30 SLP Henry VIII Vol. 5, 1948.
31 SLP Henry VIII Vol. 5, 2010.
32 SLP Henry VIII Vol. 5, 2011.
33 SLP Henry VIII Vol. 5, 2801b.
34 SLP Henry VIII Vol. 5, 2861.

35   SLP Henry VIII Vol. 5, 2878.
36   SLP Henry VIII Vol. 5, 2955.
37   SLP Henry VIII Vol. 5, 2956.
38   SLP Henry VIII Vol. 5, 2885.
39   Weller.
40   Ibid.
41   Murphy.
42   SLP Henry VIII Vol. 5, 3689.
43   SLP Henry VIII Vol. 5, 3860.
44   SLP Henry VIII Vol. 5, 4225.
45   Weller.
46   Ibid.
47   SLP Henry VIII Vol. 5, 4534.
48   Murphy.
49   Weller.
50   SLP Henry VIII Vol. 5, 4824.
51   SLP Henry VIII Vol. 5, Privy Purse Expenses.
52   SLP Henry VIII Vol. 5, 412.
53   Murphy.
54   Weaver.
55   Machyn.
56   Murphy.
57   SLP Henry VIII Vol. 5, 686.
58   Murphy.
59   Ibid.
60   SLP Henry VIII Vol. 5, 33.
61   SLP Venice Vol. 4, 823.
62   Murphy.
63   SLP Venice Vol. 4, 824.
64   SLP Venice Vol. 4, 825.
65   SLP Venice Vol. 4, 822.
66   Murphy.
67   Ibid.
68   SLP Henry VIII Vol. 5, 1627.
69   Murphy.
70   SLP Henry VIII Vol. 5, 876.
71   Murphy.
72   Weller.
73   Murphy.
74   SLP Henry VIII Vol. 7, 391.
75   SLP Henry VIII Vol. 7, 534.
76   SLP Henry VIII Vol. 7, 1507.
77   SLP Henry VIII Vol. 8, 69.

78 SLP Henry VIII Vol. 8, 268.
79 SLP Henry VIII Vol. 8, 263.
80 SLP Henry VIII Vol. 8, 909.
81 SLP Henry VIII Vol. 8, 981.
82 SLP Henry VIII Vol. 8, 687.
83 SLP Henry VIII Vol. 8, 910.
84 SLP Henry VIII Vol. 8, 911.
85 SLP Henry VIII Vol. 8, 911.
86 SLP Henry VIII Vol. 8, 1033.
87 SLP Henry VIII Vol. 8, 908.
88 SLP Henry VIII Vol. 10, 1069.
89 SLP Henry VIII Vol. 10, 908.
90 SLP Henry VIII Vol. 11, 40.
91 SLP Henry VIII Vol. 11, 108.
92 SLP Henry VIII Vol. 11, 147.
93 Murphy.
94 SLP Henry VIII Vol. 11, 148.
95 SLP Henry VIII Vol. 11, 320.
96 Weller.
97 SLP Henry VIII Vol. 11, 221.
98 SLP Henry VIII Vol. 11, 233.
99 SLP Henry VIII Vol. 11, 233.
100 Weller.
101 Ibid.
102 SLP Henry VIII Vol. 12, 164.
103 Oxford Dictionary of National Biography.
104 https://en.wikipedia.org/wiki/History_of_tuberculosis
105 Ibid.
106 https://www.gov.uk/government/uploads/system/uploads/attachment_
     data/file/363056/Tuberculosis_mortality_and_mortality_rate.pdf

9 EDWARD VI (1537–53)

1 SLP Henry VIII Vol. 12, 839.
2 SLP Henry VIII Vol. 12, 889.
3 SLP Henry VIII Vol. 12, 893.
4 SLP Henry VIII Vol. 12, 894.
5 SLP Henry VIII Vol. 12, 911.
6 Ibid.
7 SLP Henry VIII Vol. 12, 960.
8 SLP Henry VIII Vol. 12, 988.
9 SLP Henry VIII Vol. 12, 971.

10   SLP Henry VIII Vol. 12, 1020.

11   SLP Henry VIII Vol. 12, 972.

12   SLP Henry VIII Vol. 12, 1023.

13   SLP Henry VIII Vol. 12, 1060.

14   Ibid.

15   SLP Henry VIII Vol. 12, 1042.

16   Hutchinson.

17   https://www.stgeorgeswindsor.org/assets/files/LearningResources/BackgroundNotesHenryVIII.pdf

18   Nichols, *Literary Remains of Edward VI.*

19   Ibid.

20   SLP Henry VIII Vol. 13, 579.

21   Nichols, *Literary Remains.*

22   Ibid.

23   SLP Henry VIII Vol. 13, 995.

24   http://www.british-history.ac.uk/vch/herts/vol3/pp323-332

25   SLP Henry VIII Vol. 13, 1290.

26   SLP Henry VIII Vol. 13, 306.

27   Skidmore.

28   Nichols, *Literary Remains.*

29   SLP Henry VIII Vol. 14, 5.

30   Skidmore.

31   Ibid.

32   SLP Henry VIII Vol. 14, 1297.

33   Elyot.

34   Ibid.

35   http://kidshealth.org/en/teens/diseases-conditions/

36   SLP Henry VIII Vol. 16, 71b.

37   SLP Henry VIII Vol. 17, 93b.

38   SLP Henry VIII Vol. 17, 15.

39   SLP Henry VIII Vol. 18, 623 (91).

40   Clifford.

41   Skidmore.

42   Nichols, *Literary Remains.*

43   Giles.

44   Nichols, *Literary Remains.*

45   Nichols, *Testament Vetusta.*

46   SLP Henry VIII Vol. 18, 258.

47   SLP Henry VIII Vol. 18, 364.

48   SLP Henry VIII Vol. 18, 577.

49   SLP Henry VIII Vol. 19, 864.

50   SLP Henry VIII Vol. 19, 272.

51   SLP Henry VIII Vol. 19, 1019.

52 SLP Henry VIII Vol. 19, 726.
53 Skidmore.
54 Nichols, *Literary Remains*.
55 Ibid.
56 Ibid.
57 Ibid.
58 Ibid.
59 Stoughton.
60 Ibid.
61 Ibid.
62 Ibid.
63 Hutchinson.
64 Ibid.
65 Strickland.
66 Ibid.
67 Hutchinson.
68 Knecht.
69 Ibid.
70 Nichols, *London Pageants*.
71 Ibid.
72 Nichols, *Literary Remains*.
73 Ibid.
74 Ibid.
75 Ibid.
76 Ibid.
77 Ibid.
78 Ibid.
79 Clifford.
80 Ibid.
81 http://www2.warwick.ac.uk/fac/cross_fac/iatl/reinvention/issues/volume8issue2/barnett/
82 Duffy, *Voices of Morebath*.
83 Scarisbrick.
84 Ibid.
85 *Writings of Edward VI*.
86 McCulloch.
87 Pollnitz.
88 Ibid.
89 Loach.
90 Machyn.
91 Skidmore.
92 Ibid.
93 Loach.

94 Machyn.
95 Loach.
96 Nichols, *Literary Remains.*
97 Ibid.
98 Ackroyd.
99 Machyn.
100 Rosso.
101 Machyn.
102 Nichols, *Literary Remains.*
103 Ibid.
104 CSP Spain Vol. 11, July–Dec. 1553.
105 Loach.
106 Skidmore.
107 Machyn.
108 Markham.
109 Ibid.
110 Machyn.
111 Nichols, *Literary Remains.*
112 http://www.british-history.ac.uk/early-eng-text-soc/vol128/pp112-127
113 Ibid.
114 Cressy.
115 Machyn.
116 Ibid.
117 http://www.british-history.ac.uk/court-husting-wills/vol2/pp651-655
118 Weaver.
119 Ibid.

10 GUILDFORD DUDLEY (1535–54)

1 Loades.
2 Ibid.
3 CSPS Vol. 11, Apr. 1553.
4 Laird.
5 Rosso.
6 Tallis.
7 Rosso.
8 Tallis.
9 Ives.
10 Wilson.
11 Tallis.
12 Rosso.
13 Tallis.

14   http://www.british-history.ac.uk/survey-london/vol18/pt2/pp84-9

15   Adams.

16   Tallis.

17   Ibid.

18   Ibid.

19   Ibid.

20   Ibid.

21   CSPS Vol. 11, Jul. 1553.

22   Ibid.

23   Ibid.

24   Ibid.

25   Ibid.

26   Ibid.

27   Ibid.

28   Ibid.

29   Prescott.

30   http://www.british-history.ac.uk/survey-london/vol18/pt2/pp84-98

31   CSPS Vol. 11, Jul. 1553.

32   Lisle.

33   Ackroyd.

34   CSPS Vol. 11, Jul. 1553.

35   Ibid.

36   Tallis.

37   CSPS Vol. 11, 21–31 Jul.

38   Tallis.

39   Ibid.

40   Ibid.

41   CSPS Vol. 11, 16–20 Jul.

42   Ibid.

43   CSPS, 21–31 Jul.

44   Nichols, *Diary of Henry Machyn*.

45   Prescott.

46   Wilson.

47   CSPS, 26–31 Aug.

48   Wilson.

49   CSPS, 26–31 Aug.

50   Ibid.

51   Ibid.

52   Ibid.

53   Ibid.

54   Markham.

55   Ives.

56   CSPS, 21–25 Aug.

57 Ibid.
58 CSPS Vol. 12, 11–21 Jan. 1554
59 Ibid.
60 CSPS Vol. 12, 11–21 Jan.
61 Ibid.
62 Ibid.
63 CSPS Vol. 12, 6–11 February 1554.
64 Nichols, *Literary Remains.*
65 Ibid.
66 Ibid.
67 Ibid.
68 Ives.
69 Ibid.
70 Ibid.
71 Ibid.
72 Ibid.
73 Nichols, *Literary Remains.*
74 Nichols, *Chronicle of Lady Jane Grey.*
75 Nichols, *Literary Remains.*
76 Dekker.
77 Banks.
78 *Lady Jane* (1986) directed by Trevor Nunn.

11 DEATH AND THE HEIR (1450–1550)

1 Lydgate.
2 Elyot.
3 http://www.british-history.ac.uk/middx-county-records/vol1/pp2-7
4 http://tudoraccidents.history.ox.ac.uk/?page_id=177
5 Machyn.
6 Trueman.
7 This ethnic background and age range was selected as being the closest in comparison to the young men of 1450–1550 studied in this book.
8 https://www.cdc.gov/men/lcod/
9 http://www.aihw.gov.au/deaths/premature-mortality/ages-15-24/
10 http://visual.ons.gov.uk/what-are-the-top-causes-of-death-by-age-and-gender/
11 Sharland.
12 Brown.

Bibliography

Aberth, John, *From the Brink of the Apocalypse: Confronting Famine, War, Plague and Death in the Later Middle Ages* (Oxford: Routledge, 2001)

Ackroyd, Peter, *History of England, Volume II: Tudors* (Basingstoke: Macmillan, 2013)

Adams, Simon (ed.), *Household Accounts and Disbursement Books of Robert Dudley, Earl of Leicester 1558–61, 1584–6* (Cambridge: Cambridge University Press, 1996)

Anonymous (previously attributed to John Warkworth), *A Chronicle of the First Thirteen Years of the Reign of King Edward IV* (London: The Camden Society, 1839)

Anonymous (possibly John Russell), *Ingulph's Chronicle of the Abbey of Croyland with the Continuations by Peter of Blois and Anonymous Writers* (London: George Bell & Sons, 1854)

Anonymous, *Historie of the Arrivall of Edward IV, in England and the Finall Recuerye of His Kingdomes from Henry VI AD 1471*, ed. John Bruce (London: The Camden Society, 1838)

Arthurson, Ian, *The Perkin Warbeck Conspiracy* (Stroud: The History Press, 2009)

Ashdown-Hill, John, *The Dublin King: The True Story of Edward, Earl of Warwick, Lambert Simnel and the Princes in the Tower* (Stroud: The History Press, 2015)

Bacon, Francis, *History of King Henry VII, The Works of Lord Bacon, Volume I* (Cambridge: Cambridge University Press, 1838)

Banks, John, *The Innocent Usurper* (London: R. Bentley, 1683)

Bennett, James, *A Tewkesbury Guide* (Tewkesbury: James Bennett, 1831)

Bentley, Samuel (ed.), *Excerpta Historica* (London: Samuel Bentley, 1831)

Binski, Paul, *Medieval Death: Ritual and Representation* (London: British Museum Press, 2001)

Boarse, T.S.R., *Death in the Middle Ages: Mortality, Judgement and Remembrance* (London: McGraw-Hill, 1972)

Brown, Carleton, *Religious Lyrics of the 15th Century* (Oxford: The Clarendon Press, 1939)

Burgess, Clive, 'Death and Commemoration in an English Parish', in Bruce Gordon and Peter Marshall (eds), *The Place of the Dead: Death and Remembrance in Late Medieval and Early Modern Europe* (Cambridge: Cambridge University Press, 2000)

Burke, Oliver J., *The History of the Lord Chancellors of Ireland 1186–1874* (London: Longmans, Green & Co., 1879)

Calendar of the Charter Rolls Volume VI: 1427-1516, ed. A.E. Stamp (London: HMSO, 1927)

Calendar of Close Rolls, Henry VI Volume VI: 1454–1461, ed. C.T. Flower (London: HMSO, 1947)

Calendar of Close Rolls Edward IV Volume I: 1461–1468, ed. W.H.B. Bird and K.H. Ledward (London: HMSO, 1949.

Calendar of Fine Rolls, Henry VI, Volume XIX: 1452–1461, ed. P.V. Davies (London: HMSO, 1911)

Calendar of Patent Rolls 2 and 3 Edward IV

Calendar of Patent Rolls 38 Henry VI

Calendar of State Papers, Domestic Series, of the Reigns of Edward IV, Mary I and Elizabeth I, with addenda 1547–1603, ed. Mary Ann Everett Green, Lemon, Robert (London: Longman, Roberts & Green, 1870.

Calendar of State Papers Spain Volumes 1–5, ed. G.A. Bergenroth, Garrett Mattingly, Pascual de Gayangos (London: HMSO, 1865/1947)

Calendar of State Papers Venice Volumes 1 and 2, ed. Rawdon Brown (London: HMSO, 1864)

Childe-Pemberton, William S., *Elizabeth Blount and Henry VIII With Some Account of Her Surroundings* (London: Eveleigh Nash, 1913)

Clark, K.L., *The Nevills of Middleham: England's Most Powerful Family in the Wars of the Roses* (Stroud: The History Press, 2016)

Clifford, Henry, *The Life of Jane Dormer, Duchess of Feria* (London: St Anne's Press, 1887)

Comper, Frances M.M. (ed.), *The Book of the Craft of Dying and other Early English Texts Concerning Death* (London: Longmans, Green & Co., 1917)

Creighton, Charles, *A History of Epidemics in Britain from AD 664 to the Great Plague Vol. I* (Cambridge: Cambridge University Press, 1891)

Cressy, David, *Birth, Marriage and Death in Early Modern England* (Oxford: Oxford University Press, 1997)

Cunningham, Sean, *Prince Arthur: The Tudor King Who Never Was* (Stroud: Amberley Publishing, 2016)

Daniell, Christopher, *Death and Burial in Medieval England 1066–1550* (Oxford: Routledge, 2005)

Davis, Virginia, *William Waynflete, Bishop and Educationalist* (Woodbridge: Boydell Press, 1993)

Dekker, Thomas and John Webster, *The Famous History of Sir Thomas Wyat* (London: Tudor Facsimile Texts, 1914)

Dockray, Keith and Peter W. Hammond, *Richard III: From Contemporary Chronicles, Letters and Records* (Stroud: Fonthill Media, 2013)

Dockray, Keith and Richard Knowles, *The Battle of Wakefield and the War of the Roses*, www.richardiii.net/downloads/dockwray_knowles_wakefield.pdf

Duffy, Eamon, *Stripping the Altars: Traditional Religion in England, 1400–1580* (London: Yale University Press, 1994)

Duffy, Eamon, *Voices of Morebath: Reformation and Rebellion in an English Village* (London: Yale University Press, 2001)

Elyot, Thomas, *The Castel of Health* (1541)

Erasmus, Desiderius, *Epistles of Erasmus: From his Earliest Letters to his Fifty-First Year*, ed. Francis Morgan Nichols (London: Longmans, Green & Co., 1901)

Fabyan, Robert, *The New Chronicles of England and France in Two Volumes*, ed. Henry. F.C. Ellis and J. Rivington (London: F.C. and J. Rivington, 1811)

Falkus, Christopher (ed.), *The Private Lives of the Tudor Monarchs* (London: Folio Society, 1974)

Fortescue, Sir John, *De Laudibus Legum Angliae*, ed. A. Amos (Cambridge: Cambridge University Press, 1825)

Gairdner, James (ed.), *The Paston Letters, 1422–1509 AD* (Westminster: Chatto & Windus, 1898)

Giles, Rev. Dr, *The Whole Works of Roger Ascham, Volume II* (London: J.R. Smith, 1864)

Gordon, Bruce and Peter Marshall (eds), *The Place of the Dead: Death and Remembrance in Late Medieval and Early Modern Europe* (Cambridge: Cambridge University Press, 2000)

Gottfried, Robert S., *The Black Death: Natural and Human Disaster in Medieval Europe* (London: The Free Press, 1993)

Griffiths, R.A., *The Reign of King Henry VI: The Exercise of Royal Authority 1422–1461* (Stroud: Sutton Publishing, 1998)

Gristwood, Sarah, *Blood Sisters: The Hidden Lives of the Women behind the Wars of the Roses* (London: Harper Press, 2012)

Haigh, Philip, *From Wakefield to Towton: The Wars of the Roses* (Barnsley: Pen & Sword, 2001)

Hall, Edward, *Hall's Chronicle: Containing the History of England During the Reign of Henry IV and the Succeeding Monarchs to the End of the Reign of King Henry VIII* (London: J. Johnson, F.C. and J. Rivington, Longman, Green & Co., 1809)

Halstead, Caroline Amelia, *Life of Margaret Beaufort, Countess of Richmond and Derby Smith* (London: Smith, Elder & Co., 1839)

Hammond, P.W. and Anne F. Sutton, *Richard III: The Road to Bosworth Field* (London: Guild Publishing, 1985)

Harthan, John, *Books of Hours* (London: Thames & Hudson, 1977)

Haswell, Jock, *Ardent Queen: Margaret of Anjou and the Lancastrian Heritage* (London: Peter Davies, 1976)

Hicks, Michael, *Edward V: The Prince in the Tower* (Stroud: The History Press, 2003)

Hilton, Lisa, *Queens Consort: England's Medieval Queens* (London: Weidenfeld & Nicolson, 2008)

Hookham, Mary Ann, *The Life and Times of Margaret of Anjou, Volumes 1 and 2* (London: Tinsley Brothers, 1872)

Horrox, R. and P.W. Hammond (eds), *British Library Harleian Manuscript 433, Volume I* (Gloucester: A. Sutton for The Richard III Society, 1979)

Houlbrooke, Ralph Anthony, *Death, Religion and the Family in England 1480–1750* (Oxford: Clarendon Press, 2000)

Hutchinson, Robert, *The Last Days of Henry VIII* (London: Weidenfeld & Nicolson, 2005)

Idley, Peter, *Instructions to his Son* (Griefswald: Druck von J. Abel, 1903)

Ives, Eric, *Lady Jane Grey: A Tudor Mystery* (Chichester: Wiley Blackwell, 2009)

Jackson, Canon J.E., *The Execution of Ankarette Twynyho*, 1890, Catalogue of the Printed books, pamphlets etc. in the Library of the Wiltshire Archaeological and Natural History Society's Museum at Devizes

Jones, Michael K. and Malcolm G. Underwood, *The King's Mother: Lady Margaret Beaufort, Countess of Richmond and Derby* (Cambridge: Cambridge University Press, 1993)

Kipling, Gordon (ed.), *The Receyt of the Ladie Kateryne* (Oxford: Early English Text Society, 1990)

Kleineke, Hannes, *Edward IV* (London: Routledge, 2009)

Knecht, R.J., *Francis I* (Cambridge: Cambridge University Press, 1981)

Laird, Francis Charles, *Lady Jane Grey and Her Times* (London: Sherwood, Neely and Jones, 1822)

Lewis, Katherine, *Kingship and Masculinity in Late Medieval Europe* (London: Routledge, 2013)

Licence, Amy, *Cecily Neville: Mother of Kings* (Stroud: Amberley Publishing, 2014)

Lisle, Leandra de, *The Sisters Who Would Be Queen: The Tragedy of Mary, Katherine and Lady Jane Grey* (London: Harper Press, 2008)

Loach, Jennifer, *Edward VI* (New Haven: Yale University Press, 2014)

Loades, David, *John Dudley, Duke of Northumberland 1504–1553* (Oxford: Oxford University Press, 1996)

Lowe, Ben, *Imagining Peace: A History of Early English Pacifist Ideas* (Pennsylvania: Pennsylvania State University Press, 2010)

Lydgate, John, 'A Diet and Doctrine for the Pestilence', in Joseph Patrick Byrne, *The Black Death* (Westport: Greenwood Press, 2004)

MacGibbon, David, *Elizabeth Woodville: A Life* (1938) (Stroud: Amberley Publishing, 2013)

Machyn, Henry, *The Diary of Henry Machyn*, ed. John Gough Nichols (London: The Camden Society, 1848)

Mancini, Dominic, *The Occupation of the Throne by Richard III* (1483), trans. C.A.J. Armstrong (Stroud: Sutton Publishing, 1984)

Markham, Clements, *Edward VI: An Appreciation* (London: Smith, Elder & Co., 1907)

283–4, 302–4, 306

George, Duke of Clarence 27, 37–9, 61, 66, 72, 74, 103, 109, 146–50, 357, 362

Grey, Lady Jane, Queen of England 300, 301, 313–20, 322–7, 333–5, 337–40, 341–2, 343–7

Henry VI 18, 26, 28, 30, 34, 44, 45, 46, 47, 48, 52, 63, 68, 69, 70, 72, 146, 150

Henry VII 69, 86, 88, 112, 113, 121, 123–4, 131, 133, 134, 135, 136, 140, 141, 158, 160, 161–3, 167, 169, 170, 177, 182, 191, 193, 197, 200–2, 253, 356

enry VIII 141, 142, 169, 194, 204, 206, 207, 208, 214, 227, 230, 231, 234, 235, 238, 239, 240, 241, 243, 244, 245, 246, 247, 257, 60, 262, 263, 265–6, 276, 78, 279, 311, 356, 361

y Fitzroy, Duke of ichmond and Suffolk 4–224, 227, 229–3, 41, 243–51, 254–6, 350, 351

, Henry, Earl of Surrey 232, 235–6, 273

, Mary, Duchess of mond and Surrey 34, 255–6

Thomas, Third f Norfolk 229, 8, 241, 247–8, 260

picting death 11, 13, 16, –5, 87–8, 115, 0, 337

rance 52, 62, 68

Margaret of Anjou, Queen of England 30, 31, 44–53, 59, 60, 61, 62–3, 65, 67, 68, 72

Margaret, Duchess of Burgundy 131, 132, 133, 134, 135, 158, 163

Mary I 206, 211, 216, 223, 238, 240, 246, 259, 264, 266, 267, 276, 277, 279, 287, 299, 300, 302, 311, 313, 315, 320, 322, 323, 325, 327–8, 330, 334, 335, 336, 349

Mary, Queen of Scots 274–5, 276, 279, 294

Neville, Anne, Queen of England 62–3, 67, 72, 84, 103, 104, 107, 108, 109, 110, 111, 112, 118–20, 121, 151, 153

Neville, Richard, Earl of Salisbury 28, 29, 31, 32

Neville, Richard, Earl of Warwick 28–9, 31, 38, 61, 62, 63, 128, 146–9, 166

Parr, Catherine, Queen of England 271–2, 276, 277, 286, 313

Paston family 8, 48, 128–9

plague 10, 194, 265, 297, 352

Reformation, the 14, 224–5, 255, 257, 261, 279, 287–92, 301, 303–7, 308–9, 311, 330–1, 335, 342, 349

Richard III 27, 39, 65, 74, 76, 80–2, 84–91, 93, 94–5, 102, 103, 107, 108, 109, 110, 111, 112, 113, 114–7, 118–20, 121, 123–4, 130, 136, 140, 151, 153, 169, 170, 213, 279, 361–2

Richard, Duke of York 19–23, 25, 26, 28, 29, 30, 31, 32, 35–6, 44, 48, 125

Richard of Shrewsbury (later Richard, Duke of York) 76, 82, 84, 91, 92, 93, 102

Seymour, Edward, Duke of Somerset 279, 280, 288, 292, 293, 314

Seymour, Jane, Queen of England 245, 257–60

Seymour, Thomas 286–7, 292

Simnel, Lambert 91, 132–4, 136, 139, 140, 155

sweating sickness 10, 194, 220–1, 258, 266, 295–6, 297, 352

tombs 9, 37, 79, 99–100, 116, 118–9, 128, 136, 144, 150–1, 159–60, 166, 193, 197, 201–2, 248–9, 250–1, 261, 262–3

tuberculosis 247, 253–4, 302

Tudor, Arthur, Prince of Wales 131, 154, 167, 168, 170–94, 204, 235, 350, 351, 352

Warbeck, Perkin 91, 156, 157, 158, 160–1, 167, 168, 179

wills 12, 13, 97–8, 99, 127, 143–4, 159, 197–200, 225–6, 273, 281, 308–9, 342–3

Wolsey, Thomas 194, 205, 206, 207, 213, 216–20, 222, 223, 224, 228, 262–3

Woodville, Elizabeth, Queen of England 59, 62, 71, 72–3, 75, 81, 82, 137, 143–4, 172–3

MacCulloch, Diarmaid, *The Boy King: Edward VI and the Protestant Reformation* (Berkeley: Palgrave Macmillan, 2001)

More, Thomas, *The History of King Richard III* (London: William Rastell, 1557)

Murphy, Beverley, *Bastard Prince: Henry VIII's Lost Son* (Stroud: Sutton Publishing, 2001)

Napier, Henry Alfred, *Historical Notices of the Parishes of Swycombe and Ewelme in the County of Oxford* (Oxford: Oxford University Press, 1858)

Nichols, John Gough, *The Diary of Henry Machyn* (London: The Camden Society, 1848)

Nichols, John Gough, *Grants etc from the Crown During the Reign of Edward V* (London: The Camden Society, 1854)

Nichols, John Gough, *Literary Remains of Edward VI* (London: J.B. Nichols & Sons, 1856)

Nichols, John Gough, *London Pageants* (London: J.B. Nichols & Sons, 1831)

Nichols, John Gough, *The Chronicle of Queen Jane and Two Years of Queen Mary* (London: J.B. Nichols & Sons, 1850)

Nichols, Nicolas Harris, *Testament Vetusta: Illustrations from Wills (Volumes 1 and 2)* (London: J.B. Nichols & Sons, 1826)

Nichols, Nicolas Harris, *The Literary Remains of Lady Jane Grey* (London: Harding, Triphook, and Lepard, 1825)

Norton, Elizabeth, *Jane Seymour: Henry VIII's True Love* (Stroud: Amberley Publishing, 2009)

O'Flanagan, James Roderick, *The Lives of the Lord Chancellors and Keepers of the Lord Seal of Ireland, from the Earliest Times to the Reign of Queen Victoria* (London: Longmans, Green & Co., 1870)

Platt, Colin, *King Death: The Black Death and its Aftermath in Late Medieval England* (Oxford: Routledge, 1997)

Pollnitz, Aysha, *Princely Education in Early Modern Britain* (Cambridge: Cambridge University Press, 2015)

Prescott, H.F.M., *Mary Tudor: The Spanish Tudor* (1940) (London: Constable, 2003)

Rickman, Thomas and John Henry Parker, *An Attempt to Discriminate the Styles of English Architecture, from the Conquest to the Reformation* (London: John Henry & James Parker, 1862)

Roskell, John Smith, *Parliament and Politics in Late Medieval England, Volume 2* (London: Hambledon Press, 1981)

Rosso, Giulio Raviglio, *Historia* (Italy: Nell'Academia Venetiana, 1558)

Rotuli Parliamentorum Volume 6 (London: 1783)

Scarisbrick, J.J., *The Reformation and the English People* (Oxford: Wiley Blackwell, 1984)

Sharland, Elaine, 'Young People: Risk-Taking and Risk-Making: Some Thoughts for Social Work', *FQS: Forum Qualitative Social Research*, Vol. 7, No. 1 (Berlin: Freie Universität Berlin, 2006)

Skidmore, Christopher, *Edward VI: The Lost King of England* (London: Hachette, 2011)

State Letters and Papers of Milan 1385–1618, ed. Hinds, Allen B. Hinds (London: HMSO, 1912)

Stone, Lawrence, *The Family, Sex and Marriage in England 1500–1800* (London: Penguin, 1990)

Stoughton, John, *Notice of Windsor in Olden Times* (London: David Bogue, 1844)

Strickland, Agnes, *Memoirs of the Queens of Henry VIII and of his Mother, Elizabeth of York* (Philadelphia: Blanchard and Lea, 1853)

Tallis, Nicola, *Crown of Blood: The Deadly Inheritance of Lady Jane Grey* (London: Pegasus Books, 2016)

Tremlett, Giles, *Catherine of Aragon: Henry's Spanish Queen* (London: Faber & Faber, 2010)

Trueman, C.N. 'Henry VII and the nobles', www.historylearningsite.co.uk/tudor-england/henry-vii-and-the-nobles/, 2016

Underwood, Malcolm G. and Michael K. Jones, *The King's Mother: Lady Margaret Beaufort, Countess of Richmond and Derby* (Cambridge: Cambridge University Press, 1993)

Weaver, Frederic William, *Somerset Medieval Wills* (London: Harrison & Sons, 1905)

Weightman, Christine, *Margaret of York: The Diabolical Duchess* (Stroud: Sutton Publishing, 1989)

Weller, Thomas, *Inventories of the Wardrobes, Plate and Chapel Stuff* (London: The Camden Society, 1855)

Wilkinson, Josephine, *The Princes in the Tower* (Stroud: Amberley Publishing, 2013)

Wilson, Derek, *The Uncrowned Kings of England* (London: Carroll & Graf Publishers Inc, 2005)

Writings of Edward VI, William Hugh, Queen Catherine Parr, Anne Askew, Lady Jane Grey, Hamilton and Balnaves (London: The Religious Tract Society, 1836)

Wroe, Ann, *Perkin: A Story of Deception* (London: Jonathan Cape, 2003)

Index

afterlife 13, 33, 34, 36, 41, 67, 114–5, 117, 127, 224–5, 261, 279, 288, 304–5, 307–8

Anne, Duchess of Brittany 77

artwork depicting death 7–8, 41–2, 45, 68, 93–4, 348

attitudes towards death 8, 9, 10–11, 13, 35, 40, 51, 67, 243, 270, 329–33, 337–40, 348–9, 351–3, 363

Beaufort, Margaret 125, 153–4, 172, 212

Blount, Elizabeth 'Bessie' 204–6 214–6, 227

Boleyn, Anne 222, 228, 229, 231, 233, 234, 235, 237, 239, 240, 241–3, 244, 260

Catherine of Aragon 163, 167, 175, 178–91, 193–4, 204, 221, 229, 235, 240, 243, 244, 260, 262, 320

Cecily, Duchess of York 20–3, 45–6, 125, 138, 159, 160

chantry chapels 13, 39, 114–7, 261, 288, 304–5

Chaucer, Alice 125, 127, 128

Chichele, Henry, Archbishop of Canterbury 9

death in battle 11, 40–1, 67, 113–5

death rates 9, 10, 11, 96–7, 100–1, 206–7, 270, 352–7, 358–60

de la Pole, Elizabeth, Duchess of Suffolk 125, 126, 130, 132, 137, 138

de la Pole, John, Earl of Lincoln 91, 120, 122, 125–6, 129–40, 152, 154, 155, 156, 208, 350, 362

de la Pole, John, Second Duke of Suffolk 125, 126, 128, 129, 130, 137–9

diet and health 269, 351–2, 359

Dudley, Guildford 310–28, 333–5, 337, 339, 340, 341–2, 343, 351, 362

Dudley, John, Earl of Warwick 292–3, 311, 312–20, 323–33, 335, 340, 341, 342–7

Edmund, Earl of Rutland 22–33, 35–6, 37, 39–43, 44, 95, 350, 351, 357

Edward IV 21–5, 26–9, 31, 33, 35, 38–9, 44, 57, 60, 61, 63, 64–5, 78–9, 107, 148–50, 279, 350, 351

Edward V 73–96, 10' 107, 279, 350, 36

Edward VI 12, 246, 263–80, 282, 28 289–304, 312, 321, 322, 324,

Edward, Earl of 91, 102, 109 132–3, 145 151–64, 1(350, 351,

Edward of 102–22 361

Edward
Lanc
Wal
54–
8?

Eliz

Louis XI of 59–60, 61